PAINTING IMPERIALISM
NATIONALISM RED

The Ukrainian Marxist Critique of Russian
Communist Rule in Ukraine, 1918–1925

In *Painting Imperialism and Nationalism Red*, Stephen Velychenko traces the first expressions of national, anti-colonial Marxism to 1918 and the Russian Bolshevik occupation of Ukraine. Velychenko reviews the work of early twentieth-century Ukrainians who regarded Russian rule over their country as colonialism. He then discusses the rise of "national communism" in Russia and Ukraine and the Ukrainian Marxist critique of Russian imperialism and colonialism. The first extended analysis of Russian communist rule in Ukraine to focus on the Ukrainian communists, their attempted anti-Bolshevik uprising in 1919, and their exclusion from the Comintern, *Painting Imperialism and Nationalism Red* re-opens a long forgotten chapter of the early years of the Soviet Union and the relationship between nationalism and communism. An appendix provides a valuable selection of Ukrainian Marxist texts, all translated into English for the first time.

STEPHEN VELYCHENKO is a historian and research fellow at the Chair for Ukrainian Studies of the University of Toronto.

Painting Imperialism and Nationalism Red

The Ukrainian Marxist Critique of Russian Communist Rule in Ukraine, 1918–1925

STEPHEN VELYCHENKO

UNIVERSITY OF TORONTO PRESS
Toronto Buffalo London

© University of Toronto Press 2015
Toronto Buffalo London
www.utorontopress.com

Reprinted in paperback 2022

ISBN 978-1-4426-4851-7 (cloth)   ISBN 978-1-4426-1714-8 (EPUB)
ISBN 978-1-4875-4805-6 (paper)   ISBN 978-1-4426-1713-1 (PDF)

Publication cataloguing information is available from Library and Archives
Canada.

We wish to acknowledge the land on which the University of Toronto Press
operates. This land is the traditional territory of the Wendat, the Anishnaabeg, the
Haudenosaunee, the Métis, and the Mississaugas of the Credit First Nation.

University of Toronto Press acknowledges the financial assistance to its
publishing program of the Canada Council for the Arts and the Ontario
Arts Council, an agency of the Government of Ontario.

 Canada Council Conseil des Arts
for the Arts du Canada

 **ONTARIO ARTS COUNCIL**
CONSEIL DES ARTS DE L'ONTARIO
an Ontario government agency
un organisme du gouvernement de l'Ontario

Funded by the   Financé par le
Government   gouvernement
of Canada   du Canada

Canada

Vouloir leur donner la liberté avant de l'avoir nous-mêmes conquise, c'est assurer à la fois notre servitude et celle du monde entire.
Maximilien Robespierre (1792)

Save Communism from Muscovite imperialism.
Vasyl Mazurenko (1921)

Contents

Illustrations follow page 88

Foreword to the Paperback Edition

In 1918 Vladimir Lenin's Bolshevik Russian government invaded the Ukrainian National Republic (UNR), thereby sparking a war that lasted until 1923. At the beginning of this century, another Russian government under Vladimir Putin again invaded Ukraine, sparking a war that does not appear to be ending anytime soon. A century ago, Ukrainian marxists were among those who rejected renewed imperial Russian domination in Bolshevik guise and looked to join a western European state system. They imagined a third path of development – equal status in a European socialist confederation that would have included Bolshevik Russia as but one member. Today, the faith in great revolutions that would resolve all problems is no more. There is no Ukrainian Communist Party to offer a radical marxist solution. There is no socialist Europe, and Putin's Russia definitely does not represent any kind of ideal order. However, the problems that produced that faith in the need for the violent establishment of a utopian revolutionary communism are still here. Accordingly, the relevant question for today is within which bloc are these problems more intense. Does the western European liberal parliamentary capitalist order or Putin's autocratic kleptocratic neo-fascist capitalist order have a better chance of overcoming them?

This book is devoted to early twentieth-century Ukrainian communists who witnessed the reality of Bolshevik rule, were not enamoured of the Russian Bolshevik experiment and, as this book summarizes, were critical of it. They shared the critical opinions of a tiny minority of western European marxists at the time and of Bertrand Russell – opinions that have since been proven correct. They looked West. As one of these marxists, Mykola Khvylovai, wrote in 1925–6: "You ask which Europe? Take whichever you want: past or present; bourgeois or proletarian ... Europe – this is the European intellectual in the best sense of the term. It is, if you wish, the printer from Wurttemberg who showed us a great civilization and opened before us endless perspectives ... This great power is the psychological Europe upon which we must orientate ourselves." Elsewhere, he wrote, "Not the Europe that Spengler announced was 'in decline'... It is the Europe of grandiose civilization, the Europe of Goethe, Darwin, Byron, Newton, Marx and so on and so forth." In another of his works Khvylovai coined the slogan "Away from Moscow [*het z moskvy*]."

This orientation resembled that found at the opposite end of the political spectrum at the time. There, in August 1918, conservative Evhen Chykalenko also argued that Ukrainians should look West. He compared what Ukraine might become as part of a renewed liberal tsarist or Bolshevik Russian empire with what it might become as a satellite of imperial Germany, with its free trade unions, free mass political parties, parliament, and full male suffrage, and concluded that German rule was infinitely preferable to renewed Russian rule. Unlike their Russian counterparts, Germans coming to live and work in Ukraine would Ukrainize in two or three generations, as Germans had Russified in Russia, or as the English had assimilated in Ireland and then become advocates of Irish autonomy. He pointed to Prussian Poland where Poles had higher rates of literacy and national consciousness than their fellows in Russian Poland. While Finno-Ugric tribes were equal in status with Russian peasants under centuries of Russian rule, remaining illiterate and pagan, after 100 years under Baltic German landlords, Finno-Ugric Estonians and Latvians were completely bilingual, and the most literate, educated, and nationally conscious of all the tsar's subjects. Chykalenko thus wrote that "it is better to be a German slave than the comrade of a Russian." As "brothers" with Russians, Ukrainians would never be more than drunken, semi-literate, foul-mouthed, vulgar boors far removed from the Estonian or Latvian "German slave." Even when fighting against German rule Ukrainians would benefit, because in the course of learning about their enemy they would come to emulate this enemy – as had the Estonians, Latvians, and Czechs. By 1921 Chykalenko had concluded that "only Europe can build the Ukrainian state" by giving it a king as had happened in Greece and Bulgaria, countries which he thought would then carry out policies similar to those in Denmark and Norway.

Today, in hindsight, the histories of liberal, parliamentary, capitalist-based political orders, be they imperialist or not, confirm the positions of the UCP and Chykalenko because they show that, despite the despoilation, extermination, and violence committed by their elites and representatives, reform leading to change with minimal violence has nonetheless been a constant. It is difficult if not impossible, for instance, to imagine British Reform Bills, a Chartist Movement, an Irish Repeal Association (1830), or a DeGaulle, Gandhi, or Martin Luther King, in the tsarist or Soviet empire – or in Putin's Russia. As such, the European neo-liberal capitalist order appears as the lesser of two evils that Ukrainians in their majority chose after 2004, as did their ancestors 100 years ago. That "Western" order not only modernizes its subjects; it provides the possibility for reform. Popular protest and honest and persistent lawyers can force even corporate bosses to change their behaviour. There was no such possibility in Stalin's USSR and nor is there such a possibility in Putin's Russia, whose leaders deny the very existence of Ukraine, Ukrainians, and a Ukrainian state.

In light of the above, the publication of this paperback edition is timely and appropriate. The book reminds us that there were Ukrainian marxists in 1918 who rejected continued subordination to what then was a new Bolshevik Russia, and imagined Ukraine as a member of a European socialist confederation. It reminds us that Ukrainians produced a critique that remains relevant today in a country suffering not only from another Russian imperialist invasion, but from high rates of poverty, criminality, inequality, and pollution. As part of their theoretical legacy it is possible to include the following. First, they pointed out that political independence is a necessary condition for social and national emancipation and that state control of the economy in itself does not end national or social oppression. Second, although they condemned capitalism – reintroduced after 1991 in a Russian neo-liberal corporate form by politically Russophile oligarchs in Ukraine – they recognized that a "bourgeois" democratic revolution and a liberal representative democracy had to precede a socialist revolution for the latter to succeed. Third, they identified Ukraine's Russian-settler colonists as the social base of the Black Hundred–like anti-Ukrainian extremists who then controlled the Bolshevik regime in Ukraine, a group that after 2004 provided the social base of Putin's fifth column in Ukraine. And finally, they pointed out that cultural issues could not be separated from economic issues – the ownership of the means of production.

The author
March 2022

PAINTING IMPERIALISM AND NATIONALISM RED

The Ukrainian Marxist Critique of Russian Communist Rule in Ukraine, 1918–1925

Introduction

In November 1918, Stalin condemned the non-Russian "border governments" that were claiming independence from the tsarist empire as "counter-revolutionary" and "bourgeois." In October 1920, he declared that the secession from the RSFSR of "border regions" formerly ruled by the tsar was counter-revolutionary because any such region would fall under "the yoke of imperialism." This opinion was shared by those for whom the Bolshevik Russian hegemony established by 1922 within the former tsarist imperial space seemed the only viable order. Leftists in general claimed that Russian Bolshevik rule there was preferable to French or German hegemony. According to E.H. Carr, independence was not an option for the tsar's non-Russian subjects, who had only two choices: dependence on socialist Moscow, or "the bourgeois governments of the capitalist world." What these opinions ignore is that besides the non-Russian "counter-revolutionary bourgeois" governments, there were *socialist* alternatives to Russian Bolshevik hegemony. One such alternative socialist government would have been based on the left-wing Ukrainian Social Democrats (SDs). The SDs, who would later form the Ukrainian Communist Party (UCP), envisaged a European Communist Union of soviet states including those that had emerged from the tsarist empire. These states would be allied with but not be dominated by Soviet Russia or the Russian Communist Party (RCP). UCP leaders contended that only a Ukrainian communist state ruled by its own party could break the structure of dependency created during two hundred years of imperial Russian rule.

In January 1918, US President Woodrow Wilson had proclaimed a liberal-democratic version of national self-determination as one of his Fourteen Points. But, just as Lenin's Bolsheviks applied their Marxist version of self-determination selectively, so did the Entente leaders soon qualify their version of self-determination to exclude secession and did not apply the Fourteen Points to their own colonial subjects. The Entente countries retained their old imperial territories, and after 1918, they even acquired new ones, referred to as mandate territories. The Bolsheviks, for their part, after 1918 retained control over non-Russian imperial tsarist lands, which they called "republics."

In October 1918, Karl Radek and Lenin pointed out to Wilson that "we do not find among your demands the liberation of Ireland, Egypt, or India, nor even the liberation of the Philippines," while ignoring Articles 6 and 10, which accepted the territorial integrity of the Russian and Austrian empires (see figure 1, illustration section).[1] No Entente leaders, for their part, pointed to analogous discrepancies between Bolshevik words and deeds. Few then or since have asked questions such as these: Why did Russian Bolsheviks think that separate national parties in the Russian empire amounted to "nationalist counter-revolution"? Why did they not also think that national communist parties in colonies like Ireland, India, Indonesia, and Korea were an impediment to international class solidarity? And why did "Russian workers," having "renounced their rights," as Stalin claimed, to Finland, Poland, and parts of Mongolia, not do the same when it came to Ukraine?

Ukrainian Marxists living under Bolshevik rule in 1919, who considered Ukraine as much a Russian colony after 1918 as it had been before, *did* ask such questions and argued that the new Soviet state amounted to a renewed Russian-dominated empire. They asked what the difference was between Wilson and Lenin. Ukrainian Marxists exposed the double standard of the Russian Bolshevik regime on national issues and were among the first critics of the party dictatorship in the new Soviet state. In 1919, Stalin claimed there was no "soulless centralism" in the new regime. "No regime in the world," he insisted, "has permitted such extensive decentralization [for its border regions], no government has ever granted to peoples such complete national freedom as the Soviet power in Russia." Earlier that same year, Vasyl Shakhrai, the ideological founder of Ukrainian communism, who was then Commissar of War in Ukraine's first soviet government (see figure 5, illustration section), had voiced a different opinion: "What kind of Ukrainian government is this, whose members neither know nor want to know Ukrainian? That has no influence in a Ukrainian society that has never even heard their names previously? What kind of 'Ukrainian' minister [sic] of war am I, when I must disarm all Ukrainianized military units in Kharkiv, because they don't want to follow me in defence of soviet power? Our only military support in the struggle against the Central Rada is the army that Antonov brought to Ukraine from Russia, which regards everything Ukrainian as hostile and counter-revolutionary."[2]

Few scholars today know about Shakhrai, Ukrainian Marxists' critiques of Russian Bolshevism, or Ukrainian Marxism.[3] Among leftists, ignorance, methodological preconceptions, Russocentrism, Russophilism, or sovietophilism, and the notion that in empires the class identity of imperial metropolitan workers is somehow unrelated to or independent of their national identity, have led many to claim or imply that Ukrainian resistance to Russian tsarist and soviet rule was a criminal affair that sprang from a nativism unrelated to economic development. Such people considered Ukrainian nationalism a threat to the centralized soviet state socialism they considered preferable to Anglo-American or German capitalism or "balkanization." Whatever concern such people voiced for the victims of capitalism did not extend to concern for Ukrainian (or other) victims of Russian Communism, whom they discussed with aphorisms about ends and means, much as the British colonial secretary had justified his empire's use of force in 1897: "You cannot have omelets without breaking eggs" (*The Times* [London], 1 April). According to Lord Milner in *The Nation and the Empire* (1913): "But when all the crimes and follies [of the British empire] have been subtracted, there remains an immense balance on the right side."

Ukrainian communism dates from 1918, when Shakhrai and Serhyi Mazlakh wrote its first manifesto, *Do Khvyli. Shcho diiet'sia na Ukraini i z Ukrainoiu*. Russian Bolshevik leader Georgii Piatakov immediately condemned it and ordered *Do Khvyli* removed from bookstores; in March 1919, he exiled its authors and expelled them from the party.[4] Shakhrai had been the first to use the term "Ukrainian Communist Party," in December 1917, when he proposed this as the name that Ukraine's Bolsheviks should adopt for their organization; however, it was left-wing members of the Ukrainian Social Democratic Labour Party who formed the UCP (Ukr. *Ukapisty*) in January 1920. The party was dissolved in January 1925. The last vestiges of Ukrainian communism disappeared in 1933, when Mykola Skrypnyk, the leading Ukrainian Bolshevik, committed suicide, having concluded that revolutionary universalism, proletarian internationalism, and national revival were impossible under Stalin. Repression and censorship suppressed knowledge of the UCP as well as its case that Bolshevism was merely renewed Russian colonialist imperialism. By 1939, former members of the UCP were either in prison, in exile, or dead, and their writings were gathering dust in closed archives. The "anti-colonial Marxism" these Ukrainians elaborated reappeared in 1965 with Ivan Dziuba's *Internationalism or Russification;* then, after 1991, Ukrainian communism emerged as a topic of academic inquiry in Ukraine.[5] Today there is no Ukrainian Communist Party – which is not to be confused with the still-existing Communist Party of Ukraine (CPU), formed as the branch of the Russian Bolshevik party in Ukraine in 1918.[6]

At the beginning of the twentieth century, Ukrainian intellectuals seized upon Marxism as a way to mobilize their people against Russian rule, much as Asian intellectuals mobilized theirs against foreign rule. Ukrainian Marxism, like the Asian variant, was only marginally related to the working class but, also as in Asia, it served as a theory justifying industrial modernity and national liberation. Also like their Asian Marxist counterparts, Ukrainian left SDs faced the problem of state building and mobilization in an underdeveloped colonized society in which capitalism was as much an ethnic/religious as an economic problem because its agents typically belonged to a minority. In both regions, as part of empires, socialism and nationalism overlapped in ways they did not in western European national states. The UCP, however, did not win power.

Ukrainian socialists and Marxists condemned the Russocentric nature of Russian Marxism. They accused the Russian Bolsheviks of invading Ukraine, subverting its indigenous revolution, and reinforcing rather than dismantling imperial structures of domination through supposedly independent republican soviet governments. They documented how Russian Bolsheviks who were attempting to spread their principles beyond their national borders by force were, in fact, undermining those principles, just as the French Jacobins had done a century before. But whereas the former French satellites and puppet regimes had all disappeared by 1815, the personnel and structures of the Russian soviet satellite regime in Ukraine remained basically intact until

2014 despite formal political independence. For this reason, the Ukrainian communist critique of the origins and early policies of that regime is not only of historical significance, but also of contemporary political relevance.

This book is a contribution to the international comparative history of communism and imperialism. It focuses on a subject that most historians of "nationality policy," the "Russian Civil War," or "the triumphal spread of Soviet power" either ignored or treated superficially: the Ukrainian communist analysis of Bolshevik Russian policies in Ukraine as reincarnations of tsarist Russian imperialism. In 1961, Frantz Fanon wrote in *The Wretched of the Earth:* "Deportations, massacres, forced labour, and slavery have been the main methods used by capitalism to increase its wealth, its gold or diamond reserves and to establish its power." In 1920, Ukrainian Marxists would have had only to replace "capitalism" in this sentence with "Russian communism" to describe the situation in their country.

The book does not survey and analyse all Ukrainian left-wing writings, which have not yet been collected and published; rather, it focuses on critiques of Russian communism. Chapter 1 reviews the main events of the period and how contemporaries applied the imperial/colonial paradigm to Ukrainian–Russian relations. Chapter 2 examines the role of strategic-political considerations, Marxist principles, and Russian imperialist preconceptions in early Bolshevik policy towards Ukraine. It reviews the Bolsheviks' justification for their invasion of a former subject people, their occupation regime in Ukraine, and the Ukrainian Marxist condemnations of it as "Red imperialism." Chapter 3 traces the emergence of "national communism" in Russia and Ukraine. It summarizes the Ukrainian Marxist analysis of the Ukrainian revolution and the early Bolshevik order, the Ukrainian left-SD attempt to lead the anti-Bolshevik uprising of 1919, and the Russian Bolsheviks' rationale for denying membership in the Comintern to Ukrainian parties. The appendix contains documents, all translated into English for the first time, that illustrate Ukrainian communist positions.

This study defines nationalism in its broadest sense as a theory that claims that ethnic-linguistic and political borders should coincide. From such a perspective, communists who espouse political secession from empire on the basis of nationally defined frontiers, or who enact policies within national borders, are necessarily nationalists. The content of those policies is, therefore, logically distinct from the issue of the borders within which they are enacted, as is the issue of whether those policies are legal or democratic. There never has been a community that was not situated within an ethno-linguistic-cultural group on a particular territory; nor has there ever existed a class outside a specific territory inhabited by a group defined by culture and language. And finally, ruling communist elites, for all their internationalist rhetoric, used national languages to mobilize citizens by appealing to common national-cultural values. In this respect, Ukrainian communists were no different from their counterparts in other colonized nations. Russian communists, for their part, like early French or English communists, were not nationalist but imperialist because they did *not* think that political and cultural borders should coincide. Indeed, they restored imperial frontiers and extended the use of Russian as an administrative language beyond Russia's ethnic borders. Analogously, Bela Kun's Hungarian communists were not "nationalist" either insofar as they attempted to incorporate Slovakia into socialist Hungary.

This book defines imperialism and colonialism in their twentieth-century critical sense as policies advocating and resulting in the political subjugation and economic exploitation of an indigenous population by the ruling elite of another country. That domination was sometimes but not always imposed by conquest. It could be benign or brutal, and it did not always involve colonization or the presence of foreign soldiers and bureaucrats. It included the foreign control of local markets, manufacturing, and external trade, with local collaborator elites as junior partners, and was as much a class as a national phenomenon. Domination and expropriation was exercised either by direct rule or indirectly through satellite or puppet governments, which commercialized agriculture, destroyed peasant farming, and imposed policies that restricted the expansion of manufacturing and the development of skilled workers. When such regions were incorporated into the world economy, it was as peripheries of a metropolitan centre. While all empires with colonies are necessarily multinational states, multinational states are not considered colonial empires if their component parts interact with one another without central mediation, and if their populations do not perceive domination and expropriation by a foreign centre or have forgotten that these exist. Thus, while many Irish at the beginning of the twentieth century would have considered Great Britain an empire, most Scots would have regarded it as a multinational state.[7] Ukrainian SDs branded Russian communists as imperialists from 1918. They accused them of invading Ukraine and establishing there a Russian-speaking puppet regime. Strengthened by the Russian Red Army and the Russian urban-settler minority, that regime extracted resources for export to Russia, thus reinforcing instead of abolishing the pre-existing exploitative imperial structure.

Men like Tan Malaka, Mao Tse Tung, Vasyl Shakhrai, Lev Iurkevych, Serhyi Mazlakh [Robsman], Andryi Richytsky [Pisotsky], Mykhailo Tkachenko, Iury and Vasyl Mazurenko, Sultan Galiev, and Turar Ryskulov nationalized Marxism in their respective countries in much the same way that Lenin created a Russian national version of Marxism. But unlike Lenin, who belonged to a *ruling* nationality, Ukrainian Marxists belonged to a *ruled* nationality. They contended that Lenin's Bolshevism was a renewed Russian imperialism, a nationalized communism like any other rather than a universal norm from which other communisms were not supposed to diverge. Unlike the Russian Bolsheviks, but much like the French Marxists, Ukrainian and Central Asian Marxists realized that class consciousness could not transcend the national or imperial contexts within which it evolved. They claimed that the future order would be based not on classless societies but, rather, on classless nations. Only proletarian hegemony *within* nations would secure amity *between* nations.[8] For them, it was not self-evident that nationalism weakened class unity or that the "victorious industrial proletariat of the formerly ruling nation" would stop exploiting the formerly ruled nations. "The socialization of the means of production will not automatically end the domination of one nation over another," wrote Shakhrai. "For as long as one nation rules and another submits there will be no socialism even if the means of production are socialized."[9] Had they lived to see it, they would have wondered how Japan's "Greater East-Asian Co-prosperity Sphere" differed from Russia's Soviet Union.

Those unfamiliar with the details of Marx and Engels's thoughts on nationality, class, and power consider "national communism" an oxymoron and impossibility. They can point out that both men shared Enlightenment assumptions about a universal cosmopolitan civilization wherein all humans, but not all cultures, were equal, as well as German nationalists' disdain for "non-historical small peoples" and "lesser breeds."[10] From such a perspective, small peasant-nationalities were impediments to progress and were destined to assimilate because progress demands large, centralized economic units. As Adam Smith elaborated in his *Theory of Moral Sentiments* (1759), languages of "doomed peoples," like Gaelic, could be appropriate for things spiritual, but not for things of the market: "no one ever made a bargain in verse." The younger Marx and Engels inherited this Enlightenment disassociation between culture and economic life that equated "progress" not with all but only with some cultures and languages. They assumed that class consciousness was "natural" and did not elaborate on how place and community were linked to relations of production and exchange. At the turn of the century, most leftists, accordingly, thought class more important than national identity and national liberation incidental to social emancipation and economic development. Rosa Luxemburg regarded opposition to foreign domination as "mere nationalism" and not "class struggle." Nikolai Bukharin in *Imperialism* (1916) wrote that nationalism was regressive because small states were economically impossible.

National communism has a place within Marxist thought, however. Marx and Engels distinguished between "nationality," which they understood in the German ethnic-linguistic sense as a permanent feature of humanity and "nation," which they used in the French statist political sense as a transient element. They also postulated that once "the proletariat" took power, it had to "raise itself to the status of a national class [and] constitute itself as the nation." They allowed for an independent "proletarian nation state" that would be a fatherland during a necessary transition period from capitalism to communism. In their later writings they reconsidered their views on German ethnocentrism, the Irish, Poles, and Czechs, and the relationship between large economic units and nationality, and they allowed for "proletarian fatherlands" and national routes out of capitalism. Marx referred specifically to Chinese and Russian versions of socialism. In chapter 1 of the *Manifesto* he wrote that the proletariat's struggle with the bourgeoisie "is first of all a national struggle. The proletariat of each country, must, of course, first of all settle matters with its own bourgeoisie." This echoed Friedrich List, who argued that "free trade" liberal capitalism ensured the domination of wealthy industrial nations over non-industrial ones and that the latter, in response, had to develop a "national capitalism." In 1849, Engels wrote that the Czechs should not have independence because they were an "unhistorical people," but in 1893, he wrote that their wish for independence was "natural." In considering the Irish problem, he realized that what socialists of large, powerful nations called "internationalism" in fact meant national oppression for socialists in small, poor nations. While these theoretical discussions were occurring, government intervention in the form of social legislation and tariffs had improved standards of living and made national states significant to workers. By 1914, the workers of northwestern Europe were not paupers and had vested interests in their governments because socialism in practice had become more "national" than "internationalist." "National homeland" could no longer be unthinkingly equated with regimes that overtly defended class privilege. Governments that used ethnic nationalism to muster support for imperial adventures and/or to justify repression, for better or worse, reinforced this link between nationality and government. In response, socialists and liberals also resorted to nationalism to focus resistance to corporations and pro-corporate governments. Germany's Social Democratic Party in 1875 declared in its program that "the working class strives for emancipation first of all within the framework of the present-day national-state."

Marx thought that European empires brought capitalism and progress to colonial possessions (with the exception of Ireland), but that they did so at a price, and he welcomed opposition if it was not nativist and had a social program. He and Engels thought that the final liberation of colonized peoples would depend on anti-capitalist revolution in Europe rather than on local anti-imperialist revolutions against empires; even so, they supported rebellious Poles, Indians, and Irish. This line of thought was taken up by the Austrian Marxists Karl Renner and Otto Bauer as well as by Marxists from stateless nationalities who did not accept that their small nations could be ignored or would inevitably disappear or that national identity was an atavism best restricted to private life. They observed that national identity was produced by the spread of education and communications as industrial capitalism made vertical national loyalties stronger than horizontal class loyalties. Consequently, ruled nations regarded ruling nations along with capitalism as the cause of their plight. These Marxists concluded that identity and culture were plural, diverse, and permanent, that public institutions had to reflect rather than suppress them, and that there would be no social liberation without national liberation. Protectionism directed by former dependencies against former rulers was desirable, defensive nationalism was not the same as aggressive nationalism, and national conflicts were not eternal and intractable but contingent and solvable. Dominated colonial nationalities could emancipate themselves and deal with their native oppressors without the assistance of their supposed class allies within the ruling imperial nationality. Kautsky in 1895 implicitly and Bauer in 1920 explicitly stated that Austro-German workers would be acting as counter-revolutionaries if they opposed the dissolution of the Austrian and German empires. In 1920 the Comintern instructed communist parties to ally themselves conditionally with the national bourgeoisie in independence struggles.[11] Trotsky, too, distinguished between the nation as a cultural unit and as a political unit. He wrote in 1915:

> The nation will outlive not only the current war but also capitalism itself. In the socialist system, too, freed from economic dependence on the state, the nation will long remain as the most important seat of spiritual culture, for the nation has at its disposal language, the most significant organ of this culture ... To the extent that social patriots link the fate of the nation – which in itself by no means paralyses economic development and in no way prevents it from assuming a European-wide and global scale – with the fate of a closed, military-state organisation, we, the internationalists, are bound to take upon ourselves the defense of the historic rights of nations to independence and development in opposition to its conservative "patriotic" defenders.[12]

Although men like Tan Malaka are today regarded as the founders of the "national" and "anti-colonial" Marxisms, such ideas originated in Europe and were elaborated upon by Polish, Lithuanian, Jewish, and Ukrainian SDs in the Russian empire between 1900 and 1906. These forms of Marxism justified secession from empires led by a "progressive national bourgeoisie" in the name of development. This book illustrates the place of Ukrainian Marxists within this group. It was they, not the Chinese or the Yugoslavs, who created the world's second "national communist" movement. They also launched the world's first intra-communist war when they took up arms against Russian communists in 1919, fifty years before the Chinese did so. Three years before Lenin set forth his theory that the "the proletariat" should make tactical alliances with the "national bourgeoisie" in order to overthrow the old order, UCP co-founder Mykhailo Tkachenko was propounding a similar strategy: "After this common one-time fight together with the [national] bourgeoisie, when we go our separate ways, the only way for the Ukrainian proletariat to fight for the socialist ideal is that expressed in the world slogan of the world proletariat, 'workers of all countries unite.'" Perceptively, Shakhrai noted in 1919: "The Ukrainian revolutionary national movement provides (and will continue to provide) much historical material about the nature of national movements in general and their role in the epoch of imperialism and the beginning of the socialist proletarian revolution."[13]

Ukrainian Marxist writings on capitalism, national oppression, Russian colonialism, and imperialism merit attention and a place within the spectrum of anti-colonialist Marxism. They also should be included alongside the first "critical" or "Western" Marxist writings of Herman Gorter and Anton Pannekoek, who by 1920 had identified Bolshevism as a distinctly Russian national phenomenon produced by people who were ignorant of capitalism as it existed in Europe. Like the German communists Fritz Wollfhiem and Heinrich Laufenberg, Ukrainian communists labelled Bolshevism a reincarnated Russian imperialism.[14]

One reason why few today know about the Ukrainian Marxists who considered their country to be a Russian colony is that they were never a ruling party. Another is that their writings were long unavailable in German, English, or French translation. Also, the Russophilia, Russocentrism, and faith in the Russian Bolshevik experiment long shared by many foreign specialists on Russian-ruled Eurasia blinded them to Ukrainian issues. A fourth reason was the "modernization" paradigm that either ignored domination, nationality, and exploitation or considered these insignificant.[15] The impact of Lenin's *Imperialism: The Highest Stage of Capitalism* (1916), which excluded the tsarist empire, might be considered a fifth reason why Ukraine faded from the view of those interested in imperial histories. Although the book excluded Russia, was not written to explain domination, and is simply wrong in its analysis, it long set the framework for leftist and critical liberal attitudes towards empires.[16] Lenin later wrote that he had excluded the Russian empire from his analysis because of censorship. But those who used his text persisted in omitting that empire from their purview nonetheless and did not think it had to be dissolved as did empires.[17] Like Lenin, most later scholars regarded "Russia" as "multinational state" and not as an empire, rarely compared it to other empires, and judged the Russian empire differently from other empires. Very few saw through Lenin's double standards. For instance, on the one hand he condemned non-Russian socialists within the empire, insisting that parties separate from his metropolitan Russian party were "nationalists" or "chauvinists," and that his party was the empire's sole legitimate Marxist Social Democratic party. This, even though the Second International recognized between 1907 and 1914 not only an independent Ukrainian SD delegation but also delegations from five other parties representing countries that either did not exist or were not independent (Bohemia, Norway, Ireland, Poland, India).[18] On the other hand, despite his demands for one SD and later one communist party in the Russian imperial space, Lenin's twenty-one conditions for Comintern membership did not include the subordination of colonial parties in other empires to their metropolitan communist parties. Some foreign socialists went along with this centralism and thought that their empires, like the Russian one, should have a single centralized socialist party, but they could not enforce this and eventually accepted that colonies had their own independent parties – which were then members of the Comintern. Finally, leftists and critical liberals in particular were critical of Ukrainian anti-imperial separatist nationalism left or right, because, like Lenin, they regarded large economic units and ethnic assimilation as "progressive." Lenin never specified whether all empires were to be reunited after socialist revolutions had temporarily separated colony from metropole, but he did specify that all of Russia's dominated nationalities were to remain within the imperial space after a socialist revolution. He considered secession, like minority national identity, to be a temporary phenomenon. Ukrainian national liberation from this perspective was "reactionary." So Lenin rejoiced when he learned that Ukrainian socialists in Austrian POW camps through 1916 had failed to convince tsarist Ukrainian soldiers to support national independence; from this, he concluded that ethnic similarities between Russians and Ukrainians had trumped "western Ukrainian propaganda" (*galitska propaganda*). But were Marxists supposed to rejoice when spurious ideas of ethnic unity inculcated by two centuries of imperialism trumped national independence?[19] He did not apply this same logic when he praised the "bourgeois" Catholic Irish Easter Rising that same year.

Ukrainian Marxists accepted Lenin's ruminations in *Imperialism* as axiomatic. But they used them to explain the relations between Soviet Russia and Ukraine. They did not think that socialists should dismantle "bourgeois" national independence after a revolution; rather, such independence should be made the basis of the new order. They refused to subordinate themselves to a metropolitan party based in the former imperial centre, and they put their theoretical critique into practice with a short-lived armed struggle against Russian communist rule.

Ukrainian Marxists considered Ukraine before and after 1917 to be a Russian colony: a subjugated, exploited region ethnically distinct from the metropole that provided the metropole with raw materials and a market for finished goods.[20] Fundamentally, this is what differentiated them from Russian Marxists, who did not regard non-Russian territories within the empire as Russian (Great Russian) colonies. Unlike the Ukrainians, the Russians did not compare the tsarist empire, which they called "Rossiia," with other empires, except occasionally with the Habsburg Empire, which they called "Austria" and treated as a "multinational state" like Switzerland or the United States. For Ukrainian Marxists, "Russia" (Ukr. *Rosiia*) meant ethnic or Great Russia (*Velika Rossiia*) and was not synonymous with *Rossiia*. Ethnic or Great Russia as imperial metropole could not be placed on the same analytical field as Ukraine the colony, and it was not the indigenous non-Russians living on their historic lands within the empire who were "minorities." The "minorities" were the Russians living in non-Russian territories, who, insofar as they did not assimilate or acculturate with the native population, constituted *de facto* settler-colonists. Although the status of the Ukrainian provinces within the Romanov empire and of Ukraine within the Russian Soviet Republic differed somewhat from that of colonies in the major overseas empires, Ukrainian dependency before and after 1917 (as Ukrainian communists claimed) can be seen from the colonial/imperial perspective. Of the four types of colonies, the Ukrainian lands resembled the "mixed-settler" kind, which included Latin American countries, North African countries, Korea, and Ireland. Of these, Ukraine can best be compared with Ireland, in that both were geographically and culturally European.

After 1801, neither country was separated from its metropole by administrative borders, and natives from both could make careers in central government bureaucracies if they knew the imperial language. In Ireland, Catholics could work in the internal civil service as of 1829. The ruling English and Russians considered their respective nations to be agents of progress and civilization, and the Irish and Ukrainians as "doomed peoples" that could, however, be "civilized" through assimilation. Lord Milner considered the Scots, English, and Irish to be a single nation "impossible to destroy." Nationalist radicals in both nations at the beginning of the century were a minority. The fact that they spoke English or Russian rather than Gaelic or Ukrainian did not make them any less nationalist or anti-imperialist.[21] Both bemoaned how their co-nationals collaborated in their own oppression, as expressed in the aphorism "put an Irishman on a spit and you will always find another to turn him." The moderate majority sought autonomy in return for loyalty. Few settler-colonists in the Irish or Ukrainian provinces assimilated or became creole nationalist separatists on the Latin American model. Most were empire loyalists who divided the majority population that surrounded them into good ("loyal") and bad ("treasonous").[22] By 1914, few English – unlike the Russians with the Ukrainians – still harboured illusions about assimilating the Irish; yet they likely shared Winston Churchill's view that the Irish were odd "because they refuse to be English." In Ireland in 1904, extremist empire loyalists formed the Ulster Unionist Council to oppose the national movement; two years later, their loyalist counterparts in Kyiv formed the "Kyivan Club of Russian Nationalists."[23] Both groups opposed reformist moderates in their central governments. One key difference between the two countries was that Ukrainian nationalism was secular and socialist, unlike Irish republican nationalism, within which James Connolly represented a minority. Another difference: there were no paramilitary groups in the Ukrainian provinces on the eve of the war, whereas in Ireland, both loyalists and nationalists had mobilized volunteer militias approximately 100,000 strong. While English liberals accepted Irish independence, their Russian counterparts never accepted Ukrainian independence. The Treaty of Versailles did not recognize Ireland *or* Ukraine, and the words of the Irish Republic's representative in Paris in the summer of 1919 about his country being a lonely symbolic figure "tragically isolated" from the other European nations applied to Ukraine as well. If we replace "British" and "Irish" with "Russian" and "Ukrainian," the following observation might also apply to Ukraine: "Technically, at times, Ireland may not have been a colony at all; but, the forms of revolutionary and cultural activism developed by the Irish against the entrenched self-interest of its rule by the British aristocracy and bourgeoisie meant that it remained the standard bearer for all anti-colonial movements in the late nineteenth and twentieth centuries."[24]

In the 1980s there was much debate about Ireland's colonial status. The debate touched on almost all aspects of domination and dependency and their relations to Marxism, nationalism, and modernization. Most agreed that the Irish both sustained and undermined the empire they belonged to and were simultaneously colonialist and imperialist. Lines between the metropole and the regions, centre and periphery, native and foreign, were not rigid, and class consciousness could not transcend national contexts. Catholics could be imperial loyalists, Protestants could be Irish patriots. English rule had marginalized the Irish language, and it was difficult to imagine an Irishman who was not also English. Yet the country produced one of the world's strongest and longest-lasting revolutionary republican nationalist movements.[25]

The Irish case provides insights and lines of inquiry into Ukrainian–Russian relations. Particularly relevant is the idea that colonial-type dependency should not be thought of in spatial terms but as a process through which societies were integrated into a world system that after the sixteenth century was centred in northwestern Europe.[26] Geography is irrelevant to understanding the mechanism of this integration because it was the same regardless of distance and barriers. National borders defined the specific circumstances that influenced the mechanism but did not nullify the broader universal context. From such a perspective, Ireland and Ukraine can be compared not only with each other but also with Finland, Catalonia, pre-1917 Bohemia, Algeria, and Korea. The events in both countries, finally, remind us that peripheral rebellion and state fragmentation are as typical for European lands as for overseas empires. Western Eurasia prior to 1918 saw two waves of rebellions based on nationality. The first, between 1749 and 1789, involved the Scots, Greeks, Corsicans, Dutch, and Belgians; the second, between 1799 and 1848, involved the Irish, Norwegians, Finns, Belgians, Italians, and Greeks. That Ukraine emerged from the break-up of an empire only in the twentieth century and had "colonial" elements in its history normally identified with overseas colonies does not make Ukraine an anomaly in Europe. The cases of Poland, Czechoslovakia, Finland, Iceland, and Malta were similar.[27] At the end of twentieth century Ukraine was one of twenty-two of Europe's thirty-eight states that had emerged through imperial break-up between 1905 and 1991. While a colonial model is applicable to some if not all of them, Ukrainian Marxists were the first to apply this model to Ukraine.

Although colonialism and imperialism, and comparisons with non-Europeans, figured more prominently in Ukrainian than in Irish writing between 1917 and 1925 and carried more political significance, Ukrainian independence in 1991 did not lead to the kind of reconsideration of imperial links within Ukraine as had occurred in Ireland. The Ukrainian communist legacy remains little known, if at all, and has little influence even among self-proclaimed Marxist radicals. Abroad, liberals and socialists remained as little interested in Ukrainians after as they were before 1991 – much like some of their English precursors had once ignored the Irish. In 1858, the *Irishman* (28 August) observed: "Black niggers are much more attractive objects of sympathy ... Had he a white face and Irish rags your British philanthropist would think marvelously little about him." Those concerned with colonized and recently decolonized peoples continued to "think marvelously little" about the millions of Ukrainians who remained under Russian hegemony and remained reluctant, more for political than for scholarly reasons, to treat the Russian-dominated USSR as a French or British or Spanish or American-style imperialist villain.[28] Liberal-leftist interest in Ukraine heightened after the 2014 *Euromaidan* and the ensuing Ukrainian–Russian war. But Ukrainian communists would have been appalled by how many foreign, supposedly "anti-colonialist" Marxist leftists, apparently considering Russian neo-liberal corporate capitalism preferable to Anglo-American neo-liberal corporate capitalism, and refusing to see that the majority of Ukrainians did not share that opinion, supported Vladimir Putin's neo-imperialist aggression in Ukraine.[29]

Chapter One

We propose Union and they want to dominate.

Letter to the editor, *Chervonyi prapor*, 25 February 1919.

Historical Background

In the early twentieth century, the people we now call Ukrainians were much like other peoples in the world. Most were rural, did not live in independent national states, and had little influence on politics. Ukraine, like Poland, was not on any political map of Europe. There were eight Ukrainian provinces in the Russian empire, all centrally administered units with common characteristics that distinguished them from Russian territories. Like Ireland in the United Kingdom between 1801 and 1918, they retained regional particularities that allow them to be classified as a "mixed settler" colony. Ukrainian peasants spoke Ukrainian and did not practice land repartition. In 1900 the numerically small but economically powerful Polish nobility still dominated the three western provinces of Kyiv, Volyn, and Podillia.

The first significant Russian settlement into Ukrainian territories, comprising merchants, administrators, and soldiers, dated from the eighteenth century. Massive settlement of Russian migrant workers, began in the late nineteenth century. By 1900 approximately 2 million Russian speakers, most of whom were Russian, were concentrated in Kharkiv and Katerynoslav provinces. This averaged 10 per cent of the total population of the Ukrainian provinces. Declared Russians constituted 33 per cent of Ukraine's total urban population, 43 per cent

of the population in its eight largest cities, and 52 per cent in its four
largest cities. Between 40 and 50 per cent of government administrators were Russian speakers. There was no controlled border between
the Ukrainian and Russian provinces to hinder Russian in-migration
as there was between the Duchy of Finland and Russian provinces. No
border and a century of direct rule by Saint Petersburg, during which
time education, administration, the print media, and high culture were
all in Russian, meant that Russian settlers had no sense of themselves
as immigrants or colonists. They did not become an immigrant minority whose social mobility depended on learning a foreign language and
assimilating into the host community. Nonetheless, the Ministry of the
Interior in the 1897 census clearly identified Ukrainians (*Malorossy*) as
the "native [*korennoe*]" population in Kharkiv province and Russians
(*Velikorussov*) as the "immigrant population [*prishlym naseleniem*]."[1]

The Ukrainian provinces had fewer industrial workers than Russian
provinces because state policy developed Ukraine's extractive industries and agriculture while neglecting its manufacturing sector. Also
factory owners tended to hire incoming poor but semi- or highly skilled
Russian peasants, whom they preferred to local poor but unskilled
Ukrainian peasants. Many of the latter, in turn, preferred to take government subsidies and migrate to Siberia rather than risk going to a nearby
factory. Of all workers, 17 per cent came from non-Ukrainian provinces,
and of these, 70 per cent were Russian in 1897. Ukrainian speakers were
on average 73 per cent of all workers and between 30 and 50 per cent of
all urban industrial workers. Twenty per cent of all Ukrainian-speaking
workers were urban industrial workers, and Ukrainians were 70 per
cent of all workers in settlements not classified as "cities" in the census.
In terms of linguistic and socio-economic structure, "the Ukrainian proletariat was totally unlike the Russian proletariat."[2]

Although at the turn of the century, Russians who had no sense of
themselves as immigrants in the Ukrainian provinces did not have to
learn or use the local language, and few assimilated into the host community, the question of whether Ukraine's urban population would
Ukrainianize or Russify was still open. Bilingualism, diglossia, and
intermarriage kept boundaries porous and identities ambiguous, and
almost half of all incoming workers were from Ukrainian provinces.[3]
Nor was there yet direct correspondence between language use and
political allegiance. Much would depend on future governmental policies. The Polish landowning nobles and urban Russians were a dominant settler-colonist minority on Ukrainian territory. Although Polish

nobles initially supported Ukrainian autonomy, it should be noted that that support had faded by the end of 1917 as rural social radicalism brought latent mutual hatreds to the boil.[4] Rural Polish and Russian peasants tended to assimilate into the Ukrainian majority; urban Russian dwellers did not. Living in cities with no Ukrainian-language schools, churches, businesses, mass-circulation newspapers, or government offices, they had no need to learn Ukrainian or to culturally assimilate in order to obtain services, an education, a good job, and status. Most Russians, Poles, and assimilated Ukrainians, like settler-colonists and assimilated natives in any colony, looked down on unassimilated Ukrainians. Few among the Russian intelligentsia applied their humanist standards and sensitivities to Ukrainian national issues or supported Ukrainian political demands. It was the dominated indigenous majority-Ukrainian nationality for whom social mobility was contingent on learning a foreign language and adopting foreign cultural norms. All had to learn some Russian, many changed their surnames, many internalized "the colonizer's image of the colonized" by perceiving themselves as "Little Russians." Many eventually assimilated and considered themselves Russian. Many of the socially mobile ethnic Ukrainians who admired European modernity and equated it with Russian national identity, linked their own identity with the rural backwardness and poverty they were seeking to escape. Divisions ran within families: one brother might become a Ukrainian nationalist, another a Russian imperialist. Jewish political elites, for their part, by 1917 supported Ukrainian autonomy but, that support did not extend far among their compatriots, who were mostly sceptical or indifferent. "That attitude was reflected not only in comic dismissal of Ukrainian and Ukrainian-language signs; they also passively opposed Ukrainization." Jewish workers in 1917–18 volunteered for the Red Guard. None volunteered for Ukrainian units.[5]

Some bilingual Ukrainians became administrators, traders, manufacturers, patrons of the national movement, and millionaires, but they did not constitute a national capitalist class. Most of Ukraine's overwhelmingly non-Ukrainian industrialists and bankers identified with the empire. In 1920, the émigré left-SR Mykyta Shapoval noted that Russian, Polish, Jewish, Hungarian, Czech, Rumanian, Belgian, French, and English capital ruled: "In its organization *form* [sic] this is not Ukrainian but *colonial* [sic] capital. It is also colonialist [sic] in terms of its economic *aim* [sic]. It reflects the interests of the metropole and treats Ukraine only as the object of terrible exploitation." "Colonialist capital has never, in any place, built an independent state from a colony." He observed that in Ireland, "a colony of intelligent and humane English capital," the Irish had no option after more than one hundred years of struggle but to engage in "terrorist partisan war."[6]

In general, people most of the time do not think about their nationality, and before the war, linguistic-cultural borders were fluid. Educated urban elites had only begun to politicize national identities and draw boundaries between loyal "Russians" or "Little Russians" and disloyal "Ukrainians." Not every non-Ukrainian shared the anti-Ukrainian Russian-slavophile-based attitudes of the extremist imperial loyalist parties known as the "Black Hundreds." Ethnic Ukrainians and Russians who supported a loyalist "Little Russian" cultural autonomy could simultaneously condemn Ukrainian political autonomy. Difference did not disrupt everyday life. In 1917 in the town council of Vinnytsia, a typical provincial capital of around 60,000 people, of whom almost 40 per cent were Jewish, "[deputies] spoke in all languages: Polish, Ukrainian, Hebrew, various jargons, sometimes Russian, and the spokesman [of the Jewish faction] Spivak spoke in a mix of all of them."[7]

Rival elites successfully politicized identities during the revolution as attitudes hardened. Weak Ukrainian governments were too short-lived to appreciably change the views of urban dwellers with Russo-centric preconceptions of eastern Slavic and imperial political unity, who viewed Ukrainians as second-rate, inherently rural, backward, and seditious. As far as is known, most such persons after 1918 still considered Russian a higher culture, which they identified with loyalty to the Bolshevik regime, or the White one. When Anna Dobrovolska in July 1919 faced having to attend church services in Ukrainian in the re-established Ukrainian Orthodox church subject to Constantinople rather than Moscow, for example, she refused. Her imperial identity trumped her religious convictions, and she denounced the new Ukrainian church to the atheist Bolshevik government as a treasonous organization because it was linked to the Ukrainian National Republic (UNR).[8] The Ukrainian-born Russian monarchist Vasili Shulgin was extremely pleased when on his visit to Kyiv in 1925 he heard no Ukrainian in the streets. On visiting Odessa in 1921, a Ukrainian communist reported that "the Ukrainian population is small and totally terrorized … The fear is so great that they are afraid to speak Ukrainian and ask about what is happening in Ukraine in corners." When he began giving public lectures in Ukrainian, he was considered heroic "because everything Ukrainian is slandered as "Petliurism." In Mylokaiiv, another

Ukrainian communist observed that for local Bolsheviks, "there is no such thing as a Ukrainian revolution [and] the Ukrainian Communist Party is a petite-bourgeois chauvinist national organization."[9]

The leaders of the national movement were bilingual political moderates, and after 1905 they could legally form political parties. At the turn of the century, they began to disseminate the idea that the ethnically Ukrainian provinces of the tsarist empire (*Rossiia*) constituted a political, cultural, and economic entity called "Ukraine," which was distinct from Russia (*Velikorossiia*). The leaders began to build a middle-class infrastructure of literate peasants, retailers, and white-collar workers. These people began to wonder why business, education, government, and high culture in "Ukraine" had to be in Russian and not in Ukrainian.[10]

While the moderate majority of Ukrainian national activists regarded linguistic and cultural assimilation as more significant indices of Russian imperialism than economic exploitation, radicals drew attention to the latter and to the impact of industrialization and commercialization. The Jewish-Ukrainian activist Maksym Hekhter labelled Ukrainian agricultural workers "white niggers."[11] While most national leaders, like their Irish counterparts, considered capitalist urban industrial modernity a threat to Ukrainian nationality, a Marxist minority argued that Ukrainian nationality could only develop alongside capitalist modernity.[12] Before the war, self-awareness and self-assertion on the whole remained muted, although antagonisms occasionally surfaced. Ukrainian nationalists focused on cultural-linguistic rather than economic issues and were not extremists; most literate educated Russian speakers, urban white-collar professionals, and industrial workers tolerated "Little Russians" and their folk songs. Some regarded them with condescending contempt, but only the extremist imperial loyalist minority was openly hostile towards the national movement. Russian urban settlers and Polish landowners in the Ukrainian provinces, for their part, did not develop a "creole/mestizo" separatist nationalism as did European colonists in Latin and North America. Urban Russians overwhelmingly identified with the imperial metropole politically and culturally, much as Anglo-Scot loyalists in Ireland, Germans in Bohemia, and French settlers in Algeria did, rather than with their place of residence. Polish nobles, profoundly alienated by peasant land seizures in 1917, opposed Ukrainian independence (unlike their Swedish counterparts in Finland, who backed Finnish independence).

National leaders in Kyiv formed the Central Rada in March 1917.[13] That November, its moderate socialist majority proclaimed the UNR an autonomous part of Russia. Instead of declaring independence after the Bolsheviks took power, the Rada sought a federation with the Provisional government then represented by General Kaledin in southern Russia.[14] This prompted the Russian Bolsheviks to invade UNR territory in January 1918 in support of their comrades in Kharkiv, who had already on their own initiative occupied UNR cities. The Rada initially enjoyed the support of the 85 to 90 percent of peasants who were poor or struggling and who hoped it would enact land reform. The Rada's hesitation on this issue led to civil war by early 1918, which Russian Bolsheviks turned into a national war when they invaded on the side of Ukraine's Bolsheviks. The invasion prompted the Rada to proclaim independence and sign the Treaty of Brest-Litovsk with the Central Powers (see figure 4, illustration section). In April 1918, with German support, landowners and industrialists overthrew the UNR and installed Pavlo Skoropadsky as Hetman of the Ukrainian State. His regime fell in November with the collapse of Germany and was succeeded by a renewed UNR under the temporary rule of a Directory led by the centrist Simon Petliura and the leftist Volodymyr Vynnychenko. The UNR and its army collapsed in December 1919 after a second Bolshevik invasion that established the Ukrainian Socialist Soviet Republic, but, a vicious partisan war that had begun in 1919 raged on until 1922. The major Ukrainian partisan groups were affiliated with either the SRs, the SDs, the UNR, or Makhno, although they did change sides. The UNR attempted to coordinate and control as many partisan groups as possible, without much success.[15]

Russians and Russified non-Russians dominated the Bolshevik faction of the Russian Social Democratic and Labor Party (RSDLP) in the Ukrainian provinces as a "centralist" majority. The many culturally Russified ethnic Jews in that party were secular apostates who were not representative of the religious Jewish majority. As a culturally and politically Russian party in Ukraine, the RSDLP was not a party of an oppressed nation. The provincial party organizations had no ties with one another. The most important branch was in Kyiv province, but almost 65 per cent of party members were in Kharkiv and Katerynoslav provinces. By December 1917, the Bolsheviks did not yet dominate Ukraine's approximately three hundred soviets. In 1917 they controlled the soviets only in the large cities – they were 88 per cent of members in Luhansk, 60 per cent in Kyiv, 48 per cent in Kharkiv, 47 per cent in

Katerynoslav, 40 per cent in Odessa. Only forty of Ukraine's soviets present at the Second All-Russian Congress of Soviets approved the Bolshevik seizure of power in Petrograd. Only ninety of Ukraine's soviets ratified their seizure of power in Kharkiv.[16]

Among the Kyivan bolsheviks were some later termed "federalists" who differed with the "centralist" majority regarding the degree to which Ukraine was to be subordinated to Russia. Both groups cooperated conditionally with the Rada, much like communists were later to cooperate with "revolutionary anti-imperialist nationalists," until 26 October, when they declared the Rada a "counterrevolutionary bourgeois" organ. This was in reaction to the Rada's refusal to recognize the authority of Lenin's Soviet government because it represented only a minority among the country's left-wing revolutionary democrats.[17] Thereafter, Ukraine's Bolsheviks called for single-party rule in Ukraine, which they claimed was necessary to fight "Ukrainian nationalism."

Ukraine's Bolsheviks took power in Kharkiv in December 1917 with approximately 4,500 troops and Red Guards, of whom roughly 2,100 had arrived from Moscow the previous week.[18] This group, which garnered only 10 per cent of the vote in the elections to the Constituent Assembly, and which represented less than 30 per cent of Ukraine's soviets, claimed to be the government of the five Ukrainian provinces that the Provisional Government had formally subordinated to the Central Rada. Bolsheviks in Katerynoslav, Kherson, and Taurida provinces remained formally under Petrograd, not Kharkiv. The Kharkiv government arrived in Kyiv on 30 January (12 February) 1918 in the wake of the Russian Red Army (see figures 7 and 8, illustration section).The allied Ukrainian and German armies expelled it from the city in March. Ukraine's first Bolshevik government included Ukrainian-born Russians, Germans, secular Jews, some Ukrainians, a few Russians from Russia and was subordinated to Lenin's plenipotentiary in Ukraine, Sergo Ordzhonikidze.[19] This government sought more power than its central leaders were prepared to allow it, and some of Ukraine's pro-Bolshevik workers supported it as a Ukrainian and not as a Russian soviet government (see figure 5, illustration section). On 1 January 1918, the Kharkiv Bolsheviks declared: "The centre of Soviet power in Ukraine is the Central Executive Committee of the Soviets of Ukraine and its People's Secretariat ... All military units arrived in Ukraine from the north must put themselves under the authority of CEC [Central Executive Committee] of Ukraine and the activities of their commander in Ukraine can be carried out only in the name of Ukraine's CEC and the People's Secretariat."[20] Pro-Bolshevik ethnic Ukrainians in partisan units, meanwhile, may not all have been nationally conscious Ukrainians, but they did know their villages were not in Russia and, they refused to fight in Russia. They had been prepared to fight for soviet rule and land but, they mutinied or deserted when they learned that party committees had displaced the soviets, had collectivized land and, (after May 1919), had begun folding their regiments into the Red Army. "We will not fight for Russia," they told Bolshevik commissars. "But we will fight for [soviet] Ukraine."[21]

Most of Ukraine's soviets had Russian SR, Ukrainian SR, or Ukrainian SD majorities. This diversity was reflected for the last time in Ukraine's Second Congress of Soviets, held in March 1918. The Bolsheviks had not had time to stack the local assemblies that sent delegates; consequently, that Congress passed pro-Bolshevik resolutions primarily thanks to the presence of armed Russian Red sailors, who denied non-Bolsheviks the floor and threatened to shoot them. From the podium, Bolshevik delegates threatened to shoot the ninety quarrelsome Ukrainian SD representatives, which prompted fifty-five of them to leave. The Congress opened and closed with the singing of the Internationale, but delegates also sang the Ukrainian patriotic song "Zapovit" and the Ukrainian National Anthem.[22] In 1919, on arriving in Kyiv, the new government imposed on Ukraine the Russian Soviet constitution, which heavily weighted representation in favour of urban workers and soldiers. Given that the overwhelming majority of these groups in Ukraine were Russian or Russified, Bolshevik rulers thereby effectively disenfranchised the Ukrainian majority. That year, the Bolsheviks also had enough time to ensure that the people voted for them in elections. They could subsequently dominate the Ukrainian-majority villages and small towns and minimize the non-Bolshevik presence in soviets. Moreover, even though the Russian constitution stipulated proportional elections, which in November 1917 Bolshevik leaders had declared "more democratic" than majoritarian ones, in Ukraine they imposed majority voting to eliminate large non-Bolshevik minorities from the soviets.

Local agents did not refrain from force. For instance, in the village of Merefa in Kharkiv province in February 1919, the local Cheka agent referred to "my use of repression" in ensuring that a fourth round of voting established a pro-Bolshevik soviet. In the central provincial town of Horodyshche that spring, a 150-strong Cheka detachment with six machine guns arrived in the wake of the Red Army. Its commander presented the locals with lists of candidates they had to vote for. Only one list included town residents – local Bolsheviks, who were overwhelmingly Jewish. Instead of electing outsiders, the inhabitants elected the Jewish Bolsheviks.[23] As a consequence of such measures, Ukraine's Third Congress of Soviets in March 1919 was stacked with a 78 per cent Bolshevik majority, who dutifully booed one of the two Ukrainian left-SD delegates who tried to make a speech condemning centralization, Russification, and economic exploitation, forcing him to step down.

Only after they had signed the Treaty of Brest-Litovsk of March 1918 did Lenin's Bolsheviks recognize that the eight provinces claimed by the UNR constituted "Ukraine." They then ordered their Kharkiv, Katerynoslav, and Taurida (the Crimea) provincial branches to submit to Ukraine's secretariat rather than to Russia's. That same month, the Bolsheviks renamed themselves the Russian Communist Party (RCP) and permitted their branches in Ukraine to form a single territorial subunit dominated by its Russian centralist majority. The "Kyivan" minority, led by Mykola Skrypnyk, decided that April to establish instead a Ukrainian Communist Party independent of the Russian party. However, Skrypnyk backed down in May after a meeting with Lenin for which there are no minutes. Afterwards, *Pravda* (9 May 1918) proclaimed that "the Russian Communist Party Central Committee … has no objection to the formation of a Ukrainian Communist Party in as much as Ukraine is an independent state." That statement was issued only to prevent a German invasion, however. In reality, Ukraine's party remained subordinated to Moscow. This was confirmed in July, when representatives of the "provincial committees of the territories in South Russia occupied today by Germans," at a meeting attended by Lenin's deputy Iakov Sverdlov, passed a resolution specifying that Ukraine's Communist Party was to be subordinated to the Russian party. A few days later, Ukraine's Bolsheviks adopted the name Communist Party (Bolshevik) of Ukraine at a secret session of their First Congress. Senior leaders there explained that now that "the proletariat," meaning the Bolsheviks, had taken power, "the right of self-determination" and national independence were counter-revolutionary and a threat to the working class. Skrypnyk claimed that with the Bolshevik seizure of power, the period of national states had passed and nationalism had become "reactionary." He stated that the Russian party remained Ukraine's mentor: "That is why in practice the situation [of dependency] remains as it was." He added that his earlier proposal for a separate UCP belonging to the Communist International would now involve merely "formal" status. In practice, there was now an informal "unwritten constitution" that dictated that "we belong to a communist party that is one for all countries" – the Russian party. Of the CPU's 4,314 members at the time, 7 per cent were Ukrainian speakers.[24] In January 1919 the CPU proclaimed the Ukrainian Socialist Soviet Republic.

Bolshevik leaders, like Russian liberals and monarchists, sought to preserve the territorial integrity of the tsarist empire. Lenin, however, was flexible. Faced with the military power of the revolutionary Ukrainian national movement, Lenin, in his celebrated "On Soviet Power in Ukraine" and "Letter to Ukrainian workers" of December 1919, offered what he regarded as cultural-linguistic "concessions" along with governmental positions to leaders of the left-wing factions of the Ukrainian Party of Socialist Revolutionaries (SRs) and SDs. This did much to end resistance, for opposition leaders no longer saw the need for it.[25] The armed resistance that did continue, until 1922, was uncoordinated.

In early 1919 the left-wing faction of the Ukrainian SRs renamed themselves the Ukrainian Communist Party (Borotbists) and allied themselves with the Russian Bolsheviks, claiming that the excesses of the latter were but "isolated incidents" that would not have serious consequences.[26] The Borotbists had hoped to establish a Ukrainian Army, but the centralization of the Red Army limited their access to Ukrainian soldiers. On 4 May, Trotsky had ordered all Red military formations subordinated to Moscow; three days later, he ordered Red Ukrainian partisans to be either disbanded or reorganized as subunits of the Red Army. By September he had probably ordered the death of at least three Bolshevik Ukrainian commanders, who died under mysterious circumstances within weeks of one another.[27] In March 1920 the Borotbists dissolved their organization and approximately 5,000 of their 15,000 members joined the CPU. Some were given ministerial positions in May 1920.[28] Lenin admitted them into his party, but only as individuals, and he secretly instructed his people to harass Borotbists and remove them from their positions on minor or spurious legal charges. To ensure that the few who did join the CPU would have little influence, the Kremlin ordered its local leaders to form a special "temporary Central Committee" to register and exclude undesirables. By 1922 only 188 former Borotbists remained in the CPU. Similar tactics were later applied to the UCP, which also dissolved itself. As of 1924, only 23 per cent of the CPU and 18 per cent of its central committee were Ukrainians.[29]

Ukrainian communists emerged from the left wing of the Ukrainian SDs and the "Kyivans" within the CPU. The first theoretical exposition of Ukrainian communism, *Do Khvyli*, was written in December 1918 by the Ukrainian Bolsheviks Shakhrai and Mazlakh. In January 1919, left-Ukrainian SDs separated from their parent party and renamed themselves "Independentists." In January 1920 they adopted the name Ukrainian Communist Party. The head of the UNR's counter-intelligence considered Mykhailo Tkachenko, a co-founder of the UCP who died in December 1919, "the Ukrainian Lenin."[30] The UCP stood for a sovereign Ukrainian communist state with its own party independent of the Russian communist state and party. It demanded independence on the basis of categorical right, not Bolshevik imperial pragmatism. This distinguished them from the Borotbists, who, like moderate Irish nationalists, hoped only for autonomy in return for loyalty.

In 1919, pro-Bolshevik Ukrainians wanted national independence and social justice – in other words, national and social liberation within a socialist Ukraine ruled by its own party and ministries, within a supranational socialist confederation. Bolshevik leaders for their part regarded their "Ukrainian Republic" as little more than a Russian province; they did not dismantle their pre-1917 centralized party structure or the single imperial economic system inherited from the tsars. In 1923 they offered Ukraine only cultural autonomy within a nominal federation administered from Moscow as a single centralized economic and political unit through ministries controlled by a single Russian-speaking party. This was less than Ukrainians had anticipated but more than the Entente had offered the UNR – that no Entente member-state recognized.

Under immense pressure, Bolshevik leaders agreed to linguistic and cultural concessions. In early 1921 they faced the Kronstadt and Tambov revolts, conflicts in Transcaucasia, and opposition from the left and urban workers. Beginning in 1921 they had to keep almost 20 per cent of the Red Army, a million soldiers, in Ukraine; only in 1922 did the army destroy the last bastion of partisan resistance in southern Kyiv province. According to Emma Goldman, who was in Kyiv that year: "Here the very atmosphere was charged with distrust and hatred of everything Muscovite … In Kiev there was no attempt to mask the opposition to Moscow. One was made to feel it everywhere." The incomplete

Table 1 Soviet Ukraine in 1920 by nationality, residency, and literacy.

	Totals	Ukrainians	Russians	Jews
Ukraine	21,526,786	12,294,142	2,610,267	1,189,029
% of counted* (16,963,312)		73%	15%	7%
Rural	17,156,911			
Urban	4,361,595			
Literate	5,875,748	3,586,471	1,129,708	777,748
% of respective nationality		29%	43%	65%
% of all literate		61%	19%	13%
% of counted (16,963,312)	35%	21%	7%	5%
Kyiv (city)	366,279	52,743 (14%)	170,662 (47%)	117,041 (32%)
Literate-Kyiv city	247,124	31,993 (13%)	110,179 (45%)	86,843 (35%)
Chernihiv	29,995	9,151 (31%)	9,961(33%)	10,253 (34%)
Kharkiv	269,924	57,366 (21%)	136,466 (51%)	55,474 (21%)
Odessa	427,831	12,455 (3%)	191,866 (49%)	190,135 (44%)
Poltava (city)	76,648	44,222 (58%)	7,666 (10%)	21,747 (28%)

Source: *Naselenie Ukrainy po dannymy perepisi 1920 goda*. Statistika Ukrainy. No. 28 Seriia 1. Demografiia tom 1. Vypusk 11 (Kharkiv, 1922), 2, 19, 22–3, 30 31; *Naselenie Kievskoi gubernii po dannymy perepisi 1920 goda*. Statistika Ukrainy. Demografiia seriia 1 Tom 1 Vypusk 1 (Kharkiv, 1922), 20

* Only 16,963,312 of total counted indicated nationality.

statistics available at the time suggested that war and revolution had not markedly changed the national character of the cities, but that the pre-war mass migration of Russians into those cities would likely end while that of Ukrainians would continue.[31]

Perhaps such figures played a role in Stalin's decision to extend the concessions first announced in 1919, when in the Tenth Party Congress

Resolutions of March 1921, he stated that Ukrainian cities would "inevitably" become Ukrainian. The village as the "guardian of Ukrainian" would enter all Ukrainian towns "as the dominant element – just as Latvian and Hungarian in the end dominated Latvian and Hungarian cities." There was nothing artificial in supporting this process, he stressed. Rakovskii and Skrypnyk, meanwhile, were complaining about centralization and seeking maximum autonomy for their republic. In the summer of 1922 they blocked an attempt to divide Ukraine into separate economic zones. In October of that year, a CPU plenum called for the broad use of Ukrainian in schools and government: "The Ukrainian proletarian state faces a difficult and complex task: the creation of Ukrainian soviet statehood, Ukrainian schools, the equalization of the rights of Ukrainian with Russian and of the language of the Ukrainian peasant with that of the Ukrainian proletariat, hindering the Ukrainian counter-revolution, and using the Ukrainian national school for its class purposes."[32]

Against this background, the Twelfth Russian Party Congress in 1923 sanctioned extensive cultural concessions to all non-Russians under a policy labelled "indigenization." During the 1920s many viewed this as a long-term strategy to transform the Ukrainian Republic into a national republic free at last of the cultural legacies of Russian domination. Russians would thereby be transformed from settler-colonists into an acculturated immigrant minority. Stalin hoped to destabilize Poland and Romania, both allied with France, and to that end he supported the creation of a culturally thriving Ukraine to attract the disgruntled Ukrainian minorities in those countries.

Stalin, however, in the Enlightenment tradition that separated culture from market, did not match cultural and linguistic concessions with economic decentralization. Moreover, the New Economic Policy (NEP) proclaimed in March 1923 was not implemented in Ukraine until the following year.[33] CPU leader Volodymyr Zatonsky, who also saw Russification as a cultural matter unrelated to economics, avoided the colony analogy in his speeches and did not criticize economic centralism. Supposedly, Russification required only an ideological solution: make comrades stop associating the Soviet federation with Russia![34] Some of those who opposed indigenization considered it absurd precisely because it divorced language use and culture from economics and administration. In their view, Lenin's notion of national self-determination was nonsense as well, because it contradicted his plan for a centralized economic and ministerial system. Among those who backed national rights but realized that indigenization as implemented would never work was the Georgian Marxist Mdivani, who dismissed the official discourse about cultural and linguistic rights as meaningless. Without a national economy there could be no national culture or language, nor any need within the non-Russian republics to learn languages other than the one used in economic relations – which in the USSR was Russian because all the ministries were centralized. Khristian Rakovskii, a Bulgarian who in 1919 ruthlessly imposed Soviet Russian rule in Ukraine as CPU chairman, had become by 1921 an advocate of Ukrainian rights. He noted that Russian imperial tendencies could be combated only if 90 per cent of Moscow's commissariats were dissolved and their functions placed under the control of the republics. Rakovskii did not doubt the existence of Russian chauvinism, but he now considered it more than an expression of pre-revolutionary attitudes. For him, it was also the product of economic and administrative centralization, and its agents were ministry personnel: "Russian[s] and Russified Jews who [in your Ukrainian ministries] are the most consistent champions of Russian national oppression." These people's opposition to "the simple matter" of learning and using another language in addition to Russian was intense.[35] UCP spokesmen complained that indigenization was superficial. They explained in 1924 that while linguistic and cultural concessions satisfied the intellectuals, for peasants and workers the real issues were economic, political, and party organizational. It was on these that cultural and linguistic matters were based, yet the indigenization policy ignored all three.[36]

What Ukrainian communists had called Bolshevik Russian colonialism during the revolution, official representatives discussed and categorized during the 1920s as "errors" or "Luxemburgism" that "the party" and "Leninist policy" had "corrected." Even Trotsky admitted that extreme conditions had obliged him to commit excesses in Ukraine. After 1923 he opposed the imposition of Russian in Ukraine on the grounds that it would impede Ukrainians' access to world culture and the ability to learn in their own language. He favoured locating manufacturing industries near resources. At the 1923 CPU conference he said that unless people who understood Ukrainian were placed everywhere, the soviet regime faced collapse.[37] In 1924, party leaders explained that it was the pressure of war, not ideology or imperial preconceptions, that had prevented them from eliminating national oppression as soon as they came to power.[38] In June 1926 a Ukrainian party plenum resolution included even the proletariat among the guilty and Russian nationalism as a culprit. Some comrades had incorrect views on national issues, and the party underestimated their significance, that resolution stated. It named the majority of the urban population and the considerable number of Russian proletariat and party members as the source of Russian chauvinism.[39] Stalin's deputy, Lazar Kaganovich, strongly condemned Russian nationalism in a CPU Central Committee Resolution of 1928, which listed seven manifestations of Russian and Ukrainian nationalism. Russian party members and bourgeoisie were explicitly identified as the ones who wished to retain Russian domination in Ukraine, who refused to learn Ukrainian, who wanted to restrict Ukrainian identity to villages, and who exploited mistakes to condemn indigenization as a policy that "oppressed" Russians.

But neither set of "errors" was condemned as "counter-revolutionary." The critique did not label Russian Bolshevism as a form of colonial rule, and sanctions or punishments were never meted out to Russians. Key Ukrainian critics who thought the concessions did not go far enough were not arrested, though they were transferred out of Ukraine.[40] Significantly, except for some among the latter group, those involved had treated national-cultural issues as intellectual-political matters associated with "class enemies." None linked them to economic structures or centralization, except UCP critics, who applied Lenin's *Imperialism* to Soviet Russia and analysed the Russian–Ukrainian relationship in terms of empire–colony discourse.

Many cultural/linguistic proposals made their way into indigenization policies, but few of the political and economic demands contained in the UCP critiques did so. Economic centralization was not among the officially admitted "errors."[41] Ministries remained centralized, planning regions ignored national borders, and central officials refused to function in any language other than Russian. The 1929 Ukrainian constitution did not give Ukrainian official status; that same year, the All-Union Central Committee directed that all government correspondence, even at the level of the republic, be in Russian. In 1923, Rakovskii noted that anyone waiting for the comrades in Ukraine's party school to voluntarily learn Ukrainian would wait a long time. Those who worked for central ministries in Ukraine considered learning Ukrainian a waste of time. By the end of the 1920s, 43 per cent of the staff of eighteen ministry branches in Ukraine and 49 per cent of the staff of republic ministries were still totally ignorant of Ukrainian. In 1929, 85 per cent of government bureaucrats still could not function in Ukrainian.[42] Much like other colonies, Ukraine was a place where officials were ignorant of their subordinates' languages, because they expected the ruled to learn the ruler's language.

Rakovskii and Skrypnyk in 1922 well knew that a hard core of Ukraine's urban Russians were ignoring or resisting party measures intended to limit if not curtail Russian cultural domination. By that year, hundreds of requests had come in from party members ignorant of Ukrainian requesting to leave the country. Mikhail Frunze, at a 1922 CPU plenum, realized the threat this posed: "In the end everybody would leave."[43] Skrypnyk, like Galiev, asked why those "Russian chauvinists" did not argue their case publicly. In Ukraine, after voting in favour of Ukrainian-language resolutions at the 1923 Party Congress, delegates in the corridors would reply, when addressed in Ukrainian: "Talk to me in a language I can understand." Senior leaders knew that Ukraine's Russian and Russified Jewish bureaucrats were strongly opposed to learning and using Ukrainian on the job, that most delegates in Moscow for the Twelfth Congress had no conception of the national issues involved, and that Congress corridor talk was dismissing the debates as theatre. The overwhelmingly Russian or Russified delegates simply voted during the Congress as their patron Stalin had instructed them. Two years earlier, Mikhail Tomsky, at the Eighth Congress, had identified their true opinions: "I think that we will not find in this hall anyone who would claim that national self-determination and national movements are normal and desirable. We regard these as a necessary evil." At the 1923 CPU conference, Zatonsky observed that "If all comrades spoke their minds there would be a Russian stink impossible to imagine [*Russkim dukhom zapakhlo chto i govorit nichogo*]."[44] A few weeks later, the resolutions of the secret Fourth Conference of senior party activists in Moscow specified that Russian nationalists were to be dismissed from party and government posts, but made no mention of the danger of imperial Russian "great power chauvinism" that Grigorii Zinoviev had castigated during the sessions. In 1925 the purging of "great power chauvinists" from the Red Army, initiated by Trotsky two years earlier, was halted.[45] One of Stalin's assistants at the Nationalities Commissariat wrote in 1930 that in its earlier work, the commissariat "systematically violated the Leninist line [Twelfth Congress resolutions] on the national question."[46]

Indigenization was only beginning to overcome Ukraine's colonial legacy when it was halted. In 1927, Russian in Ukraine's public communications sphere had only begun to recede from its pre-1914 dominance. Only 8.5 per cent of all published titles in the USSR were in Ukrainian – well below that language's share of the USSR's total population. In terms of titles per capita, Russians in Russia had 2.4 books in Russian, while Ukrainians had 1.6 in Russian and Ukrainian. Throughout the 1920s, declared Russians averaged 10 per cent of Ukraine's population yet more than 40 per cent of published books in Ukraine were in Russian. In 1927, 4,687 titles were published in Ukraine, of which 2,135 were in Russian. Russia that same year published 21,772 titles, of which only 13 were in Ukrainian. Printed Russian books in Ukraine comprised more than 50 per cent of total copies. When broken down by subject and audience, the disproportions are stark and reflect the pre-1917 colonial reality in which Russian was the language of urban modernity. Of 1,174 titles published during the first half of 1927, 43 per cent were in Russian. However, while the number of academic titles in each language was almost equal, of the 508 Russian books, 58 per cent were for children, 37 per cent for workers, and 1 per cent for peasants. The numbers for the 603 Ukrainian books were 36 per cent, 7 per cent, and 44 per cent respectively.[47]

In 1922, 54 per cent of CPU members were Russian speakers and 11 per cent were Ukrainian speakers. At the 1923 Congress, 47 per cent of the delegates were declared Russians and 20 per cent were Ukrainians. As of 1926, 44 per cent of the members were declared Ukrainians, 30 per cent were Ukrainian speakers, and 21 per cent used Ukrainian at work.[48] An early 1926 report to Ukraine's Central Committee reported that of all Ukraine's industrial and white-collar workers, 59 per cent and 56 per cent respectively did not speak Ukrainian. In addition, 78 per cent of the former and 33 per cent of the latter were literate only in Russian. Also, 35 to 40 per cent of Ukraine's 49,689 government bureaucrats and 25 per cent of its seventy-one top ministerial personnel were totally ignorant of Ukrainian.[49] Urban Russian and Russified white-collar professionals, whose attitudes towards the majority Ukrainians were not unlike those of European settlers in Africa towards Africans and Arabs, voiced their opposition to learning and using Ukrainian throughout the 1920s in Enlightenment/imperialist Russian slavophile terms: "Ukrainian is only a language for songs"; "[the language] is vulgar and unsuited for a subject like physics … Ukraine now is nothing but a part of Russia"; "I won't Ukrainianize – the Revolution was in Russian"; "Ukrainian is a dog's language, I won't study it." Some employees who knew Ukrainian refused to use it, while a considerable number did not know it at all. While employees could be fired for ignorance of Ukrainian, apparently few were. In a letter from a Luhansk miner, we learn that in fifty-six mines in the region, where Ukrainians averaged 57 per cent of the workforce, Ukrainian was forgotten after speeches were made. Privately, officials said there was no one to Ukrainize because "all our workers are Russians." Mine committees functioned in Russian, and when Ukrainian workers complained, they were told: "Go to your honkie land [*khokhlandiia*] and talk your dog-language there." Cultural clubs functioned in Russian, and there were no Ukrainian-language manuals. Ukrainian posters and announcements were systematically torn down.[50]

In general, more Ukrainian-language materials were published after 1922 than before 1914, and the government did establish Ukrainian schools and universities. The lower the level within the government and the party, the higher the percentage of declared Ukrainians or Ukrainian speakers, and with each passing year an increasing percentage of these two groups rose through the hierarchy. Perhaps this trend would have dominated in the long term. But there would be no long term.

Indigenization was never formally condemned, but it stopped being enforced after 1933. After that year, as before 1917, Russians in Ukraine would no longer face the fate of immigrants everywhere – learning foreign languages and acculturization. They remained settler-colonists. The change was reflected in two speeches by Zatonsky that gave different characterizations of Russian settler-colonists in Ukraine. In 1926 he had considered Ukraine to be undoubtedly a colony of the Russian tsars and bourgeoisie. Both tsarism and capitalism had Russified Ukraine, and the latter had also brought skilled Russian workers into Ukraine. "The Russian proletariat went to factories built in Ukraine." In 1933 he stated that "the theory that the proletariat in Ukraine, or its majority, came from Russia is totally false."[51] Condemnation of Russian chauvinism ceased that year. Support from Russians and Russified non-Russians opposed to learning and using Ukrainian compensated Stalin for the loss of support from Ukrainian party leaders – although his elimination of the "left opposition" meant in any case that he no longer needed national republic leaders as allies.

In 1923, Sultan-Galiev strongly condemned Stalin's public rationalization of indigenization. It was absurd, he pointed out, to label opposition to Russian great-power chauvinism as "local nationalism" and then claim that the latter was the opposite of the former. Opposition to great-power chauvinism was not "nationalism" – it was simply opposition to great-power chauvinism. It was absurd, he continued, to expect the "young Russian party comrades" who staffed local administrations to fight "local nationalism" if they were "infected" with great-power chauvinism. They would only fan the flames of chauvinism while "beating" local non-Russian communists on the spurious grounds that they were "nationalists." [52] These remarks infuriated Stalin, but he did not dispense with his false syllogism. In January 1934 he declared that the "greatest enemy" in the non-Russian republics was no longer Russian chauvinism but "local nationalism," and in 1938 he ordered that Russian be made compulsory in all Ukrainian schools.[53] Policy reversals were presented as "correcting errors" – but those reversals reflected Stalin's thinking as expressed in a September 1922 letter to Lenin (see below).

By 1939, Russian dominated in urban schools, the media, and administration. Massive in-migration of Russians had begun anew. Russians and Russian speakers did not have to learn Ukrainian to receive a job, a promotion, or government services, or to be educated, informed, or entertained. Russian language use still gave status and prestige. Ukrainian language use was relegated "things spiritual" – to ethnography, rural media, scholarship on Ukrainian subjects, and private use. Moscow ministries controlled an economy they administered in Russian. The Ukrainian communist criticism of Russian Bolshevism became relevant again.

Ukrainian Anti-colonialist Thought to 1917

Modern Ukrainian nationalism emerged in tsarist Ukraine. It was given intellectual expression by tsarist subjects born there, educated in its cities, and influenced by the ideas of Herder and Mazzini. It was tsarist subjects who first imagined "Ukraine" as a single cultural/political unit that overrode existing provincial borders, who did not think Ukrainian was simply an exotic mode of expression on its way to extinction, and who formed Ukraine's first modern political organization. The Cyril and Methodius Brotherhood (1846) called for national liberation, social emancipation, and a politically autonomous Ukraine belonging to a Slavic confederation without idle rich or working poor.[54] In 1877, Pavlo Chubynsky for the first time mapped this unit as a single Ukrainian ethnographic territory. By the end of the century, national activists had begun to question whether Ukraine was reaping its share of the wealth created by imperial industrialization, given that Ukrainians were poor even though their provinces were rich in resources (see figure 2, illustration section). They concluded that the situation could only be explained politically: the central government was stifling and impoverishing outlying regions. In studying this centre/periphery relationship, they came to see the Ukrainian provinces as a single cultural *and* economic unit. In 1906, Mykola Mikhnovsky was the first to argue that Russian rule over Ukraine was illegitimate under international law; he went on to organize a nationalist terrorist group in tsarist Ukraine. He did not describe Ukraine as a "colony," but, as James Connolly did in Ireland, he placed Ukrainian issues in the context of the "oppressed peoples" of the world and argued that imperial tariffs and financial policies were discriminating against Ukraine in favour of the Russian provinces.[55] Mikhnovsky described Ukraine as one of the "oppressed nations" of the world fighting for national liberty under the flag of socialism. He asserted that only national liberation would bring social freedom and that the expropriation of property was a necessary condition of national liberty: "The proletariat of the ruling nation and that of the subjugated nation are two different classes with dissimilar interests." Who were Ukrainians, Czechs, Irish, Slovenes, and Bretons? "A rural and urban proletariat." English democracy, he wrote, never defended the Irish, the Boers, the Indians, or the African races, and English workers and farmers were not troubled by Irish dependency or by the deaths of millions of Indians as a consequence of English rule over the Raj. Analogously, Americans cared little for Negroes or Indians, German peasants and workers had no regard for Poles, and Russian socialists cared nothing for Ukrainians. European nations with colonies, he continued, behaved like autocratic tsars and were worse than the Huns in their attitudes towards native peoples. As a result of their rule, those peoples had been eliminated or were barely surviving in deserts and isolated mountain ranges. "As we Ukrainians are also an oppressed nation, fighting for our freedom, should we not extend our hand to all oppressed peoples in a common struggle?" Mikhnovsky, as Fanon would do decades later, justified the use of violence by the oppressed against the oppressor. In his 1900 pamphlet *Samostiina Ukraina* he wrote: "That inhuman Russian attitude towards us [Ukrainians] sanctifies our hatred for them and our moral right to kill the oppressor while defending ourselves from oppression."[56]

At the turn of the century the notion of "Ukraine" as a colonized country was implicit in many writings. In 1909 the conservative Ukrainian thinker Viacheslav Lypinsky labelled the Polish nobility "outsider colonists" (*prybulytsi-kolonisty*).[57] But only in 1911, for the first time in Ukrainian thought, did Mykola Stasiuk explicitly apply the term "colonialist" to the relationship between Ukraine and the central imperial government and analyse that relationship as colonialism.[58] Five years later, Max Weber compared the non-Russian territories of the Romanov empire to British colonies like Ireland and India.[59]

In 1915, Ukrainian SRs published a translation of Karl Renner's article on colonialism. It identified four types of colonies and noted that economic dependency did not necessarily exclude political independence. Ireland was an agricultural colony, and Latin America was a "debt colony," while China was a "trade colony." Renner recognized that capitalism created nations from "unhistorical peoples" in colonies. Using the example of the Czechs, he claimed that a national bourgeoisie did not necessarily require independence in order to prosper. "Autonomy within an international state" – by which he meant the Habsburg Empire – was acceptable insofar as it provided a sufficiently large economic landscape for capital. This kind of symbiosis was possible in the Austrian empire but not in the Russian one because the former was on a higher level of development and had managed to survive the threat that bourgeois minorities posed to large states. He feared that the Russian state would not survive. He thought the national bourgeoisie would continue to oppress non-Russians despite the events of 1905 and would thus trigger the collapse of the state.[60]

Familiar with German-language socialist literature on imperialism, the agricultural cooperative activist Lev Kohut in 1916 wrote an analysis of imperialism. Presumably, he was influenced by the Comtean positivist understanding of it (echoing Kautsky) as a deplorable return to the past. Kohut described Russia as an autocratic corporation whose main shareholders were the royal family and senior bureaucrats. Allied with the French and Belgian "plutocracy," it was part of a "mercantile imperialism" that, like all profit-making enterprises, had to expand and subjugate its neighbours in order to continue. Kohut anticipated Joseph Schumpeter with his claim that the political and national interests of this backward militarist bureaucratic elite explained its foreign policy. In other words, pre-capitalist politics was determining economic and cultural oppression in the Russian empire as well as impeding Russian economic development by diverting resources to expansionism.[61]

In 1917, Petro Maltsiv called Russia a "state" rather than an empire and attributed Ukraine's unfavourable position to excessive centralization rather than to imperialism or colonialism. But his detailed statistical

study made the case for colonial exploitation. It showed that as an economic unit the Ukrainian provinces between 1900 and 1914 had consistently paid more into the state budget than they received from it
and, that during those years the amount they paid rose faster than the
amount they received. Saint Petersburg and Russian culture, he continued, lived off "the countries enslaved by Russia." Maltsiv showed that
whereas Ukraine's population on average paid 17 roubles per capita in
taxes and got 8 in services, Russia's population paid 14 and got 13; it was
not clear whether these figures excluded Saint Petersburg, which, as the
author demonstrated, consumed considerably more than it contributed
to the budget. Maltsiv concluded with an examination of tariff policy
that found Ukrainian provinces paying high prices for central Russian–
produced agricultural machinery and getting low prices for grain sold
to Russia – all to the benefit of central Russia. Maltsiv did not advocate
secession as a remedy. Rather, what Ukraine needed was its own budget; the centralized empire had to become a federal "United States of
Russia." Although he did not exclude the possibility of separation, he
preferred the empire to be federalized, for then, Ukraine would spend
little on war and armaments. Stepan Kulyk estimated that taxation,
central bank interest income, foreign capitalist profits, and landowner
spending in the imperial capital annually drained 312 million roubles
from the Ukrainian provinces. Also in 1917, in what was perhaps the
first use of the term, the Ukrainian SR Joseph Maievsky published a
pamphlet titled "Red Imperialism." The great powers, he wrote, made
promises of self-determination to colonized peoples like the Ukrainians, Irish, Indians, and Vietnamese only because they needed them for
their war efforts, but those promises were empty. In the Russian empire
in 1917, "Imperialism only changed its tricolour flag into a red one."[62]

    At the Ukrainian SR conference in June 1917, Mykola Kovalevsky
explained that Russian democrats, like the Russian bourgeoisie, had
an interest in keeping Ukraine economically dependent; so did the
All-Russian Peasant Congress, which had voted against recognizing
Ukrainian autonomy because delegates saw Ukraine as a source of raw
materials. Ukrainians, meanwhile, demanded "full economic liberation
of the Ukrainian nation from foreign economic exploitation." Another
SR leader, Ivan Lyzanivsky, referring to the "imperialist policies of Russian democracy," wrote that Russia's wish for "economic union" was
just like the imperialism of Britain or Germany. These men referred to
Ukrainian events of that year as "the national rebirth of an oppressed
nation." The Ukrainian national bourgeoisie was so small that it had

little choice but to join the socialist ranks; however, the more influential non-Ukrainian bourgeoisie would cease being a threat once the revolution had destroyed the central imperial Russian state. At that point its loyalties by default would become "Ukrainian" in the territorial sense. Lyzanivsky reasoned that once national liberation had removed national oppression, the field would be clear for the development of an internationalist consciousness in Ukraine as well as for the struggle for socialism.[63] During the Bolshevik invasion, noting that the proletariat in Ukraine was small and mostly foreign, he wrote that the Bolsheviks were using the Russian Army to "nationally enslave" Ukraine – essentially a colonialism argument without the word "colonize."[64]

Thus, by March 1917, when the Rada declared it a political unit, Ukraine had already been envisaged as a cultural/national and economic unit and, there was already a body of literature examining Russian–Ukrainian relations in terms of colonialism and imperialism. The Rada issued a poster incorporating these ideas in the winter of 1917. It included statistics on raw materials extraction and taxation to demonstrate how "Muscovy for centuries has mercilessly and ruthlessly exploited our nation and reduced it today to utter ruin." Since Muscovy had always been a parasite on Ukraine, the only salvation for Ukraine lay in independence, alliance with Germany, and neutrality in the war – not federalism with Russia. The poster included a map depicting Ukrainian ethnographic territory – the first such image of Ukraine to be widely disseminated among its population (see figure 3, illustration section).

Notwithstanding all such references to imperialism and colonialism, national leaders built their movement on linguistic-cultural arguments and, in mass publications they devoted little attention to the idea of Ukraine as a Russian colony. During the years of revolution, only Ukrainian communists used anti-imperialist and anti-colonialist ideas extensively. One reason colonialism and anti-colonialism were marginal in Ukrainian public discourse was that censorship restricted the little that was published on Russian colonialism in Ukraine to specialist academic publications. A second reason was probably tactical: given the absence before 1917 of any criticism of Russian imperialism among those whom national leaders regarded as potential allies, the former would have alienated the latter had they shared and disseminated the ideas of the radicals who thought that colonized Ukrainians were suffering the same fate as Boers, Zulus, or Arabs. A third likely reason was that those who supported cultural activities and had government

jobs were unlikely to support condemnations of "Russian colonialism."
Finally, Ukrainians benefited from empire inasmuch as they served as
officers or administrators in non-Russian territories. Because national
leaders were reformist moderates, it made more sense for them to loyally uphold imperial prestige than to hope for its decline. Unlike Polish
and Finnish socialists, Ukrainians demanded only autonomy within
the borders of an empire restructured as a federated republican Russia
(*Rossiia*) – what their Irish counterparts called "imperial federation."

Bolsheviks, Colonialism, and Ukraine

Lenin sometimes intimated that tsarist Ukraine was a colony, but he
never explicitly categorized it as such. It is not known whether he
had read any Ukrainian publications on Russian colonialism. In 1914,
in a speech in Zurich that was not later published and is presumed
lost, he implied that the whole of tsarist Ukraine was a colony. He
said that Russia was "sucking out everything" from an undeveloped
Ukraine and giving nothing in return. Russian economic colonialism
was causing Ukrainian underdevelopment, so secession was justified.[65]
In December 1916 and again in June 1917, this line of thought reappeared in his remarks about his party's public support for liberation
wars: not only the Irish and Algerian uprisings, but also that of Ukraine
against Russia.[66] In his introduction to the 1917 edition of *Imperialism:
The Highest Stage of Capitalism*, published the year of the Easter Rising
in Ireland (1916), he claimed that because in the first edition censorship had obliged him to avoid mentioning Russia, he had had to refer
to Japan and Korea instead: "The careful reader will easily substitute
[in the relevant passages] Russia for Japan, and Finland, Poland, Cour-
land, Ukraine ... or other regions peopled by non-Great Russians, for
Korea."[67]

Yet Lenin never elaborated on Russian oppression as colonialist, and
in his writings on bourgeois revolutions, he did not distinguish clearly
between empires and national states, or between ruling metropolitan and colonized peripheral bourgeoisie. Notwithstanding his passing reference to Ukraine's colonial status, in the final analysis, he did
not consider it a Russian colony. In *Development of Capitalism in Russia*
(1899), he used the term "colonies" only in reference to the three south-
ernmost Ukrainian provinces, where, he argued, links between colony
and metropole were beneficial and should be maintained. Here capitalism was a necessary evil. Incorporating frequent references to southern

Ukraine, he claimed that the export of capital outside a metropolis was "progressive" because it developed capitalism in annexed regions and created large, integrated economic units. Although the empire had reached the stage of "monopoly capitalism," it remained heavily enmeshed in pre-capitalist structures. This meant that capitalism was still "progressive" and that secession would be economically regressive for non-Russians, who were therefore supposed to take part in the empire-wide anti-capitalist revolution and not stage independent anti-imperialist revolutions.

Analogously, despite his careful reading and later comments about censorship, he did not treat Ukraine in his *Imperialism* as he did the colonies of other empires. In that book he explained that links with a metropole were detrimental to a colony. He claimed, contrary to Marx and his own earlier view, that in its "monopoly" stage, capitalism was no longer "progressive," and that in colonies it was an obstacle to rather than a condition of industrialization. Secession from empires through national anti-imperialist revolutions led by a "progressive" bourgeoisie was, therefore, a precondition of industrial development in colonies. In separate articles he classified countries into groups according to the supposed strength of their "bourgeois democratic" national movements. He described the Ukrainian movement here as weak, yet, he classified Ukrainians as among an eastern European group of "oppressed nationalities" whose national movements were stronger than those in in "Asian–African colonies." This implied that the tiny Society of Ukrainian Progressivists (TUP), the only organized manifestation of Ukrainian nationalism in 1914, the year the article was written, was more influential than the Indian National Congress or the Chinese United League with their thousands of members. Logically, Lenin should have located India and China within his so-called eastern European group and Ukraine in his Asian colonial group. But he did not. He kept the Ukrainian movement analytically distinct from Asian movements. In the context of his thought, this meant that Ukraine was not "colonial," that its national movement was only that of an "oppressed nationality," and that it had no "progressive" bourgeoisie.

A second criterion Lenin used to distinguish "colonies" from "oppressed nations," besides the strength of "bourgeois democratic" national movements, was the availability of capital. Because capital supposedly existed in Ukraine, the country was not a colony and had no national "revolutionary bourgeoisie" that socialists should support. Socialists could support "anti-imperialist national revolutions" led by "progressive" petite bourgeoisie in India because capital supposedly existed there, but, in Ukraine, their task was to "unite" the workers of the oppressed and oppressor nations. Lenin's reasoning becomes even more obtuse a few pages later when he does not refer, as logically he should have, to Irish and English workers uniting against the Easter Rising that had been sponsored by the "petite bourgeoisie." In the final analysis, for Lenin, Ukrainian self-determination, unlike Indian or Chinese or Korean or Irish self-determination, did not involve a "national bourgeois revolution."

Thus, regardless of passing comparisons to the contrary, Lenin in the final analysis presents "Russia" as a multinational state with oppressed minorities rather than as an empire with settler-colonist Russian minorities scattered throughout. Within this schema, Ukrainians were not among the world's colonized peoples. While Lenin may have been the Bolshevik leader least influenced by Russian imperialist notions, nonetheless, he regarded Ukraine as an integral part of Russia. From such premises it followed for Bolsheviks that, in European overseas empires, socialists had to support the "anti-imperialist national revolutions" led by a "progressive" petite bourgeoisie. In Europe and tsarist Ukraine, their task was to "unite" the workers of the oppressed nation with those of the oppressor nations. The "right of national self-determination," Lenin additionally specified, involved only a temporary political independence. That right, moreover, could not by definition annul economic dependency, which was why capitalists who ruled empires could accept colonial political independence – they knew it would not affect their control. "Norway's 'self-determination' and secession *did not halt either* [sic] the development of finance capital generally, or … the buying up of Norway by the English." In any case, political secession would not be claimed by all, and no one was obliged to recognize the "right" to secession when it was claimed. Thus, echoing Mill, Lenin postulated that the "mass of working people" would "gravitate irresistibly towards union and integration with great socialist states" and dispense with the "seclusion" of political independence. Lenin agreed with Engels that "the victorious proletariat can force no blessings of any kind upon any foreign nation without undermining its own victory by so doing." He stressed that it was important "that yesterday's oppressors do not infringe on the long-oppressed nations' highly developed democratic feelings of self-respect." He accepted that "the proletariat," by which he meant his party, could make errors, and he assumed that such errors would "inevitably" lead to truth. But, these caveats did not negate his fundamental principle: in the long run, all political secession would eventually be nullified by the supposedly economically driven centralization of former imperial spaces.[68]

Lenin specified that any secession from the Russian empire was to be temporary, but, he never explicitly stated that that the secession of European overseas colonies would also be temporary. Only in his writings on the Russian empire – on Ukraine in particular – did he explicitly condemn all talk of "separating the workers of one nation from those of another." When he wrote about other empires, he nowhere stated that after a socialist revolution any independent socialist national states emerging from former French, British, Dutch, or Japanese empires should ultimately return to their earlier imperial spaces. Nor did he explicitly state that relationships between socialist parties in all empires should be like those he demanded obtain for the Russian empire, wherein the only legitimate workers' party and, later, communist party, would be that of the nationality of the imperial metropole. He made explicit these imperatives about the post-revolutionary centralized unity of former empires only in the case of the Russian empire – something for which Ukrainian Marxists condemned him. The SD Lev Iurkevych explained in 1917 that by organizing the proletariat in Ukrainian cities as a Russian proletariat in one imperial party, Lenin was alienating urban Russian workers in Ukraine from rural Ukrainian workers and thereby destroying the unity of the worker's movement in Ukraine. He dismissed Lenin's explanation of national self-determination as a hypocritical defence of Russian domination. If capitalism created large states and these were "progressive," then movements aimed at breaking them up had to be "reactionary" and it made no sense to support them by talking about "rights of self-determination." In1919, Shakhrai posited that the examples of Ireland and Norway showed that in Europe, which included Ukraine, talk of "internationalist class" interests was premature, because nationalism remained a mass progressive force that the proletariat had to lead. Lenin's ideas about secession, he continued, amounted to obfuscatory hypocrisy justifying imperial Russian territorial integrity by recognizing an abstract "right" to secede but not actual acts of secession: "According to Marx it is not the *right* of Ireland to separate from England that English proletarians should defend, but the *separation* of Ireland from England."[69]

In October 1917, before taking power, Lenin specified that he would not divide the Russian empire into independent socialist national states. He wanted as big a state as possible, including "the greatest

possible number of nations who are neighbours of the Great Russians."
He was quite aware of the mechanisms of imperial rule, as shown in
his comments about political independence having no impact on economic dependency. In January 1917 he referred to "the intelligent leaders of imperialism": "Sometimes the more reliable and profitable way
[to rule] is to obtain the services of sincere and conscientious advocates
of 'fatherland defense' in an imperialist war by creating *politically* independent states; we [the Bolsheviks], of course, will see to it that they
are *financially dependent!*" True to his words, within days of establishing
Soviet Ukraine, Lenin ensured it would have no national bank or cur-
rency and thus be dependent financially on Petrograd.[70]

Lenin's ideas about Ukraine resembled those of British moderates
on Ireland. Edmund Burke, who opposed Irish independence, welcomed concessions to defuse separatist demands. "Mutual affection,"
he explained in 1782, would do more for Great Britain and Ireland than
"any ties of artificial connection." No "reluctant tie" could be a strong
one, and "a natural cheerful alliance will be a far securer link of connection than any principle of subordination borne with grudging and
discontent."[71] Over a century later, Edward Cook, editor of the *Daily
Mail*, argued in *The Rights and Wrongs of the Transvaal War* (1901) that the
demands of British imperialism overrode the right of national independence of those within its sphere of influence because the British Empire
represented the highest form of liberal democracy in the world. Absorption was in the mutual interest of ruled and ruler. Secession based on
national identity was reactionary because imperialism was not at odds
with local autonomy (called "Home Rule" in Britain). While opposed,
like Burke, to Irish Home Rule "without the empire," Cook supported
"home rule within the Empire." Lloyd George also aimed to save the
empire by granting autonomy to its parts. This solution was not unlike
what Lenin proposed for Ukraine; only for Lenin such a solution would
represent the highest form of socialist democracy.

Stalin labelled the Provisional Government imperialist, but nowhere
did he imply that pre-1917 Russia might have been an empire in which
non-Russian territories were economically exploited colonies. Already
in 1904 he was analysing Russian-ruled Eurasia not as an empire but as
a "Russian state," thinking in terms of an imperial "*Rossiiskii*" proletariat that included all nationalities of the empire and defending Russian-
based centralism. This centralism did not result in exploitation of its
peripheries; indeed, he claimed, it removed any basis for national
liberation. Like many non-Russians of his time, the Georgian Iosef

Dzhugashvili identified politically and culturally with Russia because in his youth he had concluded that Russia represented cosmopolitan modernity and progress.[72] In November 1919 he declared that the right of national self-determination was an "empty slogan" that the Entente and European socialists were using to justify continued European colonial rule. Because the slogan had become "reactionary," the 1919 Bolshevik and Comintern programs proclaimed instead the "right of nations to form independent states." Nonetheless, in October 1920, Stalin explicitly condemned the secession of formerly non-Russian tsarist provinces that he termed "border regions" from the RSFSR as counter-revolutionary because any such "region" would fall under "the yoke of imperialism." This vision of revolution in the tsarist imperial space did not include the kind of alliance between communists and the "revolutionary bourgeoisie" in Ukraine that the Comintern had just approved for other parts of the world.

> We are against the secession of the border regions from Russia, because secession in that case would mean imperialist bondage for the border regions, a weakening of the revolutionary might of Russia and a strengthening of the positions of imperialism. It is for this reason that the Entente, which fights against the secession of India, Egypt, Arabia, and other colonies, at the same time fights for the secession of the border regions from Russia. It is for this reason that the Communists, who fight for the secession of the colonies from the Entente, at the same time cannot but fight against the secession of the border regions from Russia.

Within a Soviet Russia that included non-Russian territories, relations between centre and periphery would be built on regional autonomy that gave "true independence" – unlike the "artificial independence" found in Poland or Finland.[73] In 1923 he explained that "the right of self-determination cannot and must not serve as an obstacle to the working class in exercising its right to dictatorship. The former must yield to the latter. That was the case in 1920, for instance, when in order to defend working class power we were obliged to march on Warsaw."[74] He did not add that "the working class" meant only the Central Committee of the RCP, that the party was unmentioned in the Soviet constitution, or that it was a decidedly Russian party unrepresentative of non-Russians, with Russians and Russified secular Jews together averaging 79 per cent of delegates to the six RCP Congresses between 1917 and 1924.[75]

While Ukrainian Marxists could have agreed with Stalin about the desirability of a state-controlled economy free from European corporate influence, they disagreed with his rejection of the idea that independent communist parties should rule sovereign, equal, allied, socialist republics. What Stalin meant by "real independence" was to them more like typical colonial dependency. Anyone who in 1920 compared Ukraine within the RSFSR with Ukraine under the Provisional Government in 1917 would have wondered why the Provisional Government was "imperialist" while the Bolshevik one was not, what had actually changed, and whether, as Stalin claimed, "imperial bondage" existed only beyond Soviet borders. Such person would have seen that the Soviet Ukrainian government was the only new government created between 1918 and 1921 that, within a week of its formation, issued a decree stipulating that its second most important task – after supplying an army and urban working class composed overwhelmingly of nonnationals belonging to the former imperial power – was to completely and as soon as possible feed the hungry workers of another country, Russia.[76] On 27 January 1920, one month after Lenin's celebrated concessions to Ukraine, Ukraine's soviet government annulled all of its decrees regarding labour, economics, communications, and finance, declared them superseded by Russian decrees, and placed the corresponding ministries under Moscow's control.[77] Ukrainian Marxists did not consider such acts indicative of "real independence."

After 1920, internal affairs, agriculture, justice, education, and health and welfare fell within the jurisdiction of Ukraine's Council of People's Commissars, which, unlike the Rada in 1917, did not control finance, the economy, the army, the food supply, or labour. Also, unlike the Ukrainian SR and SD parties, the CPU was part of a single centralized Russian Communist Party, which was not mentioned in the constitution, was based in a foreign country, and was overwhelming non-Ukrainian in membership. After January 1920 the CPU could appoint only three commissars – for justice, education, and agriculture.[78] Ukrainian was to be the language of administration, but the Provisional Government had already conceded that point. Throughout 1919 and 1920, moreover, most of Ukraine was in practice still administered by Revolutionary Military Committees (Revkoms) directly from Moscow, not soviets subject to Kharkiv. In 1920, 10,310 (56 per cent) of Ukraine's provincial, district, and county executive committees were Revkoms responsible only to Moscow. In Late December 1919, just before his conciliatory "Letter" was published, Lenin rejected complaints from Ukrainian Bolsheviks about the mass export of Russian party members to Ukraine, condemning those complaints as a breach of party discipline. He ordered the thirty-four signatories to the complaint placed under surveillance and dispersed among other party workers.[79] Soviet Ukraine as of 1920 differed from the "oppressed" Ukraine of 1917 in that it included eight instead of five provinces. Otherwise, it had fewer prerogatives than did the Central Rada under the Provisional Government. Reflecting the perspective of a ruling settler-colonialist elite, a May 1921 conference resolution noted that the CPU was "against forcefully imposing Russian culture on the Ukrainian masses." [80] A Ukrainian party would have asserted that it was against forcefully imposing Ukrainian culture on the Russian masses.

Ukrainian communists were like that "small minority of men" condemned by the British colonial secretary in his 1897 speech (noted above) who objected to imperial massacres and occupations of territory in the name of progress. The Ukrainians labelled Stalin's "real independence" colonialism and saw little difference between a trainload of grain taken by force and sent to Germany and a trainload taken by force and sent to Russia. In Lviv in 1921 the SD Isaac Mazepa wondered how bad Western European "imperialist bondage" could be and how its exploitation of Finland or Latvia or Estonia could be compared to what was happening in soviet Ukraine. If European "capital" could not turn those small European countries into African-type "colonies," then how, as Stalin claimed, could that type of "bondage" do so with a country as large as Ukraine? Anyone who doubted the Bolsheviks' ruthlessness had only to compare it to the British response to the nationalist uprisings in Ireland, Egypt, and India.[81] The urban guerrilla war waged by a few thousand IRA militants had convinced British leaders to reject the massive repression their generals demanded and recognize the nationalist government. Fearing similar wars in India and Egypt, they conceded more autonomy to the Irish Free State than Moscow did to its Ukrainian Republic.

Despite declarations about the primacy of class loyalties, central leaders had no illusions about the strength of national loyalties and their policies reflected this awareness. In a country where few Ukrainians were pro-Bolshevik and, where in some places Russified secular Jews comprised more than 60 per cent of party and government personnel, local officials repeatedly demanded – and usually got – not "workers" but hundreds if not thousands of "Russians" from Russia to bolster their strength.[82] Some specifically demanded that Russians replace Ukrainians.[83] In the spring of 1919, for example, senior leaders were seriously considering deporting either all of Ukraine's Jews or at least all Jewish CPU members. In May 1919, central plenipotentiary M. Bunin wrote a policy paper suggesting that 90 per cent of Ukraine's Jewish communists be shipped to northern Russia and replaced by Russians brought from there. Ukraine's Politburo actually decided on 30 May to dismiss all Jews from office and desisted only on protest from Piatakov.[84] A personal letter from the Ukrainian assistant to Ukraine's Bolshevik commissar for engineering, written that June, begged Rakovskii to replace Jews with Ukrainian and Russian officials to avoid bloodshed. Two months earlier, Grigorii Moroz, a Jewish member of the central Cheka Collegium, had written to the RCP Central Committee after an inspection trip in Ukraine that he was shocked beyond description at how people identified Soviet power with Jews and hated Jews as a result. He recommended that Jews be removed from responsible positions and replaced by Russians from Russia. Russian party leader Lev Kamenev made a similar proposal to Lenin in August 1919.[85] In February 1920, in response to CPU leaders who wanted to mobilize "Ukrainian-speaking" communists in Russia for Ukraine, the RCP Politburo took upon itself to send "Ukrainian activists" – a formulation that could be interpreted to mean anyone born in Ukraine. In practice, the Russian party impeded the transfer of declared Ukrainian party members to Ukraine.[86]

Those Ukrainian military units tolerated by Bolshevik leaders as proof that soviet power was not Russian power reoccupying imperial territories were kept on a tight leash. Bolshevik leaders did not allow Ukrainians from Russia to join their 14,000 pro-Bolshevik comrades in Ukraine, and in late 1918, presumably to keep them weak, those units got less pay and supplies than imported Russian units. Between 1919 and 1922, faced with massive resistance, local commanders did not ask their superiors for more "proletarians" or "poor peasants" as reinforcements – they specifically demanded Russians. "It is necessary to implement all along the [rail] line the so-called Soviet colonization policy," wrote an official, M. Ravich, in late May 1919. "That is, to all stations along the Kazatyn–Uman [rail] line a unit must be sent composed exclusively of Russians and foreign communists supported by an armoured train ... All Ukrainian units in this region must be sent to Russia and replaced by Russian ones." CPU Central Committee member Ivan Kulyk, who was in the region at the time, concurred: "The only way to improve the situation, in my view, is to bring in Russian units." On 6 August 1919, in response to a request from Trotsky to "radically purge" the recently annexed Ukrainian lands northeast of the line Kherson–Odessa–Kyiv, Lenin ordered hundreds of Russian Cheka troops south – "the best Cheka units." Officers surrendering to the Red Army in Ukraine were to be sent to Russia and replaced by Russians.[87] Like their White counterparts, Red commanders wanted their Ukrainian recruits sent to Russia and demanded Russians instead. In 1920 no more than 11 per cent of the million-strong Red Army were Ukrainian speakers; the following year the figure fell to 9 per cent. Figures for the Kyiv province "punishment battalion" in 1919 show that 87 per cent were Russian speakers.[88]

Russian Bolsheviks may not have expropriated manufactured goods from Russian peasants. At the end of 1918 in Russia they abolished the hated Poor Peasant Committees, replaced their "food dictatorship" with a direct tax, and allowed limited private commerce. These shifts, and the fact that Russian peasants were supposed to get goods equivalent of up to 40 per cent of the value of the grain they delivered at fixed prices, while Ukrainians got no more than 30 per cent, demonstrate that policies were harsher in Ukraine than in Russia – although massive resistance there did not abate either until 1921.[89] But regardless of how economic policies compared, there was no cultural-linguistic division between exploiter and exploited in Russia.[90] That fact permitted Ukrainian Marxists to claim that Bolshevik Ukraine remained in "imperial bondage" and to condemn the extraction of resources from an occupied Ukraine as colonialism. The CPU, in short, was "not the party of an oppressed nation." As Shakhrai observed:[91]

> Objectively we [Bolsheviks – Shakhrai then belonged to the RSDLP] were a non-Ukrainian party even though living and working in Ukraine and even though the birth certificates of some of us showed that we were [almost] Ukrainian. We were a Russian, or, more properly, a Great [ethnic] Russian, party. It is not so much that we defended unity and were unenthusiastic about slogans of autonomy, federation and independence. The point is that we completely avoided the national liberation movement ...

It was not only Ukrainian communists who complained about exploitation and central commissars ignoring republican ministries. Russian SRs referred to Soviet Ukraine as a "colony" from which Russia "took everything and gave nothing." Individual Mensheviks claimed that "Bolshevik imperialism" was decidedly worse than capitalism

imperialism.[92] Russian Bolsheviks were themselves divided over centralization in late 1920, with Trotsky, Rakovskii, and Chicherin urging
Lenin to devolve authority to the Republics for reasons of expediency.[93]

Stalin advocated centralization, ignored the criticisms, and complained to Lenin in September 1922 that there was no more need for
the subterfuge and talk about independent Soviet Ukraine that had
been necessary to conquer it during the preceding years.[94] In his letter
he was effectively reminding Lenin of two secret Politburo resolutions
from April and November 1919 that nullified the concessions Lenin had
made in the public declarations titled "Soviet Power in Ukraine" and
"Letter to Ukrainian Workers." They also contradicted what he himself
had advocated in *Pravda* in 1920 where he wrote about the permanent
and principled nature of regional autonomy for "border regions": "To
think broad autonomy was temporary or a necessary evil was "fundamentally false."[95] Lenin's "Letter" of December 1919 claimed that
"Ukrainian workers and peasants themselves" would decide on the
nature of the "federal ties," and that May, he had specified that Russia would have full control over all military and economic organizations of its subordinated republics only for the duration of "the socialist
war of defense." In 1922, with the war over, Stalin reversed his position
and wanted Lenin to ignore his public statements and follow instead
the April and November 1919 resolutions that instructed party officials to "carefully prepare plans to fuse Ukraine and Russia."[96] Those
resolutions were reflected in a December 1919 Politburo instruction
to Kharkiv specifying that Ukraine could have no separate ministries
because that would complicate "the future fusion of the two republics."
Feliks Dzerzhinskii also advocated abolishing republics altogether that
year. He thought it a great misfortune that all the "borderland" governments took themselves seriously "as if they could be independent
governments."[97]

Stalin's secret 1922 note was in line with the secret 1919 decision.
With war ended, he characterized "broad autonomy" as an undesirable concession "intended to demonstrate Moscow's liberalism" that
had, "despite our intentions," created people who "demanded real
independence in all aspects." Young communists "in the borderlands
refuse to accept the independence game as a game." Stalin's associate
Dmytro Manuilsky agreed. Forming separate Republic central committees had been necessary to neutralize the "national movement." Since
then, he wrote, the NEP had pacified the villages and deprived "political separatists" of support. Accordingly, the Ukrainian Republic could

be abolished and this would engender no resistance either from the peasants, who didn't care about national issues, or from intellectuals.[98]

Lenin disagreed. In line with his 1916 ideas about the temporary nature of centralization and not "forcing blessings" or infringing upon national self-respect, he supported the "Frunze Commission." In late 1922, ignoring the secret 1919 resolution that Stalin supported, this CPU-created commission proposed structuring the envisaged USSR as a confederation. Lenin insisted on one party for the entire former imperial space but, otherwise, now thought that only War and Foreign Affairs should be common ministries. Stalin made sure that the Politburo rejected these recommendations and quashed all attempts by republic leaders to devolve ministerial functions.[99] He agreed to the term USSR and to establishing Republics, but, confident that his local appointees supported him and no longer doubting the "progressive" character of cultural-linguistic Russification, he retained much of the centralized structure established in 1919. The Union Treaty drafted by Stalin's men bore no resemblance to the Frunze Commission's proposal. The USSR was not turned into a confederation. The version presented to the First Congress of Soviets limited concessions to language and culture, kept key ministries centralized, and ensured that the non-Russian republics would be dependent on Moscow for financing and policy guidelines. Ukraine's Bolsheviks managed only to ensure that their republic was not divided into two economic regions with two local centres, as proposed by Moscow planners, but instead would be treated as a single planning unit headquartered in Kharkiv. Ukrainian communists viewed this centralized dependency enforced by a non-Ukrainian CPU as a renewed form of Russian imperialism and colonialism.

Chapter Two

We think we have shown that your internationalism has a strong Russian smell.

Shakhrai and Mazlakh, 1919

Bolshevik Politics and Ukraine

Lenin was viciously ruthless and was untroubled by paradoxes or contradictions.[1] He could support revolutionaries while simultaneously negotiating with any and all governments and businessmen. This chapter will argue that insofar as he shared Russian imperialist preconceptions of eastern Slavic ethnic unity and imperial territorial integrity – what he called Black Hundred great power chauvinism – he rarely allowed them to cloud his judgment of strategic realities. Although imperialist preconceptions and his ideological obsession with centralized control do explain his policies in Ukraine once he had invaded and annexed it, they do not explain why he invaded and annexed Ukraine in the first place. The demands of war played their part in establishing the centralized Bolshevik state, but what concerned the UCP was why that state had to include Ukraine. This chapter, accordingly, examines how one group of revolutionary Marxists ended up restoring empire by invasion and why another group of revolutionary Marxists condemned them as colonialists for doing so. It argues that for Lenin and rightist leaders, Russian imperialist preconceptions, the idea that Russia needed Ukrainian resources, and Marxist principles were only rationalizations that do not explain why they annexed Ukraine. The decision to invade Ukraine was determined by foreign policy concerns and by the unexpected initiatives of Lenin's leftist subordinates in Ukraine.

Lenin knew that Bolshevik party organizations were weak in non-Russian territories, and he was wary of supporting them if it meant threatening his hold on central Russia. In this context, his pronouncements on empires, imperialism, and self-determination could just as well serve as justifications for reincorporating former imperial territories as for their possible loss. By arbitrarily slotting a given territory into development schema that ranged from medievalism to socialism, Lenin could theoretically justify whatever policy option he deemed the moment required. The proletariat – the term the Bolsheviks used to refer to themselves – could agree either with feudal lords or with the bourgeoisie. In April 1914, Lenin referred to Norwegian–Swedish relations as "ideal and civilized." In 1917, he rationalized Finland's secession in terms of its "progressive bourgeoisie." He recognized "bourgeois" Turkey according to the same logic. He forged analogous theoretical virtue out of political prudence when he signed the 1920 Tartu Treaty with Estonia. In Central Asia, where he saw Turkestan as the door to India and to the revolution that would overturn the French and British empires, he supported Muslim socialists against the settler-colonist Russians despite their being the majority in the local RCP branch in 1919, as well as the repatriation of Russians, be it voluntary or forced.[2]

In April 1917, before he came to power, Lenin recognized Ukraine's right to temporarily secede: "Any Russian socialist who does not recognize the independence of Finland and Ukraine, is veering towards chauvinism. And he will never justify himself with any kind of sophism or references to his 'method.'" Yet there is no record of Lenin considering backing Ukrainian communists as he had backed Muslim communists against local settler-Russians, or explicitly stating that communists in other empires should recentralize all imperial territories after a revolution. Once in power, he insisted that Ukrainian independence was impossible without the tightest possible union of Russian and Ukrainian workers and peasants as well as economic union (December 1919). This was consistent with his conviction that all political secession was temporary and unrelated to economic dependency.

Lenin made decisions within a matrix of party groups and sided with one or another according to circumstances. The basic division within the leadership was between rightists who thought in terms of Russian imperial interests and leftists who thought themselves the true Marxist revolutionaries. In non-Russian territories this was complicated by a division between federalists and centralists. Most of the few declared Ukrainian Bolsheviks, like Skrypnyk or Zatonsky and some native-Russian party members like Georgii Lapchinskii, were federalists who favoured national autonomy. The majority centralists were in practice Russian provincial leaders who regarded Ukraine as at best a territorial administrative unit. These internal divisions were fluid; one side sometimes overrode its rivals and won Kremlin backing. As was typical for settler-colonist minority-based parties, Ukraine's Bolsheviks opposed or sabotaged initiatives by the metropole that they deemed unacceptable.

The resolutions of the first conference of Ukraine's Bolsheviks in December 1917 reflected centralist positions. They recognized the "fact of the Ukrainian Republic" but opposed political federalism with Russia and "economic federalism." Speakers who believed that "Russia" would not oppress nations wondered: "How can one peasant oppress another?" Overwhelmingly, Ukraine's Bolsheviks were urban Russians or Russified non-Russians from the urban settler-colonist population, and few of them had any notion of "national tasks of the revolutionary proletariat in Ukraine." In 1917, leaders in Kharkiv and Katerynoslav did not imagine they had any relationship to something called Ukraine. They regarded the territorial claims of the Central Rada as fantastical, and they sent no representatives to the December conference called by the Kyivan branch. The Kyivan-federalist idea of a Ukrainian soviet centre separate from Soviet Russia did not "enter into their understanding of the revolution in Ukraine." The rightist Kharkovians and Katerynoslavians excluded Kherson, Kharkiv, and Katerynoslav provinces from their understanding of Ukraine, they opposed the Kyivan leftists who had formed Ukraine's first soviet government that December and urged Lenin to abolish it, and they opposed war with the Rada. Lenin for his part did not know whether his regime had more loyal forces than the Rada, and the biggest threat to him was General Kaledin's army in southern Russia.

On 22 November (5 December), in reference to Ukraine and Finland, Lenin made no mention of national liberation or of letting the proletariat of each country deal with its own bourgeoisie, as Marx had proposed. Instead, sounding like Robespierre, he talked of "we Bolsheviks" extending a friendly hand to Finnish and Ukrainian workers in their fight against "their bourgeoisie and ours." Apparently, he was convinced that Finnish and Ukrainian workers wanted to "fight together" with Russian workers. By a slim majority, Kyivan Bolsheviks, following their centralist leaders, decided to stage a coup on 30 November (13 December). It failed. Over the next two days, at their provincial party conference, they decided to try again but next time to rely on Russian support. Their resolution carried no hint of invasion: "The conference calls on Ukrainian workers soldiers and peasants to unite with the workers soldiers and peasants of the other parts of Russia in a common struggle with the enemies of the people."[3] Lenin, meanwhile, kept his options open, presumably anticipating that the Kyivan Bolsheviks would dominate the upcoming Ukrainian Congress of Soviets in Kyiv. In a December 4 (17) ultimatum sent to Kyiv on the day that Congress began, of which the local Bolsheviks learned when it arrived, alongside the threat of war he hinted at an agreement with the UNR by noting his government had not opposed the national independence of the "Finnish Bourgeois Republic." On December 5 (18), Lenin instructed Antonov to begin military operations against the Rada. But that evening he revoked his order, and on December 8 (21), he ordered Antonov instead to attack Kaledin. What changed Lenin's mind was probably the note he received on 6 December from the Ukrainian Military-Revolutionary Committee of the Petrograd Soviet, which represented not only thousands of Ukrainian soldiers but also 22,000 Ukrainian sailors in the Baltic Fleet. Acting as intermediary between the Rada and the Bolsheviks, it demanded a peaceful resolution of the Ukrainian–Russian conflict as well as the transfer of all Ukrainian troops to Ukraine and sailors to the Black Sea Fleet. Lenin then learned that his Kyivan subordinates had failed to take over Ukraine's Soviet Congress.[4]

Had Ukraine's Bolsheviks been able to acquire majorities in the soviets and take power wherever they could without Russian intervention, Lenin would probably have been pleased. But in the UNR, as in Finland, they failed wherever they faced loyal forces. Meanwhile, 22,000 dissatisfied Ukrainian sailors in Petrograd presented a threat until the end of the month, when Lenin promised them immediate transfer to the Black Sea Fleet. Lenin, Trotsky, and Stalin, who had proclaimed their Bolshevik government had granted freedom to the Finnish bourgeoisie on 10 (23) December had the option of doing the same with Ukraine in early December. In the end they did not because Ukraine posed a more serious threat to Russia than Finland.[5] This was because the Ukrainian moderate majority in the Rada still thought in terms of an empire recast as a federated republic and maintained ties with Kaledin. They were encouraged by Ukraine's Bund and Mensheviks, and unlike the Finns, Ukrainians did not declare independence immediately after the

Bolsheviks took power. As *Pravda* wrote on 9 (24) December, the Rada was pursuing an "all-Russian" policy: "to establish in the whole of Russia [*Rossiia*] a regime of bourgeois power." Lenin concluded by the end of December that he had to deal with this threat and accordingly did not treat Ukraine like Finland.

Bolshevik troops had arrived in Kharkiv in late December. But the battles they fought before Lenin and the Russian Bolshevik leaders finally decided to wage war on the UNR on 30 December (January 12) were outside the five provinces the Provisional Government had allotted the Rada. Lenin at the time respected those borders and was concentrating his troops against Kaledin. Red troops did enter UNR territory in northern Chernihiv province, but their orders were to join Antonov's forces in Kharkiv and not to occupy Ukraine. They were to avoid battle unless attacked. When they came up against Ukrainian troops, the Bolshevik soldiers, Ukrainian and Russian, refused to fight and condemned Lenin's government for forcing "two brother nations" to fight each other. The operation had to be cancelled.[6] Ukraine's Red Army commander Vladimir Antonov, meanwhile, pressured by Skrypnyk and Zatonsky, despite his pleadings, got no order to march west before 30 December. It was Ukraine's Soviet leaders who effectively declared war on the Rada while Lenin was still mulling negotiations with it. Five days after establishing their Soviet republic in Kharkiv on 12 (25) December, they ordered troops to take Poltava, although they controlled no forces. Then on 25 December (7 January), they ordered the Red Guard to mobilize for operations on an all-Ukrainian front. Only on 30 December, did Lenin, after agreeing to transfer Petrograd's Ukrainian sailors south and learning the day before from Antonov that his troops controlled Kharkiv and Katerynoslav, did he end negotiations with Kyiv.[7] Even so, Ukraine's Kharkiv government explicitly called for a mass anti-UNR uprising only on January 4 (17), because until then, Lenin and Stalin had stalled, hoping that a successful Ukrainian left SR coup would topple the Rada without their assistance.[8]

Until 30 December, Lenin, the rightists, and Ukraine's centralists had considered peace with the "bourgeois" five-province UNR an option. It is not inconceivable that had the Rada declared independence in November 1917 and successfully suppressed pro-Bolshevik troops, Lenin might have recognized this rump UNR as he had Finland or Estonia or Kemal Ataturk's Turkey. Ukraine's defeated Bolsheviks would have gone into exile like their Finnish comrades. Conversely, had they succeeded in taking power in an independent five-province UNR with pro-Bolshevik forces already in Ukraine, their government would likely have remained more independent of soviet Russia than it later was. In short, Lenin was more influenced by strategic concerns than by Marxist or Russian imperial preconceptions or economic issues in his decision to destroy the UNR. The key factor on one side was pressure from leftist Ukrainian and Ukrainian-born Russian Bolsheviks for Russian help in establishing themselves in power after their failed coup. On the other side, the Rada did not declare independence immediately after the Bolsheviks took power and showed no interest in any links whatsoever with a Bolshevik Russia. Thus it presented itself as a threat to the Soviet regime, although admittedly, unlike Estonia, the UNR did not control its ports and so could not exploit in negotiations its role as a trade corridor for Russia. Faced with the leftist successes in eastern Ukraine as a *fait accompli* and with the failed Ukrainian SR coup, and having pacified the Ukrainian sailors, Lenin concluded that war against the UNR was no longer an unreasonable but necessary risk. The aim was to deprive Kaledin of an ally.

It should be noted that Lenin made his three urgent requests to his subordinates to ship food north only after the invasion had begun. This suggests that a worsening supply situation was not a primary cause of the decision to invade. Lenin's refusal to pay in gold for grain as the Rada demanded reduced Ukrainian imports to whatever his Kharkiv government could collect. But Russian cities were also getting supplies from the southeastern provinces, and the Bolsheviks had stockpiled food in Russia that they intended to export to Germany in the event of revolution there. Aleksandr Shlikhter, the Moscow Region Food Supply Commissar, told the Central Committee on 29 December, the day before Lenin decided to invade, that the food situation was improving and that "in fact there is a colossal amount of grain in Russia ... The situation was so good that the bread ration could be increased as of now." The *Sovnarkom* declared extraordinary measures to deal with Russia's supply situation only on 11 January, after the decision to invade, in the face of a Russian rail workers' strike that had halted Ukrainian imports. Lenin ordered Antonov to ship food north "for God's sake" on 15 January. That same day, he allocated 20 million roubles for the Red Army, rather than for grain purchases, and forbade any Russian organization from negotiating for food from Ukraine on its own.[9] In this light, Bolshevik accusations about Ukrainians and the Rada starving Russia had little substance, and could well have been intended as propaganda to motivate Bolshevik troops who refused to invade or fight their peaceful Ukrainian neighbour.[10]

Although Bolsheviks were not directly involved in Ireland, there, as in Finland, Poland, and Turkey and, as Lenin contemplated doing in Ukraine, they recognized the new "bourgeois" national government. Irish nationalists (Sinn Fein, formed in 1905) were moderates and federalists and were a small minority politically, like the radical socialists until 1918. It was the Irish Socialist Republican Party (1896) that first advocated independence. It was not Sinn Fein, which became a mass party representing Irish independence only in 1918, but the radical nationalist Irish Volunteers and the socialist Irish Citizens Army that staged the failed Easter Rising in 1916. The Irish Socialist Party supported independence, but it was a fringe group with no role in national politics. This comparison deserves attention because it shows the Bolsheviks were prepared to recognize Irish independence represented by political nationalists, but not Ukrainian independence represented by socialists. In 1920, before Ireland achieved independence and despite its recently signed treaty with Britain, Lenin recognized a leftist faction of the Irish socialists, the Worker's Communist Party (renamed the Communist Party of Ireland the following year), as a Comintern member. Yet he refused such membership to Ukrainian left SRs and SDs.[11]

Like the socialists, the Irish communists were a fringe group. The contrast between the Bolshevik attitude towards them and Ireland and their treatment of Ukrainians also deserves attention. Once he had incorporated Ukraine into his new republic, Lenin subjected it to centralization. From then on, his party opposed Ukrainian independence just as the British Communist Party opposed Irish independence and the French Communist Party opposed Algerian independence. Bolshevik leaders formally condemned the British party for its stand on Ireland in 1920, yet they had taken the same stance towards Ukraine. The Communist Party of Ireland, meanwhile, unlike the CPU, supported Irish independence and the "bourgeois" national state as a necessary prelude to an envisioned workers' republic – just as the left SDs did in the spring of 1919 when they temporarily supported the UNR. But whereas Lenin and the Comintern endorsed the former, they condemned the latter, in line with their 1903 decision that there could be only one metropole-based centralized SD party within the Russian empire. Had Lenin applied the same policy to Britain and Ireland as he did to Ukraine, he would have refused to recognize the independent "bourgeois" Irish Republic and the Communist Party of Ireland.

In December 1922, Lenin did decide that the Irish party should be subordinated to the British one, but the Irish comrades refused until 1934.[12]

Strategic considerations arguably resulted in policy vacillation towards Ukraine after Germany's surrender, when Lenin again considered recognizing a neutral, independent, non-Bolshevik socialist Ukraine. In March 1918, he agreed that Soviet Ukraine should include eight tsarist Ukrainian provinces. The centralist-dominated CPU described the planned status of Soviet Ukraine in a declaration of 7 March: "1. We never regarded the Ukrainian Soviet Republic as a national republic, but exclusively as only a soviet republic on the territory of Ukraine. 2. We never recognized the Ukrainian National Republic as totally sovereign and saw it only as a more or less independent unit federally tied with the all-Russian workers peasants republic."[13] It was as if the French Directory in the 1790s, instead of establishing republics in its conquered territories, had annexed them as French departments – as Napoleon later did, to his great cost. Lenin supported the short-lived Kyivan leftist–led partisan operations in Ukraine that August and their demand for local party autonomy. After the leftists failed to spark a revolt, Lenin vacillated into January 1919 between centralist rightists, who now supported his inclination to recognize the re-established UNR in a variation of the Norwegian–Swedish option he had earlier praised, and leftists, who appealed to his Marxist idealist side and wanted military help to establish a Soviet Ukraine immediately.

In November 1918, White armies threatened Moscow from the south and east, Russia was blockaded, German communists threatened to overthrow Berlin's new pro-Entente socialist government and, Polish communists wanted Moscow to invade Poland, just as Ukraine's Bolshevik leftists wanted it to invade Ukraine. Lenin concentrated his army in the southeast, apparently preferring peace to war on his western flank. Also, he was probably uncertain about the desirability of a German communist revolution led by his rival Rosa Luxemburg. If she succeeded, she would in all likelihood displace him as the leader of the socialist movement and provoke an invasion of Germany (with which Russia was at peace) by the Entente (with which it was still at war). The prospect of Franco-British armies marching east heightened when German generals around Von Seeckt prepared to abandon the Baltic countries to the Bolsheviks – contrary to the conditions of the Treaty of Versailles. In this context, the rightist position on Ukraine was reasonable. Sending the Red Army against the Polish and Ukrainian national governments would have weakened Russia's southeastern

and northwestern fronts. Lenin, accordingly, had Rakovskii and Manuilsky negotiate with German Polish and Ukrainian "militarists" and
"bourgeois democrats," as he later negotiated with nationalists Kemal
Atatürk and Reza Khan, and he instructed Ukraine's Kyivan-leftists not
to attack the UNR.

A Bolshevik treaty with the "bourgeois" UNR in January 1919 could
have been justified in terms of *Imperialism* as support for a "progressive" national liberation movement. It would have resembled Moscow's later alliance in Central Asia with Muslim communists against
local settler-Russians. Talks to this end were held in late October 1918
in Kyiv, where Vynnychenko and the Mazurenko brothers reached an
agreement with Rakovskii and Manuilsky. In return for recognition of
an independent Ukraine, the latter agreed that their party would not
interfere in its internal affairs. There is no known documentary record of
the meeting. Rakovskii's later account is different from Vynnychenko's,
and at that month's CPU conference, he made no mention of meetings
in Kyiv or that Ukrainian leaders might play a role as "progressive"
revolutionary nationalists such as Ataturk. The Bolsheviks wanted
to sign a formal document but the Ukrainians refused. This willingness to recognize a socialist UNR and to avoid war with it reflected
Lenin's focus on the south and east at the time.[14] The talks continued
even after the invasion. A draft treaty dated 4 February that recognized
the UNR as neutral in return for its recognizing Ukraine's soviets was
drafted but never signed. Zatonsky later wrote that to prevent rightists Chicherin and Vatsetis from coming to terms with the UNR, he,
Piatakov, and other leftists interrupted communications and delegate
travel between Moscow and Kyiv.[15] Leftists even changed the wording of the draft treaty the UNR had agreed to in Moscow to include its
capitulation – which, as they intended, strengthened those opposed to
the treaty.[16] War between Russia and Ukraine erupted, therefore, less
because of Lenin's revolutionary messianism, imperialist preconceptions, or a need for resources, than because Lenin and Vynnychenko
had failed to convince their associates and control their subordinates.
Ukraine's leftists, backed by Stalin, invaded in November 1918, despite
Lenin's apprehensions; meanwhile, Vynnychenko's diplomacy was
opposed by Petliura, whose officers shot any Bolsheviks they captured
and interfered with communications between Vynnychenko and his
Moscow delegation.

In November 1918, Lenin was arguably more interested in peace
with the re-established bourgeois UNR than in re-establishing a Soviet

government in Ukraine, for he realized that the UNR posed no threat to his regime. The immediate threat was from the Entente and the White Russians. Given his obsession with centralized party control, he must also have been concerned about helping German radicals establish a soviet regime in January 1919. This would have established a ruling communist party independent of his RCP and threatened to precipitate an Entente invasion. He consequently sought formal ties with the new German socialist government, which avoided open association with him while also holding secret anti-Entente talks with anti-Entente generals in Germany's War Office. He perhaps also conspired to rid himself of his rival Luxemburg. His German emissary Karl Radek, shunned by the Berlin government in January 1919, gave speeches on revolution to workers in the capital by day and, via German agent Karl Moor, secretly negotiated with generals on an anti-Entente agreement with Russia by night – the prelude to the Rapallo Treaty.[17]

Lenin, obsessed with centralized control, refused to tolerate any communist parties within the tsarist imperial space other than his own. On 25 November (OS), Sverdlov from Moscow reminded his Ukrainian comrades of Lenin's 1903 rules on party organization, which forbade non-Russians autonomy within his party – just as German SDs had refused autonomy to Silesian Poles: "We consider the creation of a separate Ukrainian party undesirable no matter what it is called or what program it adopts." Nevertheless, on 30 (OS) November 1917, Zatonsky and some Kyivans, who wanted to form an organizationally independent Ukrainian branch of the Bolshevik party, issued leaflets in a few cities declaring that they had formed such an organization in a few cities. The leaflet made no reference to political secession; it also explained that socialists in the Central Rada were not really socialists and that as "Ukrainian Bolsheviks," they would struggle to attain in Ukraine what the Russian Bolsheviks had "in Muscovy." The following month Zatonsky again stressed to local members the importance of recognizing Ukrainian autonomy and presenting themselves not as a Russian but as a Ukrainian party. Mazlakh wanted the party in Ukraine to be called the Ukrainian Communist Party. Lapchinskii noted that "territorially we are Ukrainian, [and] Ukraine is a separate distinct entity."[18] In April 1918, in the absence of their centralist rivals, the Kyivans and some left-Ukrainian SDs who had joined the Bolsheviks in December 1917 passed a resolution at a consultative conference in Taganrog to establish a Ukrainian Communist Party separate from the Russian one. It formally existed for four months. Lenin mulled that decision for two weeks, decided against, and convinced Skrypnyk to reverse it. At the first CPU Congress, held in Moscow and dominated by centralists, Skrypnyk proclaimed the official name of Ukraine's party as the Communist Party (Bolshevik) of Ukraine and stipulated that it was a provincial unit of the RCP subordinate to the latter's Central Committee. [19]

A successful German revolution led by Rosa Luxemburg would have threatened a Franco-British invasion and displaced Lenin and Russia from leadership in the envisioned Communist world order. That is why Lenin, for all his public assertions to contrary, possibly had serious doubts about a communist revolution in Germany in December 1918 that would have brought to power an independent party with a charismatic leader he could not have controlled. The failure of the Spartacist Uprising and the murder of Luxemburg allowed Manuilsky to claim in Ukraine in March 1920 that whereas before the war, the German Social Democrats had been the hegemon of the international proletarian movement, the Russian Communist Party had now taken its place.[20] Lenin admitted as much the following month when he wrote that in the event of a successful German revolution, Russia would cease to be the model and would once again become a backward country (in the Soviet and socialist sense). But he was already composing his twenty-one conditions for the Second Comintern Congress, the intent of which was to prevent revolution in an advanced country unless he controlled the party that was carrying it out. This idea was later repeated by Ukrainian communists – perhaps in eager anticipation: "It would be erroneous to forget that after a successful revolution in even one advanced country there would be a decisive breakthrough, that is, Russia would quickly thereafter become a backward country – in the soviet and socialist sense."[21] A successful German revolution would also have destroyed the "bourgeois" Germany that Lenin's government required in 1919. Luxemburg feared this strategy and condemned it as a monstrous event amounting to moral destruction.[22]

To counter the threat of Entente intervention triggered by a successful German revolution, Lenin had to maintain forces in the northwest while avoiding war in Ukraine. Given his cool judgment and his centralist penchant, it is reasonable to think that, just as he likely feared a seizure of power by a party he could not control in Berlin, whose success could provoke an Entente invasion, he was interested more in peace with Ukraine than installing a soviet regime there again by force. Peace would allow him to concentrate the Red Army on the more serious threat that the Whites posed to his regime's survival in the southeast and the threat of an Entente intervention in the northwest. That December, it should be added, Lenin would have known that in 138 of the 286 Russian counties under his control, mass armed uprisings were being provoked by requisitioning and conscription.[23]

Ukraine's leftist Bolshevik attempt to spark an uprising in August 1918 with the secret support of Russian military intelligence failed.[24] Three months later, the day after Germany surrendered, Russia's Military Soviet ordered an invasion of Ukraine by the end of November. A soviet force led by Ukrainian commander Shchors actually entered Ukraine on 13 November – but he was reprimanded for his initiative. He claimed in his defence that he had a direct order from Lenin to invade, but no one has yet found such a document.[25] Piatakov, Zatonsky, Lenin, and Stalin also decided mid-November in Moscow to create a second soviet government for Ukraine in Kursk – obviously with no mandate from a congress of Ukrainian soviets. When Piatakov, Zatonsky, and Stalin arrived from Moscow in Kursk on 19 November, Stalin told his CPU subordinates "The Central Committee of the RCP has decided to create a Soviet government – headed by Piatakov." This supposed "Ukrainian" government then published a Manifesto in Russia in Russian declaring itself formed on the 23rd – but did not disseminate it. Stalin, still considering the possible agreement with the UNR, did not permit that until the 28th.[26] Lenin, the next day, presumably to mollify Vatsetis, wrote to him explaining that he had allotted Ukraine a fictitious Soviet government so that any future attack would not look like an occupation. But Lenin never specified a date for that attack.[27] Rightist-centralists, for their part, condemned the leftist Antonov for creating "an independent Ukrainian command" – something that Antonov denied doing. Piatakov, meanwhile, the head of the Ukraine soviet government apparently did not realize he was to be totally subject to Moscow. Complaining about his prerogatives, Piatakov asked Stalin on 7 December whether the "provisional" Soviet government in Ukraine was "necessary only for fictional purposes or as a real directing centre …?" There is no known reply, but the Russian Military Council had decreed already on 12 November that Ukraine's Revkom would be totally subordinate to it. [28]

Lenin and Trotsky are on record as allocating Russian forces for the Ukrainian invasion that November. But they were actually sent only after 4 January.[29] This was more than a month after 19 November, when Antonov had ordered, on his own initiative, his 9,000-strong partisan, mainly Ukrainian force – called the Ukrainian Insurgent Army – to invade the UNR.[30] Lenin sent Trotsky to stop them. When Ukraine's leftists told Trotsky it was impossible to recall the troops, he warned them that heads would roll if their invasion failed. Only on 3 January, on the basis of an intercepted UNR report about the strength of Bolshevik sympathies on its territory, did Trotsky decide that the Ukrainian Bolshevik initiative might succeed with little cost. On the 4th, when he learned that the Entente would not recognize the UNR and had landed a huge French force in Odessa, he concluded that any alliance with the UNR was useless because its army "was powerless." He decided to commit troops that same day. Lenin agreed the following day but forbade them to advance west of the Dnipro. Faced with Entente troops in Ukraine and the likely collapse of the German revolution, Lenin accepted the leftists' *fait accompli*. But he excluded them from Ukraine's second soviet government. He stacked it with a rightist and centralist majority and specified that no party member was to go to Ukraine without the explicit permission of the RCP Central Committee.[31] The Ukrainian Insurgent Army, meanwhile, was subordinated directly to the Red Army. By the end of 1919, it had been disbanded.

Thus, in December 1917 and again the next year, broader foreign policy concerns and unsanctioned leftist initiatives in Ukraine were crucial in determining why, in the final analysis, Lenin attacked and annexed rather than came to terms with an independent Ukraine, as he had with Finland. The Bolsheviks' policy towards Poland, which they could have invaded and annexed but did not, provides another example of how strategic considerations rather than imperialist preconceptions influenced Lenin. While he was prepared to exploit opportunities that presented themselves, he preferred to err on the side of caution.

Polish Bolsheviks, like their comrades in Ukraine, were divided after November 1918 between those who sought a Bolshevik Polish SSR with Red Army assistance if necessary, and those who were prepared to subordinate themselves organizationally to Moscow only on the condition that Poland remained a separate "bourgeois" republic. That autumn, while Rakovskii was negotiating with Vynnychenko in Kyiv, Chicherin was urging Lenin to recognize not only the UNR but also the Polish "bourgeois republic" – "reactionary, but a government of the Polish masses." This was in accordance with the decision of the Provisional Government. Lenin had actually ordered troops massed on 15 November to attack Poland. Vatsetis complained there were none to spare, that the Red Army was short of supplies and, that it had to focus on the Whites in the east. On 29 November, Lenin decided against invading.

Polish Social Democrats, meanwhile, recognized as their leader the socialist Josef Pilsudski, which their leftist rivals in late December saw as a reason for an immediate invasion to save the revolution. After Polish-left SDs formed their own communist party (KPRP–CWPP) that December, they formed a Revkom and tried to raise troops in January 1919, as did the CPU, with Stalin's backing. Polish communists did not accept the principle that "bourgeois" national state independence was "progressive" inasmuch as it disintegrated empires. As they explained in February, anticipating Bukharin's theory of the offensive (see below): "The working class of each country has the right and duty to render active assistance to the workers of other countries in their revolutionary struggle; in view of this the armed help of the Russian proletariat … would be neither an invasion nor an expression of imperialist tendencies alien to the essence of socialism."

But now Stalin and Trotsky disagreed, and Polish Bolsheviks, unlike their Ukrainian counterparts, did not launch an offensive on their own initiative. In March 1919, Lenin, who thought that these Polish communists had gravely erred in not recognizing the independent Polish state, explained that communism could not be imposed by force in Poland. That same month, Lenin apparently did not think that the CPU was committing a grave error in destroying the independent Ukrainian state. At the Eighth Party Congress, while the Red Army was imposing communism by force in Ukraine, he stated: "Communism cannot be imposed by force."[32]

Faced with the CPU's *fait accompli*, Lenin did not adopt an "anti-colonialist" position for Ukraine as he did for Poland. In Ukraine he did not instruct his urban, Russian settler–based CPU to subordinate itself to pro-Bolshevik Ukrainian-left SRs and left SDs who wanted a soviet Ukraine independent of Soviet Russia and its party -- although he had been prepared to accept the UNR as an independent state. Lenin was not prepared to tolerate an independent, allied, socialist Ukraine with its own Communist party. He had no intention of permitting Ukrainian communists the same independence from Moscow as the German Spartacists under Luxemburg would have had. Ukrainian Marxists, for their part, considered the centralization that Lenin proceeded to impose on Ukraine in 1919 as reincarnated Russian imperialism and the CPU as its agent.

Russian Bolshevik centralization in Ukraine mirrored tsarist imperial practice. Soviet Ukraine in 1919 had no separate army, party, or ministries. Russia's Supreme Economic Council controlled its economy. In

April 1919, when Lenin allowed Borotbists into secondary ministerial positions, he instructed his Kharkiv subordinates to rigorously control "these little shits [*merzotniki*]." If military reversals later required that their demands for separate Ukrainian ministries be conceded, he wrote, then those ministries were to strictly implement only central orders.[33] He ordered that "if, in the course of making concessions to independentist tendencies it becomes politically necessary in the nearest future to establish within the friendly soviet republics independent commissariats ... then there must be strict directives from the corresponding [central] administrative organ explaining that all these independent commissariats work exclusively in, and in strict agreement with, the corresponding RSFSR commissariats."[34] In May 1919, when Ukraine's War Commissar concentrated his troops in the west against Makhno and Ukrainian partisans, instead of against the Whites in the east, Lenin complained that "by refusing to send all your forces and Kharkiv's mobilized workers immediately to the Donbass you are playing at independence and local republicanism. I warn you that you will be put on trial and expelled from the party unless you stop this game."[35] At the Eighth Russian Party Conference in March 1919, Lenin was juggling with the contradiction that a Ukrainian critic had pointed out two years earlier when he pointed out that economic centralization and a refusal to structure the Russian party as a federation of independent national parties was incompatible with non-Russian cultural linguistic autonomy. The conference passed concessions on language issues but rationalized them as sops, tactical necessities rather than strategic aims, to pacify "leftover nationalist feelings among the working masses of oppressed or underprivileged nations." The resolutions specified only that the proletariat of formerly oppressor nations had to be tactful and sensitive. They provided for no institutions to protect non-Russians. Only massive Ukrainian resistance and protest throughout 1919 convinced Lenin at the end of the year to rethink his dismissive attitude towards the Ukrainian national movement. But he did not rethink the causal relationship between administrative-economic centralization and cultural-linguistic Russification.

The resolutions the Bolsheviks developed for the First Comintern Conference in March 1919 reflected Lenin's obsessive centralism as well as his implicit belief that dependencies everywhere would remain within their former imperial spaces regardless of socialist revolutions – notwithstanding Estonia Finland or Poland. The resolutions made no mention of support for "progressive national bourgeois governments" or of future relationships between metropolitan and peripheral parties. Instead, they claimed that liberation for colonies was impossible without the assistance of a victorious proletariat in the metropole.[36] Zinoviev specified that, ultimately, party centralization would trump governmental federalism under socialism and, he condemned attempts to create separate national parties in the Austrian empire. According to Trotsky, only the proletariat could free the productive forces of all countries because it could unite people in economic cooperation and give them sovereignty over their national cultures.[37] This was a theoretical expression of Bolshevik practice in Ukraine, but not in Poland or Finland or Estonia, applied to the entire world.

The Second Comintern Conference, in 1920, declared the opposite. The new resolutions instructed British, French, Korean, and Dutch communists not to fight against bourgeois governments as the CPU had done in 1917 and 1919. The resolutions no longer reflected Lenin's implicit assumption that socialist revolutions should leave imperial frontiers untouched. Communists beyond the borders of Bolshevik territory were now supposed to do what the Ukrainian left SDs had wanted, for which the Bolsheviks had condemned them – that is, help the anti-imperialist national bourgeoisie establish independent governments and, by participating in them, encourage them to follow a pro-Soviet foreign policy. Lenin's *Thesis* to the Comintern of July 1920 specified that communists were to support "revolutionary bourgeois democracy" in Turkey, Persia, and, later, China. In all these places, newly independent governments were equated with "national liberation movements." This was the opposite of what he had done in Ukraine. Zinoviev that year made no comments about party centralization trumping government federalism.[38]

Before 1917, from Mexico to Albania, nationalists in dozens of countries with peasant majority populations had declared themselves independent of empire and formed national states. After 1920, the Bolshevik-dominated Comintern backed the secession of other territories from empires, whether they were led by local communists or "revolutionary national bourgeoisie" – much like what the Bolsheviks had done in Poland, Finland, and Estonia and quite unlike what they had done in Ukraine. Perhaps the general euphoria with which radicals greeted the Russian Bolshevik regime explains why none of them reflected on whether Zinoviev's 1919 assertion about the desirability of a single centralized party based in the metropole dominating the imperial space after a socialist revolution was still valid. Within the former

Russian imperial space, Bolshevik practice did follow Zinoviev's words. Bolshevik leaders condemned the radical-leftist opposition of former tsarist non-Russian subjects to reannexation into the former imperial space as "counter-revolutionary." They condemned secession and nationalism as obstacles to proletarian progress within the former Russian imperial space. Ukrainian Marxists attributed these double standards to the colonialist Russian imperialist preconceptions shared by most Bolsheviks.

Rationalizing Russian Domination

Lenin envisaged temporary secession from empires and, he might have offered Ukraine this option, just as he had offered it to Poland and Finland. But, once he did invade and annex Ukraine, he subordinated the CPU's autonomist Kyivan leftists to its rightist centralists and, through the latter, subjected Ukraine to ruthless centralization and reintegration with Russia. His foreign policy thereafter resembled that of Lord Palmerston, who seventy years earlier had supported revolution everywhere except in Ireland. Somewhat like France's Charles X, who had sent one army to fight for Greek independence and another to conquer Algeria, Lenin was conquering Ukraine while supporting independence movements in the French and British empires. Ukraine's renewed subordination to its old metropole provided the context for imperialist preconceptions held by the overwhelmingly Russian CPU membership to reveal themselves in policies and behaviour. In the wake of the Red Army's occupation, the CPU's spokesmen used those preconceptions, along with organizational, Marxist, revolutionary messianist, and realist ideas, to justify Ukraine's renewed subordination to centralized Russian domination.[39] Such rationalizations of domination provided strong evidence for the Ukrainian Marxist case that Russian Bolshevism was renewed Russian imperialism. In their view, the massive armed response to Russian Bolshevik occupation was Ukraine's true revolution and, they presented themselves as the force that would prevent right-wing parties from exploiting that response against socialism. This conflict between revolutionary Ukrainian nationalism and Russian Bolshevik imperialism was reflected even in debates on party nomenclature. For instance, the protests by Ukraine's Bolsheviks in December 1917 against Shakhrai's proposal that they call themselves the Ukrainian Communist Party had no counterpart in Moscow three months later. There, only four delegates opposed the motion that

"Russian" be incorporated as an adjective in the party's new name – the RCP. Russian Bolsheviks regarded Russia and its empire as coterminous: "Now when our country [the empire] is divided into parts by German imperialist invasion, we should not reject this word [Russia]." No one protested.[40]

In January 1918, V. Bystrianskii rejoiced that Karl Kautsky had recognized that a successful socialist revolution could occur in imperial Russia, even though it was economically underdeveloped; that he had welcomed the Bolshevik takeover in 1917; and, that Russia had displaced Europe as the country of revolutionary initiatives. Thus, to claim (as the Bolsheviks did) that the Russian proletariat led the international socialist movement was not (as the Bolsheviks' enemies said) ridiculous "imperial-slavophilism." But after Kautsky heard that Lenin had disbanded the Constituent Assembly, he condemned him and his party.[41] Bolsheviks no longer cited Bystrianskii or Kautsky when justifying Russian primacy in the Soviet republic.

That May, after the secret April decision to fuse Ukraine with Russia (see chapter 1), a special commission headed by Kamenev specified that the republic structure was a temporary organizational expedient that was to last only for the duration of the war. "And in general, Ukraine and Russia must be fused," he wrote in *Pravda,* thereby announcing the decided policy as if it were merely his personal opinion. Anonymous articles the following month dismissed the need for a separate Ukrainian party and rejected the possibility of an independent Ukraine, claiming that the tsarist economy had long ago integrated the empire into a single unit. There *was* no independent Ukraine, Soviet or otherwise, but only a German occupation that had divided Russia. Bolshevik documents referred to "the southern part of the German-occupied provinces in the east," noting that when the occupation ended the area would again be "southern Russia."[42] The first and second centralist-dominated CPU conferences confirmed this attitude, noting that there was no national liberation struggle in Ukraine, merely a "class struggle" for unity with Russia.

As party secretary in April 1919, Piatakov admitted that Ukrainians had been oppressed, but he did not see Ukraine as a colony of the Russian empire that should separate. He regretted that only "the leading element of the workers and peasants in Ukraine" were sophisticated enough to realize that only the Russian bourgeoisie had been oppressors. This legacy of national distrust had to be overcome, but a separate Ukrainian soviet state led by its own party was not the way. He

considered Ukrainian left SDs who condemned Russians as imperialists, as no better than extremist right-wing Russian Black Hundred
counter-revolutionaries. He also dismissed *Do Khvyli* that month as "a
rotten book showing how not to approach the national question, and its
authors as renegade nationalists." In any case, he continued, the book
was so badly written that it was impossible to read and almost impossible to understand.[43] The notion of an independent proletarian republic,
he claimed elsewhere, was absurd. One cannot divide the proletariat
according to nationality and then build independent states. Capitalism
had created a global economy that had been unaffected by the collapse
of the bourgeoisie and their empires, and the ongoing state regulation
of the economy that still existed was vital. In the age of "huge state-
capitalist trusts," independent small states were an impossibility. "A
Soviet state as an economically separate national state is reactionary." If
local national forces overcame centralist forces, the new Soviet republic
would collapse and an independent Ukraine would be "a call to arms
against the worker's and peasant's revolution." From such a perspective, no empire anywhere could be dissolved, and no national communist party or ministry could exist independent of a centre in the former
imperial metropole. Communist Hungary and Germany would have
had to subordinate themselves to communist Russia just like Ukraine.
But Piatakov nowhere made such claims. Piatakov saw Bolshevik-style
federalism as an interim measure to placate peasants who could not be
forbidden to express "nationalist preconceptions" any more than they
could be forbidden to pray. One had to wait until the people themselves
realized that they had to dispense with notions of national independence. "Nevertheless, in the overall scheme, federalism is preferable to
independence and, as a form of union that least provokes the national
preconceptions of the backward section of the working mass, this form
is quite acceptable." [44] These ideas were taken up by others who, like
him, did not distinguish between the cultural and political aspects of
national issues. "The proletariat cannot put political-*national* demands
in its class program." Proletarian centralization was apparently different from bourgeois centralization.[45]

Piatakov in 1918 instructed Ivan Kulyk to write a short official history of the revolution, which was published that autumn. Kulyk here
explained that Ukraine could not be independent because finance capitalism provided no basis for small, independent countries to exist. He
did not explain how small countries like Cuba, Norway, Serbia, Greece,
Estonia, Hungary, or Bulgaria could exist, nor in what sense Ukraine

was small. He went on to claim that political independence would weaken "Ukraine's proletariat" tie to Russia's proletariat, impede the rise of socialism, and heavily impact the economy of both countries – implicitly for the worse. Besides not using Ukrainian or Russian as adjectives, Kulyk did not examine whether weak ties with the proletariats of their former imperial metropoles adversely affected the proletariats of any of the above-mentioned newly independent small countries. Furthermore, small-scale Ukrainian producers would suffer under independence because customs borders would deprive them of Russian markets. Independence would benefit only intellectuals, who would work as officials, and big business interests.[46] Again, Kulyk did not consider whether this applied to other empires.

These ideas were echoed by the July 1918 CPU Resolution on Ukraine and Russia, which was formulated by centralist Emanuel Kviring on direct instructions from Lenin. It contained no ideas about national liberation and justified Ukraine's subordination to Bolshevik Russia in economic terms. It claimed that Ukraine and Russia were "indivisibly tied" economically and that separation from Russia was but a "temporary occupation." "The [soviet-led] uprising in Ukraine is developing under the slogan reestablishing the revolutionary reunion of Ukraine with Russia," and Ukraine would join the communist global order as part of the Russian Republic "on the basis of proletarian centralism." Ukrainian independence had no basis for Kviring, who stated that Ukraine should no more have a separate communist party than Samara province. Ukraine existed only thanks to German bayonets and the CPU's task was to oppose nationalist separatism "regardless of our proclaimed right of nations to self-determination … And in so far as the desire to separate [from Russia] is contrary to the economic interests of the working masses of Ukraine we must counter it and work towards union with Soviet Russia." The resolution did not mention federalism nor did it apply Lenin's reasoning in *Imperialism* to Ukraine. It postulated that "the uprising in Ukraine" would inevitably result in a "revolutionary reunion of Ukraine with Russia." Kviring concluded that the Bolshevik model of Ukrainian–Russian "union" should not be confused with the restoration of a "great-power Russia." He did not elaborate on what those differences were, nor on how Ukraine's economy was to be integrated into the empire. Perhaps he did not know that Russian "capitalists" were using the same argument as he to prove that the former imperial space had to be centralized and that Ukrainian independence was spurious. For men like Shakhrai, such reasoning was sooner Russian imperialist than Marxist.[47]

Iakovlev, as noted, bent with the wind. In December 1919, he explained that Lenin's concessions meant that party members had to deal with their inner "Russkie [katsapskii] imperialism." The reason his party had lost Ukraine that year was obvious: a mass of Russians had descended like a plague on Ukraine, where they pursued a great-power chauvinist policy. A few months later, Iakovlev appeared as a third key apologist for Russian Bolshevik rule. Now, in a series of attacks on Ukrainian communists, he made no link between tsarist Russian imperialism and political separation from the empire by oppressed peoples. He assumed that Russia was not foreign to Ukraine, and he associated the national movement only with cultural matters. There was no such thing as Soviet Russian imperialism, he now claimed. Lenin's December 1919 concessions were nothing new for the party's politics had always been correct in any case. Russian nationalism was an occasional relic, and by definition, no such thing as Soviet Russian great-power ambitions or imperialism could exist. Whatever excesses or mistakes had happened were only leftovers from the past. Beyond the borders of Soviet power, he surmised, workers were so miserable that they could have no national cultural life. To separate from Russian soviet power was therefore tantamount to separating from the revolution and turning Ukraine into a colony of Western imperialism. He dismissed the argument that Soviet power in Ukraine was an occupation regime of Russian workers as a nationalist bourgeois myth intended to compromise the revolution in their country by associating it with outside forces.[48]

Yet, for all their official rhetoric, Bolshevik leaders understood that their occupation of Ukraine amounted to a military reconquest of empire. Kamenev, referring specifically to Ukraine, said in October 1918: "We must clearly and unequivocally state that in the course of the development of the proletarian revolution in Russia [he did not use the term empire] the slogan of national self-determination turns into a tool of bourgeois counter-revolution against Soviet Russia." He attached no revolutionary significance to the Ukrainian "national bourgeoisie," and he condemned Germany for trying to smash Russia, meaning the empire, into separate parts. His call for a union of soviet Russia and soviet Ukraine was a call to restore imperial frontiers. He then claimed that the survival of the proletarian revolution, by which he meant Bolshevik rule in Russia proper, depended on the reconquest of the empire.[49] This was in keeping with Lenin's logic about the temporary nature of any secession from empire – but not the resolutions of the Second Comintern Conference, which made no calls to Irish, Algerian, Indian, or Korean radicals to remain part of their former empires after a revolution.

Epshtein explained in November 1918: "Without the Red Army not only can we not count on the success of the revolution in Ukraine, but we cannot count even on its emergence."[50] After he had taken Kyiv in 1917, Muraviev declared that "we brought this [Soviet] power from the far north on the points of our bayonets." He wrote to Lenin: "I handed the government [that I] installed with bayonets to Ukraine's Soviet."[51] The only Bolshevik leader who censured him for this was Zatonsky. In April 1919, Lenin called his takeover of Ukraine a conquest.[52] Antonov in January 1919 explained his task as follows: "We must occupy Ukraine with our armies. And fast."[53] That same month, Rakovskii described Ukrainian–Russian relations as follows: "The temporary workers' and peasants' government of Ukraine [set up in Kursk, Russia, that winter], by its essence is not sovereign ... It was labeled the Kursk [army group] by the Military Revolutionary council of the Ukrainian Soviet Army only so we could talk about a Soviet army of Ukraine and not about an advance of Russian armies." He repeated here, in as many words, the instructions that Lenin and Stalin had sent two months earlier about creating temporary *oblast* Soviet governments so that their rivals could not label the Red Army an occupation force: "Otherwise our forces in the occupied provinces would be in an impossible situation and the people would not greet them as liberators." Lecturing subordinates that December on Lenin's concessions, he explained: "We must write carefully about Ukraine in our newspapers ... When our frontline and other papers write that Ukraine is ours or Kyiv is ours, and so on, well, comrades, that does not create conditions for a favourable approach towards Ukraine. Kyiv is soviet, yes, but anything that hints at imperialist ambitions must be avoided."[54] Trotsky a few weeks earlier reminded his invading Red Army: "Firmly remember, your task is not to enslave Ukraine but to liberate it." In September 1920, in a coded letter supporting CPU requests for greater local prerogatives, he wrote: "Soviet power in Ukraine has held its ground up to now (and not well) chiefly by the authority of Moscow, Great Russian [*russkim*] communism and the Russian [*russkoi*] Red army."[55] In December 1919 the CPU's Manuilsky told delegates at the Eighth RCP Congress: "They beat us [Bolsheviks] a long time and in the end we naturally realized that banal truth, that, first, that without Russian communists, Petrograd and Moscow workers, Soviet Power cannot be established in Ukraine." In 1922, Rakovskii said: "Our [CPU] experience showed us that if we did not have behind us a power like Soviet Russia, the revolution in Ukraine would have died and today we would have had another government here … The establishment of the proletarian dictatorship in Ukraine … is possible only with the help of Soviet Russia and the Russian Communist Party."[56] In 1923, Kviring stated: "Soviet power did not triumph in Ukraine by virtue of its own strength, but only with the help of a strengthened Soviet Russia and while the German army was collapsing."[57]

The Kyivan Jewish old Bolshevik I.M. Lapidus, who in early 1920 had requested Lenin to rescind his order to reduce the number of Jews in Soviet offices, characterized Soviet rule in Ukraine as follows:

The whole course of our revolution clearly showed that in the borderlands it was not conquered [zavoevaniia] by the local proletariat but almost always was conquered [sic] by the proletariat from the center, and that soviet power in the kulak-cossack borderlands is nothing other than military occupation, in particular, in Ukraine … The honkie has more faith in his [local-born] Jew than the foreigner Muscovite because most Russians truly behave like conquerors.[58]

A fourth important Bolshevik apologist was Larik, the pen name of Ievhen Kasianenko, a former Ukrainian SD who in March 1919 joined the Bolsheviks. In two public letters he explained his choice with a convert's zeal. He made no mention of imperialism or colonialism, and he dismissed national liberation as "petite bourgeois utopianism." He wrote that the Bolsheviks rightly considered national issues trivial in light of the great tasks they faced. While in Ukraine under the Hetman, he wrote, he had hidden with workers who taught him they could never be any kind of patriots and that anyone who talked about the patriotism of Russian communists was a liar trying to undermine the common struggle against all bourgeoisie. Larik compared the Russian empire not to other empires but to the United States, and he claimed that Ukrainians should help Russia in the same way that white workers had helped the slaves during the American Civil War by joining the Union Army.[59] Drifting later that year to the CPU federalists, by 1920 Larik had become a centralist. That summer he wrote that as a class, the proletariat was not restricted to any national borders and had no territory except the world. Russia and Ukraine were only geographical expressions and on their territories each simply had a proletarian state organization. Both were the same because they were ruled by the same class. This was called political independence only because such terms made it easier to win the befuddled backward masses to communism.[60]

A final important apologist of Russian Bolshevik rule was the man in charge of imposing it, Rakovskii. In March 1919 he deftly side-stepped charges of colonial exploitation by talking about Ukrainian coal exports to Russia instead of iron ore exports. The issue was raised by a critic who had complained that Ukraine was importing shovels in return for exported ore instead of manufacturing them in Ukraine. Rakovskii argued that since Petrograd could no longer import coal from its original supplier, Britain, who could refuse to help her? He claimed that Russia sent more arms and finished goods to Ukraine than Ukraine sent grain to Russia, which was shameful. Ukrainian coal fuelled Red Army transportation, allowing it to fight the Whites, and there could be no Soviet regime in Ukraine without that Russian power. He continued that it would be an error to declare Ukrainian the official language because it was *de facto* the language of anti-soviet petite-bourgeois intellectuals and politicians. He argued that Ukrainian left SR and SD fears of Russian exploitation and domination were unfounded nationalist illusions. They had nothing to do with, and were contrary to, a socialist point of view. Surrounded by enemy armies on the offensive, Ukrainians had to accept the curtailment of formal independence and centralization. "If revolutionary Russia collapses what will remain of Ukrainian culture and Ukrainian workers' and peasants' desires for independence?" He then explained that Britain and France at Versailles had refused to recognize the UNR, which meant in practice that the only alternative to the Bolsheviks was renewed Russian rule under the Whites. Thinking about a future world socialist federation was simply dreaming. The reality at the time demanded the union and centralization of the former territories of the Russian empire around Russia; otherwise, the UNR would be back in Kyiv.

Rakovskii expressed similar rationales for Russian domination at two July 1919 CPU Central Committee meetings. Circumstances demanded union and centralization, and only Soviet rule guaranteed Ukraine independence. A UNR would be dominated by Poland just as Germany had dominated Hetman Ukraine. Ukraine needed Soviet Russian military help, Russia needed food. Someday in the future, when these circumstances changed, then union and centralization "obviously would disappear." Ukrainian language use had to be supported, he said, "but not to promulgate the class politics of the petite bourgeoisie." Ukraine had 3 million Russians and 27 million Ukrainians, and the issue was whether "the Russian revolutionary element, that is Bolshevik communists, [implements] the soviet program, or that element which is under a national Ukrainian flag implements an anti-communist program." Rakovskii refused to tolerate a revolutionary national bourgeoisie–communist party alliance in the former Russian imperial space of the kind Lenin would shortly instruct the Third International to organize in European overseas colonies, or an independent communist Ukraine allied with Russia like communist Hungary. For Ukraine, this option was dismissed as nationalism. He refuted the argument that any planned union of republics on former imperial Russian territory had to consider the future inclusion of other European countries. We see a union, he continued, "in which there is a natural solidarity formed by centuries of common struggle and aspirations, and this is a union of workers and peasants of all counties and provinces of the former Russian empire [applause]." According to this logic, the British or Spanish or any other empire also produced "natural solidarity" through "centuries of common struggle" that revolutions could not dissolve. Thus, Bulgaria would be best off within Ottoman frontiers, just as the "natural solidarity" of Irish and English workers required that the old British empire be maintained. Yet neither Rakovskii nor Comintern declarations made such assertions. Rakovskii's notion that what he called Russian–Ukrainian national solidarity trumped Ukrainian independence of even a communist nature, resembled the Russian slavophile Ivan Aksakov's notion of "natural obligations of brotherhood", that also denied Ukraine the right to full freedom granted to other nationalities.[61] Rakovskii's notion that Russian domination was the necessary form of urban worker dictatorship in Ukraine could be used to justify any imperial domination of any dependency – but the Bolsheviks applied it only to Ukraine and to former Russian-ruled territories they still controlled. The majority of workers were Russians, and "the leading revolutionary [Russian] intelligentsia, be it by chance or force of historical circumstances, has become the carrier of these communist ideas." Until a true communist Ukrainian intelligentsia was created, he continued, we had best come to terms with this *de facto* rule of urban workers. While the pro-worker Russian intelligentsia were uninvolved in national issues because there was no national oppression in Russia, "it is a fact that the cultivation in Ukrainian of issues related to the Ukrainian national movement is at the moment equivalent to out-right counter-revolution in Ukraine." These were facts, not desires or a product of his personal ideas or political partisanship. They had to be acted upon as the Bolsheviks proposed.[62]

In March 1920 the centralist Ukrainian Bolshevik Hryhoryi Petro-vsky explained that Ukraine had neither the people nor the ability to be independent. In such a context, Russians played the same role as did western European specialists who had come before the war to build factories. It was not their fault that workers were oppressed by capital-ism; nonetheless, the workers often beat or killed those specialists, thus hindering capitalist development, just as after 1917 Ukrainians beat or killed Russians, thus hindering socialist development. Since there was no material with which to build a Ukraine independent of Rus-sia, it was ridiculous to attempt to do so and a Russian alliance was unavoidable.[63]

Lesser personalities came up with other rationalizations for Russian domination. As with the above, no one applied these rationalizations to other empires, and those in Marxist form were normally Russian impe-rialist in content. It was not the fault of the international proletariat, wrote one anonymous polemicist in early 1919, that Ukraine had lost its statehood. National and cultural issues, he explained, would resolve themselves once the proletariat was victorious and all nations were socially equal. Until then, while revolution was sweeping the world, to raise issues of historical and national oppression was idiotic. It was too late historically in any case, for national needs and state sovereignty were no longer issues.[64] An anonymous T.G. claimed that a national-state economy was only a rich peasant's dream. The socialist revolution was a class revolution, there could be no national socialist revolution, and any national parties of the proletariat were only bourgeois parties. The class interests of workers in all nations were the same, and that is why they could have only one party, the Communist Party, and why it would be at the centre of a single international proletarian dictatorship. To restore the Ukrainian economy, he claimed, it was first necessary to restore "the historically created centralized economic apparatus of Ukraine and Russia." The two could not be torn into separate parts, each separately following its own economic politics. "And if fortuitous circumstances and capitalist adventurers succeeded for a time in sepa-rating this single economic unit that is why ... Ukraine is today for the most part a total morass." In T.G.'s analysis, economic exploita-tion by a Russian centre of a non-Russian periphery was not a cause of the Russian empire's collapse. The culprit was "capitalist control."[65] Regardless of the Marxist terminology, for Ukrainians in general and Ukrainian Marxists in particular, such simplifications made in Russian in Ukraine and not in Ukrainian implicitly reinforced the old imperial tsarist association of Russian and Russia with progress, modernity, and the future.

In an article on the Versailles negotiations published in late January 1919, the editor of *Izvestiia*, Iury Steklov, did not treat Russia as an empire. In his view, former non-Russian regions with their own left SDs could not be as independent of a Russian-left-SD-dominated regime as they had wanted to be of a tsarist or liberal regime. Russia was a national state with minorities who were incidental to the more important confrontation between capital and labour – and he took for granted that the Bolshevik party represented the latter. He explained that there was a war only between separate classes in Russia and that Soviet Russia had no troops on foreign territory. While admitting that "various governments" existed "in Russia" fighting between themselves, he did not view this as a war between states but rather between workers and exploiters "in Russia." There were no "national liberation wars"; instead, there was a "civil war in Russia" that "counter-revolutionaries" could fight only thanks to the Entente powers, which supported one or the other for their own imperial interests. The purpose of the Versailles Treaty was to sanction a "temporary dissolution of Russia." Ukraine had been independent only thanks to the Germans, and once they had left, and provided that no other power intervened, "Ukraine in one form or another eventually will reunite with Russia." Using Russia as a synonym for its empire, he did not specify whether his reasoning applied to other empires.

Another Bolshevik who did not think that national liberation movements should dissolve imperial ties was I. Vardin (Mgladze). In 1921, including Ukrainians within his list of small nationalities, he contended that their communist leaders had to oppose all attempts to separate from empire. Addressing the workers and peasants of "Russia's borderlands," he argued that in the interests of development and the proletarian class struggle, there had to be "full revolutionary union of all the nations of Russia." This, even though the Comintern did not envisage such post-revolutionary unions for territories of the French, Dutch, or British empires, nor did it defend ties formed by centuries of common fate within those empires. He cited only the Comintern Manifesto about proletarian revolution freeing economies from their national borders and then uniting all nations in close economic cooperation. He described Borotbism as an attempt to adopt nationalism to communism in Ukraine, but he did not think that Bolshevism represented a similar effort in Russia. Vardin followed all of this with carefully worded phrases from the Russian party program about the Bolshevik state establishing "a single economic plan with those who have already begun to build soviet power." With other nations that had not been part of the tsarist empire, however, there would be "economic cooperation." Borotbist demands for economic separation, bad enough in themselves, were also contrary to "centuries of common fate." To label Russian proletarians as imperialists was chauvinism of the worst sort. Socialism involved the erasure of all borders and required a single economic plan that, by definition, could not entail exploiting colonies. Supposedly, the socialist state would see to it that manufacturing was done where resources were located, but otherwise, for Moscow, Ukraine could not be any different from Tula or the Urals. It was "petite-bourgeois rubbish" to think that just because Ukraine produced sugar, Moscow could not do the accounting and distribution associated with its production. "A communist is not someone who under the slogan of a World Soviet Economic Council wants to create a closed Ukrainian economy. A communist is someone who realistically takes the first step towards a world economy – who creates a single economy of already triumphant workers and peasants." Given that a single, centralized ministry of world economy was unrealistic, communists in the former Russian empire had to do what they could today to realize socialism. All communists had to unite with Moscow. Soviet Russia did not need Ukraine, but Soviet Ukraine needed Russia because Bolsheviks in Ukraine were so weak.[66]

The resolutions of the centralist-dominated Fourth CPU Conference of March 1920, where only 28 per cent of the delegates declared themselves as Ukrainians, combined the above-mentioned elements into a concise justification of Russian Bolshevik domination – ignoring Robespierre, Marx, and an 1882 statement by Engels: "One thing alone is certain: *the victorious proletariat can force no blessings of any kind upon any foreign nation without undermining its own victory by so doing.*"[67] The resolution maintained that national issues – that is, non-Russian national issues – could not be placed above the fraternal alliance of workers and peasants and, that to apply national issues against the party was to complicate the task of establishing the dictatorship of the proletariat. Using the example of Ukrainian food exports to Germany and similar obligations mentioned in UNR–French negotiations, the resolution stipulated that a non-soviet Ukraine could only be a colony of inter-national imperialism. "By force of circumstances," Russia was the only soviet republic that had survived and that had the necessary resources, population, and territory to oppose counter-revolution. Russia had the right to lead the struggle of the international proletariat, a claim that no one at the Congress, where all proceedings were in Russian, seemed to think was imperialist. By definition and as an article of faith, Russian seizures of grain in Ukraine were not imperialist or colonialist seizures, as German seizures had been. "It is the revolutionary duty of all new Soviet states to enter into tight union with Soviet Russia." In the case of Ukraine, this "duty" was supposedly reinforced by similar languages, a "common" economy created under tsarism, and a "common" strug-gle against tsarism. Accordingly, "a complete separation of these two soviet states would be an artificial process [iskustvennom protsesom] at odds with the past and current struggles of the Ukrainian and Russian workers." State union involved single ministries centred in Moscow for all common affairs. Delegates thought this was compatible with Lenin's December 1919 Letter and the resolutions of the Eighth Rus-sian Party Congress. Rakovskii later specified that Ukraine should be subordinated to Russia – another assertion that no one in the Russian party considered odd or anti-Marxist.[68] Ukrainian Marxists viewed all of this as more the product of Russian imperialist preconceptions than of revolutionary messianism or the exigencies of war.

Russian Bolsheviks did not entertain the idea of an anti-colonialist alliance between Ukrainian radicals and themselves against Ukraine's settler-colonist Russians, of the kind that existed for a time in Central Asia. The First All-Ukrainian Party Conference resolutions (May 1921) supported the Irish and Indian national liberation struggles against capitalist colonialism as well as the struggle of non-Russians against great-power Russian nationalism in the tsarist empire until October 1917. Thereafter, the right of self-determination did not mean that "Ukrainian communists were to separate from Russian workers and peasants," because Ukrainian national liberation was now "counter-revolutionary." Ukrainian communists were now to "unite Ukrainian workers and peasants with their Russian brethren." The same resolu-tions went on to assert that soviet power was a-national and was not interested in supporting one nationality against another. Russification was no longer a threat because the Bolsheviks had destroyed the land-owners and urban bourgeoisie who constituted its economic base. Since only ethnic and not political borders mattered after 1917, it didn't matter whether any of the nationally defined non-Russian republics had ministries; all depended on circumstances.[69] The fact that the ministries used Russian was not discussed, nor was why internationalist soviet power spoke in Russian and not Esperanto.

Finally, Bolshevik leaders invoked an article of faith to rationalize Russian domination of non-Russian territories. Unlike Marx and Engels, who eventually abandoned hope that the English working class would dispense with its imperialist anti-Irish sentiments, Lenin presumed until his death that "the Russian proletariat" would dispense with – or not inherit from the "Russian petite bourgeoisie" – an innate contempt for Ukrainians and Ukrainian. Assuming that class consciousness was both natural and independent of ethnic-national identity, he apparently did not realize that in 1848 the German-dominated Slavs had learned that not only German elites but also the German populace as a whole looked down on them. He failed to discern the imperialist sympathies of Northern Ireland's Protestant workers. For Lenin, "the Great Russian oppressor" could not possibly be related in any way to "the proletarian business of the Great Russian workers" – and this despite his relief that the 1907 Socialist Congress had rejected the idea of a "socialist colonial policy," an idea that for him suggested that even the proletariat had been somewhat infected by the lust of conquest.[70]

This failure to recognize what might be termed plebian imperialism underlay the claim made in a February 1919 article that proletarian socialist states had no impulse to conquer nations: "The proletariat brings liberty to nations." To which someone who was in Kyiv during the first Bolshevik occupation made this response: "We well remember posters with slogans 'Death to the bourgeoisie and Ukrainians.' We have evidence of how local soviets summoned high-school teachers of Ukrainian studies and accused them of teaching a 'counter-revolutionary subject.' True, they tell us [now] that this was the mindless mass, but we say it is the result of conquest." He continued: "Clearly, the right to self-determination does not free the nations of Russia from the obligation to federate with Russia." Ukrainian Marxists regarded that kind of federalism as no different from the federalism that Hetman Skoropadsky had agreed to with the White government at the end of his rule and that Ukrainians from both sides of the political spectrum condemned as a capitulation to Russia. Bolsheviks remained unconvinced. Eight days later we read: "It is clear the proletariat cannot oppress any nation because it has no economic reason to do so." The author claimed that

Bolshevik policies in Finland and Ukraine proved this. Larik, responding to the accusation that Soviet rule had merely replaced the rule of the
Russian bourgeoisie with that of the Russian proletariat, wrote: "But it
is obvious that only under socialism will national oppression disappear. But it is obvious that the proletariat never oppressed any nation's
language because it has no economic basis do so." In May 1919, Petrovsky claimed that there could be no national oppression in a socialist
state because one class no longer ruled another, "and workers, regardless of what language, cannot enslave each other."[71]

This preconception was beyond the pale of discussion. Federalists
led by Lapchinskii submitted to the RCP in 1919, and again in February 1920 to the Kyiv branch of the CPU, memorandums condemning
RCP policy in Ukraine as colonialist (see appendices 4 and 5). The latter was used as a pretext to suspend the author from the party. At the
Fourth CPU Conference the following month, Iakovlev condemned
Lapchinskii as a renegade instead of debating his ideas. Iakovlev said
there was a line that party members could not cross. That the Russian proletariat had an economic interest in exploiting the Ukrainian
proletariat; that the RCP was dominated by Russian petite-bourgeois
functionaries and intellectuals intent on maintaining their cultural
hegemony in Ukraine; that the Russian party had occupied Ukraine, to
which the Ukrainian proletariat could only respond by establishing a
state independent from the invader, were claims "beyond the limits of
permissible discussion." When Iakovlev later elaborated on the issue
of Moscow using "colonialist methods of rule" in Ukraine, he asked
that his remarks be excluded from the minutes. "For the working class,
the proletariat of any nation and the world proletariat, any wish to
nationally oppress is totally alien," explained Petrovsky, a centralist.
Rakovskii that same year wrote: "Those who imagine federation with
Russia as covert subjugation of Ukraine to Russia, as a continuation
of tsarist policies of exploitation and Russification, intentionally ignore
the fact … that soviet power as the authentic power of the working and
peasant masses by its nature excludes the use of arbitrary power and
all Russification."[72] The RCP that same April instructed the CPU, of
which no more than 10 per cent were declared Ukrainians, to expel not
the Russian but the "déclassé demoralized Ukrainian element" from its
ranks.[73]

In May 1922, after the million-strong Red Army had finally defeated
Ukrainian partisans after a vicious three-year war and Lenin had given
up trying to impose collective farms, Kulyk wrote: "Soviet power could

not take the form of occupation because that would contradict the very essence of proletarian dictatorship, and because in a country where the Ukrainian peasants are a majority, it is a matter of life and death for proletarian power to meet the economic and cultural needs of this peasantry."[74]

In 1924 an anonymous editorialist wrote: "The proletariat does not exploit, the proletariat liberates itself and liberates. That is its nature and the nature of its revolution … The October revolution destroyed colonialist exploitation in the USSR; and the presentations and discussions of the UCP on the colonial question reflect a petite-bourgeois tendency favouring the creation of an independent bourgeois state that represents struggle against the proletariat."[75]

Bukharin's Theory of the Offensive was a Bolshevik rationalization for domination that included elements of revolutionary messianism. It echoed the idea of a "socialist colonial policy" that had been only narrowly defeated at the 1907 International Socialist Congress and the above-mentioned Polish communist ideas. It arose during the Ninth RCP Congress in September 1920, when leaders debated attacking Poland again in the spring. The general issue was not whether but *when* they as socialists should conduct offensive wars to attain revolution by conquest. Bukharin contended that offensives were permissible and condemned Polish communists who had classified the Bolshevik invasion of that year as "Red imperialism." Radek explained: "In principle we advocate that all proletarians able to bear arms must aid the international proletariat." Zinoviev similarly condemned as renegades those Polish communists who thought that "not one republic should be created with foreign bayonets."[76] In keeping with his March 1920 pronouncement against using force to spread communism, Lenin finally rejected Zinoviev's wording for the resolution on Poland, which claimed that Polish workers had accepted the Bolshevik "offensive revolutionary war."[77] Bukharin nonetheless wrote an article at the end of the year specifically justifying the use of force to impose socialist revolution. He claimed that communists in European countries who faced a Red Army invasion had to support that "importation" of socialism even when conditions might be considered unripe. Since self-determination in Europe was merely defence of "bourgeois fatherlands," revolution did not depend on class struggle in conditions where workers might believe in national liberation. It could be spread by Red Army invasion in just the same way that the French had spread revolution after 1789. "We must establish in our program that every proletarian state has the right to Red intervention ... Bayonets and rifles are also essential here. Yes, the spreading of the [Russian] Red Army is the spreading of socialism, proletarian power, and revolution. This is the basis for the right of Red intervention in those particular circumstances where it purely technically facilitates the realization of socialism."[78] The following year, Trotsky, although he had actually opposed the invasion of Georgia, in the interests of party unity implied that Moscow had just as much right to do as it willed in Ukraine, Georgia, or Lithuania as London had done and was doing in India, Egypt, or Ireland. He wrote that the soviet revolution in Georgia had been brought about "with the active participation of the Red Army." "It is only essential that this [military] support should come at the moment when the need for it has been ... recognized by the class-conscious revolutionary vanguard" – which in practice meant the Moscow-controlled and -dominated local organization of the RCP.[79] This kind of theorizing ended at the Third Comintern Congress in July 1921, where Lenin and Trotsky explained that the theory of the offensive was no longer relevant beyond Soviet borders.

Imperial and Other Preconceptions

Most Bolshevik leaders shared the younger Marx's dismissive views on nationality – his notion that large, centralized economies were progressive, that nationalism was not progressive, and that small national states were archaic. These elements of revolutionary messianism coincided with the educated opinion of the time that viewed minority nationalisms of small "doomed" peoples as anomalies and did not classify Russians living outside the thirty Russian central provinces as settler-colonist minorities. The fact that the Theory of the Offensive debate took place in the wake of an invasion of Poland and not the previous year in the wake of a failed invasion of Ukraine bears witness to this preconception. The Bolsheviks did not regard Ukraine as foreign; for them it was the non-Russians on their native territories who were the minorities, not the Russian minority settled there. Even those who accepted that a Ukrainian nationality existed subsumed it within a notion of Russian–Ukrainian ethnic unity – a notion they embraced as empirical reality rather than as a derivation of the eastern Slavic unity myth elaborated by imperial apologists. Some declared Marxists, accordingly, used ethnic-biological criteria to justify their centralization of former imperial territories. Among most Bolsheviks who had been raised and educated with the values and ideas of Imperial Russia,

Marxist principles, imperialist Russian preconceptions, and the *zeitgeist* of the times overlapped. The rationalizations and motivations derived from these reinforced one another, and it is not always clear which had primacy.

The centralist Kviring ignored Ukraine's declaration of independence in January 1918 and considered its separation from Russia to be exclusively the result of armed German imperialism. He claimed there was no basis for independence, given the country's supposed economic and spiritual proximity to Russia. It was necessary to reunite Ukraine and Russia on the basis of proletarian centralism, he stated in July 1918. "The reunion of Ukraine with Russia into one Soviet republic is an inevitable fact in the course of the social revolution."[80] To take another example, the Ukrainian-born Russified German Bolshevik Evgeniia Bosh's [*née* Miash] explanation of Ukrainian issues, written in 1918, resembled that of the monarchist Sergei Shchegolev, author of *Ukrainskoe dvizhenie kak sovremennyi etap Iuzhnorusskogo separatizma* (1912). The latter explained the Ukrainian movement as a creation of intellectuals intent on destroying "the ethnic unity of the Little and Great Russian people" in the interests of Russia's enemies. Bosh, for her part, explained that because Ukraine was so closely tied to Russia politically and economically, the national movement was dividing "two closely related people" and weakening the revolutionary struggle. She had no interest in how that tie had come about. Autocracy, in any case, had destroyed national development within the empire. Similar languages and a common economy and laws had erased national inequalities, combined Ukraine and Russia into one unit and, had united their workers and peasants in one revolutionary struggle. The "Russian revolution," which she equated with proletarian revolution, reverberated among all the oppressed nations of the borderlands and had "killed the idea of nationally uniting nations." The "borderland proletariat" had survived the autocracy and had fought for soviet power in 1917 together with the Russian proletariat. There was no national struggle, only a class struggle that Ukrainian intellectuals and bourgeoisie wanted to avoid by "establishing artificial national barriers between two peoples accustomed to each other, and disseminating into the lives of Ukrainian workers and peasants the idea of national isolation." The borderland proletariat of the "national provinces," she claimed, had no tasks separate from those of the Russian proletariat and "burns with the incontestable desire to fuse with Soviet Russia."[81] Both Shchegolev and Bosh regarded Ukrainian intellectuals and Germans as enemies of

Russia. A soviet Ukraine with its own Communist Party allied to but independent of a communist Russia was as unacceptable to Bosh as an independent Little Russia was to Shchegolev.

Like their German and English counterparts, Russian social democrats shared with Russian liberals and monarchists not only a language but a commitment to the inviolability and legitimacy of imperial borders. The Bolsheviks imagined that once they were in power, centralized monolingual Russian ministries would realize the socialist dream. Although Lenin accepted Finnish and Polish independence as a temporary condition that would allow the Bolsheviks to slowly win the trust of the most backward of the working masses in those countries, he refused this option to Ukrainians. Ukrainian independence, he claimed in December 1919, was contingent on tight economic union and the "very close union of Russian and Ukrainian workers and peasants." Unlike Otto Bauer, who in October 1918 repudiated his earlier defence of Austrian imperial borders and called on socialists to recognize the reality of their demise, Lenin thought that Russian Bolshevism was coterminous with internationalism, and he bent to pressure from party members in non-Russian territories to dismiss non-Russian opposition to central rule as "nationalism." He thereafter sided with those who waged war to keep Ukrainian lands within their restored Russian state, perhaps unaware of Robespierre's dictum: "The most extravagant idea that can be born in the head of a political thinker is to believe that it suffices for people to enter, weapons in hand, among a foreign people and expect to have its laws and constitution embraced. No one loves armed missionaries; the first lesson of nature and prudence is to repulse them as enemies."[82] Ukrainian Marxists condemned that aggression as renewed Russian colonial imperialism, pointing out that the Bolsheviks were applying one set of standards to the Russian empire and another to other empires.

One imperialist preconception that Russian and Russified radicals shared with other educated Russians, as noted, was that Russia was a multinational state rather than an empire with colonies, that its central government was a modernizing agent and, that non-Russian territories and cultures were backward and destined to assimilate. The dominant opinion among the literate was that Russian culture and language was cosmopolitan, progressive, and representative of modernity – a view shared by most of the literate in the other great powers, who imagined that only *their* respective cultures and languages were worthy of future development because only *they* were suited to the things of the

1 Indian nationalist cartoon depicting Wilson and Lloyd George excluding India from the promises of Wilson's Fourteen Points. Besides Ukraine, Ireland and Korea could have been depicted behind India. *Self-Determination for India* (London, 1918). Library of Congress.

2 Ukrainian Co-op depiction (1916) of the socio-economic order with the visibly Ukrainian "consumer" at the bottom and the Jewish "merchant" on his shoulders. Caption: "Comrade peasants! If you want throw off the yoke of exploiter-shopkeepers gather in cooperatives!" TsNB im Vernadskoho, viddil plakat.

3 Detail from Central Rada poster (February? 1918) depicting Ukraine as a national-economic unit and explaining why it is a Russian Colony. TsDAB 12638s.

4 Non-Russian nationalities of former tsarist empire leave Bolshevik Russia – depicted with a knife and a vodka bottle labelled "Bolshevik culture." Caption: "The centre: Long live the single undivided Bolsherussia. The periphery: Hey, let's not waste time, break our chains ... Let us save our homes." *Budiak* no. 3, (December 1917).

ПЕРВОЕ СОВЕТСКОЕ ПРАВИТЕЛЬСТВО УКРАИНЫ
НАРОДНЫЙ СЕКРЕТАРИАТ
(Декабрь 1917 г. — Апрель 1918 г.)

1) Артем, 2) Скрыпник, 3) Затонский, 4) Коцюбинский, 5) Бош, 6) Аусем, 7) Лугановский, 8) Терлецкий, 9) Кулик, 10) Шахрай, 11) Люксембург.

5 Ukraine's first Bolshevik government (January 1918). Vasyl Shakhrai is bottom center; Mykola Skrypnyk, top centre.

6 Russocentric Bolshevik understanding of "international solidarity" as depicted in *Pervoe maia* published by Soviet Ukraine's War Commissariat. Both Ukraine and a Ukrainian are absent. Caption: "This is how the fraternal unity of the workers is realized." *Pervoe maia* (Spring 1919).

7 Cartoon depicting Bolshevik entry into Kyiv in January 1918 on the cover of *Gedz*, a moderate socialist satirical journal. Caption: "FREEDOM brought from the north on the bayonets of the gendarme Muraviov, which is why she is bandaged." *Gedz* no. 3 (March 1918).

8 Cartoon from same issue of *Gedz* depicting stereotypical Russian and Russified Jewish urban bourgeoisie greeting Bolshevik troops entering Kyiv carrying banner "Death to Culture" (in Russian). Caption: "Comrade Kolupanov, yes we are bourgeois of sorts, but even we can thank you for educated advice." *Gedz* no. 3 (March 1918).

Українська Соціяль-Демократична Робітнича Партія.

Пролетарі усіх краïн єднайтеся!

Товариші Робітники, Селяне та Червоноармейці!

Чорна сотня, забившись десь у кутки, веде свою чорносотенну роботу серед робітників та селян. Таким способом ще в 1905 році їй вдалось, скориставшись темнотою робітників та селян, знищить здобутки революції і знову запанувать над трудящим людом. Не гнушається вона цього і тепер і вживає всіх заходів, аби розбивши сили пролетаріяту, знов впитись його кров'ю і потом. Вона натравлює трудящих людей, одної нації на таких же самих другої нації. Вона нишком шипить як гадина і вливає яд у наші серця і розум, хоче росналити наші почуття і направити нас на тих безневинних трудящих людей другої нації, котрі так же саме як і ми терпіли глум і гніт царського режиму. Вона хоче зробить еврейський погром.

ТОВАРИШІ! НЕ ПІДДАВАЙТЕСЬ НА ТАКУ ПРОВОКАЦІЮ!

Б'ючись між собою ми знищемо свої пролетарські сили, а чорній сотні і буржуазії цього тільки й треба; вона раде, коли піддаються їй провокації, ще з більшою рішучістю тоді робе і збагачує свої ряди. А хіба для нас, робітників та селян це корисно? Ні, — цим самим, коли піддамось чорносотенній агітації, пошкодимо тільки собі, давши перемогу тим, хто хоче щоб по наших спинах гуляли ще нагайки та шомполи.

Хіба ми ще мало терпіли од царів, хіба не обридли ще нам рабство, глум і гніт і експлуатація? Ні, годі! Не хочемо ми ворожнечі між працюючим людом народів! Ми в згоді хочемо жити, по братерські!

ТОВАРИШІ! НЕ ПІДДАВАЙМОСЯ ЖЕ НА ПРОВОКАЦІЮ!

Твердо пам'ятаймо, що в єднанні пролетаріяту всіх народів — його сила і могутність, що тільки з'єднавши сили свої до купи пролетаріят зможе легко боротись з ворогом — буржуазією.

Товариші! Од імені всієї Української Соціяль-Демократичної Робітничої Партії закликаємо Вас до рішучої боротьби з чорносотенною агітацією, іменем всесвітнього Пролетарського Інтернаціонала кличемо Вас, товариші, до міжнародньої пролетарської Солідарности.

Хай живе єднання Всесвітнього Пролетаріяту!

Хай живе Соціялізм.

Лохвицький Комітет Української Соціяль-Демократичної Робітничої Партії.

3 квітня 1919 року,
м. Лохвиці.

9 Ukrainian left SD leaflet warning against Russian extremist (black hundred) anti-semitic provocations, April 1919. TsDAB 12187s.

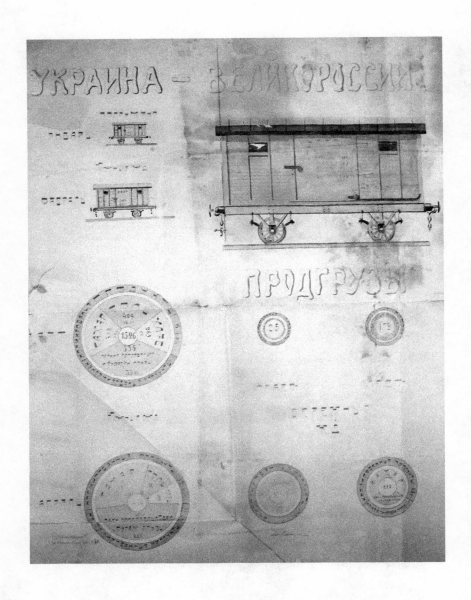

10 Detail from chart illustrating trade imbalance between Soviet Ukraine and Soviet Russia, 1919. TsDAHO f. 43 op. 1 sprava 36.

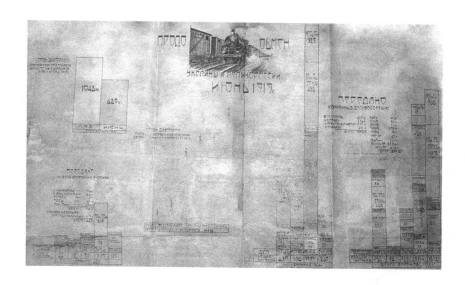

11 and 12 Charts illustrating trade imbalance between Soviet Ukraine and Soviet Russia, 1919.

13 Mykhailo Tkachenko (seated), 1918. Central State Cinefotophono Archive.

14 Iury Mazurenko?

15 Danylo Zeleny flanked by two of his officers Dmytro Liubymenko and
Vasyl Diuzhanov (1919). Reproduced in: R. Krutsyk ed., *Narodna viina*
(1917–1932).

16 Rank and file partisan from one of Zeleny's units, Panas Pustovyi with unknown woman (1919). Reproduced in R. Koval, *Otaman Zeleny*.

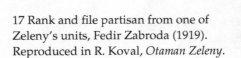

17 Rank and file partisan from one of Zeleny's units, Fedir Zabroda (1919). Reproduced in R. Koval, *Otaman Zeleny*.

18 Anarchists posing with UCP newspaper *Chervony Prapor*, 1919? (DASBU f. 6 sprava 71538fn no. 105.

22го апрѣля 1919го года

Мы организаторы Украины
1) Зеленый, 2) Соколовъ, 3) Шинкаръ,
4) Григорьевъ, 5) Ангелъ.
6) Винниченко, 7) Петлюра, и
8) Андреевъ и всѣ остальные
и всѣхъ насъ организаторовъ
на украинѣ имѣется 50 человѣкъ
и я Махно говорю вамъ если
вы жидовъ не переберете или
не вышлете въ палестину
или хотя въ свою Росiю
то вашъ дней въ Украинѣ
не устоять мы принимаемся
за оружiе въ Iюнь или въ Iюль
мѣсяцъ такъ что вы
думайте пораньше
или уходите съ украины
совсѣмъ а что вы разсчиту
ете на наборъ новобранцевъ
то даже на это и не думайте

19 and 20 (above and facing) Forged letter attributed to Makhno threatening Rakovskii with a joint Ukrainian offensive unless he "kills the Jews." TsDAVO f. 2 op.1 sprava 234, no. 103, p. 1, 2–3.

21 Anatole Richytsky's party-card with photo after he joined the CPU and just before his arrest. DASBU f. 6 sprava 32771, vol 5.

22 Group UCP members from Kyiv Province (1922). No.3 is Ukrainian writer Borys Antonenko Davydovych. DASBU f 13 sprava 423, vol.2.

market – as Adam Smith believed. Russian radicals who thought that freedom included decentralization imagined that freedom only in social terms, not in national ones. Insofar as they imagined a Little Russia or Ukraine, it was as administrative units deserving no more autonomy because of cultural-historical differences than any other unit. Imperial disintegration displeased Sverdlov in 1919: "Sometimes one is horrified by the wave of political independence coming in from Ukraine, Lithuania, Estonia, Belarus, etc."[83] Arguing against indigenization in 1923, the Russian Dmitrii Lebed said at the Seventh CPU Congress that the government should not sponsor Ukrainian culture and language; rather, it should allow the "developed" Russian urban culture to compete with the "undeveloped" Ukrainian rural culture. The Ukrainians who were present immediately pointed out that his formula repeated word for word the views of the pre-1917 Russian monarchist and extremist loyalist leader Prince Volkonskii.[84]

In *Critical Remarks on the National Question* (1913), Lenin compared the Russian empire not to other empires but to the United States and, on the basis of the American melting pot model, argued that the capitalist-driven assimilation of nations was progressive if it occurred voluntarily, without political coercion. The large, centralized state was a great step forward from medieval disunity to the future socialist unity of the entire world. Empires were "progressive" and should not be dissolved – which contradicted his arguments in *Imperialism*. Behind this ostensibly Marxist bias, however, was not only an imperial Russocentric bias but also the preconceptions of the age that had led Lenin to confuse cause and effect in this pamphlet and again in June 1917. Rather than characterizing the linguistic, historical, and character traits shared by Russians and Ukrainians as the product of pre-capitalist tsarist policies intended to eliminate existing differences in the interests of imperial unity and centralization, he assumed – like other educated Russians – that common traits resulting from tsarist rule pre-dated that rule. Thus he condemned monarchists and liberals not because (unlike them) he thought the empire should be dissolved but, because the centralism they advocated antagonized Ukrainians, thereby impeding their assimilation into the ruling nationality – a goal he shared with tsarist ministers, imperialists in general, John Stuart Mill, and supposedly, Ukrainians themselves.[85] In the same way, Zinoviev's late-1918 view that concessions to non-Russian languages were merely a form of tolerance for Ukrainian peasants raising their children in Ukrainian, only echoed a pre-1917 Russian consensus, expressed in 1883 as follows: "A local dialect should not be allowed to function as a state [official] language, nor should Russian be replaced in schools by any local dialect used only by the local common folk and undeveloped for either academic, literary, or general social use." Some twenty years later, Petr Struve would explain that "the state of affairs brought about by Russia's entire history" – that is, the hegemony of Russian culture in the empire – meant that education in Ukrainian would be a waste of time, money, and effort, because people ignorant of Russian would be marginal illiterates. The state of affairs that Struve invoked to justify his claim was, for him, "a totally natural fact," – not the product of what non-Russian national leaders considered two hundred years of oppressive, illegitimate, imperialist violence and centralizing legislation.[86] Perhaps this is why Bukharin theorized about armed "Red intervention" and Trotsky condemned carrying revolution abroad by force of arms only in 1920.[87] Neither considered their earlier invasions of Ukraine a Red intervention tantamount to international war; they viewed it as aid to local cadres against internal counter-revolution, because for them, Ukraine was an internal matter – as was Ireland for England.[88] From the Ukrainian Marxist perspective, this attitude was a variant of what Engels had called "the spirit of domination [towards Ireland that was] still dominant in the minds of some English working men." Just as Austro-German social democrats considered themselves to be the "internationalists" and their Czech counterparts "nationalists," so their Russian comrades considered themselves to be the internationalists and the Ukrainian leftists to be the nationalists. The opinion of liberal and radical Russians about Ukraine might be compared to that of Mill about the Irish: the problem was not English rule over Ireland but misrule in Ireland.

Lenin's underlying Russocentric biases also appear in his two articles about state languages. These classified Russia as a multinational state rather than an empire and Russian as a state rather than imperial language. The development of capitalism and the conditions of life and work would, he claimed, ensure that those who needed Russian would learn it without compulsion. He assumed that requirements of economic exchange would impel all to study the language "most convenient for general economic relations," and he ignored the possibility that Ukrainian migration to Ukraine's cities might make that language Ukrainian. Instead of comparing Russia with other empires, he here compared it with Switzerland, implying that, just as there different nationalities all spoke French because they were "civilized citizens of a democratic state," so, in a democratized Russian empire, everyone would adopt

Russian voluntarily.[89] But, like his French Marxist contemporaries, Lenin failed to address phenomena like proletarian nationalism and the ability of the "bourgeois state" to create a national community. He did not reflect on why Italian Swiss citizens spoke Italian in their own canton (i.e., whether that was "progressive") while educated Ukrainians spoke Russian in their provinces. He did not explain why "capitalism spoke Russian" in the empire to begin with; why only Russian should be associated with democracy; why those two forces worked to consolidate the Russian empire while dissolving others; or why anyone would want to be educated in or use their native languages if the conditions of life and work made them irrelevant to daily life. Lenin either missed or deliberately obscured the relationship between capitalism and imperial languages. He assumed that democracy and capitalism would make Russian the language of the majority in a "Russia" that he imagined as an American-style melting pot. In hindsight, his lapses are startling. He ignored how financial capital formed on a national basis; he did not ask why corporations used one language and not another; and he confused imperial languages in colonies with state languages in national states. The idea of linguistic imperialism never occurred to Lenin, who classified non-Russians in the tsarist empire as national minorities. As far as is known, neither he nor any other leading Bolshevik referred to the Irish, Koreans, Algerians, or Cubans as national minorities in their respective empires. Treating language as merely a tool of communication, he did not link it to matters of power, status, and prestige.

Those in Ukraine who questioned why they should learn or use Ukrainian: "if we are supposed to be internationalists and [already] have one common language which is Russian," were in tandem with Lenin – who had no interest in Esperanto. In 1918, in reply to a question from the mayor of Stockholm about introducing Esperanto in schools, he said, "There are already three world languages and now there will be a fourth, Russian." Bukharin and Zinoviev shared that view.[90] Most metropolitan settlers in Algeria, Vietnam, and Korea would also have wondered why they should learn the national languages of those colonies if they knew French or Japanese.

In keeping with the Hegelian Enlightenment *zeitgeist* of the time that led the educated in ruling imperial nations to equate progress and modernity with their respective cultures and languages and large states, learned imperialist ideas formed Bolshevik attitudes towards non-Russians. Most Bolsheviks belonged to the ruling Russian nationality or identified with it by choice. They had been educated in Russian,

they read Russocentric tsarist histories of the empire, and they lived
in urban centres with Russian media. The small fraction of applicants
for soviet government jobs who wrote "internationalist" in response
to the question on applications about nationality did so in Russian.
Very few Bolsheviks thought that the Russian empire should be dissolved into its constituent national parts, as they argued every other
empire should be. Insofar as the Ukrainian and other national movements celebrated the traditional and rural, many Georgian, Polish, or
Ukrainian-born who prioritized modernization rejected them and their
separatist implications for the Pan-Russian imperial identity, which
they associated with industrialization – only without the tsarism. Much
like Czech Social Democrats who opposed the formation of separate
Czech parties and unions, the Ukrainians Pavlo Tupchansky and Kon-
stantin Arabazhin claimed in 1906 that cultural similarities and economic links made political separatism impossible. Socialism, in their
view, was incompatible with nationalism, and national identity was an
invention of nationalists. People merely had cultural as well as political
and economic rights that had to be respected. A reformed democratic
Russia – by which they meant the entire empire – would end all national
oppression; "the proletariat" by definition could not engage in national
oppression.[91] The Ukrainian-born Klimentii Voroshilov (Voroshylo)
was fluent in Ukrainian and politically Russified. In November 1917 in
Luhansk, he expressed no inkling of national liberation in a letter to his
party's Central Committee about local Ukrainian activists: "In general,
this wave of chauvinism [Ukrainian national demands and declaration
of autonomy] that, fortunately for the moment, has grabbed only the
elites [*verkhi*], makes itself felt acutely. They are forcing the Rada upon
us and forbidding us to recognize the Petrograd government. Naturally, for now we spit on all this froth, but there will be unpleasantness
in the near future."[92] Almost all of Ukraine's Jewish Bolsheviks also
thought in imperial Russian rather than Ukrainian national terms. At
best, like the Ukrainophile Ivan Kulyk, some sympathized with the federalists. As apostates they did not claim to represent all Jews, nor did
religious Jews view them as their representatives.

In a Katerynoslav newspaper, a Ukrainian wrote that because national
oppression was not a historical pain in Russia, Russians could not understand it. "They are blind and deaf to the grieving of our national soul
... They don't understand because they are an imperial nation."[93] This
man would not have been surprised if he had seen the poster issued by
Soviet Ukraine's War Commissariat in the spring of 1919 depicting four

workers standing over a map of Europe and holding hands. There was no Ukrainian worker or a Ukraine on the map (see figure 6, illustration section). As Skrypnyk wrote in 1925, "For the majority of our party members Ukraine as a national unit did not exist." A 1926 CPU Central Committee report admitted that while "the city" contemptuously regarded Ukrainian as coterminous with backwardness and peasantry, by 1918 "we had full-blown hate in towns towards everything Ukrainian." Capitalism threw together into the city Ukrainian peasants and workers from Russia. The Ukrainian proletariat, as a result, "acquired Russian culture, began to internalize Russian, including its attitude to everything Ukrainian as peasant and backward. That is why the native proletariat in Ukraine turned decisively against Ukrainian nationalism and separatism, and enhanced its revolutionary tie to Russian comrades throughout the old tsarist Russia [by] reading revolutionary literature in Russian."[94] In 1927 the Russian-born Lapchinskii described anti-Ukrainian Russians in 1917 as follows: "The citizenry [of Kharkiv] were totally Russified and zoologically hostile to everything Ukrainian (to which I might add that, yet today, ten years after the revolution, we still have to beat this Russian chauvinism out of them with a club [*kiiem dovodystsia vybyvaty z neii Rossiiskyi shovanizm*])."[95]

Party members high and low shared imperialist preconceptions and biases. When in March 1918 the Seventh Bolshevik Party Conference debated removing the adjective Russian (*Rossiiska*) from its title, 90 per cent of the overwhelmingly Russian delegates voted against the proposal, for they considered "Rossiia" – which in Russian referred to the entire empire and not to ethnic Russia – to be "our country." In 1918, echoing English workers' imperialist sentiments towards Ireland, Bolshevik Russian workers in the industrial city of Katerynoslav bitterly complained that Ukraine had separated from Russia. Their delegate told the CPU's First Party Congress that he would be unleashing a scandal if he returned with the news that the Bolsheviks had formed a separate party in Ukraine. In early 1919 an enthusiastic speaker told Kyiv's arsenal workers that Ukraine and historical Rus were simply Russia: "Comrades you see how the bourgeoisie pointed at us [Bolsheviks] and shouted far and wide that we had sold Russia to the Germans. Let them look now: almost all the Rus lands have been reconquered."[96] In the summer of 1919 the first edition of Ukraine's Bolshevik *Selskaia Bednota* appeared in Poltava with an article about Zhytomir and Volyn province titled "Look Who Is Now Master in the Russian Land." In *Izvestiia* (Kharkiv) in June 1919 a Russian declared that "Moscow, the heart of worker and peasant Russia, is in our time the centre around which the gathering is taking place of all parts of the Russian empire that were destroyed and dismantled by the revolution, counter-revolution, and civil war."[97] In its 24 March 1918 edition the centralist Bolshevik *Izvestiia Iuga* wrote: "The attempt to create an independent Ukrainian state ... is counter-revolutionary by its very nature." The Russian author of a 1921 history of the Russian soviet economy, echoing tsarist opinion, compared the Russian proletariat to Tsar Ivan Kalita, in that both had "gathered the [Russian] lands." In 1919 and 1920, local activists sent numerous complaints to the UCP Central Committee complaining about imperialist preconceptions such as those made by a comrade Vasyliev, head of the Volyn (province) Party Committee. He told students at a teacher's college that "Ukraine can only be a Russian province and nothing distinguishes it from Russia." The foreign propaganda office attached to Ukraine's soviet government published nothing in Russian. The official register of foreigners in Kyiv province in 1920 did not list Russians.[98]

The Russian Bolsheviks' refusal to accept non-Russian secession from the Russian imperial space or to apply Lenin's *Imperialism* to that space was evident during the 1922 CPU October plenum, held two years after the Second Comintern Congress. Lebed explained Ukraine's dilemmas abstractly: "What can you do if for better or worse history has created a situation [in Ukraine] wherein cultural centers are centers of another culture – Russian?" Rakovskii, who had by then become a strong advocate of autonomy, also avoided the colonialism/dependency paradigm. He admitted that because the pre-1917 Ukrainian bourgeoisie and its nationalism had been essentially revolutionary, the country objectively should have ended up with an independent bourgeois national state. But he did not follow this logic and welcome the collapse of the empire. That would have led him to reiterate UCP ideas. He rather cryptically explained that "instead of the old tsarist government, power had passed to the proletariat allied with the poor peasants." Labelling Bolshevik Russia a proletarian state, he added that the circumstances created by the October Revolution had rendered Ukrainian nationalism counter-revolutionary and that the bourgeoisie was using nationalism to attract Ukrainians to their struggle against the revolution as a "Russian russifying power" – cynically ignoring both the resolutions of the Second Comintern Congress on the revolutionary role of nationalism and the existence of a Ukrainian Communist Party that, unlike the RCP, used nationalism in the interests of revolution.[99]

Bolshevik leaders did not claim that the dominated proletarians in other empires wanted to unite with the proletariats of the ruling imperial nationalities. Zatonsky complained in 1918 that Russian and Russified party members considered national self-determination fine "as long as it involved India and Egypt in as much as we [Bolsheviks] have not had to work there (there are enough problems abroad with this [slogan] already with the Tatars and Bashkirs)." Almost the entire party in Ukraine were Russians or Russified. Unable to condemn Lenin's declaration of the right of self-determination, but also unable to recognize Ukraine as Ukraine, they had to follow a party line that called for self-determination, but their hearts were not in it. So they began to wonder: "Fine, self-determine yourselves to separation ... but why here in my party fiefdom. Let an independent Ukraine exist (if it is impossible otherwise) in Australia." Zatonsky continued: "Russian communist chauvinism wanted the workers and peasants of the weaker nation not to work for the bourgeoisie of the stronger nation but for its workers and peasants. It thus creates a new form of exploitation." He stopped short of labelling Bolsheviks an imperialist settler-colonist party or pointing out that the socialists whom the Bolsheviks condemned in other empires for not being revolutionary were those opposed to the secession of their colonies. Zatonsky later indirectly criticized Lenin's December 1919 "concessions," noting that speaking in Ukrainian to Ukrainians in Ukraine was hardly a "concession. "If you go to France or Poland and speak with French workers in French and with Poles in Polish – what kind of concession is this? ... This is an old habit of comrades to look at Ukraine as Little Russia ... a habit injected into you by thousands, hundreds of years of Russian imperialism."[100]

Bolshevik leaders conflated the Russian empire with Russia across the 1917 divide and exploited Russian imperial pride in the autumn of 1918 during the successful White offensive. In November 1918, Lenin called on the previously vilified Russian petite bourgeoisie to defend Russia as patriotic Russians and for party members to accept them because soviet power guaranteed Russian independence. Russian Mensheviks, SRs, and monarchists now began joining the Bolsheviks, primarily for ethnic or nationalist rather than for Marxist reasons. In 1920, faced with the Polish offensive, leaders openly exploited Russian nationalism and imperialism to mobilize the population for war. Authors wrote about the national unity of the Russian nation, oblivious to the fact that at least half of those they ruled were not Russian and that Polish forces were distant from Russian territory. One issue of Moscow's *Pravda* contained an article about the Polish gentry in the seventeenth and eighteenth centuries ravaging Ukrainian lands inhabited by "Russian workers and peasants." As the price of his alliance with Pilsudski, it wrote, Petliura had given Poland "Russian lands inhabited by more than five million Russian inhabitants." The Jewish-born former Austrian citizen Radek was especially fervent, characterizing the war as a Russian national struggle of liberation against foreign invasion in which "Russians" were defending Mother Russia. Their goal was to "reunite all the Russian lands and defend Russia from colonial exploitation." Trotsky made speeches praising Russian officers for saving the "freedom and independence of the Russian people."[101]

Stalin conflated ethnic Russia with its empire in February 1919 when he defended Bolsheviks as restorers of "Russian unity" – by which he meant Russian imperial unity. Treating the various Bolshevik regimes outside Russia proper as if they were totally independent of Moscow and the invading Red Army, and ignoring the role of the Ukrainian left SRs in organizing Ukrainian anti-German units, he wrote that "the labouring masses of the [German] occupied regions gravitated to the Russian proletariat. The Soviet government realized that the unity of Russia [the empire], forcibly maintained with imperialist [German-French] bayonets, was bound to break down with the downfall of Russian imperialism. The Soviet government could not maintain unity with the methods used by Russian imperialism, without being false to its own nature." Ignoring the fact that the White movement, from its bases on the fringes of ethnic Russian territory, was overwhelmingly Russian, in December 1919 he explicitly identified the "nationally united" Russians of "inner Russia" as the base of the revolution, and Ukrainians, rather than Ukraine, as within the border regions that were the base of counter-revolution. In a note to Lenin in June 1920, he clearly distinguished Ukrainians from Finns and Poles on grounds that reflected great power machinations more than a Marxist rationale. While "confederal ties" with Soviet Russia would be appropriate for Finland and Poland, as well as for Hungary or Germany if soviet republics were ever established there, Ukraine would be subject to "federal ties" that effectively kept it a Russian province. This was because Ukraine as a "nation belonging to old Russia [*Rossiia*] … either did not have their own state in the past, or lost it long ago." Stalin noted that the Poles and Finns at the time of writing had governments, armies, and banking systems – as if Ukraine had lacked these in 1918–19. [102] In October 1920, Stalin explained that Russia was the hearth of world revolution and needed the resources of its "border regions" (*okrainy Rossii*).

He delineated the territories of the old empire with the terms "inner Russia," "outer Russia," and "border region," but he did not use the imperial/colonial dichotomy; instead he used Russia as a synonym for the tsarist empire. He did not explain how the "union" that was supposed to channel these resources to Russia was different from the "yoke of imperialism" that these "border regions" would supposedly otherwise suffer as "vassals of the entente" if British and American capitalists took their resources. He did not consider that common Ukrainians saw little difference between armed Russian squads requisitioning 40 million poods of grain for the good Bolshevik union, and German ones that had requisitioned 30 million for the bad imperialist yoke.[103]

There were also party members who turned with the party line. At the Second CPU Conference in October 1918, Kamenev stated: "We are united by the task of joining into one the working masses on the whole territory of the former Russian empire in order to create a single proletarian republic in its place that must then spread around the world. Borders within that unit were the result of treacherous petite bourgeois politics and German imperialism. We will not allow Russia [meaning the empire] to be destroyed by imperialist arms [or] nationalist bourgeoisie, [or] the nationalist ambitions of the bourgeoisie to destroy the proletarian revolution." The following year, when Lenin was considering a military treaty with the UNR, he phrased the necessary Politburo resolution as follows: "All talks are to be treated as an agreement with the bourgeoisie of an oppressed nation against Russian monarchism and imperialism."[104] In 1920 he again displayed no awareness of Russia as an empire composed of national units that (as Engels had argued) deserved independence. In an April meeting of Ukraine's Central Committee, he referred to the "breakup of Russia" during the revolution and took it as a given that the former imperial economic unity would benefit all when re-established. In his mind, "the Russian lands" included Ukraine just as they included Siberia. He referred to unifying "the entire economy of Russia," by which he meant the former empire, and he talked about the "interests of workers and peasants of all nationalities wherever they might be on the territory of Russia.[105]" By this kind of logic, no empire anywhere could be dissolved.

In June 1920, Vynnychenko held talks with Chicherin in Moscow, at which time the foreign minister's aide on Ukrainian matters told him: "There is not and has never been a Ukraine; everybody speaks Russian perfectly in Ukraine and everything to do with this Ukrainian question is thought-up." Despite Lenin's "concessions," Vynnychenko observed during his stay, "nothing had changed."[106] "There are words and slogans but they are not implemented," he wrote after he had left. "There is some kind of thick wall between your words and your deeds." The issue was Bolshevik Russian nationalism. This was not explicit in declarations: "But it is in your blood in the way you think and feel." What was the point of their linguistic, cultural, and educational concessions to non-Russians, he asked Bolshevik leaders, if by centralizing the economy they ensured that "in real life ... one had to know how to speak and write the master's language [Russian]"?[107]

A third influence on Bolshevik attitudes was the absence of an anti-imperialist tradition in Russian intellectual history. Even radicals like Vissarion Belinskii and Georgii Plekhanov opposed the dissolution of the empire.[108] In 1915, Trotsky – unlike Lenin, who imagined a future assimilation of nations – considered nationalities eternal entities that would outlive capitalism and ultimately be organized in a European socialist federation. But while he clearly supported Polish independence, he made no reference to Ukraine.[109] Only the anarchist Bakunin unequivocally recognized in principle a Ukrainian right to political secession from the empire.[110]

The overlap between Russian Bolshevik and Russian imperialist logic was particularly strong in arguments that used an economic rationale to justify the retention of imperial frontiers. Development, both arguments went, demanded large economic units, which meant that Soviet Russia had to dominate former imperial Russian territories. Thus, Iakovlev, like Bosh, dismissed federalist Bolsheviks because they could not see or exploit the "attraction of the mass of the population of Ukraine to soviet Russia" stemming from the fact that "Ukraine was and remains a part of Russia economically."

Lenin had actually denied this general principle in *Imperialism*. There he explained that because imperial economic unity was simply exploitative and capitalism was no longer developing colonies, bourgeois national revolutions were progressive in European overseas colonies. Nonetheless, Russian Marxists do not appear to have applied *Imperialism*'s approach to the Russian empire and studied whether central Russian workers were prosperous and imperialist *because of* cheap raw materials from the non-Russian territories and, therefore, that secession of non-Russian territories was as necessary a condition of revolution in Russia proper as in Europe's overseas empires. Notwithstanding Lenin's arguments in *Imperialism*, Bolsheviks who argued that Russia and Ukraine needed each other economically did not consider that the origins and nature of that need lay in two hundred years of tsarist policies. Marx and Engels had written that the principle of nationalism should be opposed because it contradicted the logic of capitalism and inhibited integration, but they had made exceptions for India, Poland, Ireland, and Ukraine. Russian Bolshevik leaders who claimed that Ukraine had to remain part of a soviet Russia – which was in line with Lenin's reasoning about the permanence of imperial frontiers, regardless of any possible temporary secession – did not invoke economic imperatives to argue that Poland, Finland, Estonia, or Hungary had to be part of Soviet Russia.

Piatakov in June 1917 claimed that Russia needed Ukraine:[111]

> But generally we should not support the Ukrainians, for this movement is inconvenient for the proletariat. Russia cannot exist without the Ukrainian sugar industry, the same can be said about coal (the Donets basin), grain (the black earth belt), etc. These branches of industry are closely connected with all of the rest of Russia's industry. Moreover, Ukraine does not form a distinct economic region, for it does not possess banking centres, as Finland does. If Ukraine separates itself by a customs barrier from the rest of Russia, then the industry of the Kharkiv, Chernihiv, Poltava, and other districts, which still bears a handicraft character, will successfully compete with the backward local factory industry ... which represents a retrograde step and is extremely undesirable for the proletariat.

He did not reflect on whether Ukraine needed Russia or whether Irish independence would have also been inconvenient for English workers. Ukrainian Marxists considered such reasoning the product of imperialist preconceptions that ignored how imperialist policies created economic dependency, that capitalist modernity could create as well as destroy nations, and how empires created undesirable bonds of dependency.

Piatakov's equation of the proletariat with Russia understood as empire was followed by an economic justification for Russian domination of the imperial space – something that Ukrainian Marxists dismissed as imperialist banter. Those for whom Bolshevik imperialist preconceptions might not be immediately evident might substitute Ireland, Korea, or India for Ukraine in Piatakov's quote, and England, France, or Japan for Russia, and the corresponding resources that the latter took from the former, and then imagine a Marxist in one of the colonized countries making such a claim. Only Ukrainian Marxists seemed to notice that Russian liberal Kadet Party leaders used similar logic. Ukraine's role as raw material supplier and finished goods market for Russia before the war, they wrote, meant that it could not be independent and had to belong to the empire. A CPU conference delegate who pointed out that this kind of economic logic could as easily justify Ukraine's union with Germany was ignored. Ironically, Kviring presented his July 1918 resolution on Ukraine and Russia a few weeks after Lenin had been informed about a petition sent by Ukraine's Russian and Russified capitalist industrialists and bankers to the Rada in April 1918. They had called on the Rada to sign an economic and customs union with Bolshevik Russia because "an unbreakable economic tie between Ukraine and Russia" had formed over the past century and its rupture "would be catastrophic for the economic life of Ukraine and Russia."[112]

It is not known whether those Russian Bolsheviks who thought that Russia "needed" Ukraine also thought that Korean or Irish or Indian national movements would be disadvantageous to the Japanese or English proletariat because Japan and England "needed" Korea, Ireland, and India. But it *is* known that not all Russian Bolsheviks believed that their new soviet state had an economic need for the former non-Russian imperial territories. As noted, it was not economics that motivated Lenin to invade Ukraine. Lenin, a consummate pragmatist, realized that his regime could survive without the old empire. In February 1918 he seriously considered moving his new government as far east as necessary to escape a feared German invasion, and establishing an Ural-Kuznetsk Republic: "And do you know," he lectured his critics, "we have huge reserves of coal in the Kuznetsk basin. Together with the Urals ore and Siberian grain we will have a new base." The following month, defending the Treaty of Brest-Litovsk, he said that Russia proper had sufficient resources to supply everyone with adequate means of life. In May 1918, during the First All-Russian National Economic Council in Moscow, its deputy head Vladimir Miliutin explained that since Russia had grain reserves until the next harvest and an industrial base in the Urals, it did not need Ukraine.[113] In March 1919, in response to critics who condemned him for acceding to Finnish independence because it meant that Russia had lost valuable fisheries, Lenin made his famous quip: "Scratch some communists and you will find Great Russia Chauvinists."[114] That same year, Rakovskii instructed requisitioning agents to emphatically deny that Ukrainian grain would be shipped to Russia. They were to tell the peasants that Russia was defending Ukraine "with its blood from grasping imperialists" and that Russia had enough grain of its own.[115] Fritz Platten, the Swiss representative to the March 1919 Comintern Congress and a close friend of Lenin, considered Ukraine vital to Europe as an alternative source of food in view of the American blockade. Russia, he thought, needn't concern itself with Ukraine since it had sufficient supplies in its east.[116]

Neither Marxist nor Russian imperialist preconceptions account for Lenin's decision to invade and annex Ukraine. But once he did, his obsession with and extension of centralized party control became the basis on which his party in Ukraine, under a new name and staffed largely by the Russian/Russified settler-colonist or settler-colonist-descended portion of the urban population, reimposed the old imperial structure, language, and practices. The old rationalizations of imperial rule reappeared, enhanced with Marxist terminology. The centralized party structure ensured political/ministerial centralization because party committees always dominated soviet executive committees. Once established, the soviet regime did forcibly extract resources from the new territory, but that was a result of the invasion, not a cause, regardless of how Ukraine's Bolshevik leaders rationalized that extraction. For Ukrainian communists, the issue was not that war or shortages had forced the Bolsheviks to centralize, militarize, and extract. The issue was why the Bolsheviks imposed that centralization, militarization, and extraction *on Ukraine*.

Despite Marx and Engels's support for Czech and Irish struggles, social democrats in Europe's powerful countries, like their Russian counterparts, had little sympathy for minority or dominated nationalities. At their 1910 Congress in Copenhagen, they condemned the Czechs for trying to establish a national union separate from the imperial Austrian one – they did not even use the word "empire" in their resolution. Lenin's right to national self-determination, which was condemned by many Marxists at the time, presumed reintegration after formal declarations of separation. It did not contradict Lenin's preconceptions about large centralized economic units. In any case, the right applied only to culture and language, because in the tradition of Adam Smith, who separated the spiritual from the market, most Marxists did not link culture to economics. As Iurkevych explained in 1915, Lenin, while recognizing the "right of self-determination" for the sake of appearances, actually *defended* imperial unity, believing that the advantages of large states, both from the point of view of economic progress and from that of the interests of the masses, could not be doubted.[117]

In 1919 the RCP program replaced Lenin's ambiguous slogan with the right to *political* secession, but neither right applied to peripheral SD or communist parties. Within the Russian empire, the Russian SDs, the Bolsheviks, and then the Communist Party, like all other Russian parties, presumed to represent the entire imperial space. In 1903, Lenin made it clear that his party would not be a federation of independent communist parties of the empire's various nationalities.[118] In 1919, echoing Zinoviev's comments at the Eighth RCP Conference, Sverdlov told party delegates at the Third CPU Conference in Kharkiv: "We are one Russian Communist party with various branches, regardless of how our old united Russia [*Rossiia*] will be divided, regardless of how, according to this or that political [or] international circumstance, we end up dividing the old Russia into separate Republics." Nor was anyone to doubt who would be doing the dividing: "It was we," said Sverdlov, "who created Soviet republics." That February, Lenin had instructed Rakovskii to place Ukrainian left SRs in party organizations at all levels throughout Ukraine. Their partisan formations had played a key role in the Bolshevik advance. Bolshevik control outside the major cities was weak, and Lenin, realizing compromise was necessary, forced his will on recalcitrant CPU leaders. At the conference, Russian rightist Feodor Artem amplified Sverdlov's point, leaving those who might have thought otherwise in the wake of Lenin's concession no doubt where power lay: "You Ukrainian separatists [Borotbists] will not play world politics here in Ukraine. There will be one Russian [*Rossiiskaia*] communist party and only it will make decisions." Elsewhere he drummed: "Our Ukrainian party is a now a Russian party (applause) and those who don't want to understand that understand nothing."[119]

Lenin's centralist preconceptions permitted no separate economic ministries, nor did they permit representation in the Comintern for independent non-Russian communist parties in the new soviet state. This reflected his beliefs about the temporary nature of secessions from empires and his implicit belief that imperial borders would eventually have to be re-established. Thus, Zinoviev told Comintern delegates in March 1919 that party centralization would ultimately trump governmental federalism in all empires. Nonetheless, Bolshevik leaders recognized that the Irish (if not the Indian) and British communist parties were separate bodies, as were the Indonesian, Dutch, Korean, and Japanese parties, and, they allotted each of them separate representation in the CI.[120] Only in the French empire did communists replicate the centralized imperial Russian party structure. In Algeria, a party formed in 1924 remained subordinated to the French party; indeed, it opposed Algerian national liberation, much as the Bolshevik party did in Ukraine. In South Africa, communist leaders faced workers who went on strike with the slogan "Workers of the World Unite for a White South Africa."[121]

These comparisons draw attention to the decisive role of national identity in determining attitudes and relationships between imperial centres and peripheries. In European overseas empires, communist parties initially were composed, as in Ukraine, overwhelmingly of urban settler-colonists. These were born in or, as second and third generation, identified culturally with the metropole rather than with the unassimilated indigenous population. They were concerned with maintaining rather than severing links with the imperial metropole and with maintaining their dominance over the majority native population.

In 1920, Zatonsky elaborated on the link between the imperial preconceptions of Russians and party structure in Ukraine. Because of imperial policies, Ukraine's urban Russian and Russified proletariat was alien to the Ukrainian national movement and saw it as treason. Its hostility to Ukrainian efforts to separate from Russia was soon transformed into hatred for all things Ukrainian; this hatred became what he termed Russian nationalism. Urban dwellers, he said, and even the most responsible leaders of the workers' movement in Ukraine, did not see the steppe and had no sense of the power of the Ukrainian national movement, which was not totally counter-revolutionary. They therefore based themselves on the "vulgar Russian urban proletariat." This left a legacy of mental inertia that was hard to overcome, but events had proved federalists like himself right.[122] CPU debates were in Russian, were published in Russian, and made no mention of a "progressive" revolutionary role for nationalism or a national bourgeoisie. By ignoring the Ukrainian rural proletariat, the CPU had effectively divided its nominal constituency along national lines. In the words of Shakhrai and Mazlakh: "And the reality was that the non-Ukrainian proletariat [in Ukraine] was hostile to the Ukrainian national movement, as it was to all national movements generally."[123]

Red Russian Imperialism

Once Lenin decided to annex Ukraine, his obsession with centralization created the conditions for the emergence of a Red version of tsarist Russian imperialism. This was imposed by an overwhelming

ethnically Russian party and government bureaucracy whose personnel were not as unaffected by imperialist preconceptions as their leader.
Lenin himself did not think that cultural-linguistic and political borders should coincide, and he regarded Russia – at least until 1921 – as a
stepping stone towards European if not world revolution. His Russian
opponents condemned him for this, accusing him of destroying Russia in pursuit of a communist chimera. The prominent White Russian
activist Vasili Shulgin surmised: "An internationalist communist gang
has conquered and now rules Russia that uses Russian only because
otherwise most of the population would not understand its decrees."
The Russians among them, he thought, represented Russian interests
as much as the Latvian-born Cheka chief Peters represented Latvian
interests.[124] That Lenin preferred Russian to Esperanto meant nothing
to such critics. But that some Russians were oblivious to the cultural
and linguistic Russification of almost all the non-Russian Bolsheviks,
and did not consider Bolshevism or Leninism Russian, had little relevance to non-Russians. For them, Bolshevism was Russian regardless
of the sprinkling of non-Russians in the party, and Lenin personified
Russian interests. No Bolshevik, for instance, is known to have condemned Russian as the language of General Denikin or German as the
language of the Kaiser, or to have associated Russian language and culture with anti-Bolshevik Russian political parties or bourgeois nationalists. As evident in Rakovskii's above-noted remarks, Bolsheviks did
associate Ukrainian with political groups. On 22 January 1922, *Kommunist* (Kyiv) ran an article about the prevalence of such attitudes in
Ukraine titled "The Ukrainian Language Is Not the Language of Petliura." It had little impact.

Alongside the formula "Bolshevik means Russian," current among
Ukraine's Bolsheviks and their sympathizers, party leaders introduced slavophile biological colonialist-type metaphors that discounted
national differences to justify Bolshevik rule in Ukraine. The first Bolshevik government, in its proclamations throughout 1918, used a class
discourse that avoided using Ukrainian as an adjective and that did not
single out Russians or Russia as Ukraine's disinterested benefactors.
Proclamations contained slogans such as these: "Long Live the Ukrainian German Russian and World Socialist Federated Soviet Republic";
"Our Friends – the Workers and Poor Peasants of the Entire World";
"In Complete Unity with Revolutionary Russia, the Workers of Germany and the Soviet Sections of the Former Austro-Hungarian State
You [Workers, Peasants, and Red Soldiers of Ukraine] Must Organize

Resistance and Arise Like One into the Ranks of Ukraine's Socialist Army."[125]

This changed in early 1919 with the arrival of the centralist-dominated second Bolshevik government. At Ukraine's Third Congress of Soviets, Shlikhter, in charge of food procurement, responded to a question about why Russians were coming to Ukraine to requisition grain with a Russian communist variant of Manifest Destiny or the White Man's Burden. In reply, Shlikhter did not talk about Russian workers aiding Ukrainian workers because they were of the same class. He explained that what Ukrainians regarded as invasion and exploitation was really national Russian assistance and altruism stemming from blood ties. After noting that it was not true that "brother Russians" were being fed at the cost of the Ukrainian poor, Shlikhter explained that brotherly Russia was providing not only manufactured goods but also people to "help you [Ukrainians] collect food." Russia thereby "literally shares with you its nerves brains and blood [(long prolonged applause]). It gives you the possibility of working by bleeding its local soviets in Moscow and Petrograd ... all for Ukraine!" The newly arrived Russians were not there to take grain but to "help our brothers in Ukraine when they are building soviet power (applause)." This seems to have been the first public use of ethnic biological metaphor in Bolshevik discourse about Ukraine.[126]

From their metropolitan perspective, CPU members assumed that their Ukrainian brothers wanted soviet power in the same way that advocates of empire in western Europe assumed Africans and Asians wanted European civilization. Britain's colonial secretary, Joseph Chamberlain, explained in 1897 how a sense of obligation had become part of the Imperial idea and that omelettes required broken eggs, as follows: "I maintain now that our rule does, and has, brought security and peace and comparative prosperity to countries that never knew these blessings before" (The Times, 1 April). This echoes the Russian imperialism of slavophiles like Nikolai Danilevskii, who in 1871 failed to understand why its rivals did not regard Russia's recent annexation of Caucasian territories as a victory for civilization. With their "inborn humanism," he wrote, Russians avoided the use of force and were free of hostile feelings towards others – who once part of Russia were in any case predestined to Russify and assimilate. A generation later, Vasilli Rozanov explained that those who resisted Russification had to be extirpated as people who did not understand "the joy of merging [with Russia] [radost sliianie]." Echoing such sentiments, Shlikhter in 1919

considered his Soviet Russia, which at the time included former imperial possessions, to be founded on love and fraternal links. For Shlikhter
and his comrades the annexation of Ukraine enhanced its happiness – a
logic that resembled that of Nikolai Ustrialov, who thought that Russia's annexation of Poland had only enhanced its happiness.[127]

In January 1920, Manuilsky used the biological metaphor again in
an open letter to the party condemning the recently formed UCP and
praising Russian workers. The Bolsheviks had forged an unbreakable
link between the working masses of Russia and those of Ukraine with
their sons' blood and then sent their best representatives to build soviet
power in Ukraine. He claimed that "we" – by which he presumably
meant Ukrainians – "would be ungrateful slaves if we refused help
from Russian or western European workers. Without, we would be
crushed like Hungary." Claiming that the Bolsheviks represented not
only the communism of the Third International but also the European
experience, he went on to write that "like a mighty oak," the Russian
worker stood at the head of the communist struggle, and that Ukrainian
communists were dividing the Ukrainian and Russian proletariat. The
absolute equality of all nations was incompatible with the existence of
the petite-bourgeois UCP, wrote Manuilsky. There is no record of him
applying similar logic to other countries – that is, of condemning Irish or
Indian or Korean or Hungarian communists for dividing the proletariat
within their respective empires, or for being petite bourgeois or nationally limited because they formed national parties independent of their
imperial metropoles. This reference to Russia as Ukraine's single bene-
factor appeared again that February in a proclamation by the third Bolshevik Ukrainian government. The Ukrainian soviet republic had been
restored, it noted, "only thanks to the powerful assistance of worker
peasant Russia's Red Army." "On the graves of Russia's workers and
peasants fallen for the freedom of the Ukrainian peasantry is forged for
ever *the free union of the Ukrainian working population with free workers and
peasants [sic]*." There was no analogous public dissemination of Lenin's
November 1918 letter to Vatsetis or of his March 1919 letter to his plenipotentiary in Ukraine, Ordzhonikidze. In the first, he explained that
the soviet governments he was establishing in the former imperial non-
Russian territories, including Ukraine, were only facades to prevent
their enemies from accusing the Bolsheviks of militarily occupying the
territories in question. "Otherwise … the population would not greet
[our armies] as liberators." In the second, he ordered local Bolsheviks
to quickly put a Ukrainian facade on the Red Army in Ukraine; and that

the army's commander, Antonov, accordingly add to his surname that of a distant ancestor – Ovsienko.[128]

Imperial expansion can involve state-sponsored mass violence, and the Bolshevik invasions of Ukraine certainly did. In April 1919 an anonymous author wrote in the UCP newspaper that, during Russia's communist revolution, the idea of an All-Russian or imperial statehood did not disappear: "without breaking at all with the pre-revolutionary tradition it was reborn as so-called Bolshevik imperialism that, through war and armed propaganda in the name of socialism, seeks to renew and even extend Russia's historical borders, re-annex recently separated 'borderlands' into one political unit and, to base this unnatural conglomerate on the old but even broader economic base." In Ukraine, he continued, the revolution took a different turn than proclaimed in Bolshevik slogans. "Like in Russia, where the communist revolution did not attempt to break with Russian great power traditions, so in Ukraine there is an attempt to depart as little as possible from the conditions created by 250 years of captivity." Even the gains of the 1917 "petite-bourgeois revolution" had been annulled. Political and economic independence was being destroyed, the government was sponsoring Russification despite its denials, and the result was armed opposition. The Bolsheviks shut down the paper the next day.[129]

Sergei Zorin illustrates to what lengths those Russian Bolsheviks who thought Russia lacked resources were prepared to go to control and extract resources from Ukraine. At an April 1919 CPU CC meeting, he stated that people were starving in Petrograd; he then demanded Ukrainian grain. "We do not recognize any kind of nations." If anyone opposed grain collections in Ukraine, "then send them to the other world, thousands, tens of thousands, and, if necessary, 100,000 of those idiots fools or villains [negodaev], but don't waste time." He got a round of applause. Opinion at the meeting was that the Bolsheviks had no need of Ukraine's population – only its resources for use elsewhere. [130] No one mentioned the stockpiled grain in Petrograd intended for Germany in the event of a successful revolution there.[131] In late 1920 a comrade Turkin, who commanded a food requisition unit, told a local Ukrainian communist in the town of Pavoloch: "We will burn down these damned Kyiv, Podillia, and Volyn provinces, not leaving one stone on top of another and let all know just what the Communist party is"; a comment that suggests Zorin's views circulated down the hierarchy. These recorded statements lend credence to second-hand reports about similar attitudes among other officials. In a report submitted to the Directory, a Ukrainian prisoner of war, who had travelled through Bolshevik-controlled Kyiv province during his escape in early 1920, claimed that the head of the Workers and Peasants Inspectorate of the First Cavalry Army, a man named Latipov, had told him that he didn't care if 75 per cent of Ukraine's population died of hunger. If they didn't, they would be shot anyways. That would make the remaining 25 per cent obedient: "We need Ukraine, not its people" – those were, he claimed, Rakovskii's own words. There is no known policy statement calling for the extermination of Ukrainians (as there was in the case of the Russian Don Cossacks), but it is probable that such attitudes were held by some officials. And those attitudes did reflect the social Darwinist spirit of the times.[132] For example, London's respectable *Saturday Review* (26 August 1896) stated in reference to Africa: "Permanent peace there cannot be ... until the blacks are either exterminated or driven back into the centre of Africa." Lenin, analogously, in *How to Organize Competition* (1917), dehumanized his opponents and called for their extermination – after 1918 he labelled them insects, vermin, parasites, and bugs. It was not fortuitous perhaps that in February 1919 the CPU issued a proclamation to UNR troops ensuring them that "Ukraine's Soviet socialist power ... would never allow anyone to turn Ukrainian workers and peasants into African negroes."[133]

Ukrainian left SDs in February 1918 admitted that Russian Bolsheviks had initially played a positive role in Ukraine. They expected cooperation:

> The Socialist revolution in Ukraine, indissolubly tied to the transfer of power to the Soviet of Workers and Peasants' Deputies, occurs with the help of the armed force of the fraternal working classes of other provinces and nations of the Russian Republic.
>
> This is the unavoidable result of the objective economic and social structures of a country with a weakly developed industry and strong agricultural sector, with a small working class and a large small-holding peasantry. Many efforts [finally] showed the workers of Ukraine they could not overthrow the bourgeois Central Rada itself ... A fraternal hand from Great Russia helped the Ukrainian proletariat overthrow the oppression of its Central Rada.

A year later, while CPU leaders were making speeches about Russian altruism and Ukrainian obligations, the Independentists began condemning Russian Bolsheviks as invaders and occupiers. They had established a government that called itself Ukrainian but "which we cannot and will not regard as such."[134] The Independentists condemned Bolshevik anti-imperialist discourse as nothing but talk and labelled their policies "Russian communist chauvinism." Rakovskii, scion of a leading family in the Bulgarian national movement and opponent of Ottoman rule in his country, must have infuriated them. On the one hand, as noted by Shakhrai, on 3 January 1919 he had dismissed differences between Ukrainians and Russians as insignificant and had insisted that the Ukrainian proletariat was completely Russian in origin. Six days later he contended that the Russian Bolshevik takeover of Ukraine was not an infringement of the right to self-determination: "Besides us, besides Soviet Russia, independent soviet republics have formed in Latvia, Lithuania and, most recently in Little Russia [*malorossiia* – sic], whom we regard as faithful allies and not the objects of any kind of conquest." On 13 February he said that giving Ukrainian official status would be "a reactionary totally unnecessary move," for the peasants in any case considered themselves Russians. On the other hand, he wrote a proclamation to the world on 28 January about the establishment of soviet power in Ukraine in which he used, for the first time in Bolshevik rhetoric, Ukraine in its adjectival form to describe the soviet regime: "Red Ukrainian soviet armies," "Ukrainian workers peasants government," even "Ukrainian revolution." The following February, in a propaganda leaflet to UNR troops, he tried to suggest that the Soviet regime was solicitous of Ukrainian interests, as indicated by the presence of Ukrainian socialists in government posts – but without mentioning his initial opposition to Lenin's order to appoint them.[135]

The UCP's two most important policy statements were *Do Khvyli* and the 1920 *Memorandum* to the Comintern. Both classified Ukraine as a Russian colony, but – presumably for tactical reasons – *Do Khvyli* specifically labelled only Ukraine's centralist Bolsheviks as imperialists and accused Lenin and the Russian party of imperialism only indirectly. In chapter 3, it condemned the US president: "And Woodrow Wilson manages everything himself, he has taken upon himself the role of world gendarme and hangman of the world revolution." After analysing Bolshevik policy in Ukraine, it asserted that "the Russian proletariat made a social revolution and praise and respect is therefore due it. But this does not mean that it did not inherit from tsarist Russia a bit of imperialism or of [so-called] historical and ethnographic rights." Because the overwhelming majority of Bolsheviks in Ukraine were Russian or Russified, it observed, their party logically could not

represent an oppressed nation and avoided the issue of national liberation. This book closed with the observation: "When one examines
the spread of Bolshevik Russia and the practice of self-determination
from this vantage point, it is very difficult to see to what extent your
self-determination, Comrade Lenin, differ from that of Woodrow Wilson."[136] A year later, the *Memorandum* omitted the comparison with
Wilson but explicitly referred to Bolshevik rule in Ukraine as a Russian
occupation because it ignored national issues and imagined that these
could be placated by simple "bourgeois cultural-national autonomy."
It described the CPU as totally dependent on the RCP but explicitly
accused only the former for being unable to overcome "the imperialist
legacy of old Russia."[137]

Other publications were less diplomatic and more explicit. In January 1919 the Ukrainian left SDs condemned the CPU as a "reactionary anti-Ukrainian party" subservient to the "imperialist Russian
Bolshevik regime [*rosiiskoho imperialistychnoho bolshevytskoho uriadu*]."
"It is a party that obeys the Russian imperialist Bolshevik government.
As such it is profoundly reactionary and has no place in Ukraine." "To
us, under the slogan 'power to the soviets' comes a government that
calls itself Ukrainian but which we do not and cannot recognize as
such." The CPU government proclaimed in November 1918 was not
legitimate because it had not been ratified by the Congress of Soviets.
The authors demanded that "the [newly arrived Bolshevik government in Kharkiv] must clearly respond as to whether it actively wants
to build a socialist Ukraine or whether it regards her as a Russian
colony." Party leaders considered Russian proletarians in Ukraine to
be "blinded by Russian Bolshevik chauvinist imperialism," but they
then waxed philosophical. They hoped that with time, as the Ukrainian
revolution developed, the non-Ukrainian proletariat would shed these
"old Russian leftovers" and march alongside the Ukrainian nation and
Ukrainian proletarians.[138]

In the spring of 1919 the Kyiv city executive ordered the Ukrainian
Worker's Club – which had been sponsored by the Ukrainian left SDs –
shut down because it had not hired Russian lecturers. Protesting Ukrainians asked why Ukrainian-language cultural and educational work in
Ukraine was chauvinist and inimical to Russian culture, while doing the
same work in Russian was internationalist and communist.[139] In Kyiv
the following year a Ukrainian left SD observed: "As a ruling nation
the Russians acquired various uppity ways [*panskykh zvychok*] that they
still stubbornly retain." The Russians' political parties reflected this, the

author continued; he then called on Russian communists to renounce this past. The same issue of the newspaper contained a rebuttal to an article in the Bolshevik *Kievskii kommunist* that had claimed all communists were the same and therefore could not be grouped according to "language or other zoological traits." A reporter who visited street lectures on the national question in the summer of 1919 in then Bolshevik-controlled Kyiv wrote that all groups and opinions were represented. What all speakers shared in common, however, was their claim that there was no chauvinism among Russians and that the Ukrainian of official documents was merely "Galician dialect."[140]

The Ukrainian left SR and left SD press published many articles exposing Bolshevik double standards. "Two months have passed since the Soviets took Kyiv but still we see neither real soviet power nor a proletarian dictatorship. We see only the dictatorship of the Communist party." There was no soviet Ukrainian republic because Ukraine was merely "a colony of a neighbouring northern country." In an extended reply to an article by Piatakov, a Ukrainian explained that because socialism did not yet exist, a dictatorship of one party under conditions of state capitalism meant there was a distinct threat that one country would oppress another, thereby creating a "proletarian imperialism." "Ukraine should be no more dependent on Russia than Russia should be on Georgia or a socialist France on England." The issue in Ukraine was not language but Ukrainian sovereignty and the need to come to terms with the fact that Ukrainians were an oppressed nationality. "Do you 'communists of Ukraine' with 'Russian nationalist remnants' recognize that Ukraine and the Ukrainian nation have the right to secede and form an independent sovereign state or not?"[141] In response to a Bolshevik argument that Ukrainians opposed political union with Russia because the bourgeoisie and Borotbists feared an influx of Russian petite bourgeoisie who would take jobs, a Poltava paper explained that the issue was not union, which already existed insofar as the revolution had united the Ukrainian and Russian proletariat, but restoration. What had to be avoided was the creation of a government that would restore the old Russian state. "Unite comrade workers of Russia and Ukraine," wrote the Russians. "In our workers' unity we will create a single proletarian organism." But in the hands of the proletariat, replied the Ukrainians, the state cannot be an "organism." As Marx had written, it should only be an instrument of rule that will ultimately wither. The new revolutionary state could not interfere with its real primary purpose, which was to unite the entire proletariat in a workers' republic.

"Is it so difficult for comrades from Russia or Russians to see Ukraine as a foreign state like they do Poland or Finland?"[142]

Newspapers often ran stories from various Ukrainian cities where Russian Bolsheviks had arrived as commissars and then, like conquerors, instead of learning the local language, demanded that all correspondence and work be carried out in Russian. In Kyiv in February 1918, the city garrison commander's adjutant added a note to a letter from the Chief Army Medical Commissar to the garrison quartermaster: "in Soviet Russia they write only in Russian," there was no money for translators, and the commissar should in future please write in Russian. The journalist speculated what would happen if some soviet colonel approached a communist in Berlin and told him to speak in understandable Russian because everybody talked Russian in soviet Russia.[143] "When newly arrived soviet officials demand they be addressed in Russian then this [is regarded as] deeply international-ist and in the proletarian style," wrote another. "But when Ukrainian citizens demand that soviet institutions write in Ukrainian then this is [regarded as] chauvinism and [provokes] great commotion [*istoshnyi gvalt*]."[144] In Cherkasy, the newspaper of the pro-Bolshevik Ukrainian left-SD minority wrote: "The horrific, we might even say zoological Russian great power chauvinism of some communist party members, provoked a negative attitude towards the communist party of Ukraine. A good example of this chauvinism is the [local] *Izvestiia* published by the executive committee." In a later letter we read that the same committee had appointed Russian teachers to Ukrainian schools.[145]

In Kharkiv, letter writers complained about a mass influx of Russians ignorant of the country and its language and a simultaneous impeding of returning Ukrainians, and warned that the influx would provoke anti-soviet uprisings. These Russian dregs were being given jobs, yet Borotbists were not. If this continued, once the "Ukrainian Red Army" had finished with Denikin they would have to chase out all the Russians.[146] These complaints echo those made a generation earlier about volunteer French colonial officials being drunks, sadists, and petty criminals who were turning West Africa into "a *refugium peccatorum* for all our misfits, the depository of the excrement of our political and social organism."[147]

A Russian newspaper in Zhytomir published a poem containing these lines: "Ah my little mother Russia, / how harsh is your fate." A critic observed that the paper should have been published in Ukrainian to begin with, in which case an equivalent Ukrainian verse would

have read: "Ah my dearest Ukraine, / how harsh has been your fate."
But had such lines appeared in a Ukrainian paper, it would have been
closed for "counter-revolutionary Petliurist" propaganda. As it was, no
officials took the author of the Russian poem to task for Russian imperialism. This incident, although minor, was indicative of the contempt
most local Bolsheviks held for matters Ukrainian.[148] In Kyiv, the entire
staff of the Ukrainian Telegraph Agency, except for its director, accepted
Bolshevik rule in February 1919. The new commissar appointed Russians to the agency, who then refused to learn Ukrainian and who
called Ukrainians who expected them to do so "chauvinists." As disgusted Ukrainians resigned, Russians replaced them; meanwhile, the
Ukrainian Telegraphy Agency was renamed the Kyivan branch of the
Moscow ROSTA. The staff, ignorant of Ukraine and Ukrainian, not realizing that sowing and planting times were different in Ukraine than in
Russia, and not knowing which districts were in which provinces, published much nonsense. They reported, for instance, that the Kharkiv
front was in Russia.[149] A subsection head of the National Economic
Council in Kyiv refused to accept Ukrainian-language documents. He
would cross them out and write: "Although we live in Ukraine, the
government here is Russian and that is why I can only accept correspondence in Russian." One newspaper noted that the bureaucracy
could be purged ten times, but unless top officials were included in the
purge it would not lose its "the Great Russian spirit." The underlying
cause was obvious to those with eyes to see it: "As it happened, power
in Ukraine is for the most part now in the hands of the settler Russian element and that is why the representatives of the Russian and not
the Ukrainian proletariat are building proletarian culture in Ukraine."
These representatives saw no need to free "psychologically enslaved
workers Russified in old tsarist times" from their unenviable legacy.
Their proletarian culture was simply Russian culture.[150]

In 1920, Ukrainian communists concluded that the promises of
the Eighth Congress and Lenin's December 1919 Letter had not been
fulfilled. "Instead [of Ukrainian], at the Kharkiv council of soviets
there are speeches in 'perfect Russian' about how soviet power has
deep roots in the 'Russian nation,' about patriotism, and 'the southern
capital' [Kharkiv]. There was even a speech in French, but not one in
Ukrainian. Posters for Ukrainian villages, for some reason, are painted
depicting Ukrainian peasants wearing bast shoes."[151] That same year,
Vynnychenko condemned the Ukrainian SSR as a purely fictional entity
and compared relations between Russia and Ukraine to those between

imperialist countries and their colonies. Even assuming that centralization was necessary, why did it have to take the form of "absolut-
ist Russian chauvinism and the dictatorship of Russian culture over
Ukraine?"[152]

Census takers, presumably on instruction, refused to register Ukrainians as "Ukrainian." One irate Kyivan wrote that after he explicitly
stated that he was Ukrainian, the official had said "Okay. It's all the
same. Ukrainian – that means Russian. Here there is no difference."
He then entered "Russian" as nationality, and the person concerned
would not have known had he not by chance seen the completed form.
Enumerators rewrote all forms written in Ukrainian into Russian.[153] In
1919 a Ukrainian Marxist noted that Bolsheviks did not refrain from
using force against the bourgeoisie in general; he then asked why they
refrained from applying force to make those same bourgeoisie and their
intellectuals learn the language of the people among whom they lived
and from whose work they lived. The issue concerned using or not
using violence. Behind the refusal to apply force to language use, the
writer continued, was "not very covert russification." That summer an
Independentist pointed out that since the technology required to rule
the world from a single centre did not exist, it was pointless to try, and
that the struggle for a world socialist republic was not synonymous
with the restoration of Imperial Russia.[154]

Imperialist attitudes were reflected in matters other than linguistic. Independentists in Kharkiv pointed out that in any given country,
socialist revolution reflected specific national conditions that required
the organization of independent economic organs. Citing a *Pravda*
article of 26 February about the substantial Ukrainian food exports
to Russia and about Moscow sending thousands of workers to "help
Ukrainian peasants organize," a Ukrainian author saw a blatant exploitation that Russian comrades missed. Behind the slogans of world revolution and fraternity lay the reality of vicious economic exploitation. In
return for grain, coal, and sugar, he observed, "we uneducated honks
[*khokhly*]" get Russian communist agitators and Russian propaganda.[155]

Russian communists did not understand that national movements
led by a bourgeoisie were not necessarily bourgeois. They were, on
the contrary, composed of workers and peasants.[156] Why, Independentists asked, were Ukrainian sugar workers supposed to be in one
"All Russian" union if in Ukraine there were 600,000 workers in 209
factories, while in Russia there were only 10,000 workers in 33 factories? Why, instead, was there not one "All Ukrainian" union with a

Russian subsection? Why were decrees like those issued from Moscow in the summer of 1919 unilaterally subordinating all Ukrainian ministries to Moscow limited only to the borders of the old Russian empire? Why were they not applied to all new socialist states – like Hungary? When centralists identified opposition to incorporation into Soviet Russia with a "national bourgeoisie," Independentists pointed out there was no "Ukrainian bourgeoisie" and that those behind recentralizing what the revolution had torn apart were Russified and Russian "bourgeoisie."[157]

In August 1920, in his letter of resignation, the former head of the housing section of Ukraine's Interior Ministry described the country's supposedly sovereign government. He explained that his local Bolshevik superior had declared that all of Ukraine's commissariats were merely arms of the Russian Communist Party. His ministry had no personnel, all laws and funds emanated from Moscow, and nothing could be done without consultation with Moscow. Ukrainians writing to Moscow received no replies, and correspondence in Ukrainian vanished. That October a Ukrainian communist in Pavoloch reported that the local food requisition unit was simply taking everything it could from peasants at the point of a gun. After gorging themselves on some of their takings, they would leave the rest at the train station, where what did not rot or was not stolen was then sold to speculators. The Russian Bolsheviks dispersed with threats the local educated, branding them as "Petliurites" and "nationalists." All of this utterly discredited soviet power in the eyes of the locals.[158] In Katerynoslav, Ukrainian Marxists complained about "Russian internationalists" for whom Ukraine was merely a Russian province no different from Tula and who had only disdain towards Ukrainians. "We see such behaviour in immigrant Russian citizens and from the many settled urban residents brought-up on Russian chauvinism." Another author complained that Russian Bolsheviks, like Ukrainian nationalists, could not imagine a Ukrainian communist, citing a Bolshevik article referring to Ukrainians as the "black crows of counter-revolution." He continued: "It is time for comrade Bolsheviks to understand that they, as representatives of the Muscovite communist centre in Ukraine, are based only on a part of the urban proletariat that is ideologically tied with Muscovy and, that they are very weakly linked to the Ukrainian village proletariat and semi-proletariat." Would the Russian Bolsheviks impose their party in Romania, the author asked? "That would be pure Muscovite chauvinism, and how is Ukraine worse than Romania?"[159]

Ukrainian left-SD critiques were matched by the Borotbists. Hryho-ryi Klunny in late 1919 wrote Lenin that Soviet power would triumph in Ukraine but only if it stopped "imposing Red imperialism (Russian nationalism) in Ukraine." In Rakovskii's view, he wrote, "Soviet power is Russian power; if you support it, then you are Russian." When Russians from Russia came to Ukraine, shot local party members for no other reason than that they were Ukrainian, shipped Red Army volunteers to Russia, and treated Ukraine like a colony, no one should be surprised when people supported the UNR. Klunny described invading Russian troops as "an invasion of dictators ignorant of Ukraine and with no desire to know it." In Ukraine they acted like Russian chauvinists preparing counter-revolution.[160] Ukrainian Bolshevik Pavlo Popov explained to Lenin in November 1919: "It has become the established opinion among average Russian workers that Ukraine is a Muscovite colony whose interests 'it is unacceptable' to consider."[161] Another Borotbist pointed to "Russified petite-bourgeois educated" and representatives of the Russian and Russified proletariat as legacies of imperial Russification who were totally indifferent to and ignorant of the "rural proletarianized population" that surrounded them. The result was a *de facto* privileged position for Russian culture despite declared equality. These Russian and Russified communists did not look at Ukraine from the perspective of world revolution but from that of the Russian revolution. They claimed that economic ties between Russia and Ukraine dictated political union and Russian primacy and ignored the fact that, although economics tied together all countries of the world, it did not follow that all of them had to be in one state, let alone in one dominated by a single country.[162] Soviet power would be strong in Ukraine, explained a Borotbist newspaper, when Russians stopped looking at it as a Russian province, as they had under the tsars, and when a communist party "grew" from Ukrainian conditions, as the Russian party had in Russia. And those conditions were different in Ukraine, where there was a higher emigration rate, a higher percentage of landless peasants and small landowners, no peasant commune, and no bourgeoisie. Only some of its population had experienced serfdom, and then for only sixty years.[163] Other Bolshevik federalists explained to Lenin that it was wrong to mechanically transfer personnel and practices from Russia to Ukraine because the two were so different and that Ukraine had to have its own separate ministries. Russians regarded Ukraine as a colony that could be ignored, and their leaders seemed unable to deal with that circumstance. To see Ukraine as merely a territory from which to take resources was outright colonialism. Why, they asked, did the party consistently enrol Russophile class enemies but not poor Ukrainians and Ukrainian communists?[164] Bolsheviks in Kyiv in late 1919 protested that Moscow continued to look on Ukraine as a province and its factories as spoils of war. They were for soviet power but against the centralized domination of Ukraine by Russia. Ukrainian chauvinism, they complained, had been replaced by Russian chauvinism brought by Muscovite comrades, and the "old inertia" they represented was contrary to Lenin's recently proclaimed concessions. Five days later, CPU leaders condemned these dissenters as counter-revolutionary and anti-soviet. [165] While a "Red Russian patriotism" had emerged in Russia because of the revolution, many comrades, observed Zatonsky in 1921, were beginning to see themselves as Russians first rather than communists and to value the soviet federation only insofar as it represented a renewed Russia.[166] In March 1918, when Muraviev explained to Lenin how he had lost Kyiv to the Germans, one reason he gave was that Ukrainian Bolsheviks had attempted to give him orders – something he considered the product of "narrow minded national-ism and local patriotism expressed [in the notion that] everything in Ukraine belongs not to the [Russian] federation but Ukraine."[167]

Richytsky and Mazurenko summarized Russian behaviour in a let-ter to Lenin in July 1920: Local Bolshevik leaders and the leaders of Red Army units were treating Ukraine like a hostile territory and fol-lowing Russian policies that were totally inappropriate to Ukrainian conditions. Despite six months of stability, they were still relying on Revkoms rather than soviets. Local officials were labelling everything with "a more or less Ukrainian character" counter-revolutionary. To repress the resulting hostility, they were using "Russian arms" and turn-ing what was supposed to be a class war into a war between nations. In addition, local Bolsheviks had submitted to the "old inertia" that demanded the total subordination of Ukraine to the Muscovite centre, and this had resulted in a policy to reconstruct the "single and indivis-ible [Russian empire]." For these reasons, the UCP opposed Russian communist policies and wanted "to make a Ukrainian revolution and Soviet power with Ukrainian internal forces considering its specific cir-cumstances." Mazurenko and Richytsky condemned the cynical nature of concessions extended to Ukraine and complained that local Russian chauvinist Bolsheviks emboldened by the recent victory against Poland were harassing and repressing UCP members.[168] "When soviet power is endangered or suffers setbacks 'ukrainophile' politicking begins;

that is, games with slogans about an independent Ukraine and suchlike; and they run to us for help in the political struggle against Petliura
because they feel themselves impotent. And when the front is pushed
back then, accordingly, the politics change for the worse and this, in
turn, adversely affects the front. These zig-zag Ukrainian policies result
in the masses no longer believing in any of the leaders' statements and
declarations. And one village party cell (in Osnova) characterized the
work of the CPU with this classic statement: 'our work among Ukrainians is the same as work among the Turks Arabs etc.'"

Because the Russian chauvinist wing [*russotiapske techenia*] dominated the Bolshevik party, Ukrainian communists could not focus on
the struggle against Ukrainian nationalism but had to divert their energies against Russian chauvinism. Mazurenko and Richytsky concluded
with the hope that the leader would understand what local Bolsheviks
seemed not to: that a "secret Great Russian chauvinist centralism is dis-
organizing and dividing revolutionary forces in Ukraine – and in all the
colonial [*sic*] borderlands of the former empire."

The previous month, in an earlier letter from Moscow, where the two
men had gone to submit the Ukrainian case to the Second Comintern
Congress, they had written to Kharkiv: "It is quite obvious that Moscow decides policies in Ukraine and that everything that happens there
is not the product of the local Communist Party of Ukraine types." In
Moscow, they added, people knew more about them than they thought,
but attitudes were negative. Those initially sympathetic to the Ukrainian communist case had begun avoiding them as soon as they realized
who they were. In Moscow, they continued, only power was recognized,
not principles, and the head of Ukraine's government (Rakovskii) had
informed Russian leaders that the UCP had "no real influence" – which
was why their application to attend sessions as delegates had been
rejected. They got only guest status. "The general fascination with the
Russian Communist Party was so great that to say anything against
the Russian Communist Party seems absurd."[169] To the dismay of the
Ukrainian Marxists, communism had become Russian.

Chapter Three

Wherever Communism is in power, the ruling class transforms it into an ideology whose real sources are nationalism, racism or imperialism ... If the whole world were Communist it would either have to be dominated by a single imperialism, or there would be an unending series of wars between the "Marxist" rulers of different countries.

Leszek Kolakowski, 1978

The Emergence of National Communism

Scholars have normally associated "national communism" with the countries of the old Soviet Bloc. Milovan Djilas popularized the term in his *New Class* (1957): "No single form of communism ... exists in any other way than as national communism. In order to maintain itself it must become national." A few years earlier, the then ex-communist Manadbendra Roy had noted: "Communism in Asia is essentially nationalism painted Red." However, the Dutch social democrat Pannakoek and Russian monarchists Nicholas Ustrialov and Vasili Shulgin had pointed out already in 1920 that it was the Russians who first "nationalized" communism. Lenin's Social Democratic Party was compelled to function clandestinely: it was conspiratorial, it organized through place of work not residence, it admitted full-time activists only, and it robbed banks to finance itself. Also distinguishing it from other social democratic parties was the primacy it gave to its déclassé intellectuals – as admitted by Russian delegates themselves at the 1904 socialist conference in Amsterdam. In so far as Russian Bolshevism was the product of a specific place and ethnic group, its dispersion even within the borders of the empire was bound to involve violent imposition. What the Bolshevik Russian SD and later Communist Party did share with British, French, and German SDs until 1918 was a refusal to allow separate organizations within the party for subject nationalities within the empire. Lenin claimed that his party was the single legitimate representative not just of Russia's (*Velikorossiia*) workers but of all Russian and non-Russian workers in the Russian empire (*Rossiia*), although before 1914 no more than approximately 20 per cent of all SD party members in the empire were in the Bolshevik wing of the Russian Social Democratic Labour Party – renamed the Russian Communist Party in 1918.[1]

By 1917, Lenin's party was distinctly "Russian" by virtue of the ethnic origins of most of its members and because its organizational structure and values reflected the centralized autocratic Russian political culture from which they had emerged. "The economic and political conditions of his [Lenin's] Russian background had frozen him in a kind of fundamentalism that was felt [by European socialists] to be hopelessly out of tune with contemporary reality."[2] Once in power, in much the same way as the Jacobins had renewed royal centrist étatism in France, the RCP leaders renewed Russocentric tsarist étatism within the former imperial space. This involved more than just administrative centralization. First, when tsarist bureaucrats ended their strike in January 1918 and began working for the new government, they did so in Russian, thereby effectively "nationalizing" it. Second, the Treaty of Brest-Litovsk institutionally identified the Bolsheviks with the thirty provinces of ethnic Russia, which made them, despite themselves, the creators of the first modern Russian national state. Third, as the Bolsheviks extended their control over non-Russian territories, and as educated non-Russians either fled or refused to work for them, they were compelled to rehire and/or import from Russia Russian and Russified tsarist personnel to fill their offices. These people worked in Russian and re-established the old, centralized Russian-language administration beyond ethnic Russian borders. Fourth, Lenin's appeal to Russian patriotism during the 1920 war against Poland, even though no Russian territory was involved, and then Stalin's proclamation in 1924 of "socialism in one country," explicitly legitimized the links between Russia, the Russian socialist republic, and communism. Finally, almost all of the CPU's overwhelmingly Russified or Russian members never lost the contempt for rural Ukrainians that they had inherited from tsarist times. That contempt was reinforced by an interpretation of Marxism that dismissed rural populations as "backward" and "reactionary." Such people consequently refused to learn and use Ukrainian, although they lived and worked in Ukraine. Like most of their urban non-party counterparts, Russian Bolsheviks in tsarist Ukrainian territories, can be compared to the Spanish in Latin America or the French in Algeria. That is, like typical settler-colonists they saw no need to learn or use the language of the majority among whom they lived. Within Soviet territory it was not Russians in non-Russian territories who had to become bilingual to get good jobs; it was socially mobile non-Russians. Ukrainian communists argued that under soviet, as under tsarist rule, linguistic Russification remained a first step towards cultural and ethnic assimilation. Accordingly, not all Russified Ukrainians who before 1917 viewed their origins and their parents' language as a stigma saw any reason to change their attitudes as citizens of Soviet Ukraine.

Russian Bolsheviks claimed that their values were universal. They considered themselves "internationalists," not "national communists" – a term that Lenin in *Left-Wing Communist an Infantile Disorder* (1920) reserved for parties that did not follow his dictates. Although its members were oblivious to how much of a Russian national phenomenon it was, the Bolsheviks were nonetheless the first national communist party. Former monarchists who had decided to support the RCP during the 1920s because they thought it would restore private property – as well as restore Russia as an imperial great power – described themselves and the regime as "national Bolshevik." An intellectual current rather than a political party, this group enjoyed considerable support among rank-and-file Russian party members. Trotsky, as well as Lenin, Zinoviev, and Bukharin at first, condemned this current and the idea of using Russian nationalism to build the soviet state – that is, they did not want Russian nationalism and imperialism to be painted red. But they never explained how they would keep the Soviet Russia and the soviet centralism they advocated separate from Russian interests, language, and culture. For instance, at a time when UCP stationery had Ukrainian and Esperanto letterhead, RCP leaders did not advocate Esperanto as a politically neutral All-Union alternative to Russian.[3] Stalin condemned national Bolshevism in 1923 but, having abandoned indigenization, he effectively realized its program when, after 1929, he chose to identify soviet power not only with Russian but also with select elements of Russian culture and history.[4]

One characteristic that the Russian Bolsheviks did share with British, French, and German SDs until 1918 was a refusal to allow separate organizations within the party for subject nationalities within the empire. Lenin claimed that his party was the single legitimate representative not just of ethnic or Great Russia's workers but of *all* workers in the Russian empire (*Rossiia*). When in power, Bolshevik leaders refused separate representation in the Comintern to national communist parties from any former Russian-ruled territories they controlled; thus, they quashed two attempts by Ukrainians for membership in 1920 and 1924. This was contrary to Engels's views on party organization, as expressed in his unpublished defence of the Irish claim in 1872 for separate status from Britain in the International:

> The Irish formed, to all intents and purposes, a distinct nationality of their own, and the fact that they used the English language could not deprive them of the right, common to all, to have an independent national organisation within the International ... The position of Ireland with regard to England was not that of an equal, it was that of Poland with regard to Russia. What would be said if this Council called upon Polish sections to acknowledge the supremacy of a Russian Federal Council in Petersburg, or upon Prussian Polish, North Schleswig, and Alsatian sections to submit to a Federal Council in Berlin ...? If members of a conquering nation called upon the nation they had conquered and continued to hold down to forget their specific nationality and position, to "sink national differences" and so forth, that was not Internationalism, it was nothing else but preaching to them submission to the yoke, and attempting to justify and to perpetuate the dominion of the conqueror under the cloak of Internationalism. It was sanctioning the belief, only too common among the English working men, that they were superior beings compared to the Irish, and as much an aristocracy as the mean whites of the Slave States considered themselves to be with regard to the Negroes ... If the motion [on subordination] was adopted by the Council, the Council would inform the Irish working men, in so many words, that, after the dominion of the English aristocracy over Ireland, after the dominion of the English middle class over Ireland, they must now look forth to the advent of the dominion of the English working class over Ireland.[5]

These remarks were soon forgotten, and in 1896, the British Socialist Party set a precedent when it convinced the Second International to reject separate membership for an Irish party.[6]

Ukrainian communism emerged in reaction to Ukrainian moderate socialism and Russian Bolshevik rule. A review of its forgotten writings supports the view that Russian leaders did not eliminate them or other leftist opponents because they were "counter-revolutionary," "petty bourgeois," or "nationalist." Rather, Bolsheviks branded as "counter-revolutionary," "petty bourgeois," or "nationalist" those opposed to their control, whom they decided to eliminate.[7] The colonialism that Ukrainian communists identified in their writings should not be ignored, because the colonialists they wrote about included not only the Whites, the Germans, and the French, but also, Russian Bolsheviks.

Ukrainian Marxism, like the Irish and Muslim, differed from that of imperial metropoles in that it emerged in a periphery and involved national liberation. Roy's account of the founding of the Indian party could just as well describe the situation in Ukraine: "I had only told them that driving the British out of India would be no revolution, if it was followed by replacing foreign exploiters by native ones ... Instinctively idealists, they readily agreed with my opinion and jumped to the conclusion that if the revolution had to liberate the toiling masses it would have to be a communist revolution." Ho Chi Minh admitted: "It was patriotism not communism that prompted me to believe in Lenin."[8] As a "peripheral" group, Ukrainian Marxists shared with others like them certain theoretical postulates. They regarded the exploited or colonized as a "proletarian nation"; they believed that changes in the relations of production did not automatically eliminate foreign rule; they also believed that the proletariat of ruling nations could be as imperialist, chauvinist, and exploitative in its attitudes towards former subjects as any nobility or bourgeoisie. The colonized were "proletarian" because they were dominated by a foreign ruling class, and their liberation could only be socialist in nature. National freedom and independent states would be impossible as long as international capital dominated national markets; at the same time, social liberation could not come about without national liberation and the creation of national states. "Anti-imperialism" had to include independent socialist republics and parties for every nation, and these, in the future, would be united in a confederation of socialist national states. There were two key differences between Ukrainian and Muslim communists: the latter claimed, first, that the future of the world revolution lay in colonized Eastern countries, not western Europe, and second, that alliances with the national bourgeoisie (including even religious parties) were necessary for the liberation struggle to endure. Because national liberation required the participation of the bourgeoisie, class divisions could be ignored during the struggle. To do otherwise would drive the bourgeoisie into an alliance with their imperial class allies and lead to the defeat of the revolution.[9]

A Ukrainian SD echoing one of Lenin's opinions about the workers of oppressor and oppressed nations being different because the former learned contempt for the latter in school and in life, explained in January 1919 that the destruction of the bourgeoisie as a class of exploiters did not mean the end of exploitation. The proletariat, once in power, would need decades to rid itself of the economic legacy of the bourgeoisie, and that is why Ukraine had to be an independent republic. "There is only one response [from Bolsheviks] to the demands of the Ukrainian citizen to have at least the same guarantees for [their] national and cultural rights as do the representatives of the 'fraternal nation' [Russians] here in Ukraine," complained another Independentist. "[That this demand is] chauvinism, middle-class and counterrevolutionary."[10]

Ukrainian left SDs never called themselves "national communists." Apparently, the term first appeared in August 1917, when it was used by a Russian SR criticizing Ukrainian SDs for not being "really revolutionary" like the Ukrainian SRs.[11] It was used during the spring of 1919 by Vynnychenko, who wrote that "Russian national communists lack what is most crucial: an understanding of the *Ukrainian* [sic] revolution." In April 1919, when Ukrainian left SRs were negotiating in Ukraine with the Bolsheviks for a share in the soviet government, the Bolshevik Larik labelled "Ukrainian national communism" as "the worst enemy of the communist revolution in Ukraine."[12] That summer, a Ukrainian left SR, V. Hart, used "national communism" to discredit "all Russian national patriotic communist Bolsheviks who want to create a Soviet Russia within the historical borders of the tsarist empire." He contended that they had to be stopped to prevent the emergence of a huge, centralized parasitic bureaucracy and to avoid lending credence to anti-communists who equated Bolsheviks with tsarist imperialists. Manuilsky used the term in January 1920 to discredit the UCP: "The Ukrainian bourgeoisie want to nationalize communism and restrict the workers' peasants' movement within national lines."[13] Ukrainian communists actually stressed that they were not a "national" party. An anonymous author specified in 1920 that they wanted a territorial, not an ethnic Ukrainian party separate from the Russian one that would include proletarians of all nationalities "within the borders of the Ukrainian revolution." "We decisively separate ourselves from those who solve the Ukrainian revolution from the point of view of Russian interests rather than those of the socialist revolution. We will never assist such national-economic politics in Ukraine which *will be* [sic] a politics of Russian power, a politics of disseminating national enmity." This author explained how strong capitalist states had turned weaker countries into colonies by subordinating their internal markets to foreign markets while socialist revolution would reverse this imposed pattern of exploitation and develop industries to meet the needs of the internal market. This would benefit all who lived in Ukraine and who were the product of its common historical economic and cultural conditions.[14]

Red Nationalists vs Red Imperialists

In late 1917, Ukrainian leaders differed over whether national liberation or socio-economic emancipation was more important and whether the Bolsheviks or the Don government posed the greater threat. The two biggest parties, the SDs and SRs, split. They supported independence in January 1918 but, thereafter, centrists and rightists sought association with the Entente, while leftists concluded that independence required coming to terms with the Bolsheviks. By February 1919, left SDs dominated the Kyiv city and provincial soviet together with Ukrainian left SRs. They supported soviets, government ownership, and a dictatorship of workers and revolutionary peasants; but they considered Bolshevik policies "imperialist" because they subordinated Ukraine to Russia. They specified that non-Ukrainian workers would be involved in the building of an independent Ukrainian socialist republic, while conceding that this could happen only through a non–Bolshevik-dominated soviet power "wherein workers would be guaranteed no less than one-third of the seats in all respective soviet organs." The Independents warned the Bolsheviks that by subordinating the Ukrainian revolution to Russian economic interests, they would incite war between "the urban proletariat and the poor peasantry." In April they concluded: "It is now two months since soviet power has taken Kyiv, but we have not seen either true soviet power or a dictatorship of the proletariat. There is only a dictatorship of the communist party":

> Given its present socio-economic and national-political life, imposing upon Ukraine a federation with Russia is reactionary because it deprives the Ukrainian revolution of the possibility of organically developing without imposed foreign circumstances, and disrupts the revolutionary strength of the Ukrainian proletariat and peasants introducing into its

ranks national conflicts and alienates from the socialist revolution socially
common elements opposed to the idea of uniting with Russia for national
reasons.[15]

Displeased with Bolshevik rule, the Independentists tried to come to
terms with the UNR; thus, in March 1919, in Kamianets-Podilsky, they
established a short-lived coalition with moderates called the Committee for the Defence of the Republic. This reflected Tkachenko's strategy,
outlined in 1917 (cf. Introduction, n13), about allying with a "national-
revolutionary bourgeois" government and pre-dated the adoption of
the same strategy by the 1920 Second Comintern Congress. In Marxist
terms this was a "national-liberation" alliance with the "revolutionary
bourgeoisie." The agreement condemned Russian communist power
in Ukraine as an occupation and called for an independent Ukrainian
Republic based on soviets. The country would be ruled by a coalition
of the three socialist parties that had signed the agreement; together,
they would organize the economy on the basis of a planned transition
from capitalism to socialism.[16] The committee was supported by local
Bolsheviks but dissolved itself when it learned of a planned right-wing
coup. Meanwhile, the Independentists also negotiated with the Russian
Bolsheviks. They imagined a communist Ukraine independent of Russia and wrote a proposal for a treaty between the two republics calling
for freely elected soviets, no party dictatorship, full economic, political,
and military independence, and a replacement of all imported Russian
specialists with Ukrainian speakers. They envisaged the eventual dissolution of the UNR and the CPU.[17]

During the negotiations the Independentists tried to take control
of the massive anti-Bolshevik uprisings that had erupted in March.[18]
They initially formed an All-Ukrainian Revkom under Hryhoryi Dra-
homyretsky, which they dissolved after it had achieved little. They then
formed a Central Revolutionary Committee with centrist SDs and SRs
from the UNR in Kyiv, which initially included the able military commander Iurko Tiutiunnyk. In April and then again in May, one of its
members, Oles Hrudnytsky, organized two more meetings in Pereiaslav,
where Independentists, Ukrainian Bolshevik "federalists," SRs from
the UNR, and the warlord [otaman] Mykola Hryhoriev sent representatives to try coordinate their activities. At both an informer was present.
The Bolsheviks ambushed the second meeting and captured many of its
participants.[19] More successful was a final Independentist meeting on
20 June in Uman, which was attended by almost all left-wing Ukrainian

partisan commanders. They agreed to a set of conditions under which they were prepared to ally with the UNR, similar to those formulated that March. They adopted the slogan "All Power to the Working People, Peasants and Proletarians."[20] That same month, Tkachenko and Richytsky published a draft program for a Ukrainian Communist Party. In it they condemned Bolshevik policies as catastrophic. Dominated as they were by a Russian petite bourgeoisie with a proletarian membership still befuddled by "bourgeois imperialist cravings [zabahanky]," the Bolsheviks saw Ukraine in terms of Russian rather than socialist interests. Thus, instead of using the Ukrainian national revolution in communist interests, they opposed it and sparked a national war that weakened the world communist movement. They argued for a soviet-Bolshevik Ukraine equal to and not subordinated to Bolshevik Russia either militarily, administratively, or economically.[21]

Based primarily on the forces of the partisan commander Danylo Terpilo (Zeleny), who had attended the Uman meeting, the Independentists fought the Bolshevik "Russian communist occupation regime," sometimes in combined operations with "revolutionary nationalist" UNR detachments through the summer of 1919 (see figures 15, 16, and 17, illustration section). This was not unlike the kind of alliance later advocated by the Second Comintern Congress. The initial aim was to win control of Ukraine west of the Dnipro River, but, Independentist influence was minimal, for at the time, most of the populace supported the UNR. Also, at that point Hryhoriev and Makhno remained apart. This "national liberation struggle" directed against the Russian Bolsheviks used the slogan "Soviets without Communists." Although Richytsky and Tkachenko had already made public their idea of forming a Ukrainian Communist Party, local Independentists did not use term in their leaflets and speeches, in which they labelled their enemy "communists." Perhaps, being on the spot, they realized that few if any locals knew that in March the Bolsheviks had changed their party name and imagined that their enemy was not them but some other party called "communist." Ukrainian peasants still identified "Bolshevik" favourably with the independent soviets of 1917 and early 1918 and the land redistribution, from which most of them had benefited during those months. They did not yet associate "Bolshevik" with the hated "communists" and "commissars" who in 1919 were imposing party dictatorship, conscription, requisitions, and communes upon them. In a telegram to Stalin, a Ukrainian Borotbist characterized popular opinion that spring as follows: "And so we finally got it – we were waiting for the Bolsheviks and got instead some kind of Jewish commune." Bolshevik intelligence noted: "The peasants [in central Ukraine] say that 'the communists and the Petliurites are both robbers.' In their view Communism is 'Jewish power.' They affectionately remember the Bolsheviks in Ukraine from the previous spring [1918] who disappeared to parts unknown."[22] Regardless of the terminology, in practice the Independentist uprising can be regarded as the first intra-communist war, predating the later conflicts between Stalin and Tito, Stalin and Mao, and Vietnam and Cambodia. Hrudnytsky expressed the movement's aims as follows in a leaflet: "At last the nation's patience has ended … And we, Ukrainian Bolsheviks, in order to save the socialist revolution both in Ukraine and the world announce decisive active struggle against all who speculate on communist slogans and against all chauvinists, be they Ukrainian, Russian, or Jewish … All power in Ukraine must be in the hands of the local inhabitants – Ukrainians (that is, all who live in Ukraine): we have no need of occupiers or those who speculate on communist ideals."[23] In another, we read that although Ukrainian poor peasants and workers extended the hand of friendship to Russian peasants and workers, "… the Russian communist-bolsheviks came to us with Chinese and Latvians and began to destroy the national cultural life of the Ukrainian working people … Russian communist Bolsheviks, based on hired Chinese, Latvians, and lumpenproletarians, want to turn Ukraine back into a Russian colony,"

The prospect of a radical nationalist, radical socialist, Ukrainian proto-communist alliance frightened Ukraine's Bolsheviks, who feared that Makhno would also join. In what is probably a forged letter, purportedly sent by Makhno to Rakovskii on 22 April 1919, persons unknown phrased the threat as follows: "We organizers of Ukraine, 1) Zeleny, 2) Sokolov, 3) Shiper, 4) Hryhoriev, 5) Anhel, 6) Vynnychenko, 7) Petliura, and 8) Andreev, and all the rest; and all of us organizers in Ukraine number 50, as well as I, Makhno, tell you [Rakovskii] that, if you do not kill all the Jews or send them to Palestine or at least to your Russia, you will not last in Ukraine … and not one of you [Bolsheviks] will remain alive"(see figures 19 and 20, illustration section).[24]

Iury Mazurenko (see figure 14, illustration section), the Independentist military commander, explained the positions of his party in an "Ultimatum" written that June. "The workers and peasants of Ukraine rose against you as the arm of Russian conquerors, who, under the guise of slogans that are holy to us … not only ruin [them] and destroy the true authority of the workers and poor peasants of a neighboring state but exploit them for purposes far distant from any kind of socialist order." These slogans included power to the soviets, self-determination of nations including separation, and struggle against imperialist conquerors. Russian Bolsheviks in Ukraine called themselves a worker's government, yet they took raw materials and even machinery out of Ukraine and created unemployment. Instead of ruling through soviets, they rigged elections in their favour and ruled through commissars and secret police, who were no different from tsarist governors and gendarmes. "Instead of an independent Ukrainian Republic, wherein power had to lie with the Ukrainian working nation, you have made it [Ukraine] into a Russian colony and Ukrainian workers and peasants into slaves working for Russia who send the product of their labour in return for packages of [worthless] Kerensky roubles, leaflets, and your hired agitators." This was not internationalism "but merely the subordination to Moscow of all states where workers and peasant power exists, which, as a result, opens the door for the Whites." Instead of uniting nationalities, the Bolsheviks were only intensifying the antagonism between Jews and the rest of Ukraine's population and thereby inciting pogroms. Mazurenko concluded: "Let the blood and curses of the Jewish nation fall on your head." [25] The minutes of a January 1920 partisan meeting in central Ukraine offer additional insight into Ukrainian anti-Bolshevik positions. They record support for non–Bolshevik-dominated soviets with "our people – Ukrainians" occupying all governmental positions. Participants accused communist Jews appointed by Russians of inciting quarrels between local non-political Jews and villagers and called for their dismissal. The ideal order was to include the equal franchise, national minority autonomy, and full rights for all citizens regardless of religion and nationality. "We Ukrainians must not separate ourselves from any other nation and be in accord with all nations and not only those of the Russian state."[26]

The CPU, and Piatakov specifically, accused the Independentists of anti-Semitism. This charge, however, reveals more about the Bolshevik exploitation of nationality – which they knew, despite their public rhetoric, was as significant politically as class – than about Independentist behaviour. In their correspondence, local officials wrote to their superiors requesting Ukrainians for office where the Red Army had established Bolshevik power. Where Bolshevik power was still weak, they requested Russians. In a list of pleas from thirteen Ukrainian cities for Party activists compiled in May 1919, eight specifically requested Russians.[27] CPU leaders who knew otherwise did not publicly admit that leaflets of undoubted Independentist provenance that mentioned Jews or Russians, specified these were "communist," "commissar," "chauvinist," or even "petliurite" Jews / Russians who were the agents of hated policies, and not all Jews or all Russians. Independentist rhetoric did target rich "bourgeois" Jews – but then so did Bolshevik rhetoric. The Bolshevik aim was obviously to discredit the Independentists as ideological anti-Semites who targeted all Jews.[28] Insofar as most Bolshevik-controlled provincial Ukrainian towns in 1919 were like Chernihiv, where almost all three hundred party members were secular Russified Jews, it was to be expected that furious locals resisting dispossession and requisitioning would target this particular subgroup as the agents of those policies.[29] The Ukrainian and Russian parties both had Jewish leaders, including Richytsky, and no party always controls all its members.[30] The Independentists disseminated leaflets warning Ukrainians to shun Russian extremist propaganda that tried to set them against other working people, who like themselves had suffered tsarist oppression. "They want to spark a Jewish pogrom. COMRADES DON'T FALL FOR SUCH A PROVOCATION! [sic] Fighting among ourselves will destroy our proletarian might and that is what the bourgeoisie and black hundreds want" (see figure 9, illustration section).

That unsophisticated followers were murdering non-communist religious Jews and vandalizing their property was no more directly the fault of Independentist leaders than of Bolshevik leaders. In early 1918, retreating Bolshevik troops butchered Jews in northeastern Ukraine. The Jewish historians Elias Cherikover wrote about them: "These [atrocities] were brought by a force alien to the country – Red guards and sailors from the north hiding under Bolshevik slogans." The Red Army's First Lenin Regiment staged a pogrom "to punish counter-revolutionaries." Another Bolshevik unit coined the slogan "kill all the bourgeoisie and Jews." In Uman in 1919 "there were many Jews-volunteers in the 8th [Soviet] regiment from the local criminal element – Jewish criminals – who if they did not pillage themselves showed others, for the promise of reward, the quarters of the rich, whom they knew well." The presence of Jews among Bolshevik pogromists in 1919 was recorded "with great national sorrow" by the Kyiv city Jewish Organization. In Petrograd the Bolsheviks either did not report these pogroms or did not mention their men were the perpetrators.[31] White intelligence reported that autumn that in southern Ukraine, Red Army detachments had slogans attached to their wagons proclaiming "beat the Jews, save Russia." In southern Russia, the slightest incident immediately provoked shouts of "beat the Jews."[32]

By June 1919, Independentist groups controlled large portions of Kyiv, Poltava, and Podillia provinces. Bolshevik intelligence reported that Zeleny had a well-organized intelligence and counter-intelligence and, although short of arms, had disciplined troops. A May 2 Bolshevik report noted that

> Poltava province has figured as the central base of counter-revolution, anti-semitism, and gangsterism in Ukraine. It is harder here than any-where else to impose the ideas of communism and the principles of soviet power ... The counter-revolutionary uprising in Myrhorod led by the local garrison under Dubchak, Nesiur, Ivaschchenko, and others, calling itself Independentist, derives from the counter-revolutionary organization that was supposed to lead an All-Ukrainian uprising against Soviet power, but the premature uprising in Myrhorod paralyzed the further plans of the counter-revolution.[33]

Despite this optimistic prognosis, prospects were bleak that summer for the Bolsheviks, who were importing Russians from Russia to man their punishment battalions – and then giving these units Ukrainian names to hide their origins.[34] Lenin's order to centralize all armed units in Ukraine that May had not been implemented, and tens of thousands of Ukrainians on the Bolshevik side were either refusing to fight other Ukrainians or deserting. Zatonsky observed: "Essentially, at the time, any of our regiments could have turned against us and it was not always evident why this or that unit was fighting on our side and not against us."[35] While the Borotbists remained on the Bolshevik side, the feared alliance of Ukrainian radical left groups, Hryhoriev and Makhno, actually did exist for a few weeks in mid-July. Even the "fed-eralist" Skrypnyk approached the Independentists requesting that they mediate in talks between the UNR and his group.

An Independentist delegation on 18 July came to Kamianets for talks with the UNR. Farther west that month, Poland had conquered the West Ukrainian National Republic, and its 50,000-strong army had managed to withdraw to UNR territory just before the delegation arrived. Had agreement been reached, combined Ukrainian forces would have been at least 100,000 men, with tanks and armoured trains. Centrists in Kyiv who had signed the spring agreement with the Independentists hesi-tated, however, and were not backed by UNR right-wing parties. Pet-liura still hoped for Entente recognition and had secretly just signed his agreement with Pilsudski. He disagreed with the socialist aspects of the proposed alliance and sought to take over rather than cooperate with the partisan movement. On 17 July the UNR general staff had issued a secret order to pro-UNR *otamans* in central Ukraine, as well as to Zeleny, to coordinate an attack on Kyiv. The Independentists, for their part, planned either to leave the anti-Bolshevik insurrection if they were unable to prevent the UNR from controlling it, or, to overthrow the UNR in a coup should talks fail in Kamianets.[36] When UNR military intelligence learned of their plan, it arrested the delegation on 21 July. Meanwhile, in the face of Denikin's successful offensive, Independentists in Kyiv ordered their remaining units to stop fighting the Bolsheviks just before their Kamianets delegation was arrested. Zeleny then lost a key battle at the end of July, after which he joined the UNR forces. Independentist commanders quarrelled with one another, some could not control their troops, and Makhno and Hryhoriev, despite initial promises, did not cooperate. The UNR then won over many partisan commanders; it failed, though, to unite all of them to its cause and ultimately lost popular support because until October it forbade its troops to fight Denikin. Makhno, meanwhile, fell out with and murdered Hryhoriev. When the UNR released its imprisoned Independentist leaders at the end of September, they returned to central Ukraine to fight the Whites, where they were arrested by the Bolsheviks. Considering the Whites a greater evil than the Bolsheviks, perhaps having learned of Lenin's planned concessions to Ukraine, Mazurenko on 27 December wrote to Rakovskii that his party's armed initiative had been an error. He explained that it had been an attempt to wrest from the UNR control of a legitimate armed response to anti-Ukrainian policies. As such, it was directed against "the existing regime as an occupation regime," not against soviet power or communism. Mazurenko reasserted the Independentist position on separate Ukrainian ministries but now accepted Bolshevik rule.[37] During those weeks, it should be noted, Borotbist leaders learned that Lenin's proclaimed concessions were mere rhetoric. On 26 December, the day before Mazurenko wrote his letter, a Borotbist commander wrote to his Central Committee from Kharkiv: "All the talk about a change of course in Ukraine towards independence is only talk." Lenin, meanwhile, was administratively sanctioning Ukrainian Bolshevik federalists who protested the importation of Russians to work in Ukraine.[38]

The CPU had already condemned the Independentists in February 1919, and Lenin's December concessions did not change that, nor did they prevent the CPU from deciding two months later to destroy them: "At the moment the kulak counter-revolution is conducting a nefarious demagogic policy that combines counter-revolutionary with soviet slogans hiding its rich-peasant pogromist chauvinist essence with Bolshevik phraseology [such as] 'we are Ukrainian Bolsheviks,' we are for Soviet power but against Jews and Muscovites for an independent Ukraine." In another CPU statement we read: "This entire so-called insurgent peasant movement is covered with a thick black fog of lies, provocations, and white-guardist arrogance."[39] On receiving Mazurenko's ultimatum, Rakovskii had called the uprising a "farce" that could be dealt with in a few days.[40] Informed by their intelligence agents of the differences between partisan groups, CPU leaders ordered their officials to carefully distinguish between them but did not publicize this knowledge in their propaganda. A party member mobilized in June 1919 noted in his memoirs that before his unit marched off to fight Zeleny, Rakovskii gave them a speech in which he claimed that the partisan leader was allied with the Whites. CPU posters and leaflets lumped Ukrainian SD-led revolts together with every other anti-Bolshevik movement under the term "bandits," described them as tools of the "imperialist bourgeoisie," accused them of anti-Semitism, and ignored their communist platform.[41] This condemnation of the Independentists in Bolshevik propaganda as a "bourgeois party intending to deceive the masses" reflected Lenin's refusal to tolerate an independent Communist Ukraine with its own party, analogous to communist Hungary.[42] Rakovskii's condemnation of the Independentists as a "bourgeois party intending to deceive the masses" might also be seen in the context of his attempts to ensure the survival of his party. Lenin's decision that April to "fuse" Soviet Ukraine with Russia would have left him without a job, so Rakovskii was perhaps reminding Lenin not to tolerate an independent Communist Ukraine with its own party, analogous to Communist Hungary, for this would have meant the dissolution of the CPU. That spring, given his pragmatism and the distinct possibility that the Independentists would end up taking over a sizable part of Soviet Ukraine in the wake of the successful White offensive, Lenin might have recognized them and dissolved the CPU – something he actually did do that September when he considered an alliance with the UNR.[43]

To Ukrainian Marxists, Rakovskii's condemnation was the product of those same imperialist preconceptions that had led the RCP to support the CPU, invade Ukraine, and transform its civil war into a national war between Russia and Ukraine – thereby discrediting socialism by equating it with the destruction rather than the attainment of national liberation. Russian military exigencies and food shortages might explain Bolshevik centralization and repression in Russia, but, Ukrainian Marxists saw no reason other than imperialist preconceptions to explain why that centralization and repression had to include Ukraine. There was no reason from their perspective why Lenin's Russia should not ally as an equal with a communist Ukraine ruled by its own party, just as it had done with a communist Hungary ruled by its own party and not by a Kremlin puppet analogous to the CPU.

A December 1918 UNR general staff analysis identified the Ukrainian left-SD social base: "Do the peasants and working masses want pure independence? ... No ... The majority wants cooperation with Muscovy. Obviously not subordination to it, but confederation with it." At a February 1919 meeting in Bolshevik Kyiv, the Independentists gathered more than three thousand workers for a debate with CPU centralists. At the end of the debate, the workers overwhelmingly supported the Ukrainian communist program.[44] Mazlakh wrote to his wife that spring that *Do Khvyli* was hugely in demand in Poltava province and that there was "a serious potential for a Ukrainian communist party."[45] A Bolshevik agent reported in April that Kyiv's workers were closely following Zeleny's activities, which they could, because many of them and administrative staff lived in the suburbs, commuted, and could keep abreast of events. Were he to take the capital he would have their full support. Workers were angry and they hated Jewish commissars, most of whom, the report noted, had joined the party for a "piece of the government pie" and flaunted and abused their privileges. One of their slogans was "Down with Jews, Down with horsemeat. We want bread and pork." Some workers had supported the failed Kurylivska uprising. Those who hadn't said it was only because "we were too weak." At the time of writing, a few days after the uprising, the agent contended that workers were passive only because they had no weapons.[46]

Even in early 1920, after the UCP had accepted Bolshevik rule, funding and, thus, dependency, CPU leaders feared it. The Bolsheviks controlled Ukrainian cities only tenuously; their party had only eleven thousand members, of whom no more than 10 per cent that year were declared Ukrainians, while the Borotbists had fifteen thousand and the UCP almost three thousand. CPU federalists, meanwhile, were condemning the Bolsheviks in almost the same terms as the Ukrainian Communists.[47] Russian SR intelligence reported that spring that the UCP was attracting workers who backed soviet power but disliked Lenin's communists.[48] Local officials complained that UCP attempts to control local soviets, establish their own army, and prevent "people from Russia" from controlling them amounted to "anti-communist agitation" more dangerous than that of Petliura. In response, Bolshevik leaders decided to police the UCP. They harassed its members, discredited it, and denied it publicity by not publicly debating it. The CPU sponsored a pro-Bolshevik "left" faction within the UCP, intimidated members with spurious criminal charges, and denied it funding and premises. The secret police established a special subsection to follow UCP activities throughout Ukraine and compile a detailed "Daily Information Report on the Ukrainian Communist Party."[49] In May 1920, Skrypnyk condemned the UCP and in June, after the Polish offensive had been repulsed, the Bolsheviks decided to destroy the party.[50] As described by a UCP member in August 1920: "Our affairs here in Poltava [province] are the same as yours [in Kharkiv]: In Poltava [city] they [the Bolsheviks] appear to reckon and talk with us but out in the counties 'they are cutting off our fingers, ears and noses' [and] all according to the law."[51] In a letter to CPU leaders, Mazurenko, Richytsky, and Kulynychenko complained about harassment and arrests despite their professed loyalty. Nothing had changed despite Lenin's proclaimed concessions the previous December: "You have stopped playing with the notion of an independent Ukraine and, putting all your declarations into the archives, are rebuilding a single united little Mother Russia."[52] Local CPU officials received orders: "In so far as it recognized soviet power and has its representatives in the All Ukrainian CC ... then we can include them in the work of soviet organs. But that does not mean we recognize the UCP as genuinely communist and should relate to it loyally. Absolutely not. The obligation of every communist, party organ, and primary party organization is to wage a vicious struggle against it, revealing at every possible instance its nationalist and petite-bourgeois nature." In *Ukrainska kommunistychna partia (UKP). Kommunistychna partiia Ukrainy (KPbU),* which he wrote in 1921 shortly after his return from Ukraine, Vynnychenko claimed that if it was not repressed and harassed, the UCP would double its membership within a year (see Appendix, Document 9, page 201).

CPU leaders were much perturbed by Russian-born Iurii Lapchynskii's defection from their party in 1920 – to which he had belonged since 1905. In a public letter in the UCP newspaper, he condemned the Bolsheviks as "an organization of Russian and Russified workers" that, from the start, had disassociated itself from the Ukrainian revolution and, in which the majority, even after 1917, "regarded the attempt to create a [soviet] Ukrainian territorial national state as a farce to fool

Ukrainian chauvinists and foreigners and, at best, as a tactical manoeu-
vre." It was only a minority like himself who saw "the need to fundamentally restructure the old Russian empire and, moved by a sense of
obligation to the country they had to organize and to the revolutionary
proletariat, realized that Ukraine is a distinct and separate territorial
national and economic organization." He condemned Bolshevik Russian centralization and the practice of sending Russian rejects (*otbrosy*) to
posts in Ukraine, viewing these as the reasons why counter-revolution
had triumphed in 1919. He added that Lenin's concessions had changed
nothing and that reform from within the CPU was impossible. Having seen how some newly arrived Russians had been able to suppress
within themselves "remnants of Muscovite centralism and chauvinism," he concluded optimistically that the UCP was the only alternative
for Ukraine. The Bolsheviks used his letter as an excuse to shut down
the UCP newspaper.[53]

In 1922, with strong partisan groups still active in Ukraine and UCP
members among those engaged in repressing them, CPU leaders still
feared UCP potential despite police reports to the contrary. Frunze noted
at a plenum meeting: "Even now in a proletarian region like Iuzovka 150
komsomol have joined the UCP. This is not an isolated fact but indicative [of a broader reality]." This was confirmed by Rakovskii.[54] Moreover, anti-Bolshevik partisan units formed by poor peasants opposed to
the NEP still existed. Given that the UCP had divided over NEP, with
some denouncing it as a betrayal of communist ideals and Bolshevik
pandering to the "chauvinist Russian petite bourgeoisie," such members may well have been in these units. Those who supported NEP,
meanwhile, posed just as much of a threat to the Bolsheviks. Given
that indigenization encompassed almost all of the national demands
in the UCP program, and NEP appealed to the majority of the population, the UCP was poised to increase its following. In 1924, continuing
to condemn Moscow's economic policy as imperialist and colonialist,
UCP members stood for local elections as the only non-Bolshevik candidates. By then, the UCP was the only extant non-Bolshevik party. The
party began organizing strikes and, in August of that year, formally
accepted NEP. Two months later, the Bolsheviks decided "in strictest
secrecy" to crush the UCP.[55] A CPU analysis that month warned that
the UCP wanted to create an independent Ukrainian republic separate
from Russia because "Russia looks at Ukraine as its colony." It had a
larger membership than its official figures of a few hundred indicated,
it had begun to organize low-paid metal and railway workers, and it

could very quickly mobilize "backward" workers and peasants as well as elicit mass sympathy from a broad cross-section of the population. The analysis concluded: "We must finish with that organization once and for good or in the near future we will face a serious threat." Faced with spurious arrests and censorship, the leaders decided to dissolve the party but refused to admit any "ideological errors."[56]

Ukrainian Marxists and National Liberation

Ukrainian left SDs welcomed the Bolshevik takeover in early 1918. They imagined a Ukraine federated with "the other soviet Republics of Russia" within a broader socialist confederation that they thought would eventually include Europe. They sought a "national form of proletarian culture in Ukraine," and they strived to be represented in all soviets and branches of government. They envisioned a soviet socialist Ukraine with a party, government, economy and army independent of soviet socialist Russia that would impose its own centralization and authority and, decide for itself, how to aid Russia. Within weeks they had realized that the Bolsheviks would not share power and concluded that Moscow was pursuing anti-Ukrainian policies. They then condemned Bolshevism as a reincarnation of Russian imperialism. Living in Bolshevik-controlled territory, they witnessed Bolshevik rule. After 1921, some official CPU spokesmen explained that what Ukrainian communists labelled Russian imperialism and colonialism was only the temporary unfortunate consequence of the extremist policies of the previous three years – policies that circumstances had forced upon the regime. By 1923, indigenization seemed to confirm such rationalizations. Ukrainian communist condemnations of "Russian communist colonialism" as inherent in rather than incidental to Bolshevism now seemed irrelevant, and with the demise of the UCP, they receded from the public sphere. By the late 1930s, Stalin's policies would confirm that those condemnations had been valid – but by then their authors had been arrested or executed.

Ukrainian Marxists knew that Lenin and the Politburo in the Kremlin decided policy but, inasmuch as they had legal status after 1920, they could not publicly condemn Soviet Russian leaders as unequivocally as before. Their criticism now took the form of an "evil ministers–good king" discourse that targeted the Kremlin-controlled CPU as the culprits responsible for Ukraine's ills. Ukrainian Marxists argued that their country differed from Russia because its native industrial proletariat was small and that soviet power would triumph only if it recognized the interests of the majority landless peasants and food-processing workers as represented by their territorial-based parties. The only alternative was the "dictatorship of a communist group" without ties to that majority, based on the "armed assistance of a proletariat from another place – in this case the Russian."[57] From their perspective, "the cultural national forms through which the popular masses assimilate general world values" were among the "progressive" elements of the past. Because "bourgeois despotism" had prevented smaller nations from developing to the same level as bigger nations, socialists and communists had to invent new forms to do this based on local conditions. Accordingly, any attempt to impose Russian forms on Ukrainian conditions would only transform class war into a national war and drive the majority of the population to support the national government rather than communism.[58] Applying the same logic that Lenin would apply in 1920 to the French and British empires, Ukrainians in 1919 argued that the socialist revolution that destroyed empires had to create national republics. Only in national states could socialism ultimately triumph, because within them the struggle against the bourgeoisie would not be complicated by a national question. This echoed Marx's idea that every proletariat had to deal with its own national bourgeoisie as well as Lenin's ideas in his *Imperialism*. Union of any sort with a socialist Russia was out of the question unless it was part of a broader world association of socialist republics – one that would exist only for as long as did the struggle against imperialism.[59]

An important target of condemnation was the Russian claim that economics had "unified" Ukraine with Russia and had made separatism impossible. Shakhrai and Mazlakh offered a detailed rebuttal of the idea that "under contemporary world economic conditions an independent Ukraine is impossible." If this was so, they asked, why was an independent Soviet Russia possible? Would independence also be impossible within a future socialist world economy? All great powers were bound economically to their colonies but, the "productive forces of the colonies revolt against union." Economic reciprocity, they noted, did not preclude political independence, as demonstrated by Sweden and Norway, which did not become poorer after separating in 1905. Economic relations between Russia and Ukraine were like those between great powers and their colonies, and the former were indeed bound together, just like the latter. But, that being so, what was the difference between the "centralist" Russian Bolsheviks who opposed Ukrainian

independence and "Russian counterrevolutionaries, the large landowners and capitalists," who also argued that "productive forces" united
Russia and Ukraine? Colonies and metropoles have different interests,
they continued, and, economic ties and productive forces "sometimes
lead not to political union but to political separation."[60]

In 1919, left SRs or left SDs compiled statistics that illustrated
Ukraine's colonial status within the new Soviet state (see figures 10, 11
and 12, illustration section). They showed that Ukraine exported 10,922
railway wagons of supplies to Russia (not including army requisitions)
in the first six months of that year and imported 1,737 wagons of goods.
Figures for June indicated that Ukraine exported at least 3,224 railway
wagons of primarily foodstuffs to Russia and imported no more than 689
wagons of mainly manufactured goods. That July the figures were 3,152
and 417 respectively.[61] These charts also showed that only 50 to 65 per
cent of recorded Ukrainian exports were foodstuffs as Bolshevik gangs
literally stripped everything they could from Ukraine. Bolshevik figures that April and May indicate 4,354 wagons of foodstuffs exported to
Russia and 408 wagons of imported manufactured goods from Russia –
including 13 wagons of cardboard packaging. Figures for one Ukrainian border station on 1 July 1919 show that 22 wagons of foodstuffs
and 9 of manufactured goods left the country that day, and that one
wagon of Russian manufactured goods entered it.[62] Another 1919 list,
not including gold and valuables looted from churches, showed that
almost 50 per cent of the itemized exports included commodities like
soap, matches, toothbrushes, coffee, shoe polish, laundry powder,
farming tools and machines, 456 pairs of shoes, 15,007 buckets, and
371,000 scythes – which raises the question of how much of nominally
"imported Russian" goods actually originated in Ukraine.[63] In any case,
because of massive theft en route, Ukraine's producers received little of
the imported Russian goods that did get beyond Kyiv or Kharkiv.[64]

Independentists knew that the RCP controlled the CPU and diplomatically directed their invective primarily against the "communists
in Ukraine," as they called the latter. They saw two possible paths to
soviet power in Ukraine. One was through Russian conquest and domination; the other was through a "Ukrainian socialist revolution via its
own driving forces and tasks and order of implementation that would
not exclude some possible help from Russia." Because the two were so
different, anything other than a loose alliance between the two countries
was out of the question, and even then only as part of a broader alliance
of all socialist states wherein none dominated. To think otherwise was

Russian nationalist nonsense (*zabobon*). Replying to a Bolshevik article
claiming that "proletarian wars" and the socialist state did not conquer
nations but only brought liberation to them, Andryi Mykhailychenko
suggested that the author come to Kyiv to see for himself what exactly
"the Russian conquest of Ukraine involved." There could be no liberation without independence, he concluded.[65]

In a long critique of Piatakov, Richytsky reminded him about one
pertinent point from the Eighth RCP Congress applicable to Ukraine:
"political independence for all colonized nations." In Ukraine, he
noted, deeds did not reflect words and dealing with the national question involved more than publishing a few newspapers and posters in
Ukrainian. It involved "the statehood of the Ukrainian nation." And
who among the "communists in Ukraine" recognized that, he asked?
Invoking a comparison with Hungary, he noted that nothing would
happen to soviet Ukraine if it united with a soviet Hungary, but that
if it united only with soviet Russia, "she would remain a colony for a
long time." How did Piatakov, he concluded, imagine he could establish trust between the "working masses of Ukraine and Russia" if he
was doing things like confiscating *Do Khvyli* and exiling its authors?
Richytsky saw the CPU as merely a subsection of the Russian party ful-
filling the task of keeping Ukraine under Russia's colonialist heel. He
could write a long analysis demonstrating that "communist imperialism" is no different from any other and that when a victorious proletariat tries to "sit on a foreign spine," it inevitably provokes a national war
and revolution against a socialist state. He would not, he concluded,
write that analysis, because he did not want the newspaper confiscated
and himself exiled. The following week Shakhrai, under the pseud-
onym Hryts Sokyra, criticized Bolshevik requisitioning policy pointing
out that "a 'Commune' in the eyes of the masses means occupation and
rule by foreigners and that was something the communists of Ukraine
simply don't understand."[66].

An anonymous typescript written probably during the summer of
1919 provides what might have been an official Ukrainian communist
interpretation of the revolution. A key idea in this tract was that supranational economic links did not imply the destruction of Ukrainian
political independence, if only because an independent soviet Russian
state existed even though it was linked to the world economy. That new
Russian state was, nonetheless, a "Muscovite imperialist state."[67] The
author then linked that state to the "Russian bourgeoisie," who supposedly in December 1917 plotted the war that broke out between the Rada
and Soviet Russia. While Ukraine's Russian bourgeoisie discredited

the Rada by urging it into federal union with Kaledin's government, Muscovite capitalists wanted to use the Bolsheviks to retain control of Ukraine. The Bolsheviks duly invaded as a foreign power, and they won thanks to their army and the support of Black Hundred Russian chauvinists in Ukraine. The author complained that instead of fighting Denikin and Kolchak, as Ukrainians had fought Hetman Skoropadsky, Antonov and Trotsky had attacked Ukraine. This was nothing less than a betrayal of the International. Alluding to the Rakovskii–Vynnychenko talks in the autumn of 1918, the author postulated: "If Ukraine were separated from the Russian Soviet state by the borders of a strong bourgeois state then the Bolsheviks would have recognized the authority of the national soviets and workers congress [organized by the Directory in January 1919] in Ukraine as a proletarian power and would have greeted Ukraine just as they did [communist] Hungary and not waged war against it."

Particularly significant was the observation that Russian Bolsheviks, who aimed to impose by force a federal union of Ukraine with Russia, had established their base among Ukraine's privileged Russian petite bourgeoisie and workers, as well as the Russian nobility, bureaucrats, and army. This suggests that Ukrainian SDs realized that Russian rule in Ukraine was not a matter of a simple bilateral relationship between oppressed nation/colony and oppressor nation/metropole but involved a third group: the settler-colonist minority that, as in other mixed-settler type colonies, dominated the colonized majority. Did Bolshevik not leaders see that as soon as Skoropadsky had proclaimed such a union with Russia, workers and peasants rose in revolt? What, the author asked, was the difference between these two unions? What was the difference between the Bolsheviks and the Whites? Both were counter-revolutionary, supporters of the bourgeois order and traitors to the International. Bolshevik economic policy, he continued, was mere pillaging that produced catastrophe. Moreover, he claimed, all seized goods never reached poor Russian peasants but remained in the hands of the Russian speculators who had filled Bolshevik commissariats. In short, Bolshevik policies were creating a new bourgeoisie and all power belonged only to them. They ruled a society characterized by censorship, lawlessness, and worthless money. A regime that in Ukraine was based not on the local proletariat but on a mercenary Red Army composed of "whoever was available among Latvians, Chinese, Hungarians, Russian lumpen proletariats and Jewish petite bourgeoisie." And this had nothing to do with socialism.

Richytsky wrote to Lenin just after his December "Letter" was released expressing his support, justifying his party's partisan operations that summer and explaining how the promised concessions coincided with Ukrainian communist ideas. He noted that the Bolsheviks had interpreted the refusal of some Ukrainians to fight against them to mean they had no desire for independence, and he suggested that was why Rakovskii had begun to destroy the Ukrainian national revolution. But this would now change. The CPU would dissolve and a single Ukrainian communist party would emerge in its place. A few days later he placed events in a historical context. Before the proletarian revolution could triumph in Ukraine, it had to realize the tasks of the national bourgeois revolution. This would remove the rationale behind and support for the UNR. Only then could Ukrainians liberate themselves from capitalism as part of the revolutionary international socialist movement. To that end they had to have their own Ukrainian communist party.[68] The "communists of Ukraine," he stressed, were merely "a dictatorship of the northern worker" that based itself on a thin stratum of Russian workers in a sea of Ukrainian workers and on the organized might of Russia. Isolated from the mass of the population, this dictatorship could not stand, and that was why the revolution in Ukraine had to be built around the "dictatorship of the southern worker" based on the peasant poor. By establishing a national communist state to replace the national bourgeois state, Ukrainian communists would be withdrawing mass support from the national bourgeoisie and ensuring a victorious end to the revolution. Only Ukrainian communism could successfully carry out the tasks of the national revolution and thereby end it. The simple presence of the Red Army, which forced unelected Revkoms and commissars on people, did not mean the revolution had been attained.[69]

In January 1920 the Independentists formally declared themselves the Ukrainian Communist Party. The following month, Mazurenko explained that the UCP and CPU had the same goal, except that the former acted through "our local proletariat" while the latter were "communist governor-generals." "Because of this we seem to be nationalists to you and to us you represent the metropole desirous of benefiting from the colony; although it is true our mistakes lead us towards petty-bourgeois chauvinism and your mistakes [lead you] towards bourgeois imperialism." Ukraine was of vital importance as the door to revolution in western Europe, but that door had been closed "because of the mistakes of the Russian Communist Party and its filial branch in Ukraine." Only the UCP knew local conditions, and only it could utilize the national movement against the bourgeoisie. The national movement was a tool that could be used by either the bourgeoisie or the proletariat, and to ignore it, like the Bolsheviks were doing, was childish. That movement, moreover, was not a matter of language and folk songs and culture but of economics, because that was what built or destroyed states. In all empires today, in places like Ireland and India, the revolution had "the character of national economic liberation and, within [those empires], the national movement will be a revolutionary factor if the party of the revolutionary proletariat can take charge of it and use it appropriately." This included the economic decentralization of the former empire. The national state might be undesirable in the long term, but in the short term, it was a necessary to retain power and prevent enemies from exploiting the national movement. Regarding the future, "we, the communists in a former colony can better see which paths and methods best suit the given territory than those who worked and work today in the metropole."[70]

Richytsky elaborated on differences in the treatment of "national-economic liberation," empires, and colonies in the Ukrainian and Russian party programs. Quoting *The Communist Manifesto* on the importance of national particularities, he noted that the fundamental difference between the Russian and Ukrainian parties was that the former was the party of a proletariat belonging to a ruling colonialist state nation. "The Russian Communist Party program is the program of a proletariat in a ruling metropolitan nation, the program of the Ukrainian Communist Party is that of a proletariat in an oppressed colonial nation – that is where they differ." One had to and the other did not have to deal with a national issue except as an abstraction. The Russian program referred to the soviet republic system as a model, but this ignored that in practice, the system did not work because it had not been implemented as written and because "it failed to link the national and the economic." The RCP program contained only vague generalities about colonial and national issues, whereas the UCP proposed detailed practical policies because it represented "the proletariat of the nation-colony." Unlike Russian theorists, the Ukrainians stressed that because capitalism created nations, once the war had weakened the weakest empires, the Austrian and the Russian, the communist revolution had occurred first there, based on the national units forged by capitalism. The UCP stood for a communist revolution in an independent Ukraine that the 1917 revolution had separated from imperial Russia.

Ukraine's Bolsheviks talked about autonomy and federalism, but their policies were like those of the Kadets in that both imagined an "economic unity of Ukraine and Russia." There could be no independent Ukrainian SSR if Ukraine and Russia were economically united. In a polemic with Manuilsky and Iakovlev that summer, Richytsky reiterated that the Independentist uprising not been directed against soviets but rather against the CPU occupation regime in an attempt to channel the rage that CPU policies had provoked away from the "counterrevolutionary" UNR. "We stand as guilty before the revolution [for the uprising] as do you with your russifying occupation policies in Ukraine that demoralized the proletariat and drove the peasant masses to fight against your regime." Ukrainian communists who had learned from that mistake were now waiting for Ukraine's Bolsheviks to do the same, unite with them into one party, and recognize Ukraine as a republic with its own Red Army equal (not subordinated) to Russia.[71]

These arguments were elaborated in a UCP memorandum to the Comintern that contained ideas found in the Comintern's 1920 manifesto and in later "Third World" anti-colonial Marxism. Imperialism, it explained, both developed colonial economies and created nations, while simultaneously threatening the colonized with "the destruction of their national political life as well as their national culture." Because it created a weak national bourgeoisie in backward countries like Ukraine, national liberation coincided with struggle against capitalism, and communists had to lead the national struggle to ensure that it continued into a communist revolution. Inasmuch as colonized nations represented capitalism's "weakest link," national revolutions in colonized nations had to be exploited and taken beyond their "bourgeois democratic stage." Without a preceding national liberation culminating in a national state led by an indigenous party (i.e., not one based in another country), no socialist revolution was possible. Each nation had to have its own socialist soviet republic, which would then closely ally with all others. The problem in Ukraine was that its colonial legacy had left it with a large Russian urban worker-settler population isolated from and indifferent to Ukrainian interests. As a result, the CPU leadership, imbued with "the imperialist legacy of old Russia," ignored the national revolution. Instead of supporting and carrying this revolution through its "bourgeois" stage by creating an independent state, for three years CPU leaders had opposed that state, thereby fostering counterrevolution instead of socialism. Their internal party dictatorship, centralization, and reliance on Russian workers and bureaucrats had turned their Soviet Ukrainian republic into a "Russian [Rus. *Russkuiu*] occupation regime," alienated Ukrainians from socialism and their party, provoked a "bourgeois restoration," and ignited a national war between Ukraine and Russia. Only the UCP as an independent indigenous party could reverse these developments by establishing a soviet socialist republic independent of but allied to Soviet Russia.[72]

> The task of the international proletariat [the communist party] is to draw towards the communist revolution and the construction of a new society not only the advanced capitalist countries but also the less developed peoples of the colonies taking advantage of their national revolutions. To fulfill this task, it must take an active part in these revolutions and play the leading role in the perspective of the permanent revolution, preventing the national bourgeoisie from limiting them at the level of fulfilling demand of national liberation. It is necessary to continue the struggle through to the seizure of power and the installation of the dictatorship of the proletariat and, to lead the bourgeois democratic revolution to the end through the establishment of national states destined to join the universal network of international union of the emerging Soviet republics, based on the forces of local proletarian and working masses of each country, with the mutual aid of all the detachments of world revolution.

The UCP set out its position as follows in 1924: "The Ukrainian communist party is the party of the oppressed and colonized Ukrainian proletariat, called forth by life and social evolution to solve the colonial problem in the conditions that exist in Ukraine." This could only be done via the CI, and whoever opposed this opposed the CI.[73]

Ukrainian communists characterized Moscow's local agents as men who saw Ukraine from Moscow's point of view and who judged it from the perspective of the Russian Revolution instead of world revolution. Economic ties did not require political union; in any case, the war and revolution had destroyed those ties and it made no sense to try to use them to rejoin "old state formations."[74] Developing these ideas in a letter to Manuilsky in February 1920, Mazurenko explained that communists had to use nationalism in the interests of revolution just as they used the state – otherwise their enemies would exploit it. Mazurenko here anticipated Lenin's idea expressed five months later at the Second Comintern Conference:

> For us communists from colonies the paths and means required on a given territory [to rebuild] are more visible and obvious than they are for those who worked and work in the metropole. What is now happening in Russia

will also happen in England, the Balkans, Asia and elsewhere; Ukraine, Ireland, India, Macedonia, and on and on. Revolution there will have the nature of national economic liberation and the national movement there will be a revolutionary factor, if the party of the revolutionary proletariat can take it in hand and use it as it should be used.

Decentralizing the old imperial structures was as necessary as establishing a dictatorship of the proletariat on each given territory of each given nationality that would control the economic life of each given nationality. As a temporary expedient, former imperial economies had to be decentralized and placed in the hands of national states controlled by the local proletariats. This would ensure that "capitalists" could not use those states against the "proletariat" and that nationalism would not be used to "divide the proletariat." These national states could then begin to deal not only with chauvinist tendencies within the petite bourgeoisie but also with "that section of the proletariat that still suffers from it."[75]

Another detailed exposition of Ukrainian communist views was to be found in the "Thesis" of the April 1920 second UCP conference on national and colonial questions (see Appendix, Document 10, page 209). Unlike the Comintern's thesis, which focused on centralization and which cited the Russian experience as the model for dealing with national issues, the UCP thesis linked revolution and liberation with decentralization and condemned Russian Bolshevik principles as empty rhetoric. Written by Richytsky, it begins with the standard Leninist analysis of how the national bourgeoisie in colonies fighting against their imperialist rivals for a share of the market first uses its own population but then turns the struggle for an independent national state against the native proletariat and working masses. For the latter, national independence without the overthrow of the bourgeoisie and the dictatorship of labour only means a change in owners and imperial protectors. For the proletariat, freedom means freedom from both their own and foreign bourgeoisie. The thesis then asserts that an independent state is the only means through which oppressed nations and colonies can attain their political, cultural, and economic liberation. Communist parties are to ensure the ultimate creation of a voluntary union of all nations. Distinguishing between paternalistic-feudal and early-bourgeois societies, the thesis, echoing *The Communist Manifesto*, specifies that in the latter, the proletariat can fight their own bourgeoisie if "it forms itself as a nation organized within the national framework of its country and solves its national question from the perspective of taking the bourgeois democratic revolution to completion and then struggling to establish its dictatorship." The only way a former colony can be transformed into a soviet republic, equal in status to its former metropolitan centre, is if it is independent. Each national proletariat has to free the productive forces of its own country from dependency on the "artificial industrial and financial centers of the former metropolis" and control its own economy.

The "October Revolution," which took place in a "multinational colonial empire," was the first to place this historical national program before the proletariat, but "the Russian proletariat failed to rise to the occasion." Avoiding direct condemnation of Russian party leaders, Richytsky explained that it was the chauvinist and colonialist attitudes of the "Russian proletariat," which Lenin supposedly foresaw, that had turned Ukraine's class struggle into a nationalist war that only helped imperialist interventionists. "Soviet power in many former outlying regions (Ukraine, Turkestan, Belarus), was taken by colonialist, petite bourgeois, settler-peasant, bureaucrat, and Russian intellectual elements that exploited bolshevism for their own nationalist purposes." Terminating these nationalist relationships meant destroying "single and indivisible" Russia, the psychological notion that it comprised a "centre" with "regions," and, transforming what had been the empire into a union of independent, federated, united "Soviet Republics of the East." Such circumlocutions were necessary at the time to avoid arrest and dissolution of the UCP. For the Ukrainian proletariat, the national and colonial question involved terminating colonial ties with Russia and freeing its productive forces from dependency on the old centre. The Ukrainian proletariat had to be raised to the level of a national class, and Ukraine demanded the termination of all bureaucratic ties to Moscow.[76]

The question of development of soviet statehood in forms appropriate to the national specificities of various nations, [including use of] their languages in administration was decided, formally, by the ruling Russian Communist Party in all the former outlying regions of Russia. However, because elements of the russificatory petty bourgeoisie and intellectuals usurped soviet power thanks to the weakness and low level of class and cultural development of the proletariat and workers and, the separation of the workers aristocracy of the former non-state nations from the people because of russification, this issue is still far from resolved. The entire

[governmental] apparatus of the Ukr. RSR is filled with Russifying elements, its language is Russian, it even strongly opposes using Ukrainian,
assimilating even those few Ukrainian elements in it and thus, [the appa-
ratus], bureaucratically isolated by its desks from the masses, is objectively
becoming a tool of russification. That is why the call for Ukrainian as the
state language is and long will be actual, and it is the task of the Ukrainian
Communist Party to advocate it.[77]

In an open letter to "the provincial branch of the Russian Communist
Party that calls itself the Communist Party (Bolshevik) of Ukraine" in
the summer of 1920, Mazurenko and Richytsky reiterated their positions. They pointed out that the previous year they had not fought
"soviet power" but "the existing regime as an occupation regime."
The massive uprising had been provoked by faulty Bolshevik policies,
and they had attempted to wrest the justified anger from the hands
of "counter-revolutionary groups." We Ukrainians, they stressed, distinguished between the dictatorship of the proletariat and occupation.
Although they may have been guilty for their actions in the eyes of the
revolution, they were no more guilty than the "communists of Ukraine"
whose "russifying occupation policies in Ukraine demoralized the proletariat and drove the peasant masses to fight against our [CPU-led]
regime." Having learned from their mistakes, which had resulted in
the UNR and Whites taking over most of Ukraine, they were waiting
for the "communists in Ukraine" to draw similar conclusions and unite
with them in one Ukrainian party. They explained that Ukraine had to
have its own Red Army allied with but separate from the Russian Army
and, that only an independent Soviet Ukraine could enter a Union with
Soviet Russia. Independence, they stressed, was not an end but the best
means of building socialism.[78]

In a July 1920 declaration to the Comintern, the UCP stressed that
Russian Bolshevik promises about language-use autonomy and soviet
rather than Revkom rule had been made under duress. They had been
forgotten as soon as convenient, and because of such policy "zigzags,"
no one believed any declarations any more. The Red Army, labelled
"organized foreign (Russian) military forces," had swept through
Ukraine "as if it were a foreign country." Russian Bolsheviks who dismissed everything Ukrainian as "counter-revolutionary," meanwhile,
were fanning popular resistance and turning what should have been a
class war into a national war that was "restoring the Russian empire."
The authors quoted a local Bolshevik village activist who purportedly

said: "Our work among Ukrainians is like that among Turks and Arabs etc."[79]

The situation in ministries was described in a letter of resignation sent by the UCP Minister of Housing and his assistant in August 1920.[80] Their ministry, like the rest, was simply a branch of the Russian party; it could do nothing without instructions from Moscow, and its officials totally ignored them. "The administrative division of Ukraine exists only for the eyes of the 'citizen idiot [hlupaka].'" Their department had been formally established in December 1919 and thus had existed for six months previous to their arrival in June 1920, yet it had no staff and no offices.

A major statistics-based study by Vasyl Mazurenko in 1921 criticized Bolshevik economic centralization and demonstrated what Miliutin had argued three years earlier: Russia could exist economically without Ukraine, and if Ukraine needed manufactured imports from Russia, then it was the classic result of decades of colonialist imperialism. Nothing Ukraine needed justified continued political dependency, for such needs could be met by developing manufacturing in Ukraine. Mazurenko observed that it was more rational for Ukraine to freely trade for what it needed with advanced developed countries than to force it to trade with technologically backward Russia. If for the moment it could trade only with Russia and other soviet countries, then it had to be as an equal and not as a dependency. Noting how Russian soviet publications referred to Ukraine and Poland as "western borderlands," he asked why the Foreign Ministry published books condemning England's exploitation of India while, simultaneously, the Trade and Economics Ministry published articles about "reuniting the manufacturing capacity of united Russia." Russians who talked about "reuniting our borderlands" so as to "recreate the industry of united Russia," were no different from those English who thought in terms of "our inseparable borderland India" and who contended that England would die without its colonies. Russia, if not most of the world, had been dependent on German chemicals. Did this mean that Russia and the world had to be politically subject to Germany? Why should Ukraine be dependent on Russia for wood products if the Baltic countries and Poland produced more wood products than Russia?[81] Systematically comparing production figures, Mazurenko argued that not just Russia but world communism as a whole would benefit if Russia began to build its economy around its own resources and not those of the old empire. Even in coal production, Russia could do without Ukraine

– as Miliutin had noted. The International had to be told: "Save communism from Muscovite imperialism!" From a socialist perspective, there was no economic rationale for centralization. It led to power for Moscow and dependency and exploitation for non-Russian republics. Why, he asked, was it acceptable for Russian planners and economists to think about making Russia maximally independent of materials and production from non-Russian areas while, simultaneously, endeavouring to make the latter dependent on Russian production? "From where have such imperialist ambitions on Ukraine appeared among our Russian comrades?", asked Mazurenko. He placed the blame on those non-party experts who sympathized with the new regime, hoping it would restore their empire. He hoped this "un-thought-out," very non-communist Muscovite attempt to rule new colonies would soon end, and he expressed absolute opposition to Ukrainian subordination to Russia.

Factories producing goods in Russia from raw materials imported from Ukraine did constitute an economic system, but it was one like that of metropole and exploited colony. Russian comrades who were using this kind of argument to justify Indian independence, should also be using it to justify Ukrainian independence, for only through independence would Ukraine increase its industrial power. Ukraine must have no more and no less independence than would a soviet Germany or Italy or Persia or Russia. Could anyone even imagine, he wondered, technologically backward Russia commanding and exploiting financially and administratively the industry of a soviet Germany as it did Ukrainian industry?[82]

Similar ideas were included in the UCP declaration to the Second Ukrainian Conference of poor peasant committees in February 1922:

A key reason why revolutionary forces are weak and soviet power retreated in the direction of capitalism [NEP] is the continuing repression during the entire course of the revolution of the border-colonies by ruling Russian centres, and the politics of "reuniting Russia" that is done to buy bourgeois groups for soviet power, and results in the diversion of productive and revolutionary forces to occupy the 'borderlands" and national struggles that even place the proletariat at the service of the "patriotic" interests of the petite bourgeoisie.

The remedy included dismantling the centralized bureaucratic system of economic dependency that had subordinated Ukraine to Moscow, interfered with Ukraine's economic development, and taken power from the workers and given it to the bourgeoisie. It was also necessary to end the chauvinist opposition of Ukraine's urban Russians to the cultural rebirth of the Ukrainian working people.[83]

Ukrainian left SD, "federalist," and left SR critiques of Bolshevism often coincided. In June 1919, during discussions about the political structure of the future socialist state, SR Oleksandr Shumsky explained that it had to be applicable on a world level. For that reason, a unification of soviet republics could not be imagined as merely a unification of the old Russian empire. The notion that Ukraine had to remain united with Bolshevik Russia because it had been tied economically to tsarist Russia, and that there would be time to worry about Germany and Hungary later, was current in party circles, Shumsky complained. But such ideas only reflected Menshevik Black Hundred intolerance and were "absolutely impermissible" for communists. That kind of patriotism, he lamented, "is deeply imbedded in our ranks." To try and restore economic ties destroyed by the revolution was a Kadet project, and by attempting it, the Bolsheviks were only creating opposition to themselves. To make a true socialist union possible, Bolsheviks had to dispense with two preconceptions: first, that "non-state" nations were fated to disappear; and second, that everything had to be centralized in Moscow. A Russian *sovnarkom* and an international *sovnarkom* were two different things. The collapse of empires had produced new countries, Ukraine was among them, and if the Bolsheviks centralized too quickly they would provoke resistance and conflict. Culture, by definition, was national, and it was essential to allow full national cultural development of the sort that the old empires did not allow. A highly developed national culture would bring in its wake a high level of class consciousness.[84]

In 1919, Hryhory Hrinko argued that instead of focusing resources on increasing its own industrial potential, Russia had expended them on a territorial expansion that would destroy Soviet power. Because the proletariat had taken power and the form of economic development had changed, Ukraine's role in the old empire as a supplier of raw materials should change. In the new socialist order, "wise policies" would ensure that local manufacturing developed. As had happened everywhere else in the world, revolution had disintegrated the old Russian empire into separate countries with separate economies. Those economies had to be run by each of the new proletarian countries and only coordinated by a confederated central unit. The centralized Bolshevik system, as it existed, with its more than 25,000 employees, was unable to do what it was supposed to. It was harder to destroy old imperial ties and the old habit of seeing uniformity where there was diversity, than it was to destroy the machinery of state. Under the empire, a strong Ukrainian proletariat had not emerged, but this did not mean that Ukraine needed the "military help of the Russian proletariat." It *did* mean there was no national proletariat because resources were not locally processed, because it was in the interests of the British and Russian markets to export those resources as raw materials. Thus, Ukraine was a "colony" of Russian and international capital. This was a "mistake" of capitalism that "the proletariat" had to overcome by establishing local processing and manufacturing, which would inevitably create a Ukrainian proletariat. If the Russian proletariat repeated this "capitalist mistake" and continued its colonialist policies, it would drive Ukraine back into capitalist hands.[85] The UNR was strong because it reflected the national reality that the "organization of proletarian power" had ignored. The UNR was allowing itself to be used by "world capitalism" against the "world revolution," and this would continue for as long the Russian Bolsheviks persisted in basing themselves solely on a Russified urban petite bourgeoisie that was oblivious to Ukrainian rural workers. Because the Russian proletariat did not have to deal with national oppression, it had been able to proceed directly with economic matters after taking power. The Ukrainians could not do so and thus were moving more slowly. That is why the Russian revolution was different from the Ukrainian one and why in Ukraine local Bolsheviks were only a branch of the Russian party and not the communist party of the Ukrainian masses. To triumph in Ukraine, Ukrainian communists argued, they had to create a link between the revolution and the people.[86]

Ukrainian federalist Bolshevik Mykhailo Poloz, in Moscow for the First Comintern Congress in 1919, reported that Russians there, including Lenin, knew little about Ukraine. More ominously, unlike the western European delegates, who thought of the revolution as something to be exported to Europe, Russians saw it in narrow Russian terms. Western European communists, moreover, unlike Russians, did not see Ukraine as "theirs."[87] Poloz wrote to Stalin in late 1919 that centralizing policies could be imposed in Ukraine only with the assistance of a "foreign armed power." His colleague, Hryhory Klunny, explained to Lenin in late 1919 that what had happened in Ukraine that year was as if experienced Russian chauvinists preparing counter-revolution were in charge of soviet power there.[88] Similar issues were summarized in a report by the Ukrainian group attached to the RCP's Moscow organization. After explaining Ukraine's historical differences from Russia, they demanded a Ukrainian communist centre in Ukraine with its own independent government bureaucracy. *A priori* assumptions about Ukraine as a petite bourgeois country had led to politics "that can only be classified as colonialist" and given credence to claims that they were mere "Red imperialism." They agreed to unity between Russia and Ukraine, but they stipulated that this unity was not be a continuation of the relations developed under the autocratic Russian empire.[89]

In the wake of Lenin's December 1919 "Letter to Ukrainian Workers," Borotbists reminded their Russian comrades in Ukraine that Lenin had earlier instructed them to defer to themselves. As of January 1920, they wrote, the total centralization of the economy under Moscow ministries, whose branches in Ukraine worked independently of the Ukrainian *Revkom*, was simply an expression of Russian nationalism; the situation would improve if communists deferred to Ukrainians as Lenin had instructed. Not to do so would drive Ukrainians away from Soviet power. In practice, wrote an author in Poltava, the leadership was acting as if the old empire's borders had remained untouched by events. This threatened Ukraine economically because it meant a renewal of colonial status as a supplier of raw materials to Russia. The principal aim of proletarian power in Ukraine was to economically strengthen the Ukrainian proletariat, and this required separate economic ministries to develop Ukraine's manufacturing capacity. Only then could there be a "brotherly" exchange of goods between two equal republics. If the "Russian communists" were to do otherwise, they would be acting like "Muscovite boyars."[90] At the end of that year, ex-SR CPU member Vasyl Blakytny wrote an extended critique of the CPU for its upcoming Fifth Congress. He characterized the party as divided into "colonialist" and "autonomist" wings between which members had to choose in order to restore and reform the party. The former consisted of Russified "opportunistic petite bourgeoisie" and "carpetbaggers [*torbarskii elementy*]" who were alien to Ukraine and its needs (see Appendix, Document 13, page 216).

Ukrainians and the Comintern

The UCP and the Borotbists both claimed to be the party of the Ukrainian proletariat, just as the RCP was of the Russian proletariat. They argued that a Ukrainian party could be linked to the Russian party only through the Comintern and was not to be a Russian party affiliate like the CPU.[91] Both applied to Ukraine Lenin's logic as expressed in his July 1920 speech to the Communist International in which he noted that in colonies, organizational party work and contacts with the Comintern belonged to the proletariat and workers of the colony. The Borotbists submitted a memorandum and membership request to the Comintern in 1919. It noted how Ukraine differed from Russia, how the Bolsheviks ignored those differences, and how, by imposing Russian domination on Ukraine, they threatened the success of the revolution. But unlike the UCP, the Borotbist document did not condemn Bolshevik rule as an "occupation" that had turned a class war into a national war and reimposed imperial rule – although such a view did figure among party members (see Appendix, Document 12, page 214). The document did not use the terms "Russian imperialism" or "colonialism," nor did it interpret Ukrainian national liberation as a consequence of world capitalism. It instead diplomatically noted the circumstances that had led to "the spread of the geographical base of the revolution," to the "historically unavoidable" construction of soviet power in Ukraine as an occupation, and to "the temporary organization of the Russian communist party in Ukraine which was, and essentially is, the CPU." According to the authors, the "evolution of the communist revolution in Ukraine" would result in a single communist centre separate from the Russian one.[92]

The RCP Central Committee instructed Comintern officials to reject both applications – on 29 November in the case of the Borotbists. Two weeks later, Lenin and Trotsky ordered the CPU to align with the Borotbist party while simultaneously deciding to dissolve it. [93] Then, in December 1919, they performed a charade that involved meeting the Borotbists to discuss their CI application. The meeting took place while White armies were being repulsed on all fronts. The Bolsheviks were concerned about keeping the Borotbists separate from CPU federalists, who had just issued a statement calling for an alliance with the Borotbists. The Borotbists, for their part, were trying to create a Ukrainian Red Army from Ukrainian anti-Denikin partisan units, and Zatonsky had informed the Kremlin that he feared they would soon declare an independent soviet Ukraine – a move that would win them the support of the western Ukrainian Galician Army (which had recently broken with Petliura) as well as pro-Bolshevik Ukrainians.[94] Rakovskii was the main representative of the CPU, and Hrinko of the Borotbists; Zinoviev chaired. Since the Politburo had already decided to dissolve the party, reject its application, and "carefully prepare plans to fuse [*sliianiia*] Ukraine with Russia," the meeting was pointless – something the Ukrainians did not know, for those resolutions were secret.[95] The meeting's unpublished minutes deserve attention, because they illustrate the differences between Russian and Ukrainian communists.

Both sides agreed that each country could have only one party, but arguably, the Ukrainians were at a disadvantage from the beginning because they implicitly accepted the legitimacy of the Ukrainian SSR as a "country." Either they did not know that it was founded on nothing more than Stalin's instruction to Piatakov in November 1918, or, they thought that by granting this point they would improve their bargaining position. Theoretically, the Borotbists could have adopted the same position as the Bolsheviks had towards the Rada in 1917, when they claimed that they and not the Rada really represented Ukraine. That is, the Borotbists could have claimed that they, and not the CPU, were the legitimate representatives of the Ukrainian republic. Hrinko argued that Ukraine had to have a separate party because the Russian centre, ignorant of Ukrainian conditions, could not resolve Ukrainian issues and therefore had to base itself on Russian immigrants and resort to military invasion and occupation. As a distinct cultural and economic unit, Ukraine had to have its own army and ministries. The desire for independence was not merely "petite bourgeoisie leftovers" but a powerful force that if ignored would be exploited by the UNR. Why the fiction of a Ukrainian government that had no military or economic centre, nor government administration? Because local Bolsheviks relied on Russia and ignored all of the problems related to communist revolution in Ukraine; the result had been, as experience showed, disaster.[96] The Ukrainians had welcomed Bolshevik assistance in defeating Denikin; but, they stressed, that victory had prepared the ground for a *de facto* policy of occupation and "colonialism," given that in the wake of the army, requisitioning squads had taken more from the poor peasants than from the rich and that too many people, out of intellectual inertia, had renewed their illusions about "old regime Russia." This had happened in 1917 and was happening again. They then cited Rakovskii against himself: "We have a dictatorship of Russian culture in Ukraine that we must reckon with." Hrinko closed the first day's discussions by noting that only 12 per cent of Ukraine's population self-identified as Russians but that centuries of Russification via governmental officials and the media meant that declarations about the equal status of Ukraine with Russia would remain just that – declarations.[97]

In their reply, Rakovskii and Stanislav Kossior, a Russified Polish Jew who had grown up in the Donbass, made it clear that Lenin's remark about "deferring" to their Ukrainian comrades did not encompass the possibility of an independent Ukrainian party. The two men ignored issues of empire and colony and sought to discredit the Borotbist demand for a separate Ukrainian party centre by classifying it as merely a "formal organizational-associational" matter unrelated to the more important issue of class. That is, the Borotbists were based on the peasants, and that was "dangerous," whereas the Bolsheviks were based on factory workers. They either did not know, or they ignored the fact, that as of that month, at least 22 per cent of RCP members were peasants and 30 per cent were government office workers. Nine months earlier, Zinoviev had noted at the Eighth RCP Congress that government office workers were emerging as the dominant group.[98] Rakovskii was using "Ukrainian" in the territorial sense when he claimed that the Bolsheviks were not a "Russian" party in Ukraine because they were based on the "Ukrainian proletariat" in the southeast. He accused the Borotbists of being no different from UNR leaders because they were concerned only about "protectionism" and about neutralizing Russification. Kossior added that this class essence had not been changed by the national factor. "The proletariat is ours … The revolution can triumph only if it conquers the peasants." Without explaining how or why, he asserted that the basic issue in Ukraine was "the absolute correspondence of the interests of workers in Russia and Ukraine." The Bolsheviks supported an independent Ukraine, but in light of the imperialist threat, there had to be a centralized union for as long as necessary, and what was needed was discussions not about how to develop Ukraine's productive forces, but rather about how to secure the dictatorship of the proletariat – and that was to be accomplished by Russia and its Red Army. Arguments within the Comintern about separate representation for a separate republic might perhaps be conducted later, but, Rakovskii added, such a notion was "lost in romanticism." To open those arguments now would mean ignoring the immediate need for centralization in the face of Denikin and Entente imperialism. "If Russia falls the [Soviet] Ukrainian republic cannot exist," he declared. In his view, the only mistake the Bolsheviks had made was to overestimate the peasants' revolutionary potential. If, as the Borotbists demanded, Ukraine achieved the same relationship to Russia as Hungary, it would mean "the end of the revolution." But he did not explain why.[99]

The only error that Rakovskii conceded was that his government had allowed the Ukrainians freedom to criticize their policy in the press. "I have to state that our politics from the moment we came to Ukraine [*sic*] until now were completely restrained and far from any kind of [Russian] nationalism." His remarks reflected the general view of the Bolshevik leaders that the "national question" involved only language and culture – not party organization, the economy, or the army, areas where centralization was beyond discussion. The key problem, he maintained, was that the 20,000 Ukrainian teachers in the Ukrainian Teachers Association (*spilka*) were all "nationalists" and pro-UNR. Especially nefarious were those from western Ukraine, who were "infected with fanaticism." The reality was, he continued, that Ukrainian-born communists in cities were Russian-speaking and that Russian was the language of most of the proletariat as well as the language of communism. This meant that if Ukrainian, the language of the peasants, were made the official language as demanded by the Ukrainians, a "reactionary class" would establish a dictatorship over the "progressive" workers. Thus, the only thing the Bolsheviks could do was to use Ukrainian to spread communism in the villages. By the same logic, he refused equal representation for the Ukrainians in Ukraine's Revkom. There was to be no discussion on this point. "We [Russian Bolsheviks] are the party of the proletarian dictatorship in Ukraine." Rakovskii's rebuttal of the Borotbists' demands at this meeting did not reflect the views about Ukraine he had expressed to Lenin the week before, when he admitted that his government had made serious mistakes in its economic, land, and military policies: "To deny the ethnic and state distinctions of Ukraine, to persecute Ukrainian language use and support a *Russian* [*russkii; sic*] rather than a communist-proletarian dictatorship [there] ... will result in even greater national animosity ... The tendency to fuse Ukraine and Russia is a hold-over of Russian bourgeois imperialist psychology."[100]

Zinoviev supported Rakovskii and opposed any "sovereign communist centre in Ukraine." He said that using the term "occupation" to refer to the re-establishment of Bolshevik rule after Denikin's defeat – something for which all "internationalists" had to be grateful – was uncalled for. The UNR, moreover, had nothing to do with independence and merely reflected the local petite bourgeoisie's wish to own land. He agreed that Russian comrades had to tolerate Ukraine, but, he emphasized, the Russian proletariat was not to blame for three hundred years of tsarist rule. Ukraine was not Finland, he continued, because it was tightly bound economically to Russia, and the Finns as a group hated the Russians much more than did the Ukrainians – as shown by their total boycott of the Duma elections. Nor did the Finns demand a separate communist centre from Moscow. In the future, in theory, there might be talk about decentralization, but for the present, absolute centralization was imperative.[101]

When on 17 January Zinoviev reported to the Politburo that he had voted against the Borotbists' CI application, he did not cite any of the above arguments. That same day he had received a telegram from Rakovskii with "new facts" that showed the Borotbists were organizing their own military forces and negotiating with the UNR. These he labelled "counter-revolutionary acts." The CPU, meanwhile, also on 17 January, sent the CI a note condemning the Borotbists and including Rakovskii's information. On 5 February another meeting was called to discuss terms of cooperation, with Rakovskii and Boris Sapronov on one side and Poloz, Blakytny, and Kovaliv on the other. In line with his earlier remarks, Rakovskii dismissed Ukrainian demands for separate ministries and a separate army as "nationalist, counter-revolutionary and anarchic partisan-style behaviour." Because the UNR, too, had condemned Bolshevik policy as occupation and robbery, Rakovskii accused the Ukrainian Bolsheviks of being like them. Poloz dismissed these accusations and blamed Rakovskii, not Lenin, for establishing the "dictatorship of the Russian proletariat in Ukraine." He stated that his party was enrolling larger numbers of urban proletariat, including Russians who were disillusioned with the Bolsheviks. The talks closed inconclusively with a call for another committee to review the issues again.[102]

In late January, the Borotbists learned that almost all of the partisan forces from which they had hoped to create a Ukrainian Red Army had either deserted, joined the UNR, or been forcibly incorporated into the Red Army. Then on 11 February, using a draft composed by Lenin and Zinoviev, the CPU again condemned the Borotbists in words that would later be included in the official CI declaration about them:

"Under the guise of fighting for Ukrainian independence, which found its [true] expression in the Ukrainian Soviet state, the Borotbists actively oppose the need for soviet and central economic administrative bureaucracies [*apparaty*] serving the interests of both countries. They then create economic chaos which threatens to undermine all Ukraine's and Russians' efforts to build the economy." [103]

As a consequence, on 28 February, Hrinko informed Moscow that the Borotbists had agreed to dissolve and accept "complete subordination" (*polnoe podchnineniia*). The Politburo immediately tried to stop publication of the above CI decree. The message did not reach the editors in time; on 29 February, Kharkiv's *Kommunist* did publish it. Besides the ideas in the CPU declaration, the Comintern decree stated: "ECCI expects that between those republics where soviet power triumphs the strongest possible brotherly ties should exist." A few days later, the Russian party sent 200,000 roubles to the Borotbists, and on 8 March, it allotted two Borotbists seats on the CPU Politburo. In subsequent speeches and articles about the union in Bolshevik Ukraine, there was no mention of the earlier condemnation, the subordination, or the money.[104]

In late 1924 the UCP applied again to the CI. In two letters, they pinpointed the key organizational issue between themselves and the RCP. In the first, they stated that they were being ignored because the Russian party controlled the CI. This would prevent communists from learning from problems in the old Russian empire that had parallels elsewhere in the world. "Among these we include, in part, all colonial issues presented to the proletariat by the earlier development of Russian imperialism and [its] old colonial empire." The most important of these was the existence of two parties in one country, of which one was a branch of another based in the former imperial power. Ukraine remained an oppressed colony after the revolution they wrote. This was because the Russian party, through the NEP, had made the Russian and Russified petite bourgeoisie more powerful and influential both in the party and in government. Regardless of the concessions announced by the Twelfth RCP Congress, Ukraine remained subordinated to Moscow's central administrative apparatus, "which was in the hands of non-proletarian bureaucrat elements." Just because the RCP had a certain status because it was in power, the second letter explained, did not guarantee it would not be "subjective" on matters that "by force of historical tradition" it considered internal, related to communist movements in countries "earlier subject to the Russian imperialism in its colonies, and in relation to which the normal principles of a united workers movement are displaced by a unity fetish of a specific organizational sort." This attitude was leading to many problems in workers' movements in soviet republics – problems of international significance – which were not being examined by an international communist organization. In particular, the issue of two communist parties existing in one country remained unresolved and "covered up by the single party organizational form of the RCP." Other problems included "all colonial issues placed before the proletariat [that was] oppressed by the development of Russian imperialism and [its] former colonial empire."[105] The CPU's condemnation of the UCP, sent to the Comintern that same year, did not deal with the accusations of neocolonialism, domination, or exploitation except for fleeting mention of "unfounded claims of occupation." It labelled the UCP condemnation of Ukraine's exploitation as "counter-revolutionary demagogy," and it was signed by three of Ukraine's "federalist" Bolsheviks. This CPU condemnation presumably represented a public show of loyalty on the part of its signatories in return for the promises of the Twelfth Congress. It claimed that Lenin's concessions eventually would solve all problems.[106]

Conclusion

A communist is a Marxist internationalist, but Marxism must take on a national form before it can be applied.

Mao Tse Tung, 1938

In 1791 the Girondists spread their ideals and institutions by war. Ignoring Robespierre's opposition to "armed missionaries" exporting revolutionary principles, they annexed Belgium, Savoy, and the Rhineland. By forcing their non-French subjects to copy their models, the French revolutionaries provoked resistance. Eventually, their allies began to regard what they had thought was French liberation as imperialist annexation. Despite their initial opposition to expansionist war, the Jacobins later continued it. The emergency measures they introduced brought military victory but nullified their declarations about rights. By 1815 few Europeans would have agreed with Thomas Jefferson's remark that educated men had two native countries – one of them France. For all their knowledge of the French Revolution, Bolshevik leaders repeated their precursors' errors when they used the language of republican liberty to justify invasion, annexation, and exploitation.[1] Bukharin in 1920 formulated a "theory of the offensive" and a "right of red intervention" that justified spreading the revolution by armed force. He had Poland and Germany in mind – countries that, had they taken them, the Bolsheviks would probably not have reduced to the status of Soviet Ukraine. Nevertheless, as noted in chapter 2, other leaders who disassociated themselves from his theory realized that they had incorporated Ukraine by armed conquest.

Beneath the Bolsheviks' language of liberty lay assumptions and preconceptions that can as often be traced back to imperialist Russian slavophiles as to Marx and Engels. Important as well was the Enlightenment proposition that the identities and cultures of "small peoples" were transitory and incidental – suited perhaps to spiritual matters but not to economic ones, and thus with no place in the future rational universal industrial civilization. Such notions easily led to the belief that only a successful ruling-class indoctrination of nationalism could override a supposedly "natural" class consciousness of workers. Most Bolsheviks failed to appreciate or even realize how the nationalism of the ruling Russian nationality, to which they paid little heed, could transform itself into a powerful "plebian imperialism." They, like Russian slavophiles, would have agreed with Pushkin, who in his "To the Calumniators of Russia" (1831) wrote that the Slavs would ultimately disappear into one Russian sea. The Bolsheviks, like their SD comrades in other imperial nations, identified the cosmopolitan, supposedly nonnational future with their ruling nation. With few exceptions, Russian Bolsheviks regarded non-Russian "peasant languages" much as did Russian monarchists and liberals – as unsuitable for modern urban industrial life. Russians left, right, and centre claimed that imperial economic integration made the territorial dissolution of the imperial space impossible, blithely ignoring that conscious political decisions had created that integration to begin with. Lenin's "right of national self-determination," which tolerated temporary political secession from metropoles, was not much different from Lloyd George's policy of saving empire by granting autonomy. Party leaders assumed that centralization based on metropolitan parties would nullify any future political federalism within former imperial spaces. Bolshevik leaders who were explicit about reintegrating the Russian empire after a revolution, and who once in power denied separate representation for an independent Ukrainian communist party in the Comintern, did not consistently apply the same criteria to other empires. They did not regard Russia as an empire from which non-Russians could separate to form their own "bourgeois" and/or socialist states – as could Indians, or Irish, or Chinese, or Algerians. They also allowed communist parties from colonies that existed separately from their imperial metropole parties to be independent members of the Comintern. Ukrainian communists attributed such double standards to the imperialist nature of Russian communism. If in other empires radical socialists could fight for national independence alongside a "revolutionary bourgeoisie" as a prelude to the revolutionary socialist order, then why, they asked, could Ukrainian radical socialists in the Russian empire not do the same?

With few exceptions, Russian and Russified Bolsheviks before 1917 considered "Russia" a national state with minorities rather than an empire with colonies, and they discounted the potential of anti-imperial nationalist sentiment as a revolutionary force. The urban Russians and culturally Russified non Russians who comprised the absolute majority of party members in Ukrainian lands did not represent, and were not representatives of, an oppressed nationality. Like most socialists belonging to or identifying with ruling nations, Russian and Russified socialists, to a greater or lesser degree, shared the imperialist prejudices of their ruling class, which coincided with the abstract cosmopolitanism of the younger Marx. As noted, the 1907 Socialist International Congress only narrowly avoided supporting a "socialist colonial policy." The 1910 Copenhagen Congress of the Second International, dominated by members from imperial powers, condemned the Czechs for demanding unions separate from the imperial Austrian ones. English and English cultural nationalism dominated the British labour and radical movements, with the result that English liberals, but not English socialists, supported Irish nationalists. At the First International Congress, one English delegate explained that an independent Ireland, owing to its geographical position, would threaten the security of England by inviting a French occupation. Another, critical of Marx's support for Ireland, protested that "Ireland is an integral part of the British Empire." British Marxists were English and Protestant. They long ignored the fact that the labour movement in the British Isles had started in Scotland and that the Scots and Irish were more radical than the English. For English socialists, English oppression in Ireland would be ended by English Socialists, not by an independent Irish Socialist Republican Party. This imperialist superiority also affected English socialists' relations with India. Before 1914, Spain's socialists had reconciled themselves to the loss of an empire that had collapsed during the Spanish-American War. But they still regarded Catalonia and the Basque country as rightfully Spanish. French Marxists, who nominally sympathized with France's imperial subjects, condemned Flamands, Catalans, and Basques. Japan's communists, exceptionally, made no claims on their empire's territories. Their 1921 program stated that the party would do everything possible to "liberate Korea" together with the Korean party; it also called for a common struggle with Korean patriots despite their "bourgeois ideological and nationalist preconceptions." "This is necessary not only for the Korean revolution to triumph, but to win Korean patriots to our communist principles." Only in 1928, on the instructions of the Communist International, was the Korean party merged into the Japanese party.[2]

The Russian urban settler-colonist community from which almost all of Ukraine's Bolsheviks emerged did not evolve a creole-separatist nationalism – although Artem might have become a Ukrainian creole-Russian equivalent of Simon Bolivar in the short-lived Krivoi-Rog republic. Some of Ukraine's Russians tolerated Ukrainian aspirations after 1917, but most of that community, regardless of political sympathies, identified with the imperial metropole and shared tsarist myths about Little Russian–Russian "ethnic unity." In any case, supported primarily by Ukraine's settler-colonist Russian and Russified professional white- and blue-collar workers, Ukraine's Bolsheviks were too few and too isolated from the Ukrainian majority to hold power by themselves. Without Russian troops, they would have gone the way of their Finnish and Polish counterparts – to exile in Moscow.[3] Backed by the Russian Red Army, the CPU did retain power and built the new Bolshevik order on the Russian and Russified urban minority that had not fled with the Whites. That minority might not have faced the same prospects as had the Germans in Hungary – who, Engels explained, "persist in retaining an absurd nationality in the middle of a foreign country" – even had Ukraine been independent. But they did face the unwelcome prospect after 1923 of having to learn a "peasant dialect" to get jobs or make careers in Soviet Ukraine. These people identified "Ukrainian" with "bourgeois" and "peasant-kulak" and "Bolshevik" with "Russian." They resisted indigenization, and it was they who constituted the social base of the CPU. They would have agreed with Maxim Gorky, who in 1926 refused to permit Ukrainian translations of his works. He was "amazed" how some people were trying to turn a "dialect" into a "language" and thereby "oppressing" local Russians.[4] Whether he also thought that English, Japanese, French, or whites in Africa would be "oppressed" if they had to learn Gaelic, Korean, Arabic, or Swahili or Bantu, is unknown.

Bolshevism was a Russian version of European social-democratic Marxism. Its leaders were not as forthcoming about the Russian nature of their Marxism during their early years in power, as was Mao about the Chinese nature of his Marxism. Only in 1930 did Stalin begin praising the "Russian working class;" three years later he was bestowing that praise on the "Russian [*Russkaia*] nation."[5] From the Bolshevik perspective, retaining imperial Russian frontiers was not "imperialist," but dismantling them was "nationalist" – a Russocentric distinction they shared with tsarist apologists like Shchegolev. Lenin was flexible, however. In December 1917 and again in December 1918 he pondered for a few weeks treaties with a socialist or "bourgeois" Ukraine like those he had signed with Finland, Estonia, Poland, and, for a time, Georgia. In Central Asia he had sided for a time with Muslim radicals against the local settler-Russians. It was the initiatives of Ukraine's left-ist Bolsheviks rather than Lenin's Marxist ideals or imperialist Russian preconceptions that swayed him to invade and annex Ukraine.

At the time, many believed Bolshevik propaganda because of the secrecy surrounding so many of their decisions concerning subordination and ruthless centralized extraction. This might explain why Ukrainian Marxists focused their condemnations on local agents; doing so would not alienate potential supporters of a Soviet Ukraine, who were more likely to believe that the agents, rather than the central ruler, were responsible for the evils they observed. The 1917 decree appointing Ordzhonikidze plenipotentiary, for instance, was not published until 1945. The instructions in the 1919 Ukrainian–Russian treaty that tightened centralization were also secret. Lenin specifically instructed his subordinates that June to include Ukraine's Food Supply Commissariat among the ministries subject to Moscow but to keep that subordination secret. He instructed his secretary to encipher the phrase in the telegram giving this instruction. Five months later, in another decree marked "not to be published," this instruction was repeated and applied not to "Ukraine" or "Lithuania" but to "all regions on the southern and western borders of the RSFSR liberated from occupation." Secret also were the resolutions of April and November 1919 specifying that Russia and Ukraine were to be "joined."[6]

Some CPU members viewed Bolshevik rule in Ukraine as justifiably renewed Russian rule; others justified centralization and Russian domination in determinist Marxist terms – imperial economic integration had created a large economic unit that was "progressive" and could not be dismantled. Bolsheviks did not apply that reasoning, however, to Poland, Estonia, or Finland. Nor did they claim openly that the economic integration of any other empire meant that secession from those empires would also only be temporary. Nor did Bolsheviks consistently apply Lenin's idea that the Russian empire could have only one legitimate social democratic and, later, communist party, to other empires whose colonial dependencies had parties independent of

their central metropolitan parties. Russian Bolsheviks did not envisage incorporating Communist Hungary and its party into the RSFSR
and RCP as they had incorporated Ukraine and its CPU. As noted in
chapter 2, Rakovskii expressly dismissed the idea that Soviet Ukraine
could have the same status as Soviet Hungary in July 1919, claiming
that a supposed "natural solidarity" formed by "centuries of common
struggle" made it impossible. Such thinking could justify the ongoing
subordination of any periphery to any imperial metropole, but as Russians and Russified Bolsheviks applied it only to Ukraine, Ukrainian
Marxists considered them Red imperialists. Accordingly, when Bolsheviks dismissed Wilson's national self-determination as a sham because
it left Entente empires untouched, Ukrainian Marxists considered this
hypocrisy. The pot was calling the kettle black. "When one examines
the spread of Soviet Russia and the practice of self-determination ... it
is very difficult to see to what extent your self-determination, Comrade
Lenin, differs from that of Woodrow Wilson," wrote Shakhrai.[7] That
Russian Bolsheviks worked through a locally based ethnically Russian
faction of their party in Ukraine's civil war did not change the fact that
they had invaded a foreign country.

Soon after they took power, Bolshevik leaders began applying Rous-
seau's dictum about forcing men to be free. Those opposed began
defecting from and condemning the Bolsheviks' experiment after they
dissolved the constituent assembly in January 1918. Ukrainian and
Muslim Marxists were among these early critics, but their condemnations of Bolshevik rule as renewed imperial Russian domination were
little known outside Ukraine – one key reason being that Ukrainian
Marxists published little in German, French, or English. Their ideas,
nonetheless, deserve the same attention today from historians, and
from leftists in general, as do those of the "council communists," of
Victor Serge, and of Asian Marxists. The fundamental Ukrainian position was that a Soviet Ukraine with its own party had to be as independent of its former metropole as other former dependencies were to be
independent of their former ruling imperial powers – a principle recognized by the Bolsheviks with regard to all empires other than the Russian. Ukrainian Marxists invoked imperialist attitudes to explain why
Russian communists did not leave Ukrainians to determine their own
fate, as they had Poland, Finland, Estonia, and Communist Hungary.

Ukrainian Marxists responding to Bolshevik condemnation of the
Rada summarized their position by declaring that it was not for Russian
Bolsheviks but rather for the Ukrainian working people to decide when

to re-elect and replace the Rada with soviet power. They accused Bolshevik leaders, and implicitly Lenin, of committing a colossal blunder in December 1918 when they did not instruct their centralist Russian-dominated CPU to unite with Ukrainian left SRs and SDs into a single communist party to lead the national liberation struggle and establish independence. The result would have been a federation of two soviet republics with their own parties and armies at peace with each other. Instead, the Red Army attacked Ukraine in support of the CPU and turned a class-based civil war into a horrific three-year national war between Russia and Ukraine. The refusal to realize that Ukraine was not Russia, observed a Ukrainian left SR, "was disgusting, infuriating, and unacceptable because it was directed first and foremost against the very existence as such of a Ukrainian revolutionary democracy, sovereign and independent of the Russian." In February 1919, Ukrainian-left SDs observed that they were happy to learn from the Bolsheviks: "But we do not recognize that Moscow will make a socialist revolution for Ukraine."[8]

Knowing that Lenin in *Imperialism* had included the need for resources as a cause of imperialism, Ukrainian Marxists used terms like "Russian colonialism," "proletarian imperialism," and "communist imperialism" to describe Moscow's extractive policies in Ukraine. Given, however, that Russia had the resources it needed and the Bolsheviks had no economic reason to invade, nor to exploit Ukraine as they later did, Ukrainians attached more significance to imperialist preconceptions than to economic interests as motivating forces. Their analysis of imperialism as the product not only of economic relations but also of pre-capitalistic mentalities appeared conterminously with Schumpeter's. It remains relevant today when colonialism and imperialism are understood to invoke the cultural/ideological as well as the economic.[9] Ukrainian Marxists did not accept that the centralization Lenin imposed on Russia had also to be imposed on Ukraine. If centralization was required, it was up to Ukrainian and not Russian communists to do it. They accordingly condemned Bolshevik centralization and domination as a continuation of imperial tsarist colonialism.

Significantly, they saw the Ukrainian–Russian relationship not in bipolar terms of oppressor–oppressed but rather as a three-cornered relationship within which the urban, Russified, and Russian settler-colonists constituted a distinct group located between Ukrainians and the imperial metropole. Like the French in Algeria, CPU centralists opposed or sabotaged central decisions they disliked. Like John Maclean, James

Connolly, and Jim Larkin, who condemned the Englishness of British Socialists, Shakhrai, Mazurenko, and Richytsky condemned the Russianness of the Bolsheviks and their local affiliate. Insofar as the CPU was basically a settler-colonist organization, the Ukrainian communists stressed that the new socialist metropole had to ignore it.[10] Early Ukrainian SD relations with the Russian SDs were like those between Scottish and English socialists; Ukrainian radicals and Ukrainians, like their Celtic counterparts, were ignored by European socialists. Characteristically, the great apologists for Stalin and his Russified USSR, Sidney and Beatrice Webb, were notoriously anti-Scottish and anti-Irish.

Between 1919 and 1923, Bolshevik rhetoric justifying continued Russian domination of the old empire resembled the rhetoric the Japanese produced twenty years later justifying their domination in Asia. Both discourses referred to "liberating" their claimed territories from "Western imperialism," both claimed that their respective metropoles were models that should lead because they were the most developed, and both claimed that the metropoles were not pursuing their own national or bureaucratic interests and were accommodating all interests and identities better than alternative national elites might have. Japan and Russia were not only champions of the regional nations but also leaders of broader "anti-Western" movements. The Russian elite, like the Japanese elite, distinguished their project from rapacious "Western" capitalism or native backwardness. Both discourses directed animosity not towards the subject nations but towards their elites, which were labelled incompetent, corrupt, and venal. They then abstracted this elite from "the people," who were treated as "partners" in the new order. The Greater East Asia Co-prosperity Sphere, like the USSR, was justified by the claim that all members had the same interests, which would be best served by a common supranational organization. Independence meant isolation.[11] Both discourses denied the reality of domination.

Ukrainian Marxists sought an independent socialist state with its own communist party confederated with other socialist states with their own parties. They argued they had to complete Ukraine's "bourgeois revolution" by forming a national republic. This would end national problems and focus energies on establishing the communist order. Whether that would involve centralization, expropriation, party dictatorship, and state-sponsored violence was a Ukrainian affair, not a Russian communist affair, nor an affair for Ukraine's Russian settler-colonist minority. Where they were too weak to take power, they advocated temporary support for an independent national "bourgeois" state, as the Comintern proclaimed in 1920. The Ukrainian left SD's claim that Ukraine had to have political independence achieved by a "bourgeois nationalist" revolution before a communist revolution could take place was an application of Lenin's *Imperialism* to Ukraine. From December 1918 to January 1919, and then again between March and July of that year, their attempt to ally with the UNR followed this reasoning. Thereafter, they argued, like Roy, that communists had to respect and use nationalism but not actually ally with a national bourgeoisie. Reminiscent of Trotsky's 1905 idea of "permanent revolution," and anticipating later Comintern tactics, they imagined that they would overthrow the UNR and then, as socialists, carry out the necessary "bourgeois task" of national liberation before proceeding with socialist changes. Moreover, insofar as the drive for social emancipation involved creating a state and mobilizing a population in a country where the agents of capitalism were predominantly from non-Ukrainian minorities, Ukrainian Marxists did not regard nationalism as a "deviation" but rather as a central aspect of the socialist revolution. They were not nativists, but they aspired to create a popular front led by the Ukrainian working class that embodied both national interest and internationalist solidarity and that included sympathetic non-Ukrainians. Their aim was not to expel Russian settlers but to expropriate capitalists and the native bourgeoisie. Ukrainian radicals by definition were unlike Russian communists because they considered social emancipation impossible without national liberation. In 1917, the Russian empire was so backward and its proletariat so small relative to the industrialized European countries and their empires that, from a Marxist perspective, Ukrainian left-wing social democracy was a more viable and practical alternative for Ukraine than Russian Bolshevism. Isak Mazepa argued in exile at the time that national independence, by resolving national issues, would have created optimal conditions for class struggle and socialism. Russian Bolsheviks who condemned non-Russian communists within the former tsarist empire who sought permanent secession as "petty bourgeois nationalists" did not condemn Bela Kun, Roddy Connolly, or Ho Chi Minh, who sought independence from their respective empires, kept their parties independent of the Russian, English, and French parties, and entered the Communist International separate from them.

The leading Ukrainian Marxists were Shakhrai, Tkachenko, Richytsky, and Mazurenko. The first two died in 1919. The latter made their peace with the Bolsheviks after 1925 and were ultimately executed by Stalin. Perhaps their most tragic flaw, which they shared with Ukrainian left

SR and Bolshevik federalist Marxists, was that they failed to lay aside their differences, come to terms with one another, and face the Bolsheviks as a group. Instead, each party dealt with them separately. This allowed Lenin, Trotsky, Rakovskii, and Stalin to exploit their divisions and destroy each in turn. First the left SRs, then the UCP, and finally the federalists.

Insofar as the early-twentieth-century social-democratic national states implemented pro-labour policies, workers had a stake in extending the functions of the national state and identified with it. In northwestern Europe, this interventionist state no longer fit Marx's definition of the state as the organ of the ruling capitalist class that kept workers oppressed, but not all Marxists were prepared to alter their thinking accordingly. "National communism," meanwhile, became a term referring only to communist parties opposed or subject to the Bolsheviks rather than to the Bolsheviks themselves; it was as if Russian communists were somehow not national, and unlike all others, were not born, raised, and educated in specific territories and societies speaking specific languages, and did not, as political leaders, use nationalism to mobilize their populations and justify their rule or claim to rule. Bolsheviks claimed that their Russian brand of communism represented a universal norm, and their victory predisposed all too many to accept this claim as true. However, Russian Marxists "nationalized" their communism as much as any other Marxists in other countries "nationalized" theirs and Bolshevism was not a universal norm but a particular Russian phenomenon. This was noted and condemned already in 1918 by Marxists who did not share Bolshevik russocentric conceptions about the tsarist empire.

Lenin thought he could resolve the dilemma posed by ethnic, political, and imperial borders that did not correspond with his "right of self-determination" – by which he meant imperial reunion under supposedly improved conditions. The unexpectedly strong Ukrainian reaction to invasion and centralization did not motivate him to ally with Ukrainian radicals against Ukraine's settler-Russians, a failure that arguably reflected underlying imperialist preconceptions. However, Lenin was enough of a realist to understand by the end of 1919 that he had to heed "federalist," Ukrainian left SR, left SD, and communist criticisms. These men pointed to the sorry consequences of Russian imperialist prejudices within the party that his centralization policies had unleashed, and they asked what those prejudices had to do with Marxism, socialism, and communism. Against the backdrop of strong

Ukrainian armed resistance, Lenin made concessions. They might be compared to what Napoleon did when he allowed the non-French departments of his empire to revert to Republic status.

Lenin's concessions were in keeping with his 1916 ideas about "not infringing" on national self-respect. But as implemented by Stalin, those same concessions isolated language and culture (superstructure) from economics (base), as if the latter had no influence on the former. As critics pointed out, Lenin's and later Stalin's refusal to tolerate ministries or party organizations independent of Moscow meant that non-Russian culture and language (superstructure) would be isolated from real-life politics and economics (base), which, as a result of centralization, would be conducted in non-Russian territories in Russian, the old imperial language. As a consequence, non-Russian culture and language in the USSR would recede into the private sphere, fall into disuse, become relics paraded on holidays, and be eventually forgotten. Today, critical liberals and leftists call this phenomenon "cultural-linguistic imperialism" and consider the assimilation it generates as evil as economic imperialism. Ukrainian Marxists were among the first to condemn this kind of imperialism, and accordingly, their ideas remain relevant today, when Vladimir Putin's government sponsors armed empire-loyalist extremist minority groups in eastern Ukraine, whose roots go back to the early twentieth-century Black Hundreds, to maintain by force Russian hegemony over Ukraine.

In 1922, when key CPU leaders began demanding decentralization and de-Russification, because they knew how precarious their rule was, and declared that all of Ukraine's Russians would eventually learn and use Ukrainian, they nullified much UCP criticism. Obliged to seek Ukrainian support, Bolshevik leaders antagonized many among the urban Russian/Russified minority, who saw no practical reason why they should learn and use the language of the native majority of the country if they could live, work, and play knowing only Russian. They were like the French *colons* who opposed pro-Algerian Parisian policies. As Trotsky explained in the 1923 Mayday edition of *Pravda:*

> The Russian "core" of the party dominated it. This "core" had thought through the question of relations between the Russian proletariat and the Russian peasantry. By simple analogy we [then] extend these relations to the whole of our Soviet Union, forgetting, or insufficiently taking into account, that on the Russian periphery there live other national groups, with a different history, a different level of development and, most

importantly, with a mass of grievances. Most of the Great Russian core of the party is as yet inadequately aware of the national aspects [of the alliance (*smychka*) between peasants and workers], and still more inadequately aware of the national question in its entirety.

Their fear of indigenization predisposed them to support Stalin when he decided that circumstances no longer warranted retaining any of Lenin's concessions. After Stalin stopped enforcing indigenization, Ukrainian communist criticism became relevant again.

Had Ukrainian Marxists come to power and formed a communist national state, they would likely have established a party dictatorship and used terror against their subjects much as did communists elsewhere. This seems not to have bothered conservative monarchist thinker Viacheslav Lypinsky who wrote in 1920: "Those were times for a Ukrainian Lenin. We did not find a Lenin. And here lies the tragedy of the Ukrainian republic – a tragedy whose roots lie in traditional Ukrainian democracy. Thanks to Ukrainian democracy a great Ukrainian revolutionary dictator could not appear."[12] It is likely they would have turned back the Polish army and incorporated Volyn province into their Ukraine. Whether this hypothetical Ukraine would have included western Ukraine is difficult to know. On the one hand, there were few western Ukrainian left SDs, and leaders there had little sympathy for communism. On the other hand, unable to repel the Polish invasion on their own, western leaders might have concluded that belonging to a communist Ukraine was preferable to Polish rule. Strong anti-Polish sentiment did generate western Ukrainian support for the Russian Bolsheviks in 1920. There would have been many tragedies. V. Iakovliv, a Borotbist, was deputy head of Ukraine's Cheka. He killed his own father for belonging to a Black Hundred chauvinist group before the war, and his mother committed suicide on hearing the news.[13] Perhaps Ukrainian communists in power would have done what their Russian counterparts had only planned and deported all of Ukraine's communist Jews. Perhaps they might have done the same to Russians and Polish landowners – much as their Vietnamese and Polish counterparts later deported their countries' Chinese and Ukrainian minorities. But an independent communist Ukraine would have entered the twenty-first century like other former Soviet Bloc countries. Insofar as it would have had legitimacy, like the Vietnamese and Chinese parties, because it was supported by a majority of peasants, it might even, like them, still be a ruling party today. There would have been a party dictatorship but no massive inflow of Russian settlers in mid-century, and the public communications sphere, the economy, and education would have been in Ukrainian, not Russian. Social mobility and status for immigrants and non-territorial minorities, as in any other country, would have been contingent on using the language of the titular nation – Ukrainian. Without powerful, politically Russophile, neo-soviet front groups based on the urban Russified and unassimilated Russian minority, a non-communist Ukraine, like its western former Soviet Bloc neighbours, likely would have been in the EU by 2004.

Appendix: Translated Documents

Document No. 1: Temporary Organization Committee of Independentists (Ukrainian Left-SD), December 1918 Resolution on Relations with the Bolsheviks

(*Robitnycha hazeta*, 7 January 1919; Khrystiuk, *Zamitky*, IV, pp. 55–6)

1) It [the CPU] is an anti-Ukrainian party. Being against the national and political rights of the Ukrainian people it is a party hostile to the Ukrainian state. It is a party in the service of the Russian imperialist Bolshevik government. Because of this it is profoundly reactionary and has no place in Ukraine.

2) It is a party which strives not towards a dictatorship of the proletariat and the revolutionary peasantry, but towards the dictatorship of a part of the proletariat and its party and therefore it is a party of violence that introduces, instead of the compulsion of a proletarian dictatorship over the bourgeois order, the compulsion of a small clique.

3) This party spoils and ruins the economy of Russia by its rash and disorderly way of introducing socialist reforms, and intends to do the same with the economy of Ukraine.

4) It is a hypocritical party that always breaks its own principles. Having acknowledged the principle of national self-determination it has nevertheless involved Ukraine in the war with Russia to conquer Ukraine. Having recognized at the Katerynoslav congress [March 1918] the independence of the Ukrainian workers' and peasants' republic, a miserable second voice to the Petrograd Bolsheviks, it has again taken the side of the reactionary demand for a federation, for a union of former Russia.

In view of this, the party cannot be trusted, even if it happened to change sides again and to recognize Ukrainian independence and the right of the

Ukrainian people to self-determination, until it changes organically and adopts the interests of the Ukrainian working people. Therefore any actions, agreements, candidatures, etc., with it are inadmissible.

Document No. 2: Four Ukrainian Left-SD Anti-Bolshevik Leaflets, Central Ukraine, Spring–Summer 1919

(TsDAHO f. 1 op 18 sprava 63 no. 31; TsDAVO f. 2 op 1 sprava 225 no. 9, 44; TsDAHO f. 57 op 2 sprava 398 no. 12). No. 1 reprinted in Danilov and Shanin, eds., *Nestor Makhno. Krestianskoe dvizhenie na Ukraine 1918–1921*, 116–18.

Leaflet No. 1

To the Peasants and Workers of Ukraine
  Comrades!
  You overturned the Hetman and the Directory.
  You stood for Soviet power as the power of the working people and truly that should satisfy you, but various provocateurs who want to return to the old order have usurped power.
  These little gentlemen call themselves "communists" and have started looting Ukraine's poor population and exporting everything via various speculative channels to Russia. Thus we have ended up under the heel of various "commissars" sent here who oppress us worse than did tsarist and Hetmanite policemen.
  At last the nation's patience snapped and the uprising began. The All Ukrainian Revolutionary Committee (RevKom) leads this uprising and has ordered us to be the chief military-revolutionary staff, to plan the movement. We Ukrainian Bolsheviks to save the socialist revolution in Ukraine and, thereby, in the whole world, declare an active and decisive struggle with all those who speculate on communist ideals and with all chauvinists be they Ukrainian, Russian, or Jewish.
  We chased away our Petliura but see that now other Petliuras lord over us: Russian and Jewish. These new Petliuras are just as counter-revolutionary as our [Ukrainian ones] and possibly even worse.
  That is why we proclaim:
  Down with our Petliura
  Down with Russian and Jewish Petliura-commissars
  Down with all national oppression
  Long live the world socialist revolution
  Long live the free federation of all nations
  Long live the Ukrainian soviet independent socialist republic.

We demand the following:

1) Ukraine must be independent in national-cultural and economic affairs and, as concerns federation, it must be free, that is, without any force or oppression from other nations.

2) All local power belongs to worker-peasant councils and in the center to the Council of Councils/Soviets, without any party dictatorship; that is, no party has the right to impose its program upon the nation by force [. For] us there are no parties only the class interests of the peasants and workers.

3) Power in Ukraine must be in the hands of the local Ukrainian population (that is, all those who inhabit Ukraine); we do not need occupiers or speculators on communism.

4) No one should impose Communes by force when the people do not agree to them.

5) We regard the socialist republics of the entire world as our fraternal equals, in particular Soviet Russia, and will help them with all our might to the degree that the socialist revolution requires it but with no interference in their internal affairs. When we need assistance they should also help us but, only with our permission and without interference in our domestic affairs.

6) As regards the church, this is a matter of individual conscience but no one has any right to insult the people's faith.

And so comrades defend this single correct road to liberation from all oppression and all slavery.

Your liberation is in your hands.

Whoever does not want to be under a foreigner's yoke, whoever does not want to be oppressed by phony Russian and Jewish socialists and other socialist turncoats, stand to arms and don't put them down until all power in Ukraine is transferred to real worker-peasant councils, these true representatives of your will, and not to those artificial "soviets."

Forward to true socialism.

For the Chief Military Revolutionary Staff: Otaman Bohunsky

Confirmed: Political Commissar Hrudnytsky from the All Ukrainian RevKom.

[The reprinted copy from the Moscow archive contains the following final paragraph.]

Know that we are not fighting nations, we are not fighting against Russian or Jewish Bolsheviks or other nationalities, but only against various speculators who compromise true socialism – be they ours or foreign.

Who does not want to be yoked by these phony communists and other socialist turncoats take up arms and don't put them down until all power in Ukraine is taken by true worker-peasant soviets that will reflect our will and not by the phony soviets that exist now.

Forward – towards true socialism.

For the Chief Military-Revolutionary staff: Otaman Bohunsky.

Leaflet No. 2

Comrade Red Army Men

You are led into Ukraine by Russian and Jewish commissar communists who tell you they fight for Soviet power in Ukraine but who in fact are conquering Ukraine. They tell you they lead you against rich Ukrainian peasants but in fact they are fighting against poor Ukrainian peasants and workers.

Soviet power in Ukraine had been undermined by the commissars of the Communist Party; wherever workers and peasants don't elect Russian communist Soviets they dissolve those Soviets and arrest and persecute Ukrainian workers and peasants ...

Ukrainian peasants and workers cannot tolerate the conquest and pillage of Ukraine by Russian armies; they cannot tolerate the oppression of the Ukrainian language and culture as occurred under tsarist rule.

And so they took up arms under the standard of an independent Ukrainian Socialist Republic and the rule of the workers and peasants of Ukraine – not of Russian occupiers and so-called Jewish commissars.

The All Ukrainian Committee leading the Ukrainian workers and peasants uprising assure you comrade Russian, Chinese, Latvian, and other Red Army Men, that Ukrainian workers and peasants don't need you to take Soviet power for them as they can do it for themselves.

The All Ukrainian Committee orders you to surrender your arms to the revolutionary Ukrainian workers and peasants and to return to your native countries. If you do, the All Ukrainian Revolutionary Committee will guarantee you safe conduct through Ukraine to Russia.

Brothers, don't turn you weapons against the peasants and workers of Ukraine but against your commissar communists who torture your unfortunate people as well.

Long Live the Free Union of Independent Socialist Republics – not domination and repression!

The All Ukrainian Revolutionary Committee.

Leaflet No. 3

Comrade Red Army men

You are brought by Russian and Jewish commissar-communists to Ukraine who tell you they are fighting for Soviet power in Ukraine although they are in fact conquering Ukraine. They tell you they are leading you against Ukrainian kulaks although they are in fact fighting against the Ukrainian poor, peasants and workers.

Soviet power in Ukraine is the power of commissars and the Communist Party and wherever workers and peasants elected non-Russian communist soviets, soviet power disbands them. They arrest and persecute Ukrainian peasants and workers.

They tell you it is necessary to come to Ukraine to get bread for hungry Russia, but Ukrainian workers and peasants will themselves give bread to hungry Russia in return for the manufactured goods that Ukraine needs.

If Russian communists want to take by force and loot Ukrainian peasants the only result will be civil war from which only counter-revolution will benefit.

Ukrainian peasants and workers cannot stand the conquest and looting of Ukraine by Russian armies; they cannot stand when their language and culture is pushed aside and russification is imposed like under the tsars.

And so they have taken-up arms under the standard of an independent Ukrainian Socialist Republic and the true power of workers and peasants not Russian occupiers.

The All Ukrainian revolutionary committee at the head of the revolutionary uprising of Ukrainian workers and peasants declares to you comrade Russian, Chinese, Latvian, and other Red Army men that Ukrainian workers and peasants don't need you to establish soviet power here because they will do it themselves.

The All Ukrainian Revolutionary Committee orders you to surrender your arms to the revolutionary Ukrainian workers and peasants and go back to your homes. The All Ukrainian RevKom will guarantee you safe passage from Ukraine to Russia.

You must not spill the fraternal blood of Ukrainian peasants and workers. You must either lay down your arms or turn them against your lying leaders.

Down with all conquerors of Ukraine be they French or Russian

LONG LIVE AN INDEPENDENT UKRAINIAN SOVIET SOCIALIST REPUBLIC

LONG LIVE A FREE UNION OF FREE SOCIALIST REPUBLICS AND NOT CONQUEST OR SUBORDINATION AND LONG LIVE THE INTERNATIONALE

THE ALL UKRAINIAN REVOLUTIONARY COMMITTEE.

Leaflet No. 4

ORDER no. [blank]

All power in villages counties and towns goes to SOVIETS OF WORKER AND PEASANT DEPUTIES, composed of landless and small-owner peasants in villages. In towns half of SOVIET CONGRESSES [will be] composed of working peasants and half of workers, and not exclusively by Russian looter communists as they are now, which, under the guise of communism, requisition grain cattle and horses from working peasants and export it all to Muscovy.

Until all power in Ukraine goes to UKRAINIAN WORKERS AND WORKING PEASANTS, do not recognize any foreigner communist invaders and fight as much as possible to prevent these looters by one means or another from stealing from us and then sending all that we need to Muscovy.

We should tell foreigners: comrades Out of our house. We will establish peace and order in our house by ourselves such as we want and such as befits the times. When it becomes time for communism we the literate and illiterate will deal with it as necessary without you.

Brother peasants we must unite and fight as one looting Russkies and foreigners in general.

We bolshevik UKRAINIAN INDEPENDENTISTS claim: all land must belong to the peasants who work it who should have as much as they need and can work. We declare:

LONG LIVE THE UKRAINIAN INDEPENDENT SOVIET REPUBLIC

Free with the free and equal with the equal.

LONG LIVE THE WORLD FEDERATION OF SOCIALIST INDEPENDENT REPUBLICS.

LONG LIVE SOCIALISM

Regimental Otaman
Head of the Regimental Council

Document No. 3: Leaflet Issued by Otaman Zeleny to Red Army Troops Noting His Men Are Not Anti-Semites (summer 1919).

Reprinted in: P.T. Tronko et al, *Reabilitovani istorieiu u dvadtsiaty semy tomakh. Chernihivska oblast knyha persha* (Chernihiv, 2008) 84-5.

Comrade Red Army Men!

We, the combatants of otaman Zeleny's insurrectionary unit, appeal to you comrades, to tell you about the criminal acts Russian and Jewish communists committed against the poor working peasants of Kyiv county (among us are no peasants who own more than 8 acres) that forced us to take-up arms again and, thanks to our superior spirit, get rid of [*smest*] an entire two-regiment strong punishment detachment of 3019 men.

On May 6, when we ended the uprising, Russian and Jewish communists began hunting and shooting us. They were especially interested *in our commanders* [sic] and when they did not find them at home they shot their parents, brothers or wives and burned or pillaged their houses... They burned down the villages of Trypillia, Khalepy, Krasna, Dereviana and Zlodievka. We cannot recall without resentment that our mothers, wives, and sisters knelt before these savages begging them not to burn the houses without avail. They burned down houses, barns and threshing sheds and shot at the women when they tried to put out the flames. Could we tolerate such atrocities. We rose and threw our oppressors into the Dnipro. *Comrade Red Army men, don't believe that we instigated pogroms or treated prisoners badly* [sic]. Jews who did *not participate in criminal activities and violence* [sic] against us and our families continue to work peacefully and suffer no pogroms from us as we neither engaged in them nor are we engaging in them now.

We are not fighting against individuals but against the party of Russian communists. Of the 1000 prisoners that we captured, we sent home all those who were not involved in beating or shooting our comrades, looting or burning down our villages.... *Don't stand against your fathers and brothers* [sic]. You are being provoked by those various party speculators *who know nothing of our peasant life* [sic].

Down with provocateurs and the fratricide [provoked by] Russian and Jewish communist-commissars.

Long live soviet peasant worker and soldier power

The Information Bureau of the Insurgent Regions of Otaman Zeleny.

Document No. 4: Anonymous, *Khto taki Kommunisty-Borotbysty* (Lubny, 1919?) – Excerpt

Who are the communist-borotbists?

...

And so from both parties left-wing tendencies emerged under the names: 1) the left UPSR (borotbisty) and 2) the independent leftists USDLP that completely accepted the Russian Communist Party Bolshevik program and established as their aim a stubborn struggle for the power of the rural and urban proletariat in Ukraine. The very manner of these faction's birth ensured that the most revolutionary in each party joined them. But the reaction that fell upon

Ukraine together with the Germans forced them to go underground and thus cleaned their ranks even more because all the less revolutionary could not pass this test and left. This is the condition in which the second return of Soviet power to Ukraine, after the Hetman, found the UPSR borotbists and independent-leftist USDLP. Together with the communist-bolsheviks they marched against the Hetman and Petliurist troops and alongside them took part in constructing soviet power. Already then they disagreed with the direction of Bolshevik policy in Ukraine and in the press and meetings polemicized with them.

...

III Party tactics

1 ... The communist-borotbist party recognizes that in realizing the communist program it is necessary first and foremost to meet the desires and moods of the proletariat, in this case the Ukrainian, and, when the proletariat does not want to or is unprepared to realize parts of the program, then it is only permissible to debate and to never under any circumstances to implement those parts of the program using force. Obviously, this applies only to the proletariat's wishes. We should not take account of the wishes of either the big or lesser bourgeoisie but rather fight them. And the world is now divided into many states. The conditions within them are not the same nor are the moods and desires. This means the communist program cannot be introduced the same way in all countries, as what the proletariat of one country might agree to could infuriate the proletariat of another ... The UCP borotbists considers that Ukraine differs from other countries by its conditions of life and therefore should be a separate soviet republic and have its own leader, an independent Ukrainian soviet government.

2 But this is insufficient because precisely in Ukraine fortuitous circumstances resulted in a part of its population always having been under the cultural influence of Russia – both now and under the tsars. The communist-Bolshevik party that leads the construction of soviet power in Ukraine belongs to that part of the population. The majority in this party are Ukrainian [territorially] but these Ukrainians, under the influence of Russian culture and particularly under the influence of the Russian revolution, absolutely refuse to recognize that in Ukraine the communist revolution has to follow a different path than it did in Russia. In response to all the efforts of the borotbists to point out that this or that cannot be done because in the context of Ukrainian life it will hinder the revolution, they reply "well in Russia this is has already been done." And the communists-borotbists say that it is not enough for Ukraine to be an independent republic and have its government. There must also be people in

this government who will guide it not bothering about whether this or that has been done in Russia or in other soviet states but, who will first and foremost, look at what the Ukrainian proletariat wants and then carry out policies accordingly. And while, instead, the communist-bolsheviks who now control everything in Ukraine consider primarily how soviet construction is proceeding in Russia and almost totally ignore the demands of the Ukrainian rural and urban proletariat, the communists-borotbists demand the Bolsheviks change their tactics and transfer soviet construction in Ukraine into the hands of the communist-borotbists who [unlike them] place the interests of the Ukrainian proletariat first.

3 But [while] considering the circumstance of the Ukrainian proletariat, demanding a separate government for Ukraine and that it be led by local Ukrainian activists who in the first instance would heed the Ukrainian proletariat – the communist borotbist party remains an internationalist party and disavows any nationalist enmity. It cannot support the slogan "Ukraine only for Ukrainians" or "Russkies, Poles, and Jews out of Ukraine." Nationalist enmity is a sign of counter-revolution with which the UCP borotbists will always fight with all its strength as it will against all counter-revolution. The proletariat has only one enemy – the world's bourgeoisie, and every proletarian, be he [sic] Russian, Polish or Jewish is a comrade and associate of the Ukrainian proletariat ...

IV Relations with the CPU (Bolshevik).

While communist-borotbists have the same program as the communist-bolsheviks, as already noted, they consider Bolshevik tactics, that is the methods they use to realize their program, as inimical to the revolution in Ukraine. But the borotbists conduct their dispute with the Bolsheviks only verbally, on paper. The communist-borotbists know well that there are too few communists in Ukraine and they will never allow one communist [group] to take up arms against another. Such an armed struggle would only destroy communist power in Ukraine, allow the counter-revolution to evict soviet power from Ukraine and to impose for a long time thereafter its rule over the peasant and worker. On the contrary, the borotbists support soviet power with all their might and willingly go to work in all soviet institutions where they defend the interests of the Ukrainian proletariat to the best of their abilities. And they hope the proletariat of Ukraine will judge their work, join the borotbist party and thereby allow them to peacefully realize their objectives and build a strong foundation for a new life in Ukraine.

The Lubny UCP borotbist committee

Document No. 5: November 1919 Memorandum of the
Moscow-Based Bolshevik "Ukrainian Communist Organization" to Lenin
on Need to Change His Ukrainian Policy

(TsDAHO f. 57 op 6 sprava 15 nos. 1–17) – Excerpt

To the RCP Central Committee

... The revolutionary movement in Ukraine has many particularities, as will be discussed below. To approach Ukrainian events, Ukrainian insurgency and national relations with preconceived Russian ideas [therefore] would be a grievous error. We regrettably saw much of this in Ukraine. And we consider this lack of serious attention to Ukraine's specific particularities to a great degree as the cause of the revolution's collapse in Ukraine ...

We will begin with a general overview of Ukraine's economic and political situation on the eve of the revolution. For some time now among communists it has become considered acceptable to dismiss everything in Ukraine as a country that is extremely backward economically and dominated by kulaks. Undoubtedly with regard to heavy industry Ukraine lagged behind not only Europe's leading countries but also Russia. The more or less developed heavy industry is in a small part of Ukrainian territory – the Donets Kryvyi Rih basin. Also, large industrial cities are located almost exclusively in the Black Sea littoral. The rest of the territory, excluding northern Chernihiv province, has no really big capitalist enterprises with a skilled permanent working class. On the rest of Ukraine's territory agriculture predominates ...

The fact of the matter is that the repartitional commune was almost unknown in Ukraine and therefore differentiation within villages went much further than in Russia where differentiation was tied to the commune and other precapitalist remnants ... The most communes are in Kharkiv, Katerynoslav Kherson and Tavrida provinces, but even there it quickly dissolves faster than in Russia.

Thus, the overwhelming majority of Ukrainian peasants had private land tenure.

Large landowning, meanwhile, again unlike in Russia, is primarily capitalist in nature because of favourable geographical conditions and lots of labour that could not find a place in industry.

Not able to go into statistical details, we only wish to point out that within the Ukrainian peasantry there is a very high percentage of rural proletariat and semi-proletariat – that is peasants who cannot live solely from their land and have to seek work ...

If we then add that agriculture is almost the sole occupation of the population, that non-agricultural work is limited and usually seasonal (sugar refining), then it becomes obvious that treating Ukraine as a country that is almost totally "kulak" is ridiculous and it becomes obvious why "well endowed" Ukraine is the source of most migrants to the not so very "well endowed" Siberia.

Thus we see Ukraine has a solid mass of poor, who by their social nature, cannot accept the rule of capital and are very receptive to communist ideas. An important role here as well, analogous to that of "factory plots" was played not only by sugar refineries but by large capitalist estates where hundreds and even thousands worked including locals as well as outsiders known as "migrant labourers."

The mass organized struggle of agricultural workers for improved conditions in the form of strikes was common in Ukraine.

These in general are the particularities of Ukraine's economic structure as compared to Russia. But besides these there are also historical-political factors that give the revolutionary activities of the Ukrainian masses their specific traits …

We have listed this to illustrate the complexity of the revolutionary movement in Ukraine. If practically there is no national question in Russia. If there is only a struggle between the Russian worker and the Russian bourgeoisie and, if that struggle finished in the towns as of October 1919 and moved to the village only in the fall of 1918 (according to Lenin) and, if that year the village waited and was relatively quiet then, in Ukraine affairs were fundamentally different …

1. The fundamental problem with the CPU was the lack of a leading centre organically tied to the revolutionary masses of Ukraine that could have dealt with all the issues posed by life. The existing centre could not cope with that task not because of its personnel but because of its political distance from the Ukrainian revolutionary current. It looked at everything from the perspective of the Russian centre basically ignoring that the course of the revolution in Ukraine and Russia was hardly the same, that Ukraine could not accept those forms of life developed in Russia during the course of 18 months of soviet construction that occurred in circumstances very different from the Ukrainian. The basic problems of Ukrainian life, sometimes totally unknown to revolutionary Russia, did not get proper attention. The basic practice was to mechanistically apply laws existing in RSFSR territory to Ukrainian territory.

2. In all of the CPU's policies extreme distrust of Ukrainian communist groups and an orientation on groups that, though not communist, are not infected by "separatism" and have no real influence, like the Menshevik and [Russian] left SRs, runs like a red thread. The clearest example of this are the directives given by the CPU orgburo to comrades sent to Ukraine to totally ignore the borotbists even though they controlled a huge number of insurgents and to offer aid

instead to [Russian] left SRs, who represented nothing in Ukraine and whose ideology is alien and hostile to us [Bolsheviks]. Also noteworthy is the refusal to accept borotbists into the party, while accepting the [Jewish Communist] Kom FarBand led by liquidationists.

In general we can claim that the [CPU] party has absolutely no influence in Ukrainian villages and did nothing to win the poor to its side, and instead accepted more or less Russophile petit bourgeois elements from Russian and Jewish craftsmen. The impact of these petit bourgeois elements in the party is deadly.

3. The a priori characterization of Ukraine as a kulak country incapable of independent revolutionary creativity resulted in a policy that cannot be classified in any way other than colonialist. Ukraine is seen exclusively as an object from which to extract resources, in the course of which the interests of the class struggle in Ukraine are totally ignored ...

The results of such a policy were peasant uprisings that often broke out in the most proletarianized districts (as for example Trypillia county of Kyiv district, and the Zvenyhorod, Tarashchanska and Uman districts of Kyiv province [that were led by Zeleny]). Life has shown those policies amount to cutting the branch upon which you are sitting.

Ukraine is now on the brink of a new revolutionary wave. The question of future tactics is no longer merely theoretical but takes on greater urgency. And we are convinced that continuing our previous tactics inevitably will lead to the previous results, that is, to uprisings and another collapse.

There are two theoretical possibilities: either the Ukrainian proletariat and peasant groups close to it will make a revolution and create soviet power, wherein the Russian Soviet Republic's Red Army will help them technically – or Ukraine will be helpless, counter-revolutionaries will be stronger than the revolutionaries, and it will be exclusively the forces of the Russian Soviet Republic that will chase Denikin away. In the latter instance, if there were no revolutionary movement in Ukraine, if there were a possibility that Ukraine would turn into a new Don Territory, then it would be necessary and correct to invade it to safeguard ourselves from a new counterrevolutionary neighbour and get whatever possible food coal and other resources so necessary for Soviet Russia.

But it should be obvious to all that it is not easy to take grain by force, particularly when its owner-peasants are all armed. And if there is a hope to avoid such economic measures and obtain that grain and pork-fat voluntarily, that it would be much easier both for Soviet Russia and the world revolution to do so ...

And so, looking at the present situation in Ukraine as the prelude to a revolutionary divide, and considering that there are sufficient forces in Ukraine to actively fight for Soviet power and follow a communist party, we propose the following basic principles for our party's policies.

1. The first task of Ukraine's communists is to organize the proletarian mass of the towns and villages into one communist party. With its own Ukrainian centre, organically tied with the revolutionary masses, it would be able to orientate itself within the specificities of the revolutionary struggle in Ukraine ...

As a first practical step we propose the necessity of joining two already existing communist parties in Ukraine, the CPU and the UCP (borotbists). This is particularly necessary because the borotbists, who have no ideological difference with us, have considerable support from the peasantry and play a powerful role in the uprising that is sweeping Ukraine.

2. In the struggle for soviet power in Ukraine the leading role must absolutely belong not to a Moscow centre but to a Ukrainian centre closely tied to the revolutionary movement of the Ukrainian lower orders. If this is not done then, inevitably, that struggle will be framed as Muscovite "red imperialism," as we have already witnessed, and many who can and want to fight alongside communists will be thrown into counterrevolution.

Obviously this does not exclude the possibility and need for a frontal offensive on Ukraine by the Red Army. But that offensive must be in the nature of a military-technical aid to the Ukrainian revolution. Political leadership must imperatively remain in the centre produced by the Ukrainian revolutionary current.

3. To undercut the counter-revolutionary agitation of Ukrainian nationalists, who very successfully exploit peasant's nationalist sentiments, it will be necessary to declare and realize the right of the Ukrainian revolutionary proletariat and peasants to their independent revolutionary creativity and the creation of an independent viable government apparatus ...

We firmly believe that we will thereby attain unity sooner and more surely than by using armed force against any appearance of national separatism, which only hinders class differentiation within nations ...

Document No. 6: Project of a Resolution on Party Politics Prepared by Federalists for the Kyiv City Section of the CPU, February 1920

(TsDAVO f. 2 op. 1 sprava 564 nos. 45–8)

Inscription upper right corner: copyright (not for circulation outside the party)

A project on party politics presented by members of the Kyiv city organization of the CPU at the regional meeting of February 19, 1920.

Last year soviet power did not collapse because it was destroyed by counter-revolutionary armies, but because during its existence between December and August it could not organize the working masses and poor peasants around itself or minimally organize the country's government apparatus or economy.

Greeted after the Hetman's fall with undoubted sympathy ... [the CPU then] thanks to a sleuth of errors ranged against itself those upon whom it should have relied.

Our party stands responsible for these errors. The working class and peasants of Ukraine paid for these errors with their blood.

With despair we become convinced that many party members including its present leaders learned nothing from last year's experience and forgot nothing, which will inevitably result, if not in another collapse of the proletarian dictatorship in Ukraine, then in a very slow and painful construction here of communism.

The basis of all these errors lies in the stubborn refusal to understand that the socialist revolution and communist construction in Ukraine, a country with developed agriculture and strong industrial regions with access to the sea and many natural resources, and with an appropriately significant industrial and rural proletariat, cannot be done except by the forces of that same proletariat; and, that after the national oppression of the Ukrainian nation under the Habsburgs and Romanovs, any external attempts to settle the country's fate will inevitably engender a nationalist response; that the separate parts into which dissolved the artificially constructed states like the Russian and Austro-Hungarian empires can be restored to socialist centralism not during the transitional period of the socialist revolution, but only after hard work restoring and enforcing the economic organisms of those constituent parts retarded in their development by the exploitative colonialist politics of the bourgeoisie of the previous ruling centers.

The inability of Russian comrades to understand these truths, which is undoubtedly beyond their consciousness, stems from the interest of Russia's proletariat in maintaining the earlier division of industrial regions, which, if it were restructured, could lead to Russian enterprises closing and moving to the former borderland regions. It is also explained by the ideological influence on party members of intellectuals and government officials for whom separation of national borderlands means the shrinking of their "cultural" influence on those borderlands and their replacement by locals.

As far as concerns our party specifically, it is necessary to keep in mind that its membership is basically urban and proletarian. The Ukrainian town was long ago Russified and thereby isolated from the mass of rural proletarians and poor. Having become accustomed to struggle against tsarism in the ranks of the all Russian [imperial] proletariat our party members yet still today regard the proletarian revolution in Ukraine as part of the Russian revolution.

As a result, all policies totally ignored Ukraine's social historical and national particularities. A plan [accordingly] emerged to occupy Ukraine with Soviet Russia's political and military forces that is stupid and inimical to the interests of the revolution. Party comrades closely tied to the Ukrainian revolution are taken away and replaced by others ignorant of local conditions and often contemptuous of everything local and Ukrainian. Without criticism and without accommodation to Ukrainian circumstances Russian forms of state and party building are transferred here. Finally, and this is most threatening to the success of the revolution, there is no attempt to introduce into the Ukrainian proletariat the consciousness that it, as the natural hegemon of the communist revolution, has to closely tie itself to the Ukrainian working masses and lead them. On the contrary, it is separated from that task by the transfer of all economic and professional centres beyond Ukraine's borders thereby destroying its unity, by constantly reemerging projects to separate the Donets-Kryvyi rikh basin from Ukraine, and it is taught to look at itself as a part and only a part of the Russian proletariat.

At the same time alongside the existence of the undeniable fact that Ukraine exists as a separate entity, a fact that if ignored is dearly paid for, there emerge such forms of statehood in Ukraine that make it appear as if it were an indivisible part of Russia. From this stems a politicking unworthy of a proletarian party; when we see fictitious state organs formed in the name of the working masses that in reality don't have those rights [because] they have been granted in [merely] celebratory declarations.

This warps the political consciousness of the masses and introduces total disarray into soviet construction ...

After considering these views our group has agreed to the following proposals.

1. Ukraine, previously belonging to the Russian and Austro-Hungarian empires, is a separate country united by its socio-political national and historical characteristics that can be fully developed only after the triumph and establishment of communism results in the total abolition of state power.

2. Today Ukraine must be governed by its working masses in the form of an independent and complete organization (Ukr. SSR), completely equal to other soviet republics, led by its [own] congress of soviets and worker-peasant government controlling full sovereign power in the country's economic political and military affairs.

3. The formation of fictitious organs, appearing to be independent but in fact totally subject to the RSFSR, is utterly impermissible as this befuddles the consciousness of the working masses and makes the building of proper government impossible.

4. The politically stupid idea of occupying Ukraine with the military and political forces of Soviet Russia, that is destructive of the revolution, must be resolutely opposed. The necessary military assistance against Ukraine's internal counter-revolution must be realized under the leadership and control of the local soviet authority.

5. To attain a harmonious and united realization of planned economic construction, the successful repulsion of world counter-revolution and the mutual support [provided by] the fraternal ties between the workers of the Ukrainian and Russian socialist republics, it is necessary to unite the activities of the appropriate responsible organs of the two republics via permanent or temporary federal organs so that all their plans or decisions be executed in Ukraine only by the appropriate organs of the Ukr. SSR, fully controlled by its worker-peasant government.

6. During the struggle against the counter-revolution the Ukr. SSR and Russian SFSR armed forces must be united with a common command administrative and supply apparatus via the federal Revolutionary Military Committee. The workers and peasants of Ukraine will serve in Ukrainian formations with Ukrainian commanders and commissars and military administrative organs in Ukraine (the military commissariats) will be subordinated to Ukrainian soviet power via the appropriate executive committees and, in its turn, Ukraine's military commissariat will be subordinated to Ukraine's worker peasant government and the federal Revolutionary Military Revolutionary Council.

...

8. All effort must be applied to eliminate as quickly as possible the national difference between the Ukrainian village and the russified town by the overall and energetic activity of Ukrainian proletarian culture and the widespread use of Ukrainian as the means of communist education among the Ukrainian popular mass in state social and political life.

...

10. Our party can realize all the tasks it faces only if it is completely independent and conducts all its policies on the basis of Ukrainian realities and is totally responsible for those policies. That is why it cannot simply be a part of the RCP but, as the party of the proletariat of a separate country equal to the RCP, it must enter the Communist International as its Ukrainian section and be politically subordinated only to it while being organizationally completely autonomous.

11. To unite all communist forces it is necessary to do everything possible to create a single communist party in place of the separate communist organizations that today exist in Ukraine.

...

Document No. 7: Program of the Ukrainian Communist
Party (1920) – Excerpts

Introduction

Throughout the world capitalism is in deep crisis, it is ruined, and the world-wide proletarian communist revolution is spreading.

...

(p. 7) These tendencies in capitalist development have necessarily led to the growth of militarism as a method of achieving domination in the world market. In turn militarism has become the self-fulfilling reason for the growth of industry and is the appropriate form for present-day capitalist states. However, the huge growth of heavy industry in particular has resulted in militarist needs dominating state economic life and also a growth in state borrowing, resulting in financial difficulties and an accompanying significant dislocation of economic life and increase in the cost of living.

...

(p. 16) The development of capitalism has meant the victory of strong states over the weak, the exploitation of the latter and their transformation into colonies, the destruction of their national and political life and even their national culture. Imperialism has organized the exploitation of all peoples on a global level cruelly suppressing the national liberation movements of oppressed economic entities/units.

But, having drawn all the more firmly these subordinated economic units into the world capitalist system, capitalism simultaneously strengthened their internal economy on the basis of [their] natural economic-geographic and earlier economic cohesiveness, thus increasing their ability to resist imperialism.

This is why the crisis of capitalism, the decline of economic life as a result of the world war and the accompanying weakening of imperialist ties has led to a revival in the desire of oppressed national economic units to rise up and led inevitably to an unprecedented intensification of the national struggle.

So the moment the world war ends and the transition to communist revolution comes, imperialist conglomerate states like Russia, Austria or Britain will inevitably disintegrate along the lines of the economic units of which they were composed, as well as inevitably lead to the linking of civil wars in individual countries with revolutionary wars, both in proletarian countries that are defending themselves and where oppressed peoples are fighting against imperialist yokes.

Because of this the communist revolution was to erupt first in economically weak and backward countries, weakly pasted together from different economic entities, such as Russia or Austria, and the victorious countries.

...

(p. 17) The Ukrainian revolution, prepared by and expressed by revolution in the East as a national one, by realizing its national tasks inevitably had to become a communist revolution. It was restrained by the dominance of the petit bourgeoisie supported by the big bourgeoisie, an unconscious proletariat, and a bitter national struggle caused by imperialist bourgeois prejudices still held by the proletariat in both Russia and Ukraine, that the bourgeoisie, military circles and the Russian bourgeois intelligentsia [exploited to] bluff [them] into not allowing the realization of the national aspects of the Ukrainian social revolution.

The revolution therefore still cannot fully develop into a communist one. To help this along, and to hasten the proper resolution of the national issue and combine national and social liberation, is the task of what is today the only genuine expression of the class movement of Ukraine's entire proletariat – the Ukrainian Communist Party.

The revolution in Germany, which clearly began as proletarian, was also held back by the inevitable alliance of a reactionary social democracy with the bourgeoisie, and will only become a communist revolution through bloody struggle.

...

(p. 19) Only a proletarian communist revolution can liberate mankind. It combines the tasks of the social and national liberation of workers, destroys capitalism and imperialism, and has as its primary aim increasing the productive forces in every country as much as possible, first and foremost by its own strengths and resources. Rather than worrying about external markets, it will increase the strength and importance of each domestic market.

This in turn inevitably raises [develops] the basic economic units historically tied to specific nations and leads them to an independent economic and political existence, simultaneously incorporating all the working masses into state-building and slowly transforming the state into a workers' apparatus for production and distribution. In other words, the communist revolution will inevitably occur in national economic units and be based on raising the level of national culture and economic and political consciousness of the masses.

At the same time, given the development by the previous capitalist regime of strong, worldwide economic ties, the national and social liberation of the working masses in their struggle with world capitalism can take place only on an international scale.

...

Therefore, the only leader of the proletariat in the struggle for social revolution is the International Communist Party, of which the Ukrainian Communist Party is a part.

...

(p. 20) THE NATIONAL QUESTION

7. Initially the Ukrainian revolution was a national one and the tasks of the national and political liberation of the Ukrainian people arose from the need for an appropriate development of the Ukrainian economy while it was still capitalist. That development was held back because it was exploited by imperialist Russia [that was responsible for] an unheard of enslavement and oppression of the Ukrainian people.

But as a consequence of the collapse of world capitalism, that included the partly developed capitalisms in Russia and Ukraine, the Ukrainian revolution had to become a communist one that would free the working Ukrainian masses nationally and socially on the basis of a continuous development of the productive forces of the Ukrainian economic entity, by replacing capitalist productive relations by socialist ones.

This confronts the U.C.P. with the task of providing a suitable resolution of the national problem in Ukraine thereby ending the national struggle, satisfying and realizing the requirements of the national revolution, and [then] using them to strengthen the development of the communist revolution.

8. Proceeding from the principle of the right to national independence and given the peculiarities and requirements needed for the development of the Ukrainian economic unit, and to provide balanced and continuous growth for its productive forces, the U.C.P. confirms the independence and sovereignty of the economic and political order of the Ukrainian Socialist Soviet Republic.

Simultaneously the U.C.P. recognizes the need for a close union and cooperation of the Ukrainian Soviet Republic with other soviet republics for defense and offensives primarily against bourgeois states, and for using the economic forces of each national economic unit to assist the internal construction of others, keeping in mind the interests of communist construction for all mankind.

Given that the general development of the communist revolution in Ukraine requires including the entire mass of the working population into the task of communist reconstruction and managing the state, the party supports the need for the Ukrainian Republic to have a Ukrainian national character in accordance with the overwhelming majority of the creative revolutionary mass of workers.

That involves Ukrainian as the official language in all soviet institutions and equal rights for the Russian, Jewish and Polish national minorities.

9. For these principled reasons the party rejects the passive bourgeois attitude to the nation and uplifting national cultures. Drawing the masses into the construction of the socialist state, the U.C.P. advocates active support for the development of each national culture, [but] first of all the culture of the basic mass of toiling people of Ukraine, that of the Ukrainian nationality, and then, of the national minorities – Russian, Jewish, Polish and others. Thus will be removed everything that promotes denationalization, that is, what restrains the consciousness of the masses or their cultural strength, or bitter national struggle. In the first instance this will be helped by the party appropriately resolving the issue of language use in soviet institutions.

10. In its striving for the communist reconstruction of Ukrainian society through the Ukrainian Soviet Socialist Republic the U.C.P., as the expression of the will of all Ukraine's proletariat and all its working people, including its native and most numerous Ukrainian as well as other nationalities, regards as its basic task, and precondition for the proper realization of the communist revolution, the unification and merging into a common revolutionary struggle against capitalists and landlords, the proletariat and semi-proletarians of all nationalities within Ukraine and internationally. Given the underdeveloped communist and still imperialist will of the Russian proletariat in Russia, and to some extent in Ukraine, the U.C.P. opposes all counter-revolutionary attempts to exploit this phenomenon in the interests of Russian imperialist policy towards Ukraine to foment national struggle and thus impede the inevitable development of the Ukrainian and therefore the world communist revolution.

11. The intense antagonism between town and country in Ukraine is largely the result of Russia's imperialist de-nationalization policy towards Ukraine, which led to a national and cultural separation of the town from the mass of the Ukraine's population, and thus to a national struggle. To eliminate the remnants of this policy and the cultural separation of town from village the U.C.P. considers its task to draw the proletariat into proletarian cultural creativity on an Ukrainian national basis.

Culture and Education.

12. Unlike bourgeois culture, which strengthened the dominance of capitalism, the proletarian revolution will create a new culture of the entire mass of workers. Destroying all oppression including the national, the revolution will allow the masses the possibility of cultural development and, through their own language, national culture and education, link them to world culture. Particularly

important is the continuous raising of the cultural level of the toiling masses of the Ukrainian nation, oppressed by centuries of Russian tsarist domination. That is why the soviet Ukrainian state should actively promote the development of national culture, schooling in the native language, literature, language etc.

...

(p. 46) THE NATIONAL ECONOMY.

Overall Economics ...

25. Given that the economy of the Ukrainian Soviet Socialist Republic is linked to the world economy the U.C.P. considers it necessary to broaden economic co-operation and political ties with other nations, whilst at the same time it desires to establish close ties and mutual assistance with those [nations] that have already become soviet states by consolidating and unifying state plans and the appropriate state economic organs, by organizing socialist commodity exchange etc.

...

The Organization of Production

26. The organizational structure of socialized industry should rely primarily on trade unions. They must free themselves of guild sectionalism and turn into large united organizations encompassing every single worker in each specific branch of production.

Because of the transfer of power to the workers, the trade unions will lose their character as class organizations that defend workers' interests against capital. As participants in all local and central administrative organizations in industry, they should eventually control the entire administration of the national economy as a single unit. By thus guaranteeing an unbreakable bond between the central state administration, the national economy, and the broad masses of toilers, unions should be able to draw workers directly into the running of the economy. This in turn will allow them to exercise genuine popular control over the results of production.

27. To enable the planned growth of the national economy the entire labour force must be used as much as possible. It must be properly allocated among Ukraine's different regions and the different branches of the national economy. This is a task soviet power can only accomplish in close co-operation with the trade unions. General mobilizations by Soviet power of the entire able-bodied population to execute specific public works should be done widely and frequently.

...

(p. 49) 30. Small producers and artisans must be widely employed via state contracts, and will have to be included in the general economic plan. Financial assistance will be available to them on condition that individual small workshops, workers' and producers' co-operatives and local industries combine into large industrial units that will then assist the remaining small units.

Generally, economic policy towards small and artisan manufacturing should aim at stifling artisans' capitalist ownership strivings and producing a painless transfer from those old forms of production to a superior form of mechanized industry.

(p. 52) Agriculture

...

34. In its village work the U.C.P. relies on rural proletarians, organizing them as an independent force, creates village party cells, organizes the village proletariat, brings them closer to the urban proletariat and removes them from influence of village bourgeois and small owner interests.

The U.C.P.'s policies towards kulaks and village bourgeoisie involve resolute struggle against their attempts at exploitation, and destroying their resistance to soviet policies.

As regards the middle peasantry, the U.C.P. desires their gradual and planned incorporation into communist construction. The party aims to separate them from the kulaks, draw them to the side of the workers through careful consideration of their needs, struggling against their backwardness ideologically, using no violence, and considering their national-economic structure. It seeks agreement with them wherever their vital interests are concerned, and will make concessions when determining how to realize communist reconstruction.

...

(p. 56) The Protection of Labour

40. With the establishment of the dictatorship of the proletariat, the protection of labour loses its urgency and fundamental importance, for work ceases to be a means of profit for capitalists, but instead benefits the workers' state. The protection of labour now becomes a question of guaranteeing workers the best possible conditions at work as regulated by soviet power, which will be the first in the world to introduce in full the minimum socialist party program in this regard. Legislation would be as follows:

1) the maximum eight-hour working day for all workers; for those under 18 in particularly dangerous occupations and for miners working underground, however, the maximum should be no longer than six hours;

2) a 42 hour period of unbroken rest each week for all workers;

3) as a general rule, forbidding overtime;

4) forbidding the hiring of children under 15;

5) forbidding night work particularly in dangerous industries, as well as overtime for men more than eight years [sic?], and for women;

6) no work for women for eight weeks before and after childbirth, with full wages guaranteed during this period along with free medical care, the provision for women workers of at least one-half hour every three hours for child-feeding and extra help for nursing mothers;

7) inspection of working and sanitary conditions, carried out by trade union soviets.

41. Beyond this minimum program Soviet power will also establish:

1) the participation of workers' organizations in hiring and firing;

2) a month's annual holiday with pay guaranteed for all workers of at least one year's standing;

3) state regulation of pay based on tables worked out by trade unions;

4) specific organs for the location and computation of the workforce within soviets and unions obliged to find work for the unemployed.

However, the wartime destruction of the national economy and the struggle against world imperialism force and permit soviet power to retreat in some regards from its program. Eg. to allow some overtime, allow 14 to 16 year olds to work up to four hours daily, to temporarily reduce holiday allowances from one month to two weeks, to increase night hours to seven per night, and to introduce a compulsory minimum level of productivity.

...

Document No. 8: Four Letters from Former Bolshevik Party Members Explaining Why They Joined the Borotbist or Ukrainian Communist Parties.

(*Borotbist* [Poltava], 17, 20 Feb. 1920; TsDAHO f. 8 op. 1 sprava 31 no. 114)

Letter No. 1

To the UCP (borotbist) Kyiv City Committee
from CP (Bolshevik) member Vasyl Brunst

Statement

Returning to Ukraine from Russia, to which I was evacuated with the First Reserve Regiment where I was political commissar, I prepared to devote myself totally to the new course of party work in Ukraine as expressed in resolutions of the RCP central committee.

But in Ukraine I realized that the policies of the CPU (Bolshevik) remain as before, that fine statements remain paper resolutions, and that the main focus of the CPU leadership is not on enforcing and deepening the communist revolution in Ukraine but on uniting Ukraine with Russia. That results in an atmosphere that undermines class struggle with national struggle, a clear example of which are the strained relationships of the CPU leaders with the Communist Party of borotbists and the populist [Russian] left SR party (borbists).

My earlier experience convinced me that the communist revolution in Ukraine cannot be led only by the CPU which, even before, had few links with the rural proletariat, has almost completely split off from the urban proletariat, and now, influences only the urban petit bourgeoisie and, that the final victory of the revolution in Ukraine requires uniting all Ukraine's communist parties into one, closely tied to the urban and rural proletariat.

In full solidarity with the UCP (borotbists) on this and all other questions of revolutionary tactics and, on the other hand, finding that the tactics of the CPU leadership are fixed on artificially inflaming party differences, of which a clear example is circular no. 5 issued by the Kyiv provincial committee that will not result in a uniting and strengthening but a disintegration and weakening of the communist front, which will thereby seriously impede the development of the revolution and threaten again its collapse in Ukraine, I find it impossible to remain in the ranks of that party and publicly state my departure from it.

Considering that the formation of the single communist front in Ukraine necessary to strengthen soviet power here is possible only by following the tactics proposed by the UCP (borotbist) and concentrating all communist forces within the ranks of this part, I firmly request I be accepted as a party member

Former political commissar of the First Reserve Regiment, CPU member Vasily Brunst.

Letter No. 2

Dear Editor,
    Please place the following into your respected newspaper.

Not being in agreement with the tactics of the RCP Bolsheviks I left the party. I am joining the Ukrainian Communist Party (borotbist).

Andrei Petrovych Huk.

Letter No. 3

"From the Bolsheviks to the Borotbists."

To the Kharkiv committee of the Ukrainian Communist Party (borotbist).

Former member of the Committee of 50 attached to the Central Executive Committee of Ukraine's Supreme Soviet, Alexandr Bezkrovnyi.

Statement.

As a representative of the Ukrainian working peasantry I worked for the building of socialism in the area of education as member of the Committee of 50 attached to Ukraine's Supreme Soviet to which I was elected at the All Ukrainian [illegible: Volizpolkomov?] from the Communist Bolshevik faction.

During my duties as a living link between central Soviet power and the masses I realized that the policies and tactics of the Communist Bolshevik party as regards the popular education of Ukraine's masses not only risk not achieving their goals – creating a foundation for the development of proletarian culture among the rural proletariat – the first condition of the further building of a socialist society, but risk impeding the destruction of the national prejudices noted in the paragraph on popular education in the RCP program.

On the other hand, learning about the UCP (borotbists) educational work, its policies and tactics concerning socialist construction in Ukraine, I was convinced that the UCP (borotbists) position on resolving the tasks of realizing and enforcing soviet power in Ukraine was correct.

These above mentioned reasons oblige me to submit to the UCP (borotbist) provincial committee a request to include me into the party in whose ranks I could commit all my energies to the benefit of the Socialist revolution.

Ex-committee of 50 member attached to the Central Committee of Ukraine's Supreme Soviet, Bezkrovnyi.

Party card no. 375

January 7, 1920.

Letter No. 4

To the Poltava Provincial Committee of the CPU(b)

Ia. R. Ohiia.

Statement

On account of my political differences with the CPU noted below, I wish to be considered among those who have left the party. In my opinion Ukraine's class struggle now is being waged incorrectly, just as it was previously in 1919. The lack of a Ukrainian political and economic proletarian centre produces the Petliura reaction that under the guise of independence is waging counter-revolution in Ukraine. If Ukraine had its own centre then Ukraine's masses would not regard Petliura as a liberator but as the enemy of the proletariat. Ukraine's class struggle can be waged only by the Ukrainian proletariat holding full power and not by artificially created poor peasant committees that recognize soviet power only when they get some salt. A Ukrainian proletarian worker with such an opinion would be seen not merely as mistrust towards, but as complete difference of, opinion with the CPU.

Besides that, I note that last year's horribly mistaken policies that were in the orders of the red units that entered Ukraine have remained unchanged and, like before, are being sent to Russian comrades who implement them regardless of the fact that they engender counter-revolution.

Having such political differences earlier I did not think it possible to leave the party because of the struggle with Poland but now, that talks have begun and the situation has eased, I consider it my duty to state that I request to be considered as resigned from the CPU from the date of my statement's submission and that a comrade be appointed to take-over my party duties. I stress that I remain an honorable man and can carry-out all technical duties I get as an honorable revolutionary belonging to the UCP.

To the Provincial party committee of Ukraine's Communist Bolsheviks

In connection with my resignation from the Communist party of Ukraine and shift to the Ukrainian Communist Party I consider it necessary to provide the Provincial Committee with my biography because for the whole time after the collapse of Denikin my party work in Poltava was followed by the appropriate comrades to the extent that I was followed by secret agents. My biography, moreover, will clear at least some of the fog (adventurism and counterrevolution) through which the party circles of Poltava got used to see me.

I was born in 1892 in Kobeliansk county Vrodoshchasla district. Literate, of the first guild farmstead, Ohiia. My father, a peasant, held ¾ desiatyns of land and a house. There were 9 in our family. When the family was small my father took a sheaf of grain every summer from the kurkuls with which he fed us. That grain did not last us until the next harvest because our work sufficed for only the 9 [illegible]. When the bread ran out we young ones had either to borrow or beg and then we would repay by work the following year. Such a life forced my father to send us children to work wherever he could and I ended up, when 6, herding cattle for a kulak for one rouble. The kulaks name was Serdiuk. With each successive year I got 1 rouble more – I worked for a total of 6 years. When I was 12 I was earning 7. Naturally my conditions of life gave me no opportunity for education.

Not being able to live like that any longer my father sent me to learn to be a cobbler for 4 years without pay. The master was to feed me because my father could not feed me at home. When I had learned my craft my life did not improve because a pair of shoes then cost 40 kopeks. Making that much in a day was not enough to improve my life and my ambition to own my own shop collapsed. Then I went to work for the landowner Aksiut in Alexansdrivsk county in Katerynoslav province where I made 105 roubles a year. There I worked three years ...

During the imperialist war I made boots for the old army in Reshetylivka, Poltava province, and when the revolution broke out, I moved back to my family in Kobeliaky when Kerensky was in power.

As a proletariat, for whom the foreign yoke disgusted me from my youth, I was naturally interested in politics, which is why I attended meetings when, at one of them I was elected to the Kobyliaky soviet. The soviets then met every Sunday. At one of those meetings the issue of renewing the executive committee came up and I was elected. And as I was illiterate and had no idea what to do I ended up as a courier and helper.

In 1918, seeing my interest in politics, the executive committee appointed me to the Food Supply committee where, within three months, I could take over the committee and the post of chairman.

Two parties then existed in Kobyliaky; the [Russian] left SRs and the Ukrainian SRs to which my old comrades R. Matiash and O. Spivak signed me up, that is, to the UPSR. I did not work legally in that party for long because the Germans came and I had to go underground where I worked in the UPSR Poltava RevKom with comrades Lazovsky, Buhaievych, Matiash and others ...

Petliura never really controlled Kobyliaky, to which comrade Marchenko will attest, and together with comrade Spivak we were able to form a soviet in the town and raise the red flag ...

At the fifth UPSR conference in Kharkiv, when its politics were unclear to me and it adopted the name UPSR Communist, on June 11 1918 I joined the Bolshevik communist party of Ukraine.

During my entire sojourn in the BCP [Bolshevik communist party], as the party knows, but which I here stress, my greatest contribution was in the struggle against Denikin.

During the 3 months of fighting with my brigade I moved from Volyn to Katerynoslav provinces. Me and my comrades suffered much sadness, hunger and cold, wandered in mud up to our knees, moving as much as 50 versts in a day and doing what we had to, while the Red Army moving as much as 300 versts did not see Denikin. This fighting ended, honorably, in the town of Kremechuh ...

Finishing my biography I consider it necessary to point out how difficult it is for me to see myself treated as a fortune hunter and Petliurist after such exertions. How it hurts to see myself followed as a "counter revolutionary." To see how a common speculator is taken at his word while [I] Ohiia is seen as the organizer of a gang with no consideration of my revolutionary background.

Undoubtedly after leaving the party provocations surrounding my name and surveillance of me will only increase. With this biography I give the party committee a chance to take the correct attitude concerning me.

If I had a talent for fortune-hunting, careerism or profitmaking then, as evident from my biography, circumstances would have revealed it, and, [moreover], I never had nor expected to profit from the revolution. Proof is the fact that my mother is sitting [at home] hungry, my brothers are day-labourers, and the money you think I have doesn't exist, and I eat only when a comrade brings something from the district centre.

After leaving the party I remain the revolutionary that I was, not shirking from honest work on a new path and an earlier death rather than [sitting/dying?] in a counter-revolutionary prison camp.

Document No. 9: V. Vynnychenko, *Ukrainska Kommunistychna partiia (UKP) i Kommunistychna partiia (bolshevyky) Ukrainy (KP(b)U)* (Vienna, 1921) – excerpts.

[The Ukrainian Communist Party (UCP) and the Communist Party (Bolshevik) of Ukraine (CPU)]

To a mind unaccustomed to deep analysis the course of the revolution in Ukraine seems very straightforward. Ukraine's organized proletariat took power and in keeping with its socio-historical nature is changing the productive and civil relations in Ukraine. The proletariat, usually, organizes into a party that enters events as an avant-garde and conscious collective leader of the entire working class. Or so in theory. And on this basis the concrete results: the Communist Party (Bolshevik) of Ukraine has power in Ukraine. This party is the organized avant-garde and collective leader of the Ukrainian proletariat that is leading the revolution and transforming the entire social order into a new one.

Accepting all the above it is natural to ask what sense is there for a Ukrainian Communist Party to exist alongside that party? If the revolution is represented by the CPU and all other social groups during the sharp social class struggle are hostile to the party of the revolution (counterrevolutionary), then what is the UCP?

...

First let us note that just because the CPU has power in Ukraine it cannot be concluded: 1 that this party took power for itself through the organized efforts of Ukraine's revolutionary proletariat, or that this party is the party of the Ukrainian proletariat just because it holds power.

As is known, this party took power because of a two-sided process. On one side was the spontaneous class struggle of Ukraine's working mass (primarily peasant) for its social and national liberation that was not led by this party. On the second was the military offensive of Russian communists into Ukraine that aimed at exploiting the struggle of the working mass and seizing power for themselves. Military might played the key role in overcoming the unorganized technologically ill prepared spontaneous forces of the revolutionary mass. Additionally, this military force adopted its slogans to those of the Ukrainian working current (all power to the workers peasants soviet, an independent socialist soviet Ukraine, etc.) which distracted the activity of the masses, dampened their distrust of their military ally and permitted this ally, Russian communist military power, to seize the organs of soviet and state power and take Ukraine's ruling positions. The CPU played almost no role in this. As a party and proletarian organization it was at the time completely inactive and irrelevant. Only after power had been militarily seized [February 1918] did this party appear formally as the leader of the revolution, begin to try and create a base for itself in Ukraine's working masses, try to legalize its power and ground it by unity with the Ukrainian proletariat.

But this artificial process is unsuccessful. With no deep roots among Ukrainian workers, this ex [Russian] SD organization, organizationally tied to its centre in Petrograd or Moscow, did not and could not understand the laws of the Ukrainian revolution. It looked at the Ukrainian revolution as a part of a single indivisible Russian revolution and willfully ignored all historical social national and economic differences; the particularities of the Ukrainian circumstances of the revolution. Consequently, regardless of the favourable objective circumstances, this party could not develop. After seizing power in Ukraine militarily in 1919 this organization had every chance to win over all Ukraine's proletarian revolutionary elements, all state, political, administrative and military apparatus were and remain at its disposition. All the means of propaganda agitation and organization were at its service. It appeared as if, just like in Russia, this party, a provincial branch of the single Russian party, would become very big. The numbers, however, reveal something else. At the time of writing, in a country of 40 million this party has 15 000 members. And this, I stress, when all then above mentioned circumstances are in its favour! The UCP, meanwhile, formed at the beginning of 1920, after a few short months in difficult unfavourable circumstances – without power, no special rations, no material means, no press, unable to travel by train or hold mass meetings, subject to constant harassment by the CPU, with its leading members arrested and entire local units disbanded – within 3-4 months of its formation had 2000 members. These were registered and gone through all necessary party preparation and not merely noted in a book as is usually the case with entrants to the CPU. How to explain this?

Basically, the CPU is not the organization of Ukrainian workers [sic]. Neither by its social nature, membership or tactics. This is the party of the militarist bureaucratic petit-bourgeois white-collar educated [intelligentsia] with a sprinkling of Russian or Russified workers who live on Ukrainian territory. This becomes obvious in light of the following. The party has 15 000 members. Ukraine has more that 15 000 governmental positions. So obviously, the party represents functionaries and bureaucrats. That these functionaries are neither urban nor rural workers, but educated white-collar personnel is demonstrated by facts evident to anyone who has been in Ukraine.

...

The majority in the party are Jews. Without fear of error it can be said 60% of the CPU are Jews, 20-25% Russians, and 10 % Ukrainians (the remainder of the Borotbists who merged with the CPU). The Jewish majority is explained and proven by the following. The Russian bourgeoisie and democratic-minded educated persons hid from communist persecution during the civil war in Ukraine and usually fled with the Whites – Denikin or Wrangel. Very few remained and adapted to the regime. The Ukrainian educated also hid from persecution with some fleeing with Petliura and other hiding in villages. Only the Jewish educated could not flee either with the Russian or Ukrainian Whites, nor hide in villages where judeophobic [sic] attitudes were intensifying, Thus, whether or not they wanted to, the Jewish educated had to be on the Bolshevik side.

Trade, law, private medical practice, journalism, in a word, all the professions earlier occupied by the petit-bourgeois Jewish educated were annulled. That mass in these professions were left without work and means of sustenance. Hunger forced them to work for the soviets. And since only party members could hold a better position with good rations and pay, all these ex- doctors, lawyers, petty-traders, clerks, small shopkeepers and suchlike began joining the party and taking government jobs. Thus, by force of national and economic circumstances, appeared the abnormality that, within the Ukrainian worker-peasant socialist republic with its 40 million population, a 15 000 strong party rules, 60% of which is composed of petty-bourgeois Jewish educated, alien by nationality to the Ukrainian working population, alien by its social nature to the working classes, and uncertain in terms of its political allegiances.

This party's Russian element is also made up primarily of the local educated bourgeoisie, including whiteguardists tacked-on to communism, Russian secular functionaries from Russia; people also nationally alien to the Ukrainian working masses, tied to them neither by origins, nor interests. There remains an insignificant Ukrainian element of ex-borotbists that has no significance either in the party or the government; first because of its small size and second because of the policies of the ruling Russian communists.

...

Talking about the tactics of such a party [CPU] is impossible because this organization has only the name of an independent party. In reality it is not even autonomous part of the single Russian Communist Party let alone independent. The fact that the Central Committee of the RCP delegates the CPU's Central Committee via telephone from Moscow is the best proof of just how much independence this party has in reality. This is the administrative apparatus of the RCP Central Committee in Ukraine that for diplomatic reasons is called "a party."

Obviously, such an organization cannot have its own tactics but is the carrier and expression of RCP tactics. These tactics, moreover, are in fundamental opposition to the principles of the revolution. The very fact of this party's creation, as we noted, is a denial of the basic demands of the revolution. This "party" implements the directives of Ukraine's military occupation [regime]. That is its fundamental task; not the organization of Ukraine's economy on socialist principles, or the organization of the proletariat and its revolutionary energies. It only organizes an apparatus to maximize the extraction of Ukraine's resources.

...

The RCP's colonialist policies in Ukraine suit the [CPU's petit-bourgeois] professionals extremely well and that is why, not only through fear but because they benefit, they eagerly and carefully support and implement [those policies]. For their part, their tendentious reports to Moscow reinforce these policies as they variously demonstrate how such policies are necessary "for the revolution" in Ukraine. That is why the very idea of soviet power as a form of proletarian dictatorship exists in Ukraine only in declarations, as in reality, all power, absolute and unchallengeable, belongs precisely to these "delegated" petit-bourgeois professionals – commissars.

...

Let us now look at the UCP.

This organization cannot be bureaucratic because it is not a ruling party. Members are in soviet institutions but they are few and not in responsible posts, because the basis of any colonialist policy is not to permit a significant number of natives to administer their own country. There are also few white-collar professionals in this party and, indeed, there cannot be many; 1, overall there are few Ukrainian white-collar professionals, 2, a sizable number of them either emigrated or left with the Directory, or dispersed in villages. Thus most of its members are working people.

...

And this is inevitable because the UCP carries the principles of the revolution. The masses cannot but see that the CPU is only Moscow's technical-bureaucratic apparatus; an organization of commissar-functionaries and not a class organization of working masses. The masses cannot but see that the primitive single purpose of this technical apparatus is to exploit the country without the slightest regard for its economic commercial and political development. The feelings and survival instinct of the masses tell them that this kind of organization spells doom for the revolution, the country, and themselves. Accordingly, from one side distrust and reluctance to join irrespective of attendant material privileges – which explains why there are so few members despite the favourable circumstances. On the other side, for these reasons existing CPU organizations are disintegrating and the best from them join the UCP. That same instinct in the masses tells them that the UCP is the organization that can give them the true expression and realization of their class desires. They correctly sense that this is a mass revolutionary workers-peasants party, that its tactics are totally in accord with the principles of the revolution, that it places the main basis for the triumph of the working population not on technical military or bureaucratic power, but on the organization of the country's internal revolutionary and productive forces, and, that without a strong class organization and awakening of the working masses, without their intense active participation in the construction of new social, political, national and productive relations, the revolution cannot be consolidated and developed.

...

The moral levels of both parties also differ. The very nature of the CPU, its specific tasks, the character of its power, its policies, all inevitably <u>must demoralize its members</u> [sic]. The practice of giving its members material privileges, and then, usually in view of non members, must serve as a temptation and also demoralizes [*musyt sluzhyty spokushaiuchym i rozkladaiuchym*] . This party is joined for rations, money, cars, power, the opportunity to take bribes, the possibility of exploiting subordinates in a system of total irresponsibility of the powerful and their agents towards the collective. In light of the system of "delegation," centralization, and ignoring the most elemental demands of worker democracy, even idealistic and decent party members become demoralized ... Without anyone except another bureaucrat-commissar and "utilitarian communist" like himself to supervise him, thanks to the bureaucratized delegatory RCP centralized system, he [the CPU party member] worries only about "not crossing superiors" and placating them with "sharing" if they do.

Theft, bribery, malfeasance and counter-revolution in government work, the mockery of socialism and communism in the daily life of these CPU "party" members, all *must* [sic] be the result of the RCP's national and government policy in Ukraine. And it is not as much that these individual members are demoralized as that the entire system demoralizes them ... And in Ukraine it is even worse. Here all the various "activists" have a free hand. Here from Russia are sent the unworthy corrupted element unwanted in Russia but which cannot be sent to the secret police. Here gather the eager and cunning element desirous of "feeding." Central leaders are far away, Ukraine is a "counterrevolutionary" country not in the leadership's favour, so, do as you wish. The more vicious you are the more you will be seen as diligently working for the revolution and thus "a real communist."

We repeat this is the inevitable "natural" logical result of the RCP's colonialist Ukrainian policies. *This policy* [sic] brings division, debauchery, and moral and political filth into the apparatus of its CPU and into all Ukraine's political and social life.

Naturally, in the UCP none of this exists and cannot exist. No positions, no privileges, no luxuries, no power. The party cannot give its members any such things ... And one must have the courage of their convictions, a deep sense of honour, much courage and fortitude, in disregard of the unfavourable circumstances, to be a member of a persecuted organization out of power.

Indeed, there must be much thoughtfulness and conviction in one's *communist* [sic] convictions to have the fortitude to oppose such a recognized communist authority as the RCP. But this fetishization of the RCP must end and it must be understood that the RCP is not the source or cause of the revolution, but only one of its manifestations, and that historical national social psychological and a host of other factors can so change the internal nature of even such a renown phenomenon as the RCP, that only its authority and form would remain of its former content and essence.

...

Ukrainian communists abroad did not understand the UCP's historical importance and role. Without experience and facts they cannot yet critically analyze the existing authorities. The UCP is something they either cannot understand or simply anti-revolutionary. This is the attitude of idealist communists. We have no doubt that if they remained as such in Ukraine they would have to change their opinion and join that UCP they now cannot understand. "Utilitarian communists" have a totally different opinion. They have a negative opinion because it does not hold power, has no governmental significance or positions and cannot offer any crumbs from its table [*lakomstv neshchasnykh*]. They have a theory that UCP tactics are unsuited to "the Ukrainian issue."

It supposedly makes more sense to join the CPU and get positions and influence in Ukraine; become "true communists," win Moscow's trust and then betraying it, change its policies in Ukraine. We say nothing about the last sort of utilitarian communists who don't think about changing policies but merely attach themselves to communism for its perks and privileges or to assuage their personal ambitions. Only the ruling CPU can give them positions and perks so, accordingly, the UCP is a "counterrevolutionary party and they are sincere communists and revolutionaries. So, long live the RCP, the CPU, the occupation, the colonization, and of everything that in this mess allows catching a few crumbs [*v kalamutni vodi lovyty 'lakomstva neshchasni*] ...

Summing up. The CPU is an imported temporary phenomenon; the result of the unnatural and difficult evolution of the revolution in Ukraine. This is an interim and even perhaps [illegible] result of Ukraine's socio-economic and historical conditions.

The UCP is a phenomenon directly indissolubly and organically tied with Ukraine and its working masses. This is a process resulting from historical inevitability passing through all the stages of normal development and with time will root itself ever more firmly into the mass of Ukrainian workers.

The CPU by name and according to its officially declared program, its formal tasks (and because of the inertia inherited from its once revolutionary period), is communist and revolutionary. In reality, that is, objectively according to the essence and content of its concrete activity, its methods, and the nature of its tactics, it is anti-communist and counterrevolutionary.

The UCP, having basically the same program as the CPU, nonetheless appears truly communist and truly revolutionary because its tactics and concrete activity is totally in agreement with its program and does not depart in stark contradiction from the basic principles of revolutionary socialism and revolution.

The CPU is an artificial institution and technical apparatus, and tool of a foreign will standing apart from Ukraine's organic life. It is an obedient temporary bureaucratic machine only named "communist party" so as to win the trust of the masses.

...

The UCP is a natural historical and organic necessity. This party did not drop into Ukraine [illegible] riding in train wagons on Red Army bayonets. It emerged from the loins of Ukrainian workers through the stage of old Ukrainian social democracy taking from there the best and most energetic not breaking its link with the worker revolutionary tradition and being the most vibrant continuation consequence and product of the Ukrainian proletarian movement ... Regardless of whether the revolution in western Europe evolves faster or slower – upon which as noted, depends whether the Ukrainian revolution will be freed from the muscovite bureaucratic centralism that is throttling it-- or whether reaction triumphs for a shorter or longer time in Ukraine, the UCP will not disappear because of this, nor will the Ukrainian proletariat in towns and villages. Its members will not flee Ukraine because it is an indigenous product [plot vid ploti] of the Ukrainian working people, because the issue of the revolution in Ukraine is their issue, inseparable from their being, and not merely a temporary posting, something "for feeding," or a place to play the role of an occupation power.

...

The UCP is indeed now a small weak organization out of power. But this reflects the history of the Ukrainian working people that, for centuries on its fertile lands and despite its natural riches, was poor tattered and exploited by the occupational power of every Russian regime. And that is why the UCP regards world socialist revolution as the best way to liberate the Ukrainian working masses socially and nationally. It aspires to this as for a messiah as the single true liberator. And if only by virtue of this, it is more revolutionary and internationalist than those bureaucrats, archaic russifiers, masked black-hundreds and Russian nationalists with which the CPU overflows and who make its party-citizen opinion, who give this institution the real daily tone of all its work, and who in their simple nationalist naivety imagine the world revolution as only a bigger territory for their Russian occupationism [sic].

Such is the reality of Ukraine's two communist organizations. Their ideological and organizational struggle is a profound, organic, unavoidable phenomenon, which, with roots in ancient history, is now reflected in the principled struggle of the UCP that represents the principles of worker democracy, and revolutionary socialism with the CPU that represents the principles of modernized centralized absolutism and national despotism ...

Document No. 10: Resolution on the National and Colonial Question (1920) Adopted by the 2nd UCP Congress

(TsDAHO f. 8, op. 1, sprava 48, no. 50)

1. The Communist party stands on the historical class positions of Marxism concerning the national and colonial questions, in contrast to the mendacious formulations of bourgeois democracy about abstract judicial equality in general and national equality specifically. It therefore considers first, the concrete historical conditions, in particular the economic situation, the state of historical development of the given nation or colony; second it clearly distinguishes between the interests of the exploited classes of workers and those of the exploiters, from the general understanding of national interests, which inevitably means those of the ruling class; and third, it clearly distinguishes between exploited unequal dominated nations and ruling, exploiter nations.
...

4. The capitalization of [dominated exploited colonial] agrarian countries and "unhistorical peoples" naturally promotes their economic development, overturns social relationships and creates new classes, the bourgeoisie and the proletariat. On the basis of their geographical conditions economic centers emerge in colonies that become centers of political national and class struggle. Focused directly against foreign capital this struggle poses the issue of statehood which then becomes a slogan for the various social groups of exploited nations and colonies. In so far as this struggle is directed against imperialism it is a revolutionary factor in the fight against the European bourgeoisie; in so far as it internally unites different social groups it is bourgeois and represents, thereby, the bourgeois democratic period in the evolution of the national or colonial movement. The national bourgeoisie becomes the expression and leader of this movement that appeals to the nationally oppressed mass and its hatred of imperialism which it uses in its own class interests. These involve a national struggle and competition with a foreign bourgeoisie for markets. A colonial national bourgeoisie is made up mostly of representatives of trade or industrial capital or small land ownership [added in margin] and so its "national" demands against the metropole's finance capital is "democratic" – which deceives the working masses of the oppressed nation.

5. During the epoch of social revolution and capitalist collapse the struggle of a colonial bourgeoisie and oppressed nation for an "independent" state inevitably turns into a struggle against the indigenous working population and proletariat, for whom national independence without the overthrow of the bourgeoisie and dictatorship of labour, results in nothing but a change in owners. The Ukrainian (particularly western Ukrainian), Finnish, Georgian, Latvian, Polish and Czechoslovak [added in margin] experiences proves this in practice. Similarly, a colony's wish for independence on the basis of capitalist relations only pulls it into international imperialist combinations that, in the best instance, can end only with a change in imperialist protectors. For communists, therefore, who represent the class interests of the proletariat and working masses, the true meaning of the national liberation of the workers and national equality involves the destruction of classes through the dictatorship of the proletariat and soviet power.

...

9. The bourgeoisie through its colonialist policies directed capital and concentrated industry into artificial centers separated from their sources of raw materials – which are supplied by colonies. By controlling all of a colony's economy, imperialist-colonizers make it one-sided, [that is, it is] held and exploited as a source of raw materials and producer of semi-finished goods processed in the metropole's industrial centers. Finance capital imposed railroads [according to its interests] onto the national economy of the dependent countries. The proletarian revolution must free colonial productive forces so they can fully and rationally develop, it must redistribute economic regions, relocate production in proximity to resources, equalize colonies' industrial development and disassemble the old industrial centers. The proletariat will thereby destroy any possibility of economic exploitation and inequality and organize a planned world economy.

10. In its dealing with colonies and dependent nations the communist party must distinguish patriarchal feudal countries with peasant populations from developed capitalist nations recently become bourgeois democracies with their slogan of independence. In as much as the former, bypassing capitalism, will be pulled into the communist economy by the industrialized proletarian countries, the latter, ready to fight with its own bourgeoisie that has just constituted itself as a nation, as phrased in the *Manifesto*, organizes within the national borders of its country and resolves its national question by carrying the bourgeois democratic revolution to its conclusion by establishing its own dictatorship. (*The separation of industrial colonies from the imperialist countries that exploit them is absolutely necessary to free the colonies' productive forces from foreign financial-capitalist pathways, which in the transitional period of the proletarian revolution, means the necessary creation of new states from former colonies, as well as separate*

organizations of the colonial proletariat with their own administrative centers, as a condition for the existence of the proletarian dictatorship [added in margin]). The essence of the fastest possible attainment of independence for colonies, as prophesized by Engels to the leading proletariat, lies in the transformation of colonies and former metropoles into equal soviet republics and their [subsequent] union.

11. The October revolution in a multinational colonial empire first presented the proletariat with the concrete task of realizing its national program, and the Russian proletariat failed to rise to the occasion. Remaining great power tendencies, a blooming of colonialism and "Russian chauvinism" in the "borderlands," and attempts to sit on foreign backs, as foreseen by Lenin in his articles on the national question, often led to disasters for the proletarian revolution in the "borderlands" that the imperialist Entente exploits in its intrigues with Petliura, the Dashnaks, Musavatites, and others, who helped the Entente encircle the Soviet republics with a ring of bourgeois "borderland" states, and mire Soviet Russia in wars. The Russian proletariat could not implement the slogan of "self-determination" and thereby complicated the revolutionary process, hindered class differentiation in the "borderlands," and sowed enmity among the worker-peasant masses.

Because of this, in many of the old borderlands (Ukraine, Turkestan, Belorus) colonizer, petit-bourgeois, settler kulak, bureaucrat and Russian professional [intelligentsia] elements took soviet power and used Bolshevism to their own [Russian] nationalist ends. This often turned the class struggle into a nationalist conflict. The elimination of these national relationships is closely tied to the elimination of Russia [*Rossiia* – the empire] as "the single indivisible" with its psychology of "center-borderland" and its transformation into the union of independent federated and Unitarian soviet republics of the East.

12. For the Ukrainian proletariat the national and colonial questions have internal significance as a problem involving the elimination of colonial ties with Russia, liberating the productive forces of Ukraine's economic organism from their artificially created dependency on the industrial and financial centers of the former metropolis, and leading the popular masses out of the fog and cultural oppression left over as a legacy of capitalism. Raising the Ukrainian proletariat to a national class and organizing it on a national Ukrainian level will hasten its inevitable class growth. Towards this end, the Ukrainian Communist Party demands the elimination of Moscow's economic political professional and party bureaucratic supervisory organs. By putting an indigenous proletarian content into the UkrSSR [the UCP] aspires to transform it into a fully equal soviet republic within an international union. It is also attempting to obtain direct representation for the Ukrainian proletariat in the Communist International.

13. The second task of the UCP's national policy is to struggle against the influence of the Ukrainian nationalist bourgeoisie on the worker-peasant masses, and to reveal the total mendacity of the slogan of an "independent Ukrainian National Republic" as only a weapon in the Entente's hands against the revolution. Together with the dictatorship of the bourgeoisie it includes the national-cultural oppression of workers. Simultaneously the UCP struggles with the Russificatory and colonialist tendencies of soviet power [whose organs] are filled with petit-bourgeois trader elements and aspires to replace them with class-trained proletarians tied to the mass of Ukraine's working population.

14. [hand-written] The issue of developing soviet statehood in forms appropriate to the national-circumstances of various nations with their languages used in administration has been resolved in theory by the ruling Russian Communist Party in all of Russia's old borderlands. But in light of the seizure of the soviet apparatus by Russifying petit-bourgeoisie and professionals due to the weakness and low cultural and class level of the proletariat and working population, and because of the Russified worker-elites of the former non state nations who live apart from the national mass, this question [of appropriate state forms] in practice remains far from resolved. The Ukr SSR's entire apparatus is stuffed with these russifying elements and not only does the Russian language totally dominate, but it even opposes the adoption of Ukrainian, assimilating even those few Ukrainian elements within. [The apparatus] thus objectively becomes a tool of russification and a bureaucratic officialese isolated from the masses. That is why the slogan Ukrainian as the state language is still and will continue to be very relevant for some time yet and the Ukrainian Communist Party's task is to propound it.

[signature] And. Richytsky.

Document No. 11: Anonymous, *Vzgliad na polozhenie na Ukraine* (1920?)

(TsDAVO f. 2 op. 1 sprava 564 nos. 32–6)

A Consideration of the Situation in Ukraine.

Before presenting my opinion please consider

1. I am practically familiar only with Chernihiv and Poltava provinces.

2. I do not have the time, or perhaps the education, to present my views in a scholarly fashion.

3. I don't consider them immutable, but think that every party member has the right to think and circulate within the party his opinion on tactical issues …

I. Party building

There would be no Ukrainian question if Ukraine did not have profound and deep differences from central Russia. That is why the correct resolution of the Ukrainian question depends in the first instance on the clear exposition of those differences, and second, on decisive and logical conclusions. I personally consider these to be the major differences.

1. THE NATIONAL MOMENT.

This has two characteristics. On the one side, *Ukraine's population, to its lowest orders, including the considerable number of workers and urban dwellers who are linguistically Russified, identified themselves* [sic] as Ukrainian and very clearly juxtapose themselves as a nation and a state to Russians and Russia. Thanks to the work of a few but systematically energetic conscious Ukrainian intellectuals it, that is the population, learned much about national oppression and can well deal with it, reacting particularly sharply to economic oppression. On the other side, the most revolutionary but most [illegible] to the majority of the Ukrainian population according to the communist party is composed of a clearly Russified element with a distinct social characteristic. And it is this half-bandit half-anarchist element, because of a lack of a true proletarian element, that had unwarranted influence in the party. The result, first of all, is that those few more or less conscious proletarians in Ukraine began avoiding the party. A further consequence was that the party is incapable of growing. This element constitutes a quantitative and qualitative majority in the party able to destroy but not to build organizational life. They have no talent for it and are like a fifth wheel [*kak u vybytykh iz kolei*]. Their work is based almost totally on examples taken from their earlier life. The major shortcoming of this group that sets the tone in the party, unfortunately, is their total refusal to recognize any laws above themselves, just like our Cheka. They never consider themselves guilty ... they are obsequious towards their superiors and expect their subordinates to behave towards them similarly; themselves incompetent they are great masters of revolutionary phraseology and consider all calm systematic work petit-bourgeois.

3. [SIC] THE ORGANIZATIONAL MOMENT.

I do not support any one particular system or tactic ... In our party organization the example of the RCP is copied completely. That same dictatorship of the party summit in the form of the most powerful party leaders; that same dictatorship of party committees, the same kind of conferences that must rubber-stamp decisions previously made by the leaders ... In Russia, as far as I know, the group of individuals leading the party are geniuses. That can't be said of Ukrainian leaders. Maybe in Russia party committees are so competent and developed as contrasted to the rest of the party that they can completely run it, but this is not evident in Ukraine ...

SOME CONCLUSIONS.

I. In national matters it is imperative to accept the following: 1. There will be no agreement for as long as the party and the population suspect each other of treason. Relations must be more sincere; 2. Ukraine's proletariat at its current level of development, as it exists today, cannot ignore national issues in the name of internationalism; 3. ... From this it is obvious that the party must openly and firmly adopt a national program and make itself native for the Ukrainian proletariat, that is, it must Ukrainianize and totally throw out all background ideas about chauvinism and Petliurism that in practice are only a subsidiary factor for true [*nastoiashchie*] social petliurites.

...

III. With regards organizational matters the conditions of party life in Ukraine not only have not yet produced geniuses or even talent ... Our party leaders feel this and constantly turn to the RCP for instructions; this is a false path. The RCP central committee, leaving aside the geniality of its individual members, can only issue principled conceptual guidelines and aims. It cannot detail how to realize those aims in Ukrainian conditions because they themselves know nothing of those conditions and the information they get from the responsible Ukrainian workers, because of the above noted characteristics of their nature and work, present Ukraine from a distance higher than a bird's eye view [*s vysoty bole chem pticheskogo polete*].

No. It is possible and necessary to compensate for the shortage of geniuses by the collective supervision and creativity of the entire party. And this requires the introduction of the widest possible democracy within the party and the development of a strict constitution of party relationships ...

Document No. 12: Ivan Vrona (ex Ukrainian SR), Resolution on Russian Bolshevik Colonialism passed by the Volyn Provincial Conference of the CPU (Autumn 1920)

Cited in Popov, *Narys istorii Komunistychnoi partii (bilshovykiv)*, 251–2.

The CPU, originated from the depths of a non-Ukrainian current, the RSDLP (Bolshevik) and the urban proletariat, that experienced no national oppression and developed the revolution within the framework of the old unified single Russia [i.e., empire]. It regards itself also as a single undivided section of the general all-Russian revolutionary current; it is not organically tied with the Ukrainian masses and their national revolution. From the very beginning [for that reason] it took the wrong path. It could only get support from and orientate towards the Russian center and advance on Ukraine as an external foreign power that carries revolution from above and looks upon the national issue as an annoying complication and misunderstanding. [The CPU] regards the national movement as Petliurism and exclusively as a counter-revolutionary movement that has to be combated, or, in the best instance, ignored. It did not think it could trust the local Ukrainian forces and masses treating them as if they were infected with nationalism and chauvinism.

Adopting such a hopeless tactical approach to the socialist revolution in Ukraine, and in particular to the national revolution, the CPU inevitably had to isolate itself from a socio-economic base, the Ukrainian masses, and develop an ever more intensive colonialist occupation policy. This policy viciously centralizes the entire party and soviet apparatus, subordinates them to the Russian centre and destroys all of their initiative and independence. Forced by the course of events of the revolution in Ukraine to create separate party and soviet-state centres in Ukraine (the CPU and the Ukr SSR) to better fight against the bourgeoisie and the Ukrainian national movement, this tendency [from the Russian centre] nonetheless does not regard these centres seriously but as a temporary charade. It attempts to recreate the economic system within the framework of the old empire, dissolve the CPU into the national structure of the RCP (by opposing Ukrainian federalist borotbist and other tendencies in that party), and to progressively de-nationalize the Ukrainian masses with urban Russian and Russified colonizer elements.

The great-power colonialist policy that now dominates in Ukraine is extremely harmful to the interests and development of the communist revolution. In as much as it ignores the natural and rightful national emergence of the hitherto enslaved Ukrainian working masses it is totally reactionary and counter-revolutionary. It is a reflection of the old unforgotten Russian imperialist chauvinism and is enacted by the representatives of an oppressor nation against the oppressed nation that the Ukrainians had been [sic].

Document No. 13: Vasyl Blakytny (ex–Ukrainian SR). Analysis of CPU Submitted as Discussion Document for the 5th CPU Congress (November 1920) – Excerpts.

Kommunist 17, 19 November 1920. Reprinted *Suchasnist* no. 1 (1994), 146–55.

"The Communist Party of Ukraine and How to Strengthen it."

… During the revolutionary wars (1917–18) a considerable number of the best proletarian elements quit the party; the Donetsk miners, Kyiv's Arsenal workers, the Kharkiv drovers etc, died with the retreat of Ukrainian Soviet power, defending its borders against the Hetman, and during the following offensive.

What remained, with an addition of carpetbaggers, advanced from the RSFSR into Ukraine during the Second Soviet regime and, without appropriate central control, formed the CPU in 1918–19.

Filled with bourgeois carpetbagger elements and "predatory [*lovki*] fellow travelers" it was unable to control the revolutionary wave, lost touch with the workers, never made contact with the rural semi-proletariat. It was unable to carry out the fundamental tasks of destroying the Petliura regime or the warlords [*otamanshchyna*] and creating a strong base in the village by dividing it according to class, and, *ultimately*, again began to fall apart.

…

There are two basic views on how to reform the CPU into a single monolithic organization within which the "leaders" and the "mass" differ only in the level of their communist consciousness, revolutionary experience and fortitude. These two opposing tendencies exist within the party, for the most part furtive or unconscious, and our task is to objectively study and discuss them – without obfuscation or concealment. The first of these, which we shall call the "colonialist," is a result of the weakness of Ukraine's proletariat and is based on the shared nationality of most of Ukraine's urban proletariat with Russia's proletariat, semi-proletariat and petit-bourgeoisie. It demands building the RSFSR's state system in the restored borders of the old empire within which Ukraine was a part, a full levelling of the CPU into the RCP, and the dissolution and digestion of all the young proletarian forces of this "non-historical nation" into the Russian section of the Communist International.

The natural base of this tendency is in the RCP, particularly among those who one way or another did not break with the opportunistic bourgeoisie, within which is found most of the old national inertia, and who comprise a considerable proportion of force behind of this tendency. In Ukraine its leader is naturally those urban industrial workers unassimilated to Ukrainian conditions, and, more importantly, the mass of urban Russian or Russified petit-bourgeoisie that composed the mechanism of Russian bourgeois rule in Ukraine. It is natural, therefore, that in the party this tendency is based on elements whose social origins are from that part of the urban proletariat which did not loose its tie to the Russian national movement [*stykhiia*], russified craftsmen and urban petit bourgeoisie, bureaucrats, traders and other similarly class-suspicious groups. In as much as this complex cannot constitute a propitious base for a proletarian party, it is absolutely necessary to send strong proletarian cadres from the RCP to reinforce the CPU and become the main agent of party life. Being directly tied to Russia, these thousands of live threads would tie the CPU with the RCP, dissolving the former into the latter and negating the opposing tendency [within the CPU].

...

Based on a view of Ukraine as a Russian periphery, a staging area in the present, and a reserve of raw materials and grain in the future, the "colonialist" tendency sees the rebuilding of Ukrainian economic life from a presentist centralist perspective – not relating the economic system to the best possible organization and development of Ukraine's natural productive capabilities. Instead, it threatens a continued vertical integration of the Ukrainian periphery with the Russian economic center.

...

Nationality policy is characterized by the fact that the "colonialist" tendency has positively decided about a slow but full denationalization of a compact mass of about 30 million Ukrainian peasants, semi-proletarians and proletarians by using Russian nationals and their colonies in Ukraine [*sylamy natsionalnoi stykhyii Rossii ta ii kolonii*]. From this stems the policy of hindering the development of Ukrainian language and culture, the dispersion and assimilation of intellectuals-specialists, and protecting Russian culture and its bearers in Ukraine. This does not exclude using Ukrainian for propaganda nor does it formally infringe upon the equality of the "Ukrainian national minority."

...

In military policy the result of the principles of this tendency is the refusal to form Ukrainian national units, and forming and reinforcing units on Ukrainian territory with exclusively non Ukrainians etc. ...

Document No. 14: A. Richytsky, "The Economy and Culture" (*Chervony Prapor* 11 July 1920)

In our arguments with communists of the "All Russian variety" about organizing the Ukrainian proletariat as the ruling class, that is, about the organization of the Ukrainian proletarian state, we can hear that such organization is impossible and deleterious as concerns the economy, because, supposedly, it is unavoidably necessary to centralize the economy and subordinate various economic organisms to the "center", that is, Moscow – but, as concerns language and culture, then here... "self-determination including separation."

Obviously, for any worker who has at least heard of Marx, about the science of historican materialism, which teaches that at the root of social evolution, its socio-political organization and development of its culture lies the development of productive forces, that is, the economy, — that, for such a worker, it might seem odd that these "communists" and "marxists"separate culture from the economy, the economy from politics and so on.

To justify this [notion of] separating culture from the economy that dominates the psyche of "All Russian" communists only in the "borderlands", that is in Russia's colonies, and only in regards to nations oppressed by the Russian empire ... they must turn to history, and look for historically created unity etc.

And here these "marxists" and "dialecticians" have to think metaphysically, and taking what was – make the conclusion: that is what must be. They turn to history, to the past, not to trace the process of historical *development* [sic] as a historical materialist should, but in order to use history to tie upon that history what they want.

But the historical process went precisely in the direction of capitalist development of colonies and oppressed nations, and this development, with *historical* [sic] inevitability led them to free themselves from the imperialist *unity* [sic] imposed upon them, the unity of parasites and oppressors with the exploited and oppressed, and to create another unity of a different kind on the basis of ties with the world economy.

It is because of this "historical unity" that when capitalism collapsed we saw not only the dissolution of ... economic ties, but the collapse of colonial states. ... And all this talk we recently hear about the development of Ukrainian culture language schools etc. and cultural independence alongside [talk of]economic subordination and the dismemberment of Ukraine's economy – hearkens back to those "democratic freedoms" that the bourgeosie gave under capitalism.

In reality how is it possible to *independently* [sic] develop one's culture school and language etc when there are no economic means for it, because they must be imported from abroad or "the center?" Obviously, "center" can either give or not give, and if it does not, where then is the free development of culture?

Once the so called "center" controls the economy then it will bring the culture of "the center." When this center talks about the free unfettered cultural development of the "borderlands" these are but empty words for the masses behind which is nothing that will turn [those] words into action.

Only those can talk about cultural self-determination and free national cultural development who understand this as a free national-economic development, who recognize and create an independent proletarian state organization.

Notes

Introduction

1 J. Degras, ed., *Soviet Documents on Foreign Policy* (London, 1951), 116. Article 3 of Wilson's draft of the League Covenant, which did allow for the self-determination of British and French possessions, did not make it into the final version. A US delegation showed Wilson's Fourteen Points to Lenin in early January. He allowed the Americans to distribute over five million copies in German, Russian, Polish, and Ukrainian throughout the former empire. E. Sisson, *One Hundred Red Days* (New Haven, 1931), 210–11. The Entente leaders' refusal to grant independence to their colonies turned many elites in the colonies from liberal moderates into radical Marxist nationalists and members of the Comintern. E. Manela, *Wilsonian Moment: Self-Determination and the International Origins of Anticolonial Nationalism* (New York, 2007).

2 J.V. Stalin, *Works* (Moscow, 1953), IV: 165, cited in H. Lapchynsky, "Pershyi period Radianskoi vlady na Ukraini, TsVK ta Narodnyi Sekretariat," *Litopys revoliutsii* 1 (1928): 171.

3 J.C. Young. *Postcolonialism: An Historical Introduction* (Oxford, 2001), 124, classifies the Soviet Union as "at once colonial and anti-colonialist." He recognizes the significance of James Connolly, Sultan-Galiev, Tan Malaka, and M.N. Roy as anti-colonial Marxists but makes no mention of any Ukrainians. Ivan Dzuiba is not in the bibliography. A. Dirk-Moses, ed., *Empire, Colony, Genocide: Conquest, Occupation, and Subaltern Resistance in World History* (New York, 2008), has no chapter on Soviet internal policies. M. Kohn and K. McBride, *Political Theories of Decolonization: Postcolonialism and the Problem of Foundations* (Oxford, 2011), omit Russian-ruled Eurasia. National and Ukrainian communism is ignored by M. Dreyfus et al.,

Le Siecle des Communismes (Paris, 2000) and *A Dictionary of 20th Century Communism* (Princeton, 2010).

4 *Kommunist* (Kyiv), 5 April 1919; *Chervonyi prapor*, 17 April 1919. The Russian edition was confiscated. One hundred Ukrainian copies were allowed into stores – in Saratov. It has yet to be reprinted in Ukraine. *Do Khvyli* was translated: P. Potichnyi, ed., *On the Current Situation in Ukraine* (Ann Arbor, 1970). Shakhrai also published a survey of Ukrainian history, *Revoliutsiia na Ukraine* (1918), as well as a critique of Lenin's treatment of self-determination: ed., *N. Lenin. Statti po natsionalnomu pytanni Pereklad z Rossiiskoi na Ukrainsku* (Saratov, 1919), i–xxviii. On line: https://vpered.word press.com/2014/12/22/shakhrai-preface/

5 There are fourteen editions of Dzuiba's book, including three in English, three in Ukrainian, one in Chinese, and one in Catalonian. The major English-language works are C.P. Ford, "Outline History of the Ukrainian Communist Party (Independentists): An Emancipatory Communism 1918–1925," *Debatte* 2 (August 2009): 193–246; J. Mace, *Communism and the Dilemmas of National Liberation* (Cambridge, MA, 1983); and I. Maistrenko, *Borotbism: A Chapter in the History of the Ukrainian Revolution*, 2nd ed. (Stuttgart, 2007). The only published memoir of a UCP member is I. Maistrenko, *Istoriia moho pokolinnia. Spohady uchasnyka revoliutsiinykh podii v Ukraini* (Edmonton, 1985). Most UCP leaders' police files were moved to Moscow before 1939 and have not been used by any historian.

6 M. Popov, *Narys istorii komunistychnoi parti (bilshovykiv) Ukrainy*, 3 editions (Kharkiv, 1927–30); I. Maistrenko, *Istoriia komunistychnoi partii Ukrainy* (Munich, 1972).Overwhelmingly ethnic Russian and Jewish until the 1950s, the CPU was founded to administer the interests of the metropole on its periphery. It was a settler-colonist party of an unrepresentative urban minority. Its leaders still advocate reintegration with Russia and still think in terms of the Russian imperial space. Their mentality is reflected on the first page of the 4 January 2006 edition of their newspaper. Above the title "Kommunist," a picture of Lenin, and the slogan "Workers of the World Unite," we read: "Greetings on the occasion of Christ's birth" – all in Russian. Below, a picture of and greeting from the party leader is flanked by a picture of the Metropolitan of the Ukrainian branch of the Russian Orthodox Church giving Christmas greetings – in Russian.

7 Since all states are created using similar methods, whether they are subsequently labelled "empire" or "national state" or "multinational state" depends on how their elites see them and how these terms were defined at the time of formation. Until the establishment of the League of Nations mandate system in 1919, public opinion considered colonial issues a

matter of internal policy. Rule over colonies was legal in international law, which did not apply to colonies. After the Second World War, colonies became subjects under international law and the legality of "colonialism" was disputed. By mid-century, the pejorative connotation of imposed control resulting in economic exploitation that was initially associated with the word "empire" by intellectual critics had become part of its accepted definition in all languages. I.S. Lustick, *State-Building Failure in British Ireland and French Algeria* (Berkeley, 1985); idem, *Unsettled States Disputed Lands* (Ithaca, 1993); M. Beissinger, "The Persisting Ambiguity of Empire," *Post-Soviet Affairs* 11 (1995): 149–84; C.Q. Quayle, *Liberation Struggles in International Law* (Philadelphia, 1991), 82–121. On empires as structures, see M. Motyl, *Imperial Ends* (New York, 1992).

8 This idea was implicit in Marx and Engels wrote in 1843: "Give me 200 000 Irish men and I will overthrow the entire British monarchy." In the 1890s French Marxists wrote about two nations within each nation, "nation class" and French "proletarian patriotism." K. Marx, F. Engels, *Ireland and the Irish Question* (Moscow, 1971), 43. R. Stuart, *Marxism and National Identity: Socialism, Nationalism, and National Socialism during the French Fin de Siecle* (Albany, 2006), 90–2.

9 V. Skorovstanskii [pseud. Shakhrai], *Revoliutsiia na Ukraine,* 2nd ed. (Saratov, 1918), xi. Iurkevych drew attention to this danger in his 1917 pamphlet *Russkie sotsial demokraty i natsionalnyi vopros.* English translations: M. Yurkevych, *Journal of Ukrainian Studies* (Spring 1982): 57–78; on line: http://thecommune.co.uk/ideas/what-is-capitalism/imperialism/the-russian-social-democrats-and-the-national-question/. It is unknown if Ukrainian Marxists knew of Kazimierz Kelles-Krauz, the Polish PPS theoretician who in the early years of the century also advocated linking national liberation to proletarian struggle.

10 There are two basic perspectives on nationality. Those who are influenced by Enlightenment cosmopolitism and classical economics (Voltaire, Adam Smith, advocates of neoliberal capitalism) ignore domination and dependency. From this perspective, European-type industrialization, urbanization, and civilization is a desirable universal norm that all will adopt voluntarily or otherwise. Cultural differences are ephemeral and are destined to be replaced by a universal rationalist civilization represented by the country to which the advocate belongs. "National liberation" is "anti-modern." Those who refuse to adapt and assimilate or to "rationally" exchange goods on the "free market," which disregards borders, are "irrational" and to be ignored or repressed. The past is only "tradition" and is an impediment to progress best forgotten or relegated to holidays. Nationalism is atavism, and there are no "liberation wars," only "rebellions."

Those influenced by Romanticism and mercantilism (Herder, Alexander Hamilton, Friedrich List) justify opposition to foreign domination as rational and desirable on the grounds that all peoples should have a national state, within which they should find their own way to modernity and social justice. Cultural/national difference is a primordial human attribute that cannot be ignored. Unity is not uniformity.

11 R. Rosdolsky, "The Workers and the Fatherland: A Note on a Passage in the 'Communist Manifesto,'" *Science and Society* 3 (1965): 330–7; J.P. Himka, ed. and trans., *Roman Rosdolsky: Engels and the "Nonhistoric" Peoples: The National Question in the Revolution of 1848* (Glasgow, 1986); R. Munck, *The Difficult Dialogue: Marxism and Nationalism* (London, 1986); R. Szporluk, *Communism and Nationalism: Karl Marx versus Friedrich List* (Oxford, 1988); E. Brenner, *Really Existing Nationalisms: A Post-Communist View from Marx and Engels* (Oxford, 1995); Stuart, *Marxism and National Identity*.

12 L. Trotsky, *Sochineniia* (Moscow, 1927), IX: 209–10.

13 *Robitnycha hazeta* (30 March–6 April) 1917, reprinted in V. Verstiuk et al., *Ukrainskyi natsionalno-vyzvolnyi rukh. Berezen-Lystopad 1917 roku. Dokumenty i materialy* (Kyiv, 2003), 105. Shakhrai, *Statti*, ii.

14 The only Ukrainian included in the most recent work on the subject is Roman Rosdolsky. M. Van Der Linden, *Western Marxism and the Soviet Union: A Survey of Critical Theories and Debates since 1917* (Leiden, 2007). No Ukrainian is represented in R.B. Day and D. Gaido, eds, *Discovering Imperialism: Social Democracy to World War I* (Leiden, 2012).

15 D. Rowley, "Interpretations of the End of the Soviet Union: Three Paradigms," *Kritika* (Spring 2001): 395–426. "Dependency theory" ignored Russian-ruled Eurasia.

16 Lenin wrote to explain why war between capitalist states was unavoidable and why real wages could rise in Europe and keep workers loyal to their national governments – which Marx had incorrectly claimed was impossible under capitalism. Lenin ignored that workers in colonies (Australia, Canada) and in countries without colonies (Denmark, Sweden) could prosper, while workers in imperial countries (Spain, Portugal) could be poor. Because workers in Britain had high wages, supposedly because of colonial profits, secession would impoverish and radicalize them. Lenin did not explain how owner profits were turned into the wages of skilled workers. He incorrectly claimed a direct relationship between imperial profits and imperial sentiment, failing to see that willingness to profit from empire was rarely matched by willingness to pay for empire. To justify secession, he claimed that imperialism impeded development in dependencies. Marx specified that capitalism could profit from dependencies but

did not need them. B. Warren, *Imperialism Pioneer of Capitalism* (London, 1980); A. Brewer, *Marxist Theories of Imperialism: A Critical Survey* (London, 1980).

17 The Ukrainian Bolshevik Volodymyr Zatonsky specifically denied the applicability of Lenin's theory to imperial Russia. Unlike English workers, the Russian proletariat could not be "imperialist," because Russia was itself a colony and its capitalists could not use profits, which went to Belgium and England, to "buy off" Russian workers. All workers in the empire were therefore equal, and Russian culture dominated because it was part of their revolutionary consciousness. V. Zatonsky, *Natsionalnaia problema na Ukraine* (Kyiv, 1926), 32–4.

18 O. Vysotsky and A. Holub, "Zarodzhennia sotsial-demokratii v Ukraini i mizhnarodnyi sotsialistychnyi rukh," *Politolohichi chytannia* 2 (1994): 114–15.

19 "I vse zhe blizost k velikorusam brala verkh!" Lenin, *Polnoe sobranie sochinenii*, 55 vols. (Moscow, 1959–65) IL: 377. Lenin supported the Boers in South Africa but not the Bantus whom "imperialist" Britain had recently freed from slavery.

20 "Internal colony" is a modern term implying that the jurisdiction of the ruling metropole over a given periphery is legitimate. In so far as Russian rulers conquered Ukrainian territory in 1709-1712, 1919-1921 and 1944-47 those opposed to Russian rule can consider it illegitimate. From this perspective Ukraine can only be a colony – not an "internal colony." It is not an "occupied territory" because Russia claimed permanent sovereignty over it.

21 The leading radical populists of *Narodna Volia* (Andrei Zheliabov, Semen Iakhnenko, Mykola Kylbachych, Sofiia Perovska, Semen Barannikov, Valerian Osynsky) were Ukrainian-born. Like the Irish Fenians and Republicans, they wanted to decentralize the empire and achieve autonomy for Ukraine – for which their Russian counterparts condemned them. *Literatura sotsialno-revoliutsionnoi partii "Narodnoi Voli"* (n.p., 1905), 163–4.

22 P. McMahon, *British Spies and Irish Rebels: British Intelligence and Ireland, 1916–1945* (Woodbridge, UK, 2008), 163–74; D.W. Miller, *Queen's Rebels: Ulster Loyalism in Historical Perspective* (Dublin, 1998); G.K. Peatling, *British Opinion and Irish Self-Government 1865–1925* (Dublin, 2001); E.G. Lengel, *The Irish through British Eyes* (London, 2002); M. de Nie, *The Eternal Paddy. Irish Identity and the British Press, 1798–1882* (Madison, 2004).

23 The Kyivan Club, the Party of Legal Order, and the Russian Brotherhood were explicitly anti-Ukrainian organizations. They did not constitute a single coordinated extremist imperial loyalist group in the Ukrainian

provinces as did the Ulster Unionists in Ireland. Dozens of loosely related loyalist groups, termed "Black Hundreds," appeared throughout the Russian empire after 1904. The largest was the Union of Russian People.

24 E. Childers, "Might and Right in Ireland," *English Review* (June 1919): 512–14; Young, *Postcolonialism*, 302.

25 L. Kennedy, *Colonialism, Religion and Nationalism in Ireland* (Belfast, 1996); C. Carroll and P. King, *Ireland and Postcolonial Theory* (Cork, 2003); K. Kenny, *Ireland and the British Empire* (Oxford, 2004); S. Howe, *Ireland and Empire: Colonial Legacies in Irish History and Culture* (Oxford, 2000); T. McDonough, *Was Ireland a Colony?* (Dublin, 2006). See also T.E. Hachey, *Britain and Irish Separatism* (Washington, 1984).

26 J. Cleary, *Outrageous Fortune: Capital and Culture in Modern Ireland* (Dublin, 2006), 11–35.

27 In 2000 the UN had 188 member countries. In 1900, 125 of them had been dependencies and/or colonies. Another 17 were European countries that had belonged to the Tsarist, Habsburg, or Ottoman empires. D.B. Abernathy, *The Dynamics of Global Domination* (New Haven, 2000), 411–16.

28 D. Chioni-Moore, "Is the Post- in Postcolonial the Post- in Post-Soviet? Toward a Global Postcolonial Critique," *PMLA* 30 (January 2001): 111–24.

29 S. Velychenko, "The Strange Case of Foreign Pro-Russian Radical Leftists," http://ucipr.kiev.ua/publications/the-strange-case-of-foreign-pro-russian-radical-leftists/lang/en. http://krytyka.com/en/solutions/opinions/leftists-liberals-and-ukraine-tale-double-standards.

Chapter 1

1 *Pervaia vseobshchaia perepis naseleniia Rossiiskoi imperii 1897 g. Kharkovskaia guberniia*(St Petersburg, 1904) 46: xiv.

2 B. Krawchenko, *Social Change and National Consciousness in Twentieth Century Ukraine* (London, 1985), 17-19, 41-43; I. Mazepa, *Bolshevizm i okupatsiia Ukrainy. Sotsialno-ekonomichni prychyny nedozrilosti Ukrainskoi revoliutsii* (Lviv, 1922) 4-29. Mazepa labeled the Ukrainian provinces with its Russian settlers a Russian colony and "Ukraine's Ulster," 149. K. Kononenko, *Ukraine and Russia: A History of Economic Relations between Ukraine and Russia (1654-1917)* (Milwaukee, 1958), based primarily on 1920s Soviet publications, is the best account in English for the argument that the Ukrainian provinces were colonies of the Russian metropole. There is no study on Russians as settler-colonists in Ukraine analogous to David Prochaska's *Making Algeria French: Colonialism in Bone, 1870-1920* (Cambridge, 1990).

3 M. Porsh, *Ukraina i Rossiia na robitnychym rynku* (Kyiv, 1918).

4 The Polish nobility in these provinces might be compared to the late-nineteenth-century British in India. Both groups retained attitudes, behaviours, and customs that had disappeared among their counterparts in England and the central Polish provinces. Unlike their counterparts in the Lithuanian provinces, with rare exceptions, they met protest with repression instead of reform and thus never won support or sympathy from the surrounding peasant population. B. Hud, *Ukrainsko-Polski konflikty novitnoi doby. Etnosotsialnyi aspect* (Kharkiv, 2011), 235–7.

5 I. Cherikover, *Antisemitizm i pogromy na Ukraine1917–1918 gg.* (Berlin, 1923), 115–16. Jewish soldiers were willing to serve in Ukrainian units.

6 "Munyvshyna i buduchyna Ukrainskoi vyzvolni borotby." Reprinted in *Kyivska starovyna* 5 (1993): 47–8. On an emerging regional interest among Ukraine's industrialists and bankers critical of central policies they thought discriminated against them, see O. Shliakhov, "Stavlennia pidpryiemt-siv pivdennoukrainskykh gubernii do polityky imperskoho tsentry na pochatku XX st.," *Problemy istorii Ukrainy XIX st.* no. 23 (2013) 159–71.

7 Cited from the memoirs of a Jewish socialist Duma delegate: O. Lohinov, L. Semenko, *Vinnytsia u 1917 rotsi,* (Vinnytsia, 2011) 247.

8 Tsentralnyi derzhavnyi arkhiv vyshchykh orhaniv vlady ta upravlinnia Ukrainy (hereafter TsDAVO) f. 2 op 1 sprava 531. Attached to her letter addressed to Rakovskii was a petition signed by 880 like-minded Kyivan faithful opposed to Ukrainians within their parish holding services in Ukrainian.

9 V. Shulgin, *Tri stolitsy* (Moscow, 1991), 125; Tsentralnyi derzhavny arkhiv hromadskykh obiednan Ukrainy (hereafter TsDAHO) f. 8 op 1 sprava 76 nos. 5–6; sprava 75 no 10v. "Petliurism" was a Bolshevik term intended to disparage Ukrainian independence by associating it with a single person rather than the UNR.

10 After censorship was eased in 1905, the educated could popularize the notion of "Ukrainians," and of "Ukraine" as a place, in postcards and posters as well as through cheap editions of Shevchenko's poems. In 1896, private publishers were allowed to print postcards. M. Zabochen et al, *Ukraina u starii lystivtsi* (Kyiv, 2000), passim.

11 M. Hekhter, "Nashi bili nehry," *Rada* 14 (27) July,1909.

12 For the history and platforms of Ukraine's parties: Maistrenko, *Borotbism: A Chapter in the History of the Ukrainian Revolution*, J. Borys, *Sovietization of Ukraine, 1917–1923*, 2nd ed. (Edmonton, 1980), 73–97, 121–70; V. Shevchenko, ed., *Ukrainski politychni partii kintsia XIX – pochatku XX stolittia* (Kyiv, 1993); R. Vetrov, *Likvidatsiia bahatopartiinosti v Ukraini (1920–1925 rr.)* (Dniproderzhynsk, 2007); O. Liubovets, "Natsional-kommunizm

iak politychna alternatyva revoliutsiinoi doby 1917–1920," in *Ukraina v revoliutsiinykh protsesakh pershykh desiatylit XX stolittia*, ed. V. Lytvyn et al. (Kyiv, 2008), 439–514; O. Liubovets,*Ukrainski partii revoliutiinoi doby 1917-1920 rokiv: narysy istorii ta prohramni dokumenty* (Kyiv, 2012).

13 Three basic surveys in English of the political history of the period are A. E. Adams, *Bolsheviks in Ukraine: The Second Campaign 1918-1919* (New Haven, 1963); J. Reshetar, *The Ukrainian Revolution 1917-1920* (New York, 1972); and Borys, *Sovietization.*

14 Few in 1917 thought the Bolsheviks could retain power. They had only 10% of the Ukrainian vote for the Constituent Assembly.

15 Notwithstanding earlier claims to the contrary, historians today think that the UNR had little if any control over more than a few of the major partisan formations in Soviet-controlled Ukraine. Iu. Tiutunnyk, *Zymovyi pokhid 1919-20 rr.*, (Kolomyia, 1923); O. Dotsenko, *Zymovyi pokhid 6.XII.1919–6.V.1920*, 3rd ed. (Kyiv, 2001); M. Kovalchuk, *Nevidoma viina 1919 roku* (Kyiv, 2006), 91.

16 Iu. Hamretsky, "Bilshovyky ta ikhni politychni protivnyky na Ukraini v 1917 r.," *Ukrainsky istorychnyi zhurnal* no. 11 (1987), 92–3. Voting statistics do not indicate nationality, but given the Russian majorities in the big cities, where their support was concentrated, it can be assumed that the Bolshevik vote was overwhelmingly from the urban Russian-settler population which paid little notice to Ukrainian national issues.

17 V. Manilov ed., *1917 god na Kievshchine* (Kharkiv, 1928) 329. Ukrainian SDs Tkachenko and Porsh formulated the resolution.

18 The Bolsheviks held nineteen of the forty seats on the Kharkiv City Soviet Executive in early December, when they got it to drop its earlier support for the UNR and align with Moscow. In October 1917, the Ukrainian provinces had 15,000 Red Guards.

19 Two weeks later, the Russians made Zatonsky a member of their *Sovnarkom* with "a deciding vote in all matters relating to Ukraine." From that point until the Germans vanquished the Bolsheviks in Ukraine, the *Sovnarkom* made no decisions on any Ukrainian issues. Iu.N. Amiantov et al., *Protokoly zesedanii soveta narodnykh komissarov RSFSR. Noiabr 1917–mart 1918 gg.* (Moscow, 2006), 130, 199.

20 *Bolshevitskie organizatsii Ukrainy: organizatsionno-partiinaia deiatelnost* (fevral 1917–iul 1918g.) (Kyiv, 1990), 533. For details of the differences between Ukrainian and Russian Bolsheviks, see H. Iefimenko, *Vzaiemovidnosysny kremlia ta radianskoi Ukrainy: ekonomichnyi aspekt (1917–1919)* (Kyiv, 2008) 45–106.

21 TsDAHO f. 57 op 2 sprava 281 no. 31. Claims that the lack of national consciousness among Ukrainian peasants was a major weakness of the national movement during the revolution are dubious. Little or no national consciousness among Bulgarian, Romanian, and Serbian peasants did not impede the establishment of independent Bulgarian, Romanian, and Serbian governments.

22 An eyewitness reported that it was standard Bolshevik practice to surround soviet congresses and executive committee plenums with loyal troops to intimidate critics. *Robitnycha hazeta* 15 (NS), 1 February, 3 March, 12 April 1918. Convened during the German offensive, the congress did not include delegates from Kharkiv, Katerynoslav, or Taurida provinces and was not "All Ukrainian" despite its title. Mazepa, who was present, made no mention of such troops in his memoirs, written twenty-three years later. I. Mazepa, *V ohni i buri revoliutsii,* 3rd ed. (Kyiv, 2003), 55–8. For different versions of the proceedings, including rejected motions: "Materialy pro druhyi VseUkrainskyi ziizd Rad," *Litopys revoliutsii* no. 2 (1928): 240–75; TsDAHO f. 57 op 2 sprava 168.

23 *Tretii VseUkrainskii sezd sovetov (6–10 marta 1919 g)* (Kyiv, 1919). The Third Congress did not include delegates from UNR-controlled territories. Local officials also reported that after having such soviets thrust upon them, people would ignore them and hold meetings on their own. TsDAVO f. 2 op 1 sprava 272 no 16–17. Cited in I. *Kuras* et al., *Politychna istoriia Ukrainy XX stolittia u shesty tomakh* (Kyiv, 2003), II: 342–3. How Bolsheviks ensured Bolshevik majorities in soviets is described in E.A. Sikorskii, *Iz istorii utverzhdeniia v Rossii diktatury Bolshevikov. (po materialam vserossiiskim i smolenskim)* (Smolensk, 2009), 150–61.

24 Skrypnyk also feared that his centralist opponents would split the Ukrainian branch of the Party if he did not withdraw his earlier demand. V. Iurchuk et al., *Pervyi siezd kommunisticheskoi partii (bolshevikov) Ukrainy* (Kyiv 1988), 127–9, 166–68; TsDAHO f. 57 op 2 sprava 488 no. 46, 53–5; M. Frolov, *Kompartiino-radianska elita v USRR (1917–1921 rr.): stanovlennia i funkstsiovannia* (Kyiv-Zaporizhzhia, 2003), 31.

25 Lenin offered concessions and, as Shakhrai observed, not "independence" but merely the "right" to independence. H. Iefimenko, *Status USRR ta ii vzaiemovidnosyny z RSFSR: dovhyi 1920 rik.* (Kyiv, 2012), 95–115.

26 *Nove Zhyttia* (Poltava), 15 March 1919.

27 Ivan Tsiupa, "Taiemnytsia smerti nachdyva Shchorsa," *Kyiv,* no. 11 (1988): 117; J. Meijer, ed., *The Trotsky Papers* (The Hague, 1964), I: 350, 393; Ia. Dashkevych et al., *Istoriia Ukrainskoho viiska* (Kyiv, 1996), 115n, 120–1.

Orders issued on 1 May called for "no stopping short of the most savage methods" to bring partisan forces under control. In June, Trotsky sent Semion Aralov, head of military intelligence, to serve as Chief of Staff of Ukraine's newly formed 12th Army. He began accusing Shchors of indiscipline and UNR sympathies. TsDAVO f. 2 op 1 sprava 175. On 6 August, Trotsky received permission to conduct a "radical purge" in Ukraine, as well as a detachment of five hundred special Cheka troops to carry it out. On 28 June, and again on 9 August, he ordered Aralov to purge with "molten steel" insubordinate commanders in Ukrainian formations that contained too many "Petluirite partisan and Otaman [warlord] elements." Trotsky probably also ordered the arrest and/or execution of commanders Dumenko, Sharyi-Bohunsky, Tkachenko, Bochkin, Bozhenko, Hrebenko, and Cherniak.

28 Borotbist Oleksandr Shumsky stated that his party's anti-Bolshevik "slogans" were only tactical expedients and did not reflect its program. *Borotbist* (Poltava), 30 March 1920. The offer of positions on Revkoms in December 1919 served to separate the few who had achieved power from the majority who had not. V. Nahorny, "Bilshovyzm ta Ukrainskyi natsional kommunizm v dobu revoliutsii (1917–1920 rr.)," Kandydatska dissertatsiia Kyivskyi derzhavny linhvistychnyi universytet (1995), 185–9.

29 Frolov, *Kompartiino-radianska elita v USRR,* 132; *Kommunist* (Kyiv), 24 April 1920; Lenin, *Polnoe sobranie,* XXXXII: 174–5.

30 *Chervonyi prapor* (special issue), no. 6 (18 February 1920). In Tkachenko's obituary, co-founder Andryi Richytsky expressed amazement at how Russian communists totally failed to understand the Ukrainian revolution and resorted to military occupation.

31 The table excludes Volyn province, four *povits,* and some *volosts.* Counted total includes 85 per cent of the population of tsarist Ukraine in 1917 borders. Urban population includes 617,301 people in small towns counted as "villages" in 1897. The estimated total was 25,621,463 (20,886,682 rural; 4,726,501 urban – including. 770,269 small towns). Only 16,963,312 of the total counted indicated nationality. The highest numbers of declared Russians were in Donetsk (885,471) and Odessa (436,984) provinces (51 per cent of total). The highest numbers of Jews were in Odessa (313,606) and Kyiv (321,401) provinces (53 per cent of total). In reality, the percentage total of ethnic Ukrainians was higher and of Russians was lower than indicated because an unknown number of Ukrainians and Jews declared themselves Russians. As more urban than rural residents could be counted, most of the 4 million excluded were Ukrainian. Enumerators in Kyiv and probably other towns pressured Ukrainians to declare themselves Russians

and/or subsequently changed forms to read "Russian" where persons wrote "Ukrainian." *Chervonyi prapor* (Kyiv), 21–2 March 1919.

32 E. Goldman, *My Disillusionment in Russia* (New York, 1923), 214. TsDAHO f. 1 op 1 sprava 92 nos. 81–2. Postwar published collections of CPU resolutions did not include this preamble to the directive. *Desiatyi siezd RKP(b) Mart 1921 goda. Stenograficheskii otchet* (Moscow, 1963), 213; 604, 606–7.

33 In 1919, Lenin expected Ukraine to send to Russia 50 million poods (903,000 tons) of grain. In 1921, the targetof 57 million was not lowered until December.In April 1921, Rakovskii explainedthat "there will be absolutely no changes in quotas or deadlines, and any rumours to the contrary are idle speculation." Repression was intensified, and included the use not only of the Red Army but also of more than 206,000 men organized into punishment battalions and requisition squads. P. Isakov, "Spivvidnoshennia tsin ta realnykh dokhodiv hromadian v Ukrainskomu seli … ta rozhortannia selianskoho povstanskoho rukhu," *Siverianskyi litopys*, no. 4 (1998): 138–45; S. Kulchytsky, *Komunizm v Ukraini. Pershe desiatyrichchia (1919–1928)* (Kyiv, 1996), 193–9. M. Lytvyn et al,*Vidnosyny derzhavy suspilstva i osoby pid chas stvorennia radianskoho ladu v Ukraini (1917-1938)* (Kyiv, 2013) II: 172-76.

34 Turkistan delegates at the Tenth Congress presented their region as a Russian economic colony where the dictatorship of the proletariat in the hands of the local Russian proletariat continued the old colonialist relationships. A "thin stratum of the [local] Russian population" ruled politically and culturally, irrespective of class, because they dominated economically and were under the influence of "colonialist ideology." Ukrainians who argued like this were not in the Ukrainian branch of the Party or at the Congress. *Desiatyi siezd*, 195–8, 203–5, 209.

35 *Vosmoi siezd RKP(b), Mart 1919 goda. Protokoly* (Moscow, 1959),80–1, 95–7. *Dvenadtsatyi siezd RKP(b)*, 498, 531–2, 595–6, 693–7. In 1923, at the Seventh CPU Congress, Rakovskii noted that while the older generation of Ukrainians were inclined to regard Ukrainian as "a slave language," the younger were not and were introducing their language into education and public life – a matter of vital importance. TsDAHO f. 1 op 1 sprava 98 no. 99–100.

36 P. Bachynsky, ed., *Dokumenty trahichnoi istorii Ukrainy (1917–1927)* (Kyiv, 1999), 523–5.

37 L. Trotsky, *Sochineniia* (Moscow, 1927), XXI: 324. He does not specifically mention Ukraine, but in reference to the Transcaucasus, he writes that for its people to see the intrusion of the Red Army as an occupation would be a great error against the Revolution. He suggests that "on afterthought," the intrusion was accepted – as had been the vicious food-procurement policies

– as a lesser evil necessitated by the circumstances to save the area from "imperialism." "Deiatelnost tsentralnogo komiteta partii v dokumentakh," *Izvestiia TsK KPSS*, no. 5 (1991): 160. TsDAHO, f. 1 op 1 sprava 97 no. 61.

38 *Zvit robitnyche-selianskoho uriadu Ukrainy za 1923-24 rik* (Kharkiv, 1925), 12–13. Skrypnyk also avoided the terms "colonialism" and "imperialism" and the issue of economic decentralization. He attributed pre-1923 policies to "erroneous" interpretation of theory. He defended Ukrainian autonomy within the USSR as well as the harnessing of Ukrainian nationalism to the interests of socialism, but he accepted subordination to Russia. He did not regard the Bolshevik seizure of power as a purely Russian affair, nor did he believe thata bourgeois national state had to precede a socialist state. M. Skrypnyk, *Statti i pisma* (Kharkiv, 1930), I: 136, 147–63.

39 Bachynsky, ed., *Dokumenty*, 578–81. Russification was beneficial because it made urban organization and "revolutionary struggle" easier. V. Zatonsky, *Natsionalna problema na Ukraine* (Kharkiv, 1926), 35, 90–1, 96. The pamphlet appeared in Russian and Ukrainian in a total press run of 10,000.

40 Frolov, *Kompartiino-radianska elita*, 148, 177, 180, 184.

41 TsDAHO f. 1 op 20 sprava 2248. Detailed stenogram, statistics, and reports of the 1926 Ukrainian CC discussion of Ukrainization.

42 *Visti TsK KP(b)U*, no. 13 (1929) 3; *Dvenadtsatyi siezd RKP(b), 17–25 Aprelia 1923 goda* (Moscow, 1968) 573, 596, 615; TsDAHO f. 1, op. 20, sprava 2250 no. 3; op 1 sprava 98 no. 45.

43 TsDAHO f. 1 op 1 sprava 92 no. 55.

44 *Vosmoi siezd RKP(b) Mart 1919 goda. Protokoly* (Moscow, 1959), 82; TsDAHO f. 1 op 1 sprava 98 no. 76. An estimated 80 per cent of all Party members in Ukraine were of the centralist/rightist "Katerynoslav" faction. M. Ravich-Cherkasskii, *Istoriia kommunisticheskoi partii Ukrainy* (Kharkiv, 1923), 54. Former Jewish SDs (Bundists) who had joined the CPU were the most hostile to indigenization. Non-Party Jews took it in stride.Maistrenko, *Istoriia moho pokolinnia*, 183, 221–2.

45 B.F. Sultanbekov, ed., *Tainy nasionalnoi politiki RKP* (Moscow, 1992), 222–4, 282–6; Dashkevych et al., *Istoriia*, 236, 238, 244; V.M. Danylenko et al., *Ukrainizatsiia 1920–30kh rokiv: peredumovy zdobutky uroky* (Kyiv, 2003), 47–8.

46 S. Pestkovsky, cited in Nahorny, "Bilshovyzm ta Ukrainskyi national kommunizm," 48.

47 *Knizhnaia produktsiia SSSR v 1927* (Moscow, 1930), 8, 13, 28–9, 50, 88; *Statystyka knyzhkovi produktsii USRR. Biuleten*, no. 5 (October–December 1927).

48 *Itogi partperepisi 1922 goda* (Kharkiv, 1922), I: xii; TsDAHO f. 1 op 20 sprava 2248, nos. 42–6.

49 TsDAHO f. 1 op 20 sprava 2248 no. 27, 83–5; op 1 sprava 98 no. 118. Overall, 50 per cent of white- and blue-collar workers considered themselves Ukrainian; 33 per cent used Ukrainian.

50 Cited in E. Borisenok, *Fenomen sovetskoi ukrainizatsii 1920–1930e gody* (Moscow, 2006), 136–42; *Izvestiia VUTsVK* (Kyiv), 3 January, 23 and 24 May, 21 June 1930.

51 Zatonsky, *Natsionalna problema,* 29–30; *Kommunist* (Kharkiv), 23 August 1933.

52 He was specifically referring to Bashkeria. Stalin either ordered him arrested nine days later because of these words or agreed to his arrest when it emerged that Galiev had been forming a secret organization. He was the first Party member arrested by the Party. Whether Stalin ordered surveillance because of their ideological differences and only wanted a pretext for arrest, or whether the cause of arrest was his breach of Party discipline as revealed in letters allegedly discovered accidentally, is unclear. There was no subsequent purge, and Stalin afterwards was prepared to release him. H.G. Gizzatullin and D.R. Sharafutdinov, eds., *Mirsaid Sultan-Galiev. Izbrannye trudy* (Kazan, 1998), 437.

53 T. Martin, *The Affirmative Action Empire: Nations and Nationalism in the Soviet Union, 1923–1939* (Ithaca, 2001) 20-27, 75–125, 344–70; H. Iefimenko, *Natsionalno-kulturna polityka VKP (b) shchodo Radianskoi Ukrainy (1932–1938)* (Kyiv, 2008), 24–39, 93–106. No one was arrested or executed for not knowing Ukrainian or opposing indigenization. The number of declared Ukrainians in responsible positions declined during the 1930s. As of 1937, the appointment of Ukrainians was no longer a priority and knowledge of Ukrainian was unnecessary for a government job.

54 G.S. Luckyj, *Young Ukraine: The Brotherhood of Saints Cyril and Methodius in Kiev, 1845–1847* (Ottawa, 1991).

55 How widespread such ideas were at the time is unstudied. Ivan Zabolotnyi, for example, gave speeches in the First Duma about all the oppressed of the world having to unite against oppressors. A socialist revolutionary belonging to the *Trudoviki* faction, his words reflected his deeds, as in South Africa he had fought on the Boer side against the British. M. Boiovich, *Chleny gosudarstvennoi dumy* (Moscow, 1906).

56 The Ukrainian National Party (1902) that Mikhnovsky organized was small and not influential. He published its program in 1906. In 1917, he changed its name to the Ukrainian Party of Sovereignist Socialists. It had members in the Central Rada, and it dropped its earlier internationalist–anti-colonialist perspective. Shevchenko, ed., *Ukrainski politychni partii,*

60–3. The Revolutionary Ukrainian Party (RUP) also called for independence but did not compare Ukraine with European colonies.
57 Cited in Hud, *Ukrainsko-Polskii konflikty*, 243.
58 S. Velychenko, "The Issue of Russian Colonialism in Ukrainian Thought,"
   Ab Imperio no. 1 (2002): 323–66.
59 M. Weber, *Politische Schriften* (Munich, 1921), 90. The speech was not published until 1921.
60 K. Renner, *Problemy skhodu. Natsionalne pytannia na Skhodi* (n.p., 1915)
   14–15, 19, 28, 32–4. The highest form of colonialism occurred when the
   metropolis sponsored local manufacturing. Lenin condemned Renner, but
   the USSR had similarities to Renner's "autonomy in an international state"
   in that it gave the Russian national economy, controlled by Russian intellectuals and engineers rather than by private capitalists, broad economic
   scope for state capital.Paul Leroy-Bealieu was the first to subdividecolo-
   nialism into"settlement" and "exploitation," *De la colonisation* (Paris, 1902).
61 L. Kohut, *Ukraina i Moskovskyi imperialism* (n.p., 1916) 96, 155–6. Schumpeter lectured at Chernivtsi (Chernowitz) University, where Kohut was
   a student, between 1909 and 1911. His *Sociology of Imperialisms* (1919)
   explained imperialism not as the "most advanced stage of capitalism" but
   as the clear sign that pre-capitalistic (feudal) aspects survived in capitalism. Thus, capitalists remained subservient to state rulers. Kautsky linked
   colonialism to the pre-capitalist Prussian nobles who ruled Germany. *Die
   Neue Zeit* (March, 1898).
62 P. Maltsiv, *Ukraina v derzhavnomu biudzheti Rossii* (Lubni, 1917), 13, 26.
   Forty-five per cent of taxes raised in Ukraine came from liquor and 12
   per cent from direct taxation. S. Kulyk, "Iak Rossiia vyzyzkuie Ukrainu,"
   Pamiatkova knyzhka Soiuz Vyzvolennia Ukrainy i kalendar na 1917 rik (Vienna,
   1917), 101; I. Maievsky, *Chervonyi imperiialism. Po shliakhu kontr-revoliutsii*
   (Kyiv, 1917), reprinted in *Khronika 2000*, nos. 27–8 (1999): 286–96.
63 *Borotba* (Kyiv),20 June/3 July 1917, 6, 14–15; 6 and 19 October 1917, 5.
64 *Borotba*, 31 December 1917, 13 January 1919.
65 Velychenko, "The Issue of Russian Colonialism," 333. P. Kravchuk, *Pid Pro-
   vodom blahorodnykh idei* (Toronto, 1969), 28–29. In April 1914, Lenin called
   relations between Sweden and newly independent Norway "civilized" in
   an article implying that this was a model for Ukrainian–Russian relations.
   Lenin, *Polnoe*, XX: 222.
66 Lenin, *Polnoe*, XXX: 264; XXXII: 251–2; see also D. Boersner, *The Bolsheviks
   and the National and Colonial Question (1917-1928)* (Westport, 1981).
67 Lenin, *Polnoe*, XXII: 188, 298.

68 Lenin, *Polnoe*, XXII: 150–2, 337–9, 353; XXIII: 42–55; XXIV: 130; XXVII: 68; XXX: 50–1, 90–106; XXVII: 68, 260–2; XXX: 34–7.

69 Iurkevych called Ukraine a colony but did not call Russia an empire. L. Rybalka [pseud.], "The Russian Social Democrats and the National Question," *Journal of Ukrainian Studies* 1 (1982): 58, 68, 72, 77; Shakhrai, *Statti*, xi, xx, xxiv.

70 Lenin, *Polnoe*, XXIII: 263; XXVI: 176.

71 J.A. Woods, ed., *The Correspondence of Edmund Burke* (Cambridge, 1963) IV: 460; P. Langford, ed., *The Writings and Speeches of Edmund Burke* (Oxford, 1991), vol. IX.

72 Stalin, *Works* , I: 35–40, 48; E. Van Ree, *The Political Thought of Joseph Stalin: A Study in Twentieth-Century Revolutionary Patriotism* (London, 2002), 62–9. On his exploitation of Russian imperial sentiment to centralize the Soviet state: S. Blank, *The Sorcerer as Apprentice: Stalin as Commissar of Nationalities, 1917–1924* (Westport, 1994).

73 Stalin, *Works*, IV: 385, 364. In November 1918, while Rakovskii and Manuilsky were negotiating with Vynnychenko on a treaty of mutual recognition between Bolshevik Russia and a post-Hetman socialist Ukraine, Stalin, supported by Ukraine's leftist Bolsheviks, was calling for invasion. *Works*, 171, 179.

74 Stalin, *Works*, IV: 364–6; V: 270; *Desiatyi siezd*, 183–5, 186–7, 600–2. In the RSFSR, which included most of the former empire's non-Russian territories, Stalin in 1921 asserted that there were no rulers and ruled, no metropole, and no colonies. Since imperialism stemmed from capitalism, the Bolshevik government could not be "imperialist." Workers throughout the former tsarist empire naturally chose to remain linked to the Soviet Russian state. The new RSFSR was a "voluntary" federation whose non-Russian members "voluntarily refrained" from exercising the right to secede.

75 1917 – 71 per cent, 1919 – 78 per cent, 1920 – 80 per cent, 1921 – 83 per cent, 1922 – 80 per cent, 1924 – 75 per cent. *Shestoi siezd RSDRP(b) avgust 1917 g.* (Moscow, 1960), 294; *Vosmoi siezd RKP(b)*, 451; *Deviatyi siezd RKP(b) mart–aprel 1920 g.* (Moscow, 1960), 480; *Desiatyi siezd RKP(b)*, 760; *Odinnadtsatyi siezd RKP (b) mart–aprel 1922 goda* (Moscow, 1961), 716; *Trinadtsatyi siezd RKP(b) mai 1924 goda* (Moscow, 1963), 711. A breakdown of delegates by nationality was not provided for the Twelfth Conference (1923).

76 Iefimenko, *Vzaiemovidnosysny Kremlia ta Radianskoi Ukrainy*, 126–9.

77 A week earlier, this government had revived all its earlier decrees. The sudden change was probably dictated from Moscow, but I have found no evidence. Rubach et al., *Radianske budivnytstvo na Ukraini v roky*

hromadianskoi viiny (Kyiv, 1957), 47, 55. The published RCP CC protocols from that week are incomplete.

78 V. Iurchuk et al., *Komunistychna partiia Ukrainy v rezoliutsiiakh i rishenniakh z'ïzdiv, konferentsiĭ i plenumiv TsK. Tom pershyi* (Kyiv, 1976) , 70–1; TsDAHO, f. 1 op. 1 sprava 57 no. 3. Ukrainian Bolsheviks were displeased with their limited jurisdictions and were extended greater prerogatives for their republic in the Union Treaty of December 1920. A November 1918 resolution, which avoided the term "Ukraine," placed "all regions on the southern and western borders of the RSFSR liberated from [German] occupation" under the direct authority of the Russian Commissar for Food Supply. It included this note: "not for publication." TsDAHO, f. 57 op. 2 sprava 76 nos. 166, 179.

79 N. F. Bugai, *Chrezvychainye organy Sovetskoi vlasti: revkomy 1918–1921* (Moscow, 1990), 86–7, 288–93. Likewise, local food supply commissars and Cheka personnel were subject only to their Moscow superiors. Someone in the accompanying note to Lenin's instructions labelled the request "irresponsible politicking." Lenin, *Polnoe*, LI: 95–6.

80 *Kommunistichna partiia Ukrainy v rezoliutsiiakh i resheniiakh siezdov i konferentsiiakh* (Kyiv, 1958), 134–5.

81 Mazepa, *Bolshevizm*, 147.

82 R. Krutsyk, ed., *Narodna viina 1917- 1932* (Kyiv, 2011) 82-83. On line: http://www.narodnaviyna.org.ua

83 In April Kharkiv requested ethnic Russians for all its reserve civilian police and CHEKA troop detachments TsDAVO f. 3204 op 1 sprava 6, no. 7.

84 TsDAHO f. 1 op 20 sprava 35 no. 69; sprava 124 no. 6, sprava 106 no. 84; Iefimenko, *Vzaiemovidnosyny Kremlia ta Radianskoi Ukrainy*, 122.

85 TsDAVO, f. 2 op. 1 sprava 241. S.A. Pavliuchenkov, *Voennyi kommunizm v Rossii: Vlast i massy* (Moscow, 2007), 256, 259.

86 Kulchytsky, *Komunizm v Ukraini*, 80–1. A Borotbist arrived from Russia at the time reported that local authorities were hindering declared Ukrainian Bolshevik party members as much as they could from going to Ukraine, while simultaneously sending native Russians who had never before lived there.

87 TsDAVO f. 2 op 1 sprava 234 no. 165. Lenin's decision was not included in the published RCP Politburo protocols: "Deiatelnost tsentralnogo komiteta partii v dokumentakh," *Izvestiia TsK KPSS*, no. 2 (1990): 151. TsDAVO f. 2 op 1 sprava 233 no. 91, 98. "Deiatelnost tsentralnogo komiteta partii v dokumentakh," *Izvestiia TsK KPSS*, no. 12 (1989): 153.

88 Krutsyk ed., *Narodna viina*, 82-83. V.Zh., Tsvetkov, *Belye armii iuga Rossii 1917-1920 gg,* (Moscow, 2000), 51–2; Dashkevych et al., *Istoriia*, 132–7,

163–4, 245–7. L. Hrynevych, "Dynamika natsionalnoho sklad chastyn i ziednan Ukrainskoi voienoi okruhy u mizhvoiennyi period," *Problemy istorii Ukrainy*, no. 15 (2006): 351–2. In 1919, Red Army strength in Ukraine was 188,000. There is no known record of how many ethnic or declared Ukrainians this figure included. In 1920, the Red Army in Ukraine numbered 1,200,000; 48,000 declared Ukrainian Red Army men served in Russia. Latvians, Chinese, and Hungarians comprised the bulk of Ukraine's "internationalist" units (10,000 strong, total), whose principal task was not front-line combat but suppressing civilian resistance,.

89 *Izvestiia TsK KPSS*, no. 12 (1989): 136; O. Figes, *Peasant Russia Civil War: The Volga Countryside in Revolution 1917–1921* (Oxford, 1989), 258; L. Lih, *Bread and Authority in Russia 1914–1921* (Berkeley, 1990), 260; T.V. Osipova, *Rossiiskoe krestianstvo* (Moscow, 2001); O. Mykhailiuk, *Selianstvo Ukrainy desiatylittia XX st.: Sotsiokulturni protsesy* (Dnipropetrovsk, 2007), 239. Ukrainian grain sent north in 1919 (not more than one million poods) represented less than 1 per cent of Russia's increase in procurement to almost 59 million poods for that year over 1918. Each pound of bread sold in state stores in Ukraine at 45 kopeks cost the government 25 roubles.

90 No one has yet compared Bolshevik policies in Ukraine and Russia. A higher proportion of Ukrainian than Russian lands, for instance, were owned as estates – approximately 27 per cent. The Bolsheviks in 1919 did not divide those estates and excluded the horses and ploughs of wealthy farmers from the expropriation intended to centralize production and maximize exports. In response, peasants revolted within weeks of the Bolshevik takeover rather than within months as in Russia. R. Zakharchenko, N. Zemziulina, and O. Nesterov, *U Pokhodi za voliu* (Kyiv, 2000), 39–50.

91 Potichnyi, ed., *On the Current Situation in Ukraine*, 97.

92 TsDAVO, f. 2 op 2 sprava 300 no. 2; Z. Galili, ed., *Mensheviki v 1921-1922 gg.* (Moscow, 2002), 68, 111.

93 These men claimed that the breakdown of central control and the need for a nominally "independent" Ukraine in talks with Poland required the devolution of authority to Kharkiv. Rakovskii's defence of Ukrainian interests in 1920 included complaints to Lenin that Ukraine was being "systematically cheated" by Russia. Iefimenko, *StatusUSRR*, 225–315; idem, "Evoliutsiia derzhavnoho statusa USRR naprykintsi 1919-u 1920 rr.: Netradytsiiny pohliad," *Ukrainsky istorychnyi zhurnal*, no. 6 (2011): 80–101.

94 A classified pamphlet allegedly published by the Kyiv Military District intelligence unit in 1921 includes similar ideas. *Politicheskii banditizm na*

Ukraine ego prichiny formy i borba s nim (1921) listed two tactics to control
Ukraine, one of which was the "ideological disarming" of those considered
to be national leaders in small towns and villages: the educated, teachers,
doctors, medics, and co-op activists:

Here we must do the following; shoot some of them and give the rest
a "bribe" ... consisting of what they are fighting for. We must make them
agree that Soviet Ukraine is a Ukrainian state. They want Ukrainian in
schools and government offices – we will give it to them. We will disband
their nationalist private cultural organizations [*prosvity*] but in their place
we will create other Ukrainian, I stress, Ukrainian cultural centres, in villages and towns. We will closely watch them [Ukrainian activists], but will
allow for the moment those who are now organizing the village to expend
their energies working in them. Now we cannot give economic concessions
to the peasants who refuse to surrender grain, but we can and must give
"ideological concessions" to the rural educated, give them illusions that
in the future the political leadership in Soviet Ukraine will be theirs and
to thereby deflect their interests into a direction different from those of the
rural masses. When the need for this passes we will send them to the devil
and place our trustworthy communists.

I was unable to locate the original. The citation is from Iuryi Holis-
Horsky, *Spohady*, 2nd ed. (New York, 1977), 13. Horsky was a former partisan commander who claimed he got the booklet before he fled to Polish-
controlled territory. He claimed that the ideas were based on a June 1920
speech by Lev Degtiarev, chief political officer of the Kyiv Military District.

95 "Iz istorii obrazovaniia SSSR," *Izvestiia TsK KPSS* (1989) 9: 193, 199. Lenin,
Polnoe, XXXIX: 334-6; 40: 41. Also reproduced in L.S. Gatagova et al, *TsK
RKP(b)-VKP(b) i natsionalnyi vopros. Kniga I 1918-1933 gg*. (Moscow, 2005)
30.

96 Iu. A, Amiantov et al, V. I. Lenin, *Neizvestnye dokumenty 1891-1922* (Moscow, 1997) 306-07. Lenin, *Polnoe*, XXX: 335-36; 38: 400. Lenin's speech on
this issue at the 8th Russian party congress and related comments are not
published and might have been lost. Opponents were prohibited from protesting at the 4th CPU conference in March 1920.

97 Cited in: Iefimenko, "Evoliutsiia derzhavnoho statusa USRR," 84. This
instruction was not included in the published protocols: *Izvestiia TsK KPSS*
no. 7 (1990) 168. A.A and A.M. Plekhanov eds,. *F.E. Dzerzhinskii, Predsedatel
VChK-OGPU: 1917-1926* (Moscow, 2007) 135

98 Stalin, *Works*, IV: 371. "Iz istorii obrazovaniia SSSR," *Izvestiia TsK KPSS*
(1989) 9: 193, 199. Bachynsky ed, *Dokumenty*, 461-62.

99 V. Swoboda, "Was the Soviet Union Really Necessary?" *Soviet Studies* 5 (1992): 775–6. Stalin stipulated in item 6 of his original resolution that the Central Committee decision to create a centralized RSFSR was not to be published. It was to be sent as a directive only to the non-Russian Central Committees, telling them to instruct their respective Soviets to demand the formation of the RSFSR at the next Congress of Soviets. This would make Stalin's plan appear as the expression of the popular will. Item 6 itself was to be excluded from the copies of the resolution sent to the non-Russian CCs. "Iz istorii obrazovaniia SSSR," *Izvestiia TsK KPSS*, no. 9 (1989): 193, 215.

Chapter 2

1 P. Holquist, *Making War, Forging Revolution: Russia's Continuum of Crisis 1914–1921* (Cambridge, MA, 2002); J. Ryan, *Lenin's Terror: The Ideological Origins of Early Soviet State Violence* (London, 2012).
2 Institutionally expressed in Moscow's backing of the Muslim Bureau and Bashkir RevKom against local Russians. R. Pipes, *The Formation of the Soviet Union: Communism and Nationalism, 1917–1923* (Cambridge, MA, 1997), 166, 198; J. Smith, *The Bolsheviks and the National Question, 1917–1923* (London, 1999), 90; A. Khalid, "Turkestan v 1917–1922 godakh," in *Tragediia velikoi derzhavy*, ed. G.N. Sevostianov (Moscow, 2005), 214–20. On Estonia, see Lenin, *Polnoe sobranie*, XL: 90–1. Lenin forbade Trotsky to invade Estonia. Meijer, ed., *The Trotsky Papers*, I: 719–47.
3 V. Maiorov, ed., *1917 god na Kievshchine. Khronika sobytii* (Kharkiv, 1928), 539–40. In *Izvestiia* (Petrograd) on 24 November, Trotsky wrote that the Bolsheviks would accept Ukrainian self-determination in whatever form it took.
4 Lenin, *Polnoe*, XXXV: 116, 182. Amiantov et al., *Protokoly zesedanii soveta narodnykh komissarov RSFSR*, 87–9, 153; I. Mikhutina, *Ukrainskii Brestskii mir* (Moscow, 2007), 82–6.
5 Stalin, *Works*, IV: 24.
6 M. Kovalchuk, " Proloh pershoi Ukrainsko-radianskoi viiny: nastup 1-oho Minskoho revoliutsiinoho zahonu na Bakhmach," in: *Zahartovana istorieiu. Iuvileinyi zbirnyk na poshanu profesora Nadii Ivanivny Myronets*, P. Sokhan, et al (Kyiv, 2013) 89–99.
7 Lenin, *Polnoe* XXXV: 213. Skrypnyk. *Statti i promovy*, I: 176-77. A. Zdorov, "Do istorii viiskovykh syl Ukrainskoho radianskoho uriadu v pershyi period ikh isnuvannia," *Kyivska starovyna* no. 6 (2005) 86-88. Lenin and Stalin waited four days before recognizing the Kharkiv government.

Notes to pages 58–61

V. Zatonsky, "Uryvky z spohadiv pro Ukrainsku revoliutsiiu," *Letopis revoliutsii*," no. 1 (1925) 161-63. P. I. Pavliuk et al, *Bolshevistskie organizatsii Ukrainy v period ustanovlenniia i ukrepleniia sovetskoi vlasti (noiabr 1917-aprel 1918 gg.)* (Kyiv, 1962) 13-23.

8 The December 30 decision was published only in Petrograd papers the next day. On January 2 Stalin wrote to Antonov that the decision had not yet been sent to Kyiv and assured him that "the war with the Rada would absolutely be continued." Cited in V. Soldatenko, *Revoliutsiina doba v Ukraini 1917-1920* (Kyiv 2011) 142. Skrypnyk later condemned the anti-Ukrainian behaviour of Russian Bolshevik troops. He noted that Kharkiv province was still legally part of Russia – which is why Lenin did not think sending troops there amounted to war against the UNR.

9 Lenin paid his Kharkiv government with worthless soviet rubles printed in Moscow that it then used to buy grain from Ukrainians, thereby avoiding requisitioning. In this way, he got Ukrainian food for nothing. Through December 1917, local Ukrainian forces in Kharkiv ignored the Rada's orders not to ship grain north. Lenin, *Polnoe*, L: 28, 30; Amiantov et al., *Protokoly*, 203, 211, 224; *Protokoly zasedanii Vserossiiskogo Tsentralnago Ispoln. Komiteta Sovetov R.,S.,Kr. i Kaz. Deputatov II Sozyva* (Moscow, 1918), 192. On stockpiles: V.A. Kondratiev, "Otkliki na oktiabrskuiu revoliutsiiu v Sovets-koi Rossii," in: *Noiabrskaia revoliutsiia v Germanii. Sbornik statei i materialov*, ed. V.D. Kulbakin (Moscow, 1960), 439–56; N.P. Okunev, *Dnevnik Moskvi-cha. 1917–1924* (Paris, 1990), 234.

10 Among those who opposed the invasion were Kharkiv province Bolsheviks who did not consider their province part of Ukraine and who preferred peace with the Rada. M. Kovalchuk, "Proloh pershoi Ukrainsko-radianskoi viiny," in: *Zahartovana istorieiu*, 89–99; M. Frenkin, *Zakhvat vlasti Bolshevikami v Rossii i rol tylovykh garnizonov armii: Podgotovka i pro-vedenie oktiabrskogo miatezha 1917–1918 gg.* (Jerusalem, 1982); V. Antonov-Ovsienko, *Zapiski o grazhdanskoi voine* (Moscow–Leningrad, 1924–35), I: 53–7, 131.

11 J. MacLaughlin, *Reimagining the Nation State: The Contested Terrains of Nation-Building* (London, 2001). In Ireland by 1914, the majority of peasants had land and livestock and were more interested in independence than in redistribution of wealth. Also, the clergy dampened radical proclivities in favour of national issues. In 1918, there was no large group of radicalized landless rural labourers.

12 M. Milotte, *Communism in Modern Ireland: The Pursuit of the Worker's Repub-lic since 1916* (Dublin, 1984), 43, 54, 59, 64. Lenin did not instruct the Irish

party to turn itself into a subsection of the Northern Ireland branch of the Communist Party of Great Britain. The Irish party remained a Comintern member independent of its Northern Ireland members.The Irish communists had no organization in Northern Ireland, where the anti-Irish British Socialist party dominated.

13 Bachynsky, ed., *Dokumenty* , 63; G. Lapchynsky, "Z pershykh dniv vseukrainskoi radianskoi vlady," *Litopys revoliutsii*, no. 3 (1927): 48; V. Zatonsky, "Iz spohadiv pro Ukrainsku revoliutsiiu," *Litopys revoliutsii*, no. 5 (1930) 168–9. Kharkiv Bolsheviks under Artem then established a Krivoi-Rog Republic. As over half the party's members in Ukraine would be in this republic, it would have much weakened Russian influence in the rump UNR and any future Soviet regime including only the rest of Ukrainian territory. Lenin opposed the initiative and ordered the republic incorporated into Soviet Ukraine. V. Nahorny, "Bilshovyzm ta Ukrainskyi national kommunizm v dobu revoliutsii (1917–1920 rr.)," Kandydatska dissertatsiia, Kyivskyi derzhavny linhvistychnyi universytet (1995), 152.

14 V. Mazurenko, "USDRP i soiuznaia okkupatsiia," in *Chernaia kniga. Sbornik statei i materialov ob interventsii Antanty na Ukraine v 1918- 1919 gg.*, ed. A.I. Shlikhter (Kharkiv, 1925), 277; F. Rudych et al., *Vtoroi siezd Kommunisticheskoi partii (bolshevikov) Ukrainy. Protokoly* (Kyiv, 1991), 15–16, 113. Kamenev condemned "nationalist bourgeoisie" for trying to divide Russia and the proletarian revolution, apparently ignorant of these secret talks. Rakovskii argued Lenin's case against war in Ukraine that autumn.

15 Kh. Rakovsky, "Illich i Ukraina," *Ukrainsky istorychnyi zhurnal*, no. 4 (1989): 112. Originally published in January 1925, it does not say that Lenin agreed. Zatonsky, "Iz spohadiv pro Ukrainsku revoliutsiiu," 150, 153, 155, 157, 162, 164, 171. In Minsk on 17 January 1919, Mazurenko confirmed that the talks had taken place with the knowledge and agreement of their governments but that the verbal agreement was never written down. R. Symonenko and O. Reient, eds., *Ukrainski-Rossiiski perehovory v Moskvi (sichen-liutyi, 1919) Zbirnyk dokumentiv* (Kyiv, 1996), 33. Vynnychenko conducted the talks on his own as his party opposed them. P. Solukha, *Dohovir z Moskoviu protiv Hetmana Pavla Skoropadskoho* (n.p., 1973), 37–45.

16 S. Posse, "Ukrainska Dyrektoriia ta ii zovnishna polityka," *Litopys revoliutsii*, no. 5-6 (1929): 9–16. The head of the UNR delegation in Moscow confirmed the division of opinion among the top Russian leaders: Symonenko and Reient, eds., *Ukrainski-rossiiski perehovory*, 79. On 23 January, Ukraine's Bolsheviks still feared a UNR–Moscow agreement and explained to Lenin in a long letter that day why he should avoid such a move. Antonov-Ovsienko, *Zapiski*, III: 127.

17 G. Felshtinskii, "Byl li prichasten K. Radek k gibeli K. Libknekhta i R.
   Liuksemburg?", *Voprosy istorii*, no. 9 (1997): 3–35; J.F. Fayet, *Karl Radek
   (1885–1939). Biographie politique* (Paris, 2004), 267–86. Felshtinskii does not
   link Lenin to Luxemburg's assassination but, if Radek was involved in
   the plot, it could not have been on his own. It is also unclear when Radek
   began his talks with German generals and politicians. Once Gustav Noske
   became Minister of War on 29 December, it was clear that the government
   would repress the communists and that the Entente would not intervene.
   Lenin would have learned of that decision within the week. With a secure
   western border, and unchallenged in the communist movement, he agreed
   to support Antonov's invasion on 5 January. L. Kochan, *Russia and the Wei-
   mar Republic* (Cambridge, 1954), 16–18; I. Jedrzejewska, *Wspolpraca Armii
   Czerwonej i Reichwehry w latach 1917–1933* (Warsaw, 2005), 21; K. Maklak,
   Radziecko-niemiecka wspolpraca wojskowa w latach 1917–1932 (Warsaw, 1997),
   20–1; J. Braunthal, *History of the International, 1914–1943* (London, 1967),
   II: 134. Information on German-Soviet talks that December may also be in
   Entente intercepts of Bolshevik radio messages. American intercepts are in
   the Hoover Institute archives.
18 Zatonsky's proclamation in *Kommunist Ukrainy*, no. 4 (2002): 32–3; Zatonsky's call attracted approximately 1000 sympathizers in south-east Ukraine
   but they dispersed after a few months. The leaflet is reproduced in: *Ukrainsky istorychnyi zhurnal* no. 7 (July 1989) 50–1; M. Ostrohorsky, "Z istorii
   bilshovytskoi orhanizatsii …Donbasa (1901–1918)," *Litopys revoliutsii* no 5
   (1930) 106–10. Lapchynsky, "Pershyi period Radianskoi vlady na Ukraini.
   Litopys revoliutsii, no. 1 (1928): 160.
19 V. Soldatenko, "Do otsinky orhanizatsiia Ukrainskykh bilshovykiv,"
   Ukrainsky istorychnyi zhurnal, no. 6 (June 1989): 64–6. For speeches and resolutions at the first congresses of soviets in Kyiv and Kharkiv reproduced
   in full: *Kommunist Ukrainy* no. 4 (2002): 34–5; "K otchetu o 1 Vseukrains-
   kom siezde sovetov R.S.I.K.D.," *Letopis revoliutsii*, no.1 (1928): 282, 288–90.
20 *Borotbist* (Poltava), 28 March 1920. Liebknecht and Luxemburg opposed
   the idea of a Third International and made no mention of the Bolsheviks
   in their January 1919 program of the German Communist Party (KPD).
   In 1916, they had formed an international group in Berlin whose call to
   replace the Second International anticipated Lenin's Comintern. Although
   their declaration specified that each national proletariat was to deal with
   its own national bourgeoisie, in 1918 Luxemburg dismissed Ukraine as
   part of Russia – namely, the terrain of the Russian Revolution with no
   national proletariat. Ia.S. Drabkin, *Komintern i ideia mirovoi revoliutsii*.

Dokumenty (Moscow, 1998), 73–7; R. Looker, ed., *Rosa Luxemburg: Selected Political Writings* (New York, 1974), 235–43.

21 Lenin, *Polnoe*, XXXI: 21; *Chervonyi prapor* (Kyiv) [now mimeographed monthly], July 1924; TsDAHO f. 8 op 1 sprava 113 no. 9.

22 Luxemburg characterized the anti-Entente talks between Germany and the Bolsheviks begun in August 1918 as a "grotesque coupling of Lenin and Hindenburg ... A socialist revolution supported by German bayonets ... under the patronage of German imperialism." Looker, ed., *Rosa Luxemburg*. She joined the uprising thinking it had been started by the government. Throughout 1919, while in and out of prison, Radek negotiated with generals and politicians who believed that cooperation with Bolshevik Russia would make Germany a world power again. J. Wheeler Bennet, *Brest-Litovsk, The Forgotten Peace* (London, 1939), 427–46; V. Vourkoutiotis, *Making Common Cause: German-Soviet Secret Relations, 1919–22* (London, 2007); M. Agursky, *The Third Rome: National Bolshevism in the USSR* (London, 1987), 215.

23 T.V. Osipova, *Krestianskyi front v grazhdanskoi voine* (Moscow, 1996), 109–15.

24 Ukraine's Bolsheviks were not involved with the mass anti-Hetman uprisings between April and August 1918, which were organized by the Ukrainian left-SRs. Lenin was lying on July 1 when he claimed in an interview that in Ukraine "Bolshevism was becoming national." O.I. Bondarenko, *Povernennia iz zabuttia* (Kyiv, 2012) 464–7.

25 Lenin's orders of 11 October to prepare an army to invade must be seen in light of his note of 3 October, which specified that he did not expect to have a 3 million-strong army ready to aid the German people until the spring of 1919. On 22 October, he said that Ukrainian comrades would have to wait: "We shall take care that our interference [in Germany] will not harm their revolution." Lenin's relationship to the 12 November Russian Military Soviet's order to invade Ukraine by the end of the month is unknown. On 29 November, in a telephone conversation, he mentions establishing soviet power in Ukraine as soon as possible. The published protocols of the Military Soviet do not indicate voting and those of the RCP Central Committee between October 1918 and January 1919 are incomplete. T.F. Kariaeva, ed., *Revvoensovet Respubliki. Protokoly 1918–1919* (Moscow, 1997), 101–2; Lenin, *Polnoe*, XXXVII: 99, 121; V. Soldatenko, *Ukrainska revoliutsiia. Istorychnyi narys* (Kyiv, 1999), 585–6; Ia. Dashkevych et al., *Istoriia Ukrainskoho viiska* (Kyiv, 1996), 141–3.

26 M. Rubach, "K istorii grazhdanskoi borbe na Ukraine," *Letopis revoliutsii* no. 4 (1924) 164; Zatonsky, "Iz spohadiv," no. 5 (1930) 153-56. V. Soldatenko ed., *Revoliutsiina slava Ukrainy. Fotoalbum* (Kyiv, 1978) 179.

27 Antonov wrote that, after a meeting with Lenin on 24 November, when
   he became infuriated with him for proposing a formal attack on Ukraine,
   Sverdlov told him: "Don't worry. We will set things straight … There is
   so much intrigue around him … To be frank, there is a lot of disorder in
   the Revoensoviet and no agreement with other agencies. There is fog to
   be sure … and not without perfidious intention [*i ne bez zadnikh myslei*]."
   V. Antonov-Ovsienko "Na Ukrainu," *Litopys revoliutsii* no. 4 (1929) 195–7.
   These sentences were censored out of Antonov's book (*Zapiski* III: 30).
28 Cited in: Kuras et al, *Politychna istoriia Ukrainy*, II: 327; cited in: "Iz spohadiv," 155. Lenin, *Polnoe*, XXXVII: 234. Bachynsky, ed., *Dokumenty*, 87–91;
   TsDAVO f. 2 op 1 sprava 1 no. 8; Karaieva, ed., *Revvoensovet Respubliki*, 104.
29 Dashkevych et al, *Istoriia Ukrainskoho viiska*, 131–75; N.E. Kakurin and
   I.I. Vatsetis, *Grazhdanskaia voina 1918–1921*, 2nd ed. (St Petersburg, 2002),
   167; G.A. Belov et al., *Direktivy glavnogo kommanduvaniia krasnoi armii
   (1917–1920)* (Moscow, 1969), 198, 207, for full list of Russian units in
   Ukraine; Antonov-Ovsienko, *Zapiski*, III: 14, 27, 37–8. Antonov explicitly refused to accept Ukrainian volunteers from Russia and insisted on
   troops from Russia. On 1 January, Vatsetis instructed him not to attack
   Kharkiv. He did so regardless, and took the city two days later. Belov et
   al, *Direktivy*, 200–1, 205; Meijer, ed., *The Trotsky Papers*, I: 236–8. Lenin's
   telegram of 3 January to Trotsky expressing doubt about sending troops
   to Ukraine is not in volume 50 of the *Polnoe Sobranie*. The telegram of
   5 January sanctioning the attack is reproduced in: Antonov-Ovsienko,
   Zapiski, III: 115–16.
30 Approximately 50,000 Russian workers from Ukraine had joined the Russian Red Army in late 1918. The two divisions of the CPU's Ukrainian
   Insurgent Army (*Ukrainska Povstanska Armiia*), which included the Red
   Cossacks, were formed in Russia mainly from anti-Hetman Ukrainians.
   Ukrainian was used in only one regiment. The men agreed to fight only in
   Ukraine. Lack of supplies and officers limited recruitment. Russians were
   added to the Insurgent Army beginning in the summer of 1919. O. Bozhko,
   "Povstanska armiia Ukrainy (osin 1918r.): stvorennia, orhanizatsiia struk-
   tura sklad," *Ukrainsky istorychny zhurnal*, no. 4 (2009): 118–25. Antonov-
   Ovsienko, *Zapiski*, III: 17, 53.
31 Stalin supported Piatakov and the leftists. Lenin's dismissal of most of this
   group was supported by Trotsky, who opposed Stalin's attempt to appoint
   his clients, particularly Voroshilov, to Ukraine's second soviet government.
   V. Krasnov and V. Daines, *Neizvestnyi Trotskii. Krasnyi bonapart* (Moscow,
   2000), 143–5.

32 Cited in K. Trembicka, *Miedzy apologia a negacja* (Lublin, 1995), 24–5; Lenin, *Polnoe*, XXIX: 175; Drabkin, *Komintern*, 128; I.V. Mikhutina, "Kto gotovil sovetizatsiiu Polshi v 1918 godu?", in *Revoliutsionnaia Rossiia 1917 goda i Polskii vopros: Novye istochniki, novye vzgliady*, ed. M. Volos and A. Orekhov (Moscow, 2007), 268–79. The Polish position reflected the ideas of the First Congress of the Comintern but not the second.

33 Iefimenko, *Vzaiemovidnosysny kremlia ta radianskoi Ukrainy: ekonomichnyi aspect* 120, 181. On the appointment of centralists to Ukraine's second government, see 108–14. On 23 April 1919, Moscow secretly instructed the CPU to begin examining when and how to fuse (*slivat*) Ukraine with Russia. Kulchytsky, *Komunizm v Ukraini*, 87. The passage cited by Kulchytsky was not in the Politburo protocols selection published in *Izvestiia TsK KPSS*, no. 12 (December 1989): 152–3.

34 TsDAHO f. 1. op 6 sprava 1 no. 4. Lenin stipulated that Moscow was to send all financing directly to its local agencies and not to Ukraine's soviet government. Upon implementation, Ukraine's Politburo recorded: "The formally independent HQ of the Ukr SSR railways must be subordinated to the RSFSR." TsDAHO f. 1 op 6 sprava 4 no. 24.

35 *Vosmoi siezd*, 46–9, 78–81, 105, 398, 425. Lenin, *Polnoe*, L: 308. The letter was not published until 1965.

36 These applied to the rest of the world ideas expressed in the summer of 1918 in reference to Ukraine by Radek, Mikhail Pokrovsky, and Stalin's associate Sergei Bakinsky, who claimed that "objectively" bourgeois nation states were no longer possible. They would inevitably fall subject to one empire or another and exploit the proletariat. The class conscious proletarians after the successful seizure of power would not dissolve their empires but ally with each other against their bourgeoise. *Kommunist* (Moscow) 1918 no 1-2: 8-9, 21; no. 3-4: 5-6, 11-12.

37 *Vosmoi siezd*, 286; Boersner, *The Bolsheviks and the National and Colonial Question*, 66. Recognizing a "bourgeois" UNR, as "bourgeois" Finland had been and Turkey would be, was a policy option again in August 1919 when the Bolsheviks lost Ukraine to the Whites and the UNR. As in the spring of 1918, faced with the possible loss of central Russia, Lenin and Trotsky again considered shifting their main political and military focus from the west to the east and moving their base to the Urals. Meijer ed., *The Trotsky Papers*, I: 625–7.

38 With Lenin dead, Zinoviev reverted to his 1919 centralism and began extending the control imposed on non-Russian party subunits within Soviet borders onto communist parties beyond. When Polish communists

in 1924 disagreed with Stalin's campaign against Trotsky, he told them:
"We will break your bones if you try go against us." Cited in S.D. Gupta,
Comintern and the Destiny of Communism in India, 1919–1943 (Calcutta,
2006), 58.

39 A collection of their later essays about the events of 1918–19 is in TsDAHO
f. 57 op 2 sprava 285. Many were published throughout 1928 in *Letopis
revoliutsii.*

40 Manilov, ed., *1917 god na Kievshchine* 430–3; *Sedmoi ekstrennyi siezd RKP(b).
Mart 1918 goda* (Moscow, 1962), 155–8.

41 *Vistnyk Ukrainskoi Narodnoi Respubliki* (Kharkiv), 19 January 1918; *Robitnycha hazeta*, 1 March 1918; Ukrainian translation of Kautsky's article,
ibid., 12 and 14 November 1918. Kautsky argued that in Europe, national
independence was in the interests of the proletariat because it would foster
industrial development. He opposed the disintegration of Russia's empire
along national lines and doubted the existence of a Ukrainian nationality.
Die Vereinigten Staaten Mitteleuropas (Stuttgart, 1916).

42 *Pravda*, 24 May and 30 June 1918. That spring, Ukraine's Red Army commander repeatedly referred to Ukraine in his orders as southern Russia.
Antonov-Ovsienko, *Zapiski*, II: 27, 43, 47, 85, 237, 247, 261.

43 "Problemy natsionalnoi osvobozhdenie," *Kommunist* (Kyiv), 15 and 18
April 1919. ("*Vprochem i etu storonu dela dovolno trudno razgliadet; takoe
nitovernoe kolichestvo vsiakoi balaganshchiny i slovesnoi trukhi ona soderzhit
chto prochetat ee tselikom net nikakoi vozmozhnosti*"; 5 April). Piatakov in July
1918 had backed Skrypnyk's failed bid to form a Ukrainian party separate
from the Russian and then the failed Bolshevik uprising in Ukraine that
August. Perhaps these articles were intended as "penance."

44 *Kommunist* (Kyiv), 1 May 1919.

45 *Kommunist*, 25 March; 3 and 26 April 1919.

46 I. Kulyk, *Ohliad revoliutsii na Ukraini. Chastyna persha berezen 1917r.–kviten
1918 r.* (Kharkiv, 1921), 9–10. Kulyk noted but did not reflect on the colonialist implications of massive Russian settlement in Kharkiv and Katerynoslav, the isolation of those city populations from Ukrainian issues,
or the rivalry of Russian and Ukrainian bourgeoisie (15, 19). The booklet
first appeared, serialized, in the August to December 1918 issues of the
Moscow-based *Vistnyk Ukrainskoho viddilu narodnoho komysariiatu sprav nat-
sionalnykh*. In the later edition, he made no mention of the 1920 Comintern
proclamations on the progressive role of anti-imperial colonial national
bourgeois independence and how communists were obliged to support
such movements.

47 Iurchuk et al., *Pervyi siezd kommunisticheskoi partii (bolshevikov) Ukrainy*, 125–7, 175–80. Shakhrai condemned Kviring in the *Vistnyk Ukrainskoho viddilu* (September 1918), 14. He called for a united independent sovereign Ukraine in an article preceded by an editorial disclaimer. On Lenin's role in formulating the resolution, see F. Riazanov, *Nezabutne, Spohady pro Pershyi sziizd KP(b)U* (Kyiv, 1958), 120.

48 *Vosmaia konferentsiia RKP(b), Dekabr 1919* (Moscow, 1934), 77, 84; *Kommunist* (Kyiv), 19, 21 and 24 February 1920; *Kommunist* (Kharkiv), 14 December 1920.

49 Rudych et al, *Vtoroi siezd*, 115, 120, 122–3.

50 Antonov-Ovsienko, *Zapiski*, III: 12.

51 Antonov-Ovsienko, *Zapiski*, I: 157; *Izvestiia* (Kyiv), 30 January 1918. This proclamation was reprinted by most Kyiv newspapers. L. Hrynevych ed., *Slidcha sprava M.A. Muravïova: dokumentovana istoriia* (Kyiv, 2001), 33, 97, 223. Muraviev was arrested for his excessive brutality in Ukraine, and Dzerzhinskii condemned him for doing more harm to the Bolsheviks there than their enemies. He was released and exonerated for lack of evidence.

52 Lenin, *Polnoe*, XXIX: 317.

53 Cited in Kuras et al., *Politychna istoriia*, II: 327.

54 *Vosmaia konferentsiia RKP(b)*, 97. Lenin, *Polnoe*, XXXVII: 234; The instruction was secret and was not published until 1942. The English version translates the verbs incorrectly, using the past conditional instead of the future conditional.

55 *Levyi es-er*, 18 December 1919. S.M. Korolivsky, ed., *Grazhdanskaia voina na Ukraine* (Kyiv, 1967) II: 517; 1920 message reproduced. Cited in Borys, *Sovietization of Ukraine, 1917–1923*, 295; Iefimenko, *Status USRR ta ii vzaiemovidnosyny z RSFSR*, 294.

56 *Vosmaia konferentsiia*, 109. Kh. Rakovsky, "Piat rokiv Ukrainskoi radianskoi vlady," *Chervonyi shliakh* nos. 4–5 (1923): 92; TsDAHO f. 2 op. 1 sprava 16–17.

57 *I siezd KP(b)U. Stati i protokoly* (Kharkiv, 1923), 14. Federalists during the 1920s could not admit that Russia had conquered Ukraine as that would have undermined their own legitimacy. To justify broader concessions from Moscow, they had to argue they had led an indigenous revolution.

58 Cited in: V. Verstiuk et al, *Narysy istorii Ukrainskoi revoliutsii 1917-1921 rokiv* (Kyiv, 2012), bk. 2: 331.

59 *Kievskii kommunist*, 9, 18 March 1919. He thought that northern workers had fought to free the slaves even though they were starving because their factories were receiving no cheap southern cotton.

60 *Kommunist* (Kyiv), 7 July 1920.

61 K.S. Aksakov, *Polnoe sobranie sochinennie* (Moscow, 1886) III: 7. "Dnieper [central and eastern] Ukraine ... are parts of the living flesh of Russia; here there is no room for questions or arguments."

62 *Tretii Vseukrainskii sezd sovetov*, 47–8; TsDAVO f. 1 op 1 sprava 11 nos. 24, 26, 29, 42–3, 94–7 (21 June 1919 TsVK protocols). He did not admit that Bolshevik policies had provoked resistance. He instead claimed that problems had stemmed from the fact that the party had been unable to organize a solid block of 10,000 to 15,000 stalwarts into effective requisitioning squads, whose members would have explained to the peasants what was what and thumped the Kulaks. He did not concede that his attitude towards Ukrainian issues had been careless until that November, when Lenin had also changed his mind. At the meeting of May 19, Trotsky said that no matter how bad Soviet rule might be for Ukrainian peasants, it would have been twenty times worse under some other government. Cultural rights did not require dividing military resources. Idem, sprava 10, no. 177–9. Also in *Kommunist* (Kharkiv), June 1920, 11.

63 V.S. Lozytsky et al., *Chetverta konferentsiia Kommunistychnoi partii (bilshovykiv) Ukrainy 17–23 bereznia 1920 r. Stenograma* (Kyiv, 2006), 142–3. In his *Revoliutsiia i kontr-revoliutsia na Ukraine* (Moscow, 1920) written before the Second Comintern Conference, Petrovsky did not consider Ukraine a colony, Russia an empire, or nationalism a progressive force. Independence had failed not because of a Russian Bolshevik invasion but because of an indigenous social revolution. Petrovsky saw no alternative to Soviet Russian rule. His survey has no theoretical or comparative perspective.

64 *Kievskii kommunist*, 8 February 1919.

65 *Kommunist* (Kyiv), 25 April 1919.

66 *Kommunist* (Kyiv), 3, 7, 9 March 1920.

67 Cited in Lenin, *Polnoe*, XXII: 352.

68 Lozytsky at al, *Chetverta konferentsiiai*, 444–8. There were 242 voting delegates at the congress, but apparently only 16 voted on this resolution, with 8 for and 6 abstaining. Kh. Rakovskii, "Othoshenniia mezhdu sovetskami respublikami Rossiia i Ukraina," *Kommunist* (June, 1920), 11. See also TsDAVO f. 2 op 1 sprava 564 nos. 25–8; *Kommunist* (Kyiv), 3 March 1920. In the latter article he proposed a single, united proletarian state with no Ukrainian or Russian republics.

69 This was the first set of conference resolutions to include a section on the international situation. That section explained that capitalism had outgrown national states and was now imperialist. *Kommunistichna partiia*

Ukrainy v rezoliutsiiakh i resheniiakh siezdov i konferentsiiakh (Kyiv, 1958), 124–5.

70 Bachynsky ed., *Dokumenty*, 583. The socialist colonial policy issue is discussed in Day and Gaido, eds., *Discovering Imperialism: Social Democracy to World War I* , 24–9. In 1932, almost a decade after Ukrainian and Asian Marxists noted that workers could be chauvinist extremists, Karl Renner took this idea further and identified workers as among the strongest of Hitler's supporters. G. Botz, "Austro-Marxist Interpretations of Fascism," *Journal of Contemporary History* 11 (1976): 136.

71 *Kievskii kommunist*, 12 and 20 February 1919; *Chervonyi prapor*, 14 and 15 February 1919. Bolshevik federalism, wrote another, was but a cover for Russian nationalism; 9 March 1919. *Kommunist*, 27 February and 10 May 1919.

72 Lozytsky et al., *Chetverta konferentsiia*, 35–7, 102, 133, 471, 151; *Kommunist* (Kyiv), 3 March 1920.

73 Lozytsky et al., *Chetverta konferentsiia*, 476–7. This order came two weeks after the Borotbists were allowed to join the CPU and was used to keep the vast majority of them out of it.

74 *Chervonyi prapor* (Kamianets-Podilsky), 9 May 1922.

75 *Biuleten tsentralnoho biura livoi fraktsii UKP*, 15 September 1924, 2–3. The relationship between "the proletariat" and the party was not breached. Overall, 50 per cent of white- and blue-collar workers considered themselves Ukrainian, but only 33 per cent *used* Ukrainian.

76 *Deviataia konferentsiia RKP(b) sentiabr 1920 goda* (Moscow, 1972), 57–61, 69, 230. Lenin's offensive speech was not published here. R. Pipes ed., *The Unknown Lenin* (New Haven, 1996) 94.

77 Drabkin, *Komintern*, 206. Lenin equivocated on whether his party should spread socialism by force. In 1915, he used the phrase "raise up the socialist proletariat." In July 1920, he explained that the triumphant proletarian should "help and aid with all the means at their disposition." He noted that the idea of an offensive war against Poland had not been expressed in formal resolutions but rather in informal talks among the leadership. Before the congress, despite defeat at Warsaw, he still advocated "using bayonets." *IV Vsemirnyi kongress Kommunisticheskogo Internatsionala: Izbrannye doklady, rechi i rezoliutsii* (Moscow, 1923), 195–6; Lenin, *Polnoe*, XXVII: 51, 91; XIL: 246; Amiantov et al., *V.I. Lenin Neizvestnye dokumenty*, 368, 373–4.

78 Reprinted in Drabkin, *Komintern*, 223–7. The idea did not appear in his *Diktatura proletariata v Rossii i mirovaia revoliutsiia* (Odessa, 1920), which only supported use of violence in defence of revolution by the "Russian

[*Russkii*] proletariat" and "Russian [*Russki*] soviet government." Nor did it appear in propaganda issued by the CPU's Polish Section in June 1920 to the invading Polish army. Here Polish communists wrote that Soviet Russia wanted peace because it knew capitalism would inevitably shortly collapse. Russia had more than enough of its own land, its own problems, and no need to "make a revolution in Poland for the workers." They could do it themselves and "don't need a nanny." *Do walki o pokoj* (Kyiv, 1920) 7, 11.

79 L. Trotsky, *Social Democracy and the Wars of Intervention in Russia, 1918–1921* (London, 1975), 93–4, 100–1. Trotsky did not go into the details of the decision to invade. He was not present at the meeting, but Stalin advocated it against Lenin's hesitations.

80 TsDAHO f. 57 op 2 sprava 488 no. 61.

81 S. Shreiber, "K protokolam pervogo vseukrainskogo soveshchaniia bolshevikov," *Letopis revoliutsii*, no. 5 (1926): 74–8, 80; E. Bosh, *Natsionalnoe pravitelstvo i sovetskaia vlast na Ukraine* (Moscow, 1919), 2, 5, 9, 53.

82 A. Vermorel, ed., *Oeuvres de Robespierre* (Paris, 1866), 222.

83 TsDAVO f. 57 op 2 sprava 285 no. 2.

84 TsDAHO f. 1 op 1 sprava 98 no. 70. Trotsky and Stalin in Moscow a week later condemned Lebed. "Deiatelnost tsentralnogo komiteta partii v dokumentakh," *Izvestiia TsK KPSS*, no. 5 (1991): 160.

85 Lenin, *Polnoe*, XXV: 342. Mill in his *Considerations on Representative Government* (1861), referred to inferior and superior nationalities and that absorption of the former into the latter was desirable. "Nobody can suppose it is not more beneficial to a Breton or a Basque ... to be members of the French nationality ... than to sulk on its own rocks, the half savage relic of past times, revolving in its own little mental orbit, without participation in or interest in the movement of the world." Some years later Russian liberal Anastasia Kairova wrote: "Let the Little Russians remain Little Russians and they will quickly turn into real Russians not only in name but in essence." N.S. "Lvovskyi protsess," *Vestnik evropy* no. 10 (1882) 850–1.

86 Popov, *Narys istorii komunistychnoi partii (bilshovykiv) Ukrainy* 240; V. I. Modestov, *Statti dlia publiki* (SPB, 1883) 200; R. Pipes ed., *P. B. Struve Collected Works* (Ann Arbor) IX: 185-87.

87 No biographer of Trotsky examines why he opposed exporting revolution by force of arms to Poland and Georgia but not Ukraine. I. Deutscher, *The Prophet Armed. Trotsky: 1879-1921* (London, 1954), 470–4; P. Broue, *Trotsky* (Paris, 1988) 269.

88 Trotsky made this comparison in July 1920, after Ireland had declared independence. Meijer ed., *The Trotsky Papers* II: 229. Although the

Comintern by then had proclaimed "bourgeois" nationalism "progressive" the Bolsheviks did not apply the principle to Ukraine. Their publicists obfuscated the reality of foreign invasion: "And Ukrainian communists with the support of Russian armies ended-up waging a long and deadly struggle for Soviet power." A. Pryideshky, "Zhovten na Ukraini i borotba za Radiansku vladu," *Zhovten na Ukraini. 1917-1920. Zbirnyk stattiv* (Kharkiv, 1920), 6.

89 This echoed the opinions of tsarist officials like Aleksander Troinitskii, who fifty years earlier had argued that forced linguistic russification would be counterproductive as it would provoke defensive counter-reaction. V.S. Borodin ed., *T.H. Shevchenko i tsarska tsenzura* (Kyiv, 1969), 155–6. Lenin, *Polnoe*, XXIII: 423–6; XIV: 294–5. The English-language translation of the 1912 article rendered state language as official language, thus obscuring the distinction between state and empire; XX: 71.

90 Cited in Borisenok, *Fenomen* , 138; U. Lins, *Die Gefahrliche Sprache. Die Verfolgung der Esperantisten unter Hitler und Stalin* (Gerlingen, 1988), 191–2; Aleksander Bogdanov did declare Esperanto compulsory in schools but the decision was never implemented. On the spatial aspect of capital, see D. Harvey, *The Urbanization of Capital* (Baltimore, 1985), 32–61.

91 P. Lukashevich [pseud.], "Ukrainskie natsionalnye partii," *Vestnik Zhizhni* no. 1 (1906): 36–40; K. Ne-ia [pseud.], "Deshcho pro natsionalizm ta sotsializm," *Vilna Ukraina*, nos. 1–2 (1906): 88–96.

92 V.V. Anikeev et al., *Perepiska sekretariata TsK RSDRP(b) s mestnymy partiinymy organiztsiiamy. Sbornik dokumentov* (Moscow, 1957–74), II: 287; P. Hryhorenko, *Spohady* (Kyiv, 2007), 164. This section is omitted without indication in the English translation of Hryhorenko's memoirs.

93 *Ukrainsky proletariat* (Katerynoslav), 29 February 1920. Even if they don't understand, they must, because that is what the revolution demanded.

94 Skrypnyk, *Statti*, I: 291; TsDAHO f. 1 op 20 sprava 2242, no. 80, 140. In 1926, declared Russians and mostly Russified Jews made up 15 per cent of Ukraine's population and 51 per cent of the CPU.

95 Lapchynsky, "Pershyi period radianskoi vlady na Ukraine." *Litopys revoliutsii*, no. 1 (1928): 166.

96 The idea of a separate party was condemned and the CPU was established as a Russian subunit. Iurchuk et al., *Pervyi siezd*, 176; *Chervonyi prapor*, 17 April 1919.

97 *Shliakh borotby* (Poltava), 14, 19, and 21 June 1919.

98 TsDAHO f. 43 op 1 sprava 65 no. 13, cited in Mazepa, *Bolshevizm*, 82–3; *Derzhavnyi arkhiv Kyivskoi oblasti* (DAKO) f. 846 op 1–59.

99 TsDAHO f. 1 op 1 sprava 92 no. 53, 81. Rakovskii began to change his centralist Russificatory opinions in November 1919. Iefimenko, *Status USRR*, 105.

100 V. Zatonsky, " Iz nedavnego proshlogo," *Kommunist* (Moscow), July 1918, 57–8. In the previous issue, Radek had declared the right of national self-determination passé; *Vosmaia konferentsiia*, 105.

101 *Chervonyi prapor*, 16 May 1920 and 11 July 1920; *Pravda*, 12 May 1920; Lenin, *Polnoe*, XXXVIII: 206–18. Agursky, *The Third Rome*, 203–13, 215–20. Zinoviev and Bukharin condemned this exploitation of Russian imperialism. Bukharin, who saw no relationship between it and the new proletarian soviet fatherland, called on Polish workers to support the first proletarian fatherland against their own capitalist fatherland. *Pravda*, 10 July 1920.

102 Stalin, *Works*, IV: 234, 297–8; Drabkin, ed., *Komintern*, 183.

103 The figures are Stalin's, who regretted that the government could not extract the expected 160 million; *Works*, IV: 46, 311, 363–76. He saw no third alternative. A year later (p. 297) he referred to Russia (*Rossiia*) – that is, the entire former Russian empire – as a "colony." Lenin never called Russia a "colony," presumably because he did not think a "colony" could lead the world socialist revolution.

104 Rudych et al., *Vtoroi siezd*, 6–7. The October 1919 resolution was not in the published protocols: *Izvestiia TsK KPSS* no. 3 (1990): 186; reproduced in Kovalchuk, *Nevidoma viina*, 384.

105 TsDAVO f. 1 op 1 sprava 10 nos. 84, 92, 98, 102.

106 V. Vynnychenko, *Shchodennyk* (Edmonton, 1980), I: 430, 438. In late December 1919, Lenin and Trotsky invited Vynnychenko to take a top position in Ukraine, hoping thereby to strengthen the federalists in the CPU. This was to counter the *"desysty,"* who called for inner-Party democracy, and to attract more Ukrainian support for the Bolsheviks in the face of Petliura's alliance with Poland. In November 1920, after the Polish offensive and Molotov and Lebed were placed in charge of the CPU, Lenin's support for Vynnychenko ended. V. Lozytsky, *Politburo TsK Kommunistichnoi partii Ukrainy* (Kyiv, 2005).

107 *Nova Doba*, 28 November 1920. He here published a letter he had not sent to Bolshevik leaders when in Bolshevik territory.

108 Plekhanov hated Mykhailo Drahomanov and Taras Shevchenko and condemned Engels in 1891 for referring to Ukrainians as a nation distinct from and conquered by the Russians that should freely be able to choose its political fate. Himka, ed. and trans., *Roman Rosdolsky: Engels and the*

"Nonhistoric" Peoples, 184, 189. On Belinskii, see "V.G. Belinskii, 'Gaida-maki,' Poema Tarasa Shevchenka," *Polnoe sobranie sochinenii* (Moscow, 1953–9), VI: 172–4; XII: 436–42; V. Swoboda, "Shevchenko and Belinsky," *Slavonic and East European Review* (1961): 168–83; A. Rutherford, "Vissarion Belinskii and the Ukrainian National Question," *Russian Review* 4 (October 1995): 500–15.

109 Trotsky, *Sochineniia*, IX: 214–15. Capitalism made nationally defined frontiers obsolete politically and economically, not culturally.

110 "I demand only one thing: that every tribe, great and small, be given the full opportunity and right to act according to its will. If it wants to merge with Russia and Poland – let it merge. Does it want to be an independent member of a Polish or Russian or general Slavic federation? Then let it be so. Finally, does it want to separate completely from every other people and live as a totally separate state? Then God bless it! Let it separate." Cited in Himka, ed. and trans., *Roman Rosdolsky*, 170.

111 Manilov, *1917 god*, 104.

112 *Izvestiia soiuza promyshlennosti torgovlia finansov i selskago khozaistva Ukrainy* no. 1 (April 15/28). The group pointed out, up to the Hetman's fall, that "the separated parts of Russia" had to be united and that there already existed Russian associations, soviet and private, working towards this end: the Bureau of United Russian Manufacturing and Co-op Organizations in Ukraine and, in Russia, the private Russia Union of Importers and Exporters. Ibid. (December 2/19). That September, the group formed a subcommittee on the issue – "*Obiedenennoe obshchestvo po tovarobmenu s velikoi Rossii*" – which later added the prefix "*Vseukrainskogo*" to its title. The April statement was reported to Lenin in June by an adviser attached to the Russian peace delegation in Kyiv. TsDAHO f. 57 op 2 sprava 76 no. 514. The most sophisticated presentation of the economic case against Ukrainian independence was not made by a Bolshevik but by Naum Iasny, *Mozhet-li Ukraina byt ekonomicheskoi nezavisimoi* (Kharkov, 1918). Like the Bolsheviks, he labelled Ukraine's allegedly unavoidable economic dependency on Austria and Germany, but not on Russia, as colonial. 29

113 The full speech and debate is reproduced in P. Khrystiuk, *Zamitky i materialy do istorii Ukrainskoi revoliutsii 1917–20*; reprint ed., New York, 1969 [1921], IV: 186–9. See also P.V. Miliutin, *Chy Velykorosiia bez Ukrainy mozhe ekonomichno istnyvaty* (Vienna, 1921).

114 *Vosmoi siezd*, 106; L. Trotskii, *O Lenine* (Moscow, 1924), 88–9; Lenin, *Polnoe*, XXVII: 160–1. Although he confuses the terms *Rus* and *Rossiia*, he is

referring in this speech to the Russian borders established by the Brest-Litovsk Treaty.

115 M. Vladimirov, ed., *Spravochnik prodovolstvennogo agenta Ukr. Sots. Sov. Respubliki* (Kharkiv, 1920), 6–7. Nothing was to be requisitioned from those with less than three desiatins (approx. 9 acres) of land. The UNR requisitioned nothing from those with 15 desiatins or less. M. Bal, *Pro realizatsiiu (uborku) urozhaiu* (Kamianets-Podilsky, 1919).

116 *Proletarska borotba* (Zhytomir), 31 November 1919.

117 Lenin made no sense when he claimed that demands for secession could not fragment big states or create small ones. Lev Yurkevych, "Iesuits'ka polityka," in *Tysiacha rokiv ukrains'koi suspil'no-politychnoi dumky*, ed. T. Hunchak and R. Solchanyk (Kyiv, 2001) VI:187.

118 *Vosmoi siezd*, 143, 160.

119 Cited in Nahorny, "Bilshovyzm," 163–79; S. Hurenko, ed., *Tretyi ziizd Komunistychnoi partii (bolshevykiv) Ukrainy (1-6 berezen 1919 roku)* (Kyiv, 2002), 27, 54, 63. Lenin in May 1919 issued secret instructions to restrict and ultimately destroy the Borotbist party, whose participation in Bolshevik commissariats varied with the fortunes of war. The end came in February 1920. Members were allowed to join the CPU only as individuals and their influence was limited to cultural affairs. Ibid., 200–1.

120 In 1913 the British Labour Party (including the British Socialist Party as of 1916) recognized the Irish Labour Party as a separate party. This led to the formation of a Belfast Labour Party, which was not recognized by the British party. The Socialist Party of Ireland was separate from the British Socialist Party. The latter, as well as British Communists, opposed Irish independence in 1918. The Indian Communist Party, formed in 1920, was independent of the British Party. The ICP disappeared into the Communist Party of India, formed in 1925. In 1929, Moscow subordinated the CPI to the British Party. The Anglocentric imperialist superiority of the latter and the deferential obsequiousness of the former resembled the relationship between the RCP and the CPU. Milotte, *Communism in Modern Ireland*, 36–48; G.M. Adibekov et al., *VKP(b) Komintern i Koreia 1918–1941* (Moscow, 2007); idem, *VKP(b) Komintern i Iaponiia 1918–1941* (Moscow, 2001); Gupta, *Comintern*.

121 Dutch radicals formed the Indonesian Party. By the time it joined the Comintern they were a tiny minority in it. The Vietnamese Party was separate from the French. As in Ukraine, the membership in Algeria was overwhelming settler/colonist. In 1935 the Algerian Party separated from the French; in 1956, it advocated independence. The Russians condemned the French in Algeria for opposing independence and backed the small

pro-independent faction – the equivalent of the UCP they condemned in Ukraine. In 1922, when local communist leaders claimed that a Muslim revolution would mark a return to feudalism and that a French revolution was a precondition of an Algerian revolution, Trotsky condemned them as having a "slave-owner mentality." A. Drew, "Bolshevizing Communist Parties: The Algerian and South African Experiences," *International Review of Social History* 48 (August, 2003): 181–9; E. Sivan, *Communisme et nationalisme en Algerie 1920–1962* (Paris, 1976).

122 *Kommunist* (Kharkiv), 14 December 1920. He added that, by default, this left the millions of peasants in the hands of nationalist leaders. Zatonsky never went further than calling for a different approach in Ukraine from Russia on grounds it was more backward than Russia. *Borotba*, 23 December 1919.

123 Potichnyi, ed., *On the Current Situation in Ukraine*, 44.

124 Cited in D. I. Babakov, *Gosudarstvennye i natsionalnye problemy v mirovozzrenii V.V. Shulgina* (Moscow, 2012), 123.

125 Korolivsky, ed., *Grazhdanskaia voina*, I, pt 1: 35, 49, 101, 12, 25–53, 378, 462; Pavliuk et al., *Bolshevistskie organizatsii Ukrainy v period ustanovlenniia i ukrepleniia sovetskoi vlasti*, 16–17.

126 Ukrainian left-SRs also used ethnic/cultural discourse, but not to justify centralization. In the spring of 1919, we can find reference to "fraternal" ties with the Russian proletariat but, at the same time, central control from Moscow is condemned. *Borotba* (Kyiv), 3 April 1919.

127 *Tretii VseUkrainskii siezd sovetov (6-10 marta 1919 g.)*, 33, 86. D. Rancour-Laferriere, "Assimilationism in Relation to Ethnic Hatred among Russian Nationalists," *Ab Imperio* no. 1 (2000): 139–40. S.M. Sergeev, ed., *Natsiia i imperiia v Russkoi mysli nachala XX veka* (Moscow, 2004), 100–4, 114–30, 143–4.

128 TsDAVO f. 2 op 1 sprava 564 nos. 30–1; *Tretii VseUkrainskii sezd sovetov*, 33, 86; Korolivsky, ed., *Grazhdanskaia voina*, I, pt 1: 458; pt 2: 728. The authors, Manuilsky, Petrovsky, and Zatonsky, claimed that a "Ukrainian Red Army" had joined the Russian force to make it appear that the Red Army was not almost 90 per cent Russian. On 22 January 1920, Ukraine's third Soviet government stressed the importance of directing as many Ukrainians and Ukrainian speakers as possible into the army that had just occupied their country. Ibid., 675; Lenin, *Polnoe*, L: 50. Hrynevych, "Dynamika natsionalnoho sklad chastyn," *Problemy istorii Ukrainy* no. 15 (2006): 351–2.

129 *Chervonyi prapor*, 25 April 1919.

130 TsDAVO f. 1 op 1 sprava 10 no. 98 and nos. 113–17. Nikolai Podvoisky, Ukraine's Military Commissar, said: "I did not come to cultivate Ukrainian independence but to create an organization whose aim is to use Ukrainian resources."

131 "Rossiia i soiuzniki," *VTsIK* (Moscow) 25 and 31 January and 4 February 1919. Stockpiling began in October 1918 and does not appear to have been secret (Cf. n.9). Despite food shortages that year, the Bolsheviks earmarked a 200,000-ruble monthly stipend for Polish communists in January 1919; over 10 million rubles for European communist parties in August; 5 million for a Comintern office in Kharkiv in January 1920; and another 15 million for agents in Germany that December. Drabkin, *Komintern*, 128, 150–2, 157, 219.

132 TsDAHO f. 8 op 1 sprava 40 no. 61; TsDAVO f. 1113 op. 2 sprava 200 no. 4.

133 Holquist, *Making War*; Korolivsky, ed., *Grazhdanskaia voina*, I pt. 1: 643.

134 *Vestnik Ukrainskoi Narodnoi Respubliki* (Kyiv), 19 and 20 February 1918, reprinted in *Litopys revoliutsii*, no. 5 (1928): 135–6; *Chervonyi prapor* (Kyiv) 5 and 6 February 1919; Khrystiuk, *Zamitky*, IV: 82.

135 Potichnyi, ed., *On the Current Situation*, 115–18; TsDAHO f. 57 op 2 sprava 314; Khrystiuk, *Zamitky*, IV: 173; Korolivsky, ed., *Grazhdanskai voina*, I pt. 1: 591, 642.

136 Potichnyj, ed., *On the Current Situation*, 9, 65, 97, 106, 165, 176. The reference is to Rakovskii's claim in the summer of 1918 that Soviet Russia was the direct successor of the former Russian empire and that Russian colonization made the Donbass Russian (146). If there is no Ukraine, the authors wondered, why should a Communist Party of Ukraine and a Soviet Ukrainian government exist (52)?

137 Bachynsky ed., *Dokumenty*, 535–6, 544. English translation: C. Ford, "Memorandum of the Ukrainian Communist Party to the Second Congress of the III Communist International July–August 1920," *Debatte* 2 (August 2009): 248–262. The memorandum was published as a pamphlet in Vienna in 1920.

138 Cited in Khrystiuk, *Zamitky*, IV: 55–6, 72. *Chervonyi prapor* (Kyiv) 6, 9, and 12 February 1919. *Rosiiskoho* in Ukrainian means "Great Russian."

139 *Chervonyi prapor*, 24 April 1919.

140 *Chervonyi prapor*, 12 February 1919; *Chervonyi stiakh* (Kyiv), 27 May 1919.

141 *Chervonyi prapor*, 3, 6, 9, and 17 April 1919.

142 *Shliakh borotby* (Poltava) 12 June 1919. Others saw centralization as the main reason why the new Soviet bureaucracy was so big and filled with ex-officials and Russian nationalists, and argued that decentralization was the solution. *Levy es-er* (Kyiv), 27 December 1919.

143 *Chervonyi prapor,* 13, 20, 23, 25, 26, and 27 February and 13 March 1919. *Proletarska borotba,* 20 November 1919.

144 *Chervonyi prapor,* 13 and 27 February 1919; also in *Chervonyi stiakh,* 29 July 1919.

145 *Chervonyi stiah,* 5 and 8 June 1919.

146 *Proletarska Pravda* (Kharkiv), 6 and 7 January 1920.

147 Cited in F.P. Fonge, *Modernization without Development in Africa* (Trenton, NJ, 1997), 66.

148 *Borotba,* 3 February 1920. Bolshevik propaganda sought to belittle and delegitimize the Ukrainian national movement and the UNR by referring to them by the name of the leader of the government.

149 *Chervonyi prapor,* 4 March 1919; *Chervonyi stiah,* 11 and 18 June 1919.

150 *Chervonyi prapor,* 11 April 1919.

151 *Chervonyi prapor,* 29 April, 1920. Ukrainian peasants did not wear bast shoes.

152 V. Soldatenko, *U poshukakh sotsialnoi i natsionalnoi harmonii. Eskizy do istorii ukrainskoho kommunizmu* (Kyiv, 2006), 424–30. Two months later, he published another letter in Moscow's *Kommunist* that condemned the regime's militarization, centralization, and Russian chauvinism but did not use the word "colony." In both he expressed hope for reform. Bachynsky ed., *Dokumenty,* 313–16. Vynnychenko organized a Foreign Group of the UCP in Vienna. Disillusioned, after his trip he began condemning the regime. Mazurenko in an open letter then broke with the group, explaining that the Ukrainian Party differed from the Russian on the colonial issue and the organizational form of the Ukrainian revolution and that this was a purely internal communist affair. TsDAHO f. 8 op 1 sprava 41 no. 100.

153 *Chervonyi prapor,* 21 and 22 March 1919. The published results consequently recorded an increase in the number of declared Ukrainians (from 12 per cent in 1917 to 24 per cent) and a slight decline in declared Russians (50 per cent to 42 per cent). *Chervonyi prapor,* 31 July.

154 *Chernovy prapor,* 15 February 1919. Nahorny, "Bilshovyzm," 139.

155 *Chervonyi prapor,* 9 March and 17 April 1919.

156 *Chervonyi prapor,* 25 February 1919.

157 *Chervonyi stiah,* 25 May and 3 and 5 June 1919.

158 TsDAHO f. 8 op 1 sprava 40 nos. 61–2; sprava 20 nos. 1–2; sprava 23 nos. 1–2.

159 *Borotba* (Katerynoslav), 3 February 1920; *Ukrainskyi proletar,* 15 February 1920.

160 TsDAHO f. 43 op 1 sprava 46 nos. 1–3.

161 TsDAHO f. 1 op 20 sprava 129 nos. 49–50.
162 *Borotba* (Kyiv), 3 August 1919.
163 *Borotbist* (Poltava), 1, 2, and 4 January 1920.
164 Nahorny, "Bilshovyzm," 179. The memorandum is reprinted in *Ukrainsky proletar* (Katerynoslav), 15–25 February 1920. The signatories included Popov and Larik (Kasianenko). TsDAHO f. 57 op. 2 sprava 383 nos. 10–12. Other letters are reproduced in Iefimenko, *Vzaiemovidnosysny*, 184–206.
165 Bachynsky, ed., *Dokumenty*, 263–5, 269.
166 *Desiatyi siezd*, 203.
167 TsDAHO f. 57 op 2 sprava 76 nos. 71–2.
168 TsDAHO f. 8 op 1 sprava 41 nos. 3–6; no. 100. There is no known response to this letter.
169 TsDAHO f. 8, op 1 sprava 41 nos. 68–9. Richytsky complained he learned little and talked with few delegates because the only foreign language he knew was Russian. In the future, he wrote, delegates had to have translators with them. Only the Finns supported the Ukrainian cause in the Comintern.

Chapter 3

1 I.N. Kiselev et al. "Politicheskie partii v Rossii v 1905–1907 gg.: chislennost, sostav, razmeshchenie." *Istoriia SSSR*, no. 4 (1990) 71–87; V.V. Shelokhaev, ed. *Politicheskie partii Rossii konets XIX – pervaia tret XX veka. Entsiklopediia.* (Moscow, 1996).
2 N. Harding, *Leninism* (Durham NC, 1996), 51.
3 For example, TsDAHO f. 43 op 1 sprava 65.
4 Karl Radek coined the term National Bolshevism in Berlin in 1919; German left SDs then used it to refer to the anti-Entente movement they were trying to organize. Whites who had joined the Bolsheviks hoping to restore imperial Russia called themselves *Smenovekhovtsi*. Lenin in 1920 condemned "German National Bolshevism," and in 1922 classified *Smenovekhovtsi* ideas as an ideology of bourgeois restoration. M. Agursky, *The Third Rome: National Bolshevism in the USSR* (London, 1987).
5 Marx and Engels, *Collected Works*, (New York, 1975–2005) XXIII: 154–7. It is unlikely anyone would have known about this speech in turn-of-the-century Russia or Ukraine.
6 Lenin condemned the federal structure of the Austrian SD party. "No, we won't have any of that nonsense [*merzosti*] in Austria here. We won't allow it! And we have more of our brother ethnic Russians here [in the empire, than there are Germans in Austria]. We won't allow this 'Austrian spirit' with our workers." Lenin, *Polnoe Sobranie*, XXXVIII: 162.

7 *Leninskii Sbornik* (Moscow, 1945), XXXV: 94. Lenin, whose party by then had more déclassé intellectuals and clerks than workers, instructed his underlings in December 1919 to discredit UCP members by documenting the origins of its non-proletarian members.

8 M. N. Roy, *Memoirs* (Delhi, 1984), 464; J. Lacoutre, *Ho Chi Minh* (NewYork, 1968), 32.

9 Sultan Galiev was writing at the same time as the Ukrainian communists. Already in 1919 he was condemning Columbus, "freedom loving America," and cosmopolitan Europe, because they were built on the bones of millions of Africans and Amerindians. Gizzatullin and Sharafutdinov, eds., *Mirsaid Sultan-Galiev. Izbrannye trudy*, 141–5, 198–203.

10 *Robitnycha hazeta*, 7 January 1919; *Chervonyi prapor*, 9 March 1919.

11 Nahorny, "Bilshovyzm ta Ukrainskyi national kommunizm v dobu revoliutsii (1917–1920 rr.)," Kandydatska dissertatsiia, 61. Radek used it in December 1919 to criticize the German Communist Party for cooperating with the German right against the former Entente powers.

12 V. Vynnychenko, *Vidrodzhennia natsii* (Vienna/Kyiv, 1920), III: 302; *Komunist* (Kyiv), 1 April 1919.

13 S. Barannyk et al., *Istoriia KP(b)U v materiialakh ta dokumentakh 1917-1920 rr.*, 2nd ed. (Kharkiv, 1934), 630; *Borotba* (Kyiv), 21 January and 28 June 1919.

14 *Chervonyi prapor*, 4 April 1920.

15 *Chervonyi prapor*, 20 and 22 January and 3 April 1919. TsDAB, Lystivky, no. 11021s.

16 Mazepa, *Ukraina v ohni i buri revoliutsii*, 116. For the text of the proposed agreements with the UNR, see Khrystiuk, *Zamitky i materialy do istorii Ukrainskoi revoliutsi*, IV: 111, 131–2; Bachynsky, ed., *Dokumenty*, 122–4, 156. The anonymous criticism of the UNR and opposition to cooperation is reproduced on 159–60. Bela Kun in Hungary also allied with SD "bourgeois nationalists."

17 Bachynsky, ed., *Dokumenty*, 156–9. The documents are undated.

18 The uprisings were provoked by the tens of thousands of Russians from Russia sent to expropriate and requisition as well as by the exclusion of large estates, sugar beet plantations, cattle, and inventory from redistribution. In 1919 approximately 30 per cent of Ukraine's arable land was still in noble hands. Nesterov, Zemziulina, and Zakharchenko, *U pokhodi za voliu*, 36–45.

19 O. Iurenko, "Za mandatom holovnoho otamana," *Poltavska petliuriana*, no. 3 (1999): 54–7. Hrudnytsky claimed to be in touch with organizers in Kyiv and Makhno. His initial ally, Ukrainian Bolshevik Oleksandr Sharyi-Bohunsky, denounced the plan to Antonov on April 2. TsDAVO f. 2 op

1 sprava 241 nos. 16–17; V. Danilov and T. Shanin, eds., *Nestor Makhno. Krestianskoe dvizhenie na Ukraine 1918–1921. Dokumenty i materialy* (Moscow, 2006), 116. Hrudnytsky escaped and joined the Borotbists.

20 TsDAHO f. 1 op 20 sprava 39 nos. 126–7. M. Kovalchuk, "Rol Vseukrainskoho revkomu ta Holovnoho povstanskoho shtabu v antybilshovytskomu povstanskomu rusi," *Pamiat stolit* no. 5 (2000): 94–107.

21 M. Tkachenko, A. Richytsky, *Proekt prohramy Ukrainskoi Komunistychnoi Partii* (1919). Richytsky's police file contains little about his pre -1923 activities. By 1932 he had become a zealous Stalinist who brutally enforced collectivization. V. Vasiliev et al, *Partiino-radianske kerivnytstvo USRR pid chas holodomoru 1932-1933 rr.:Vozhdi Pratsivnyky Aktyvisty* (Kyiv 2013) 289-400.

22 Individuals who had been to and seen Russia in 1918 did explain to Ukrainians that it was the Bolsheviks who were responsible for the repression and dictatorship. "It is not isolated individuals rising up there but peasants in many counties who, with their wives, children and elders, face Latvian and Chinese bullets and bayonets because they see no other alternative." Bachynsky, ed., *Dokumenty*, 114; Danilov and Shanin, eds, *Nestor Makhno*, 73, 82, 111, 202.

23 TsDAB, lystivky, 11908c; Derzhavnyi Arkhiv Sluzhby Bezpeky Ukrainy (DASBU) f. 13 sprava 40 no 57.

24 TsDAVO f. 2 op 1 sprava 234 nos. 103–5. This letter appeared just after Kamenev arrived in Kharkiv with instructions from Lenin to "fuse" Ukraine and Russia and Trotsky and Lenin had decided to militarily aid Hungarian communists. Between 10 and19 April, Trotsky decided Makhno was a greater threat than the UNR and ordered the Red Army to destroy him. This nullified the alliance with Makhno that Rakovskii supported – which the letter was supposed to discredit. The letter is suspicious because Makhno never advocated killing Jews. Although he was formally neutral towards the UNR and in contact with Ukrainian SDs and Hryhoriev, Makhno decided on 17 May not to ally with the latter because he tolerated the slaughter of Jews. The handwriting in this letter does not correspond to that in Makhno's genuine letters, and the text is not a transcript because it lacks the standard obligatory phrase "true to the original" at the end. A.V. and V.F Belash, *Dorogi Nestora Makhna* (Kyiv 1993), 175–218; Danilov and Shanin, eds, *Nestor Makhno*, 104, 121. Makhno letters are reproduced in: V. Golovanov, *Nestor Makhno* (Moscow, 2008)

25 TsDAB, lystivky no. 12131s. Copies in TsDAHO f. 8 op 1 sprava 21 nos. 8, 10 and in f. 57 op 2 sprava 355 contain this additional phrase: "It is not Russian Bolsheviks who will save Ukraine's workers. Ukraine's proletariat must liberate itself." I am unaware of any collection of Independentist

Revolutionary Council documents. Some related letters are reproduced in Bachynsky ed, *Dokumenty,* 125–6, 148, 156–8.

26 Reproduced in Tiutiunnyk, *Zymovyi pokhid,* 75–7.

27 Russified atheist Jews comprised the entire Podillia provincial and Chernihiv city party memberships . TsDAVO f. 2 op.1 sprava 241 nos. 21, 61; TsDAHO f. 57 op 2 sprava 283 no. 16.

28 Barannyk et al., *Istoriia,* 464–9; TsDAB lystivky nos. 7417s, 4347s, 13512s, 13918s. At the time, associating "Jew" with financial predation did not imply ideological anti-Semitism because speculators or usurers of all races and creeds were routinely condemned as "Jews." Associating all Jews with Bolshevism likely reflected similar imprecise colloquial usage. Stuart, *Marxism and National Identity,* 116. Among those who considered Bolshevism Jewish was Winston Churchill (*Illustrated Sunday Herald,* 8 February 1920). Ukrainian peasant violence against Jews, moreover, cannot be reduced to the ideological anti-Semitism disseminated in tsarist Ukraine by imperial Russian extremist Black Hundreds. The issue also involved the restoration through violence of customary social boundaries that Jewish officials had breached as agents of Bolshevik-style modernization. D. Engel, "What's in a Pogrom? European Jews in an Age of Violence," in *Anti-Jewish Violence: Rethinking the Pogrom in East European History,* ed. J. Dekel-Chen et al. (Bloomington, 2011), 30–3. See also S.N. Kalyvas, *The Logic of Violence in Civil War* (Cambridge, 2006). Ukrainian SDs did not explain the phenomenon biologically and knew well there existed a Jewish proletariat.

29 TsDAHO f. 1 op 20 sprava 35 no. 64. S. Velychenko, *State Building in Revolutionary Ukraine* (Toronto, 2011), 189–94.

30 Elias Heifetz attributes two thousand dead to Zeleny's men for all of 1919 and claims that he instigated pogroms in Trypillia (*The Slaughter of Jews in the Ukraine in 1919* [New York, 1921], 177–9). The more reliable Elias Cherikover [Tcherikower] specified that it was communist Jews who sparked pogroms and that Zeleny forbade pogroms in his native Trypillia. He attributes approximately one hundred Jewish deaths to Zeleny's men during the five months he fought as an Independentist and another hundred to his lieutenants. *Di ukrainer pogromen in yor 1919* (New York, 1965), ch. 9. English translation: http://www.berdichev.org/the_pogroms_in_ukraine_in_1919.htm. Sartre, Fanon, and Memmi all condemned subaltern genocide against foreigners. But, they considered this "revolutionary violence of the colonized" a predictable, regressive, and unavoidable consequence of the demoralization produced by imperial rule – not by nationalism.

31 Cherikover, *Antisemitizm i pogromy*, 25, 143–6, 151; N.A. Ivnytskii, ed., *Grazhdanskaia voina v Rossii* (Moscow, 2002), 452; DAKO f. 3050 op. 1 sprava 37 no. 58; S.I. Gusev-Orenburgskii, *Bagrovaia kniga; pogromy 1919–1920 gg. na Ukraine* (Kharbin, 1922; 2nd ed., New York, 1983), 92–3. The Bolshevik edition of this book, titled *Kniga o Evreiskikh pogromakh na Ukraine v 1919 g.* (Petrograd, 1923 – reprinted 1972, 1983, 1989), omitted one hundred pages from the original that covered Bolshevik pogroms; also omitted was an introduction by Gorky about Red Army pogroms. M. Agurskii, ed., *Maksim Gorkii. Iz literaturnogo naslediia. Gorky i evreiskii vopros* (Jerusalem, 1986), 304.

32 A Russian peasant-born Red Army commander got married in a church and played tsarist anthems during the reception. Drunk, he toasted the revolution and shouted, "Beat the Jews." One of the honoured guests was his Jewish commissar, who upon hearing this drew his gun. The commander drew his, and the two men shot each other. V. Amfiteatrov-Kadashev, "Stranitsy iz dnevnika," *Minuvshee* 20 (1996): 594.

33 Bolshevik intelligence reported that the Independentist centre was in Kyiv, that it had ties with Hryhoriev, was well organized and was supported by local soviets. Its commanders shot captured non-Ukrainian Red army soldiers. TsDAVO f. 5 op 1 sprava 20 nos. 8–9, 14; f. 2 op 1 sprava 252 no. 17v; sprava 234 nos. 110, 120. By contrast, centrist Ukrainian SDs at the time doubted the council's ability to control anything, as well as its degree of popular support. O. Bozhko, ed., "General –khorunzhyi Armii UNR. Nevidoma avtobigrafiia Iu. Tiutiunnyka," *Z arkhiviv VUChK GPU NKVD KGB*, nos. 1–2 (1998), 44–7; P. Fedenko, "Povstannia natsii," in *Zbirnyk pamiaty Symona Petliury (1879–1926)* (Prague, 1930), 89–97; B. Kozelsky [pseud. Bernard Holovinsky], *Shliakh zradnystva i avantur* (Kharkiv, 1926), 19–21, 27–8. Kozelsky gives no sources but, he was a top counter-insurgency operative in the early 1920s. On Zeleny, see R. Koval, *Otaman Zeleny*, 2nd ed. (Kyiv, 2011).

34 Ukraine's Ministry of Defence Archive (DAMOU) f. 3796, op 2 sprava. 6 nos. 85–9, reproduced in R. Krutsyk, ed., *Narodna viina 1917-1932*. 82-83.

35 Cited in Belash and Belash, *Dorogi*, 216. TsDAVO f. 2 op 1 sprava 234 no. 133. Bolshevik intelligence reports that summer confirm their shaky hold over both the population and their own troops. TsDAVO f. 2 op 1 sprava 86; Danilov and Shanin, eds., *Nestor Makhno*, 109–10.

36 Independentists hoped to unite the Ukrainian left during a successful partisan struggle and then win over the Borotbists and CPU "federalists." A small group opposed to the anti-Bolshevik revolts broke with the main party, named itself "independentists-leftists," then in August joined the

Borotbists. TsDAHO f. 8 op 1 sprava 2 no 1-3. Bachynsky., ed., *Dokumenty*, 157–8 mistakenly attributes Richytsky letters to the "leftists."

37 *Chervonyi prapor,* 27 December 1919 and 11 March 1920. English translation by C. Ford, *Critique* no. 4 (December, 2010), 607–11. The one file on Mazurenko in the Ukrainian SBU archive has little about his revolutionary activities. DASBU f. 6 sprava 36546fp vol 2.

38 The Politburo had decided on concessions on 2 December. Lenin, *Polnoe*, XXXV: 334–7. Bachynsky, ed., *Dokumenty*, 247, 251–3.

39 TsDAHO f. 1 op 1 sprava 20 nos. 56–7; Barannyk et al., *Istoriia KP(b)U*, 447, 449, 464. *Kommunist* (Kharkov) 14 February 1919. Lenin that spring apparently ignored his plenipotentiaries' condemnations of the policies that had provoked Ukrainian resistance: see David Gopner's letter of 13 March; Joffe's letter of 9 April; M.I. Kulkova et al., *Ekonomicheskie otnosheniia sovetskoi Rossii s budushchimi soiuznymi respublikami 1917–1922* (Moscow, 1996), 65–75; Danilov and Shanin, eds., *Nestor Makhno*, 109. Genrik Iagoda, then head of the Cheka special section, noted on the margin of a critical report submitted that May by a military intelligence officer that it was to be ignored. Danilov and Shanin, eds., *Nestor Makhno*, 131–5.

40 *Kievskii Kommunist*, 7 February 1919; TsDAVO f. 1 op 1 sprava 11 no. 63.

41 DAKO f. 4823 op1 sprava 7 no. 26; Kolektsiia lystivky i plakativ op 5 nos. 28 and 29. The aim of the "bandits" was to weaken Russia by not sending grain; this would make it easier for them to destroy soviet power in Ukraine and take peasant lands for themselves. TsDAHO f. 57 op 2 sprava 210 no. 75; TsDAVO f. 5 op 1 sprava 17 no. 47v. A returned Red Army soldier reported on 11 July that as a prisoner he had heard Zeleny making a speech saying he would attack Denikin. TsDAVO f. 2 op 1 sprava 234 no. 121.

42 Given his pragmatism, Lenin might have recognized an Independentist-ruled Ukraine had they controlled a sizeable territory when his regime faced collapse in face of the successful White offensive. By that spring Rakovskii and the CPU leaders had evolved enough of a territorial self-interest to oppose Lenin's plan to "fuse" Ukraine with Russia. H. Iefimenko, "Istoriia stovrennia ta avtentychnyi zmist 'voienno-politychnoho soiuzu' mizh USRR ta RSFSR," *Ukrainskyi istorychnyi zhurnal* no. 1 (2014) 139–44.

43 The willingness to ally with the UNR that October ended with the White threat. Kovalchuk, *Nevidoma viina*, 158-60.

44 Cited in V. Soldatenko, *Vynnychenko i Petliura. Politychni portrety revoliutsiinoi doby*, (Kyiv, 2007), 264; *Borotbist*, 28 February 1919.

45 TsDAHO f. 39 op 4 sprava 128 no. 7.

46 TsDAVO f. 1078 op 2 sprava 34 no. 117; f. 2 op 1 sprava 272 nos. 64–5. Although claiming that workers would have supported Zeleny, it also claims that politically, they were split between Monarchist and Menshevik supporters. The report was written one week after the uprising, which Kozelsky linked to the Independentists.

47 Frolov, *Kompartiina-Radianska elita*, 31, Appendix 5. Federalist resolutions submitted for discussion to the Fourth CPU conference of March 1920 were not accepted and were not included in the published proceedings. TsDAVO f. 2 op 1 sprava 546 nos. 50–8.

48 As of 1921 almost 50 per cent of CPU members were Red Army men. No more than 13 per cent were workers. Frolov, *Kompartiino-radianska elita*, 30, 271. TsDAVO, f. 2 op 2 sprava 300 no. 4; f. 43 op 1 sprava 77 no. 1–3, contains 148 applications from all regions, completed in early 1920. This sample suggests that workers, peasants, and local educated professionals each comprised about 33 per cent of UCP membership.

49 R. Podkur, V. Chentsov, *Dokumenty organov gosudarstvennoi bezopasnosti USSR 1920-1930-kh godov*, (Ternopil, 2010) 211-12. TsDAHO f.1 op 20 sprava 1757 no 188. The reports are now in Moscow. Supporting a dissident minority with promises of concessions to split a larger party, destroying the majority and then the minority, was a standard Leninist tactic. He used it in April 1914 against Ukrainians in his party who had wanted to create a Ukrainian SD party. Lenin, *Collected Works*, 35: 135, 137. Russian SR leader Victor Chernov's description of this tactic in early 1921 was characterized by Cheka head Dzerzhinskii as "clear and concise." K. V. Gusev, *V. M. Chernov. Shtrikhi k politicheskomu portretu* (Moscow, 1999) 170. Borys, *Sovietization of Ukraine*, 432-433.

50 In reply to Mazurenko, who noted that the Ukr SSR was not independent and had no ministries, Skrypnyk said it was independent of the bourgeoisie and capitalism and that "we" did not need a state independent of the Russian proletariat. M. Skrypnyk, *Vybrani tvory* (Kyiv, 1991), 144–7; TsDAHO f. 1 op 18 sprava 58 no. 11; op 6 sprava 7 no 43. The editor of the CPU's *Kommunist* had suggested to Rakovskii in July 1919 that he proceed to divide and destroy the Independentists. Iefimenko, *Vzaiemovidnosyny*, 183.

51 TsDAHO f. 8 op 1 sprava 31 no. 56. This fond contains letters from provinces complaining of and recording arrests and harassment.

52 TsDAHO f. 8 op 1 sprava 13 no. 24.

53 *Chervonyi shliakh*, 11 July 1920. Reprinted as a pamphlet in 1921: TsDAHO f. 8 op 1 sprava 38. English translation in Ford, *Debatte*, 612–4.

54 TsDAHO f .1 op 1 sprava 92 nos. 56 and 59. DASBU f. 13 sprava 193 no 76; sprava 260 no 44.

55 The destruction of the UCP – and, earlier, the Borotbists – might be regarded as the first applications of tactics later used to destroy, subordinate, purge, and Russify Comintern member parties. G.M. Adibekov et al., *Organizatsionnaia structura Kominterna 1919–1943* (Moscow, 1997); A. Thorpe, "Comintern 'Control' of the Communist Party of Great Britain, 1920–1943," *English Historical Review* (June 1998): 643–62; W.J. Chase, *Enemies within the Gates? The Comintern and the Stalinist Repression* (New Haven, 2001).

56 TsDAHO f. 1 sprava 129 nos. 207 and 225; *Proletarskii proletarii* (Vinnytsia), 23 April 1921; V. Chentsov, *Politychna represiia v Radianski Ukraini v 20-kh rokakh* (Ternopil, 2000), 339–44; D. Arkhireiskyi and V. Chentsov, "Vlada i selianstsvo v Ukraini u 20-ti rr.," *Z Arkhiviv VUChK GPU NKVD KGB*, nos. 1–2 (1999): 106–7; Iu. Diriavko, *UKP: stvorennia, diialnist ta likvidatsiia ii bilshovykamy (1920–1925)*, candidate dissertation, Dniproderzhynsk National University, 2006.

57 *Borotba* (Kyiv), 3 April 1919.

58 *Borotba* (Kyiv), 17 June, 13 August, and 24 December 1919. The major spokesman for the Borotbists was Vasyl Blakytny.

59 *Chervonyi prapor* (Kyiv), 9 and 25 February 1919. Modified later in the Party program that proposed a union of socialist republics in a confederal arrangement.

60 Potichnyj, ed., *On the Current Situation in Ukraine*, 60–6.

61 *Chervonyi stiakh*, 21 July 1919; *Chervonyi prapor*, 22 August 1919. Nahorny, "Bilshovyzm ta Ukrainskyi," 169. Bolshevik totals showed that Ukraine received 8,500 wagonloads of finished goods over the first six months of 1919. In 1918 officials had planned to exchange three wagonloads of goods for four of produce – twice the tsarist wartime average – but could not. In Russia in 1918, 80 per cent of shipped goods were stolen. A. Iu. Davydov, *Nelegalnoe snabzhenie Rossiiskoho naseleniia i vlast 1917–1912 gg.* (Moscow, 2002), 206–7.

62 TsDAVO f. 340 op 1 sprava 43 no. 129, 178; idem sprava 441 no. 227, 312.

63 These figures were released at about the same time CPU leaders were claiming that trade between Russia and Ukraine was equitable – using weight, monetary value, and item quantity, rather than wagonloads, as units of measurement. Barannyk et al., *Istoriia KP(b)U v materiialakh ta dokumentakh*, 457. There is no comprehensive study of imports/exports using comparable units of measurement, nor of how widespread a practice it was to give items confiscated from targeted groups in one area to favoured groups in another nearby. A report from Poltava county (*povit*) in July 1919 indicates that it ostensibly received from Russia 140 ploughs, 1300 scythes, 185 harrows, 10 reapers, 3,600 pounds of nails, and 2,270 pounds of axle

grease, but without recording recipients. TsDAVO f. 2 op 1 sprava 252 no. 87; TsDAHO f. 43 op 1 sprava 36 no. 1. Wagonloads shipped to Russia rose from 145 in January to 6,575 in June.

64 When the Russian CC issued this instruction, the average fixed price for grain was 15 to 17 rubles for 40 pounds. On the urban black market, 40 pounds of flour ranged from 450 to 600 rubles. Soviet rubles represented nothing to the government, which simply printed as many as it needed. Iefimenko, *Vzaiemovidnosysny*, 70, 133.

65 *Chervonyi prapor,* 9 and 14 February 1919. Rakovskii dismissed Ukrainian issues when he met the Kyiv city soviet on 13 February to present Bolshevik policy.

66 *Chervonyi prapor,* 17 and 24 April 1919.

67 TsDAHO f. 8 op 1 sprava 21 nos. 11, 12, 14–20. The first pages are missing.

68 *Chervonyi prapor,* 21 and 23 December 1919.

69 *Chervonyi prapor,* 25 and 26 December 1919; 4 January 1920. Reprinted in his *Nash Spir* (Kharkiv, 1921).

70 *Chervonyi prapor*, 8 February 1920.

71 *Chervonyi prapor,* 4 and 26 March; 19 June 1920. Also in *Nash Spir*.

72 Bachynsky, ed., *Dokumenty*, 537–45. English translation by C. Ford, " Memorandum of the Ukrainian Communist Part to the Second Congress of the III International July August 1920," *Debatte* 2 (August 2009): 248–62.

73 *Chervonyi prapor* (Kyiv) [mimeographed monthly], May 1924. The article was preceded by a quote from Zinoviev, who, that February, had said that the communist parties of those countries whose bourgeoisie oppressed colonies should spend 50 per cent of their time on colonial issues; otherwise, they could not be considered communist.

74 *Chervonyi prapor,* 25 February 1919.

75 Mazurenko reasoned that the Bolsheviks were responsible for the pogroms because they had placed communist Jews in positions of authority to implement hated polices that benefited only themselves. TsDAHO f. 8 op 1 sprava 13 no. 21. Published in *Chervonyi prapor*, 11 March 1920.

76 TsDAHO f. 8 op 1 sprava 48 nos. 42–44, 47–8; J. Degras, ed., *The Communist International, 1919–1943* (London, 1955) I: 138–44.

77 TsDAHO f. 8 op 1 sprava 48 no. 51v.

78 *Chervonyi prapor*, 16 May, reprinted 19 June 1920. Also in *Nash Spir*.

79 Given the Darwinian classification of peoples current at the time, this was hardly complimentary to any of them. TsDAHO f. 8 op 1 sprava 41 nos. 78–81.

80 TsDAHO, f. 8 op. 1 sprava 20 nos. 1–3; Those concerned were M. Avdienko and O. Iaroshchenko.

81 V. Mazurenko, *Ekonomichna samostiinist Ukrainy v tsyfrakh* (Vienna, 1921), 8, 11, 13, 16–17; G.M. Krzhizhanovskii, ed., *Voprosy ekonomicheskogo raionirovaniia SSSR. Sbornik materialov i statei (1917–1929)* (Moscow, 1957), reproduces articles by central planning commission (*gosplan*) planners from 1920 to 1924 that reflected the thinking Mazurenko condemned. They juxtaposed Russocentric "economically rational" central planning to planning around "leftovers of lost sovereign rights" (72). Regarding the USSR as a single Russian unit rather than the sum of theoretically "independent" parts, it referred to "the rebirth of the Russian national economy" (120, 208) and "the future Russian economy." "The national economy of the USSR" meant "the entire economy on the territory of Russia" (224).

82 Mazurenko, *Ekonomichna*, 27, 30, 34, 38, 40, 49.

83 TsDAHO f. 8 op 1 sprava 90 no. 1.

84 TsDAVO f. 1 op 1 sprava 10 nos. 255–9. Zatonsky rebutted with the official rationalization. In light of the successful White offensive, centralization was imperative and thinking about federalism would have to be done some other time.

85 K. Barbachenko [pseud. H. Hrinko], "K voprosu ob ocherednykh zadachakh i razvitie revoliutsii na Ukraine," *Ukrainsky kommunist* (Moscow), no. 1 (1919): 5–12; "Ekonomicheskaia polozhenie Ukraine i ei perspektivy v sostave sovetskogo stroia," 12–17. *Borotba*, 21 February 1919.

86 *Borotba* (Kyiv), 23 July and 3 August 1919. *Proletarska Pravda*, 16 January 1920.

87 *Proletarska borotba* (Zhytomir), 31 November 1919.

88 Bachynsky, ed., *Dokumenty*, 114–16, 175–8, 233–6.

89 Nahorny, "Bilshovyzm ta Ukrainskyi," 179. The memorandum was published in *Ukrainsky proletar* (Katerynoslav), 15–25 February 1920. The signatories included Popov and Larik. TsDAHO f. 57 op. 2 sprava 383 nos. 10–12.

90 *Proletarska Pravda* (Kharkiv), 7 January 1920; *Borotbist* (Poltava), 11 January 1920.

91 Between 1920 and 1922 the Russians dominated the CI but it was not "bolshevized." National Party Congresses were held before the World Congress, National Congresses elected representatives to the World Congress, the representatives were bound by mandates and, national parties at times ignored central resolutions as there were no centrally dispatched emissaries ensuring compliance.

92 Bachynsky ed., *Dokumenty*, 195–210; TsDAHO f. 57 op2 sprava 260 nos. 121–86. Extended version, nos. 184–6. The circumstances consisted of socio-economic particularities, ties between the Ukrainian and Russian proletariats and, the difficult struggle against world counter-revolution. Borys, *The Sovietization of Ukraine*, 437–8.

93 TsDAHO f. 57 op 2 sprava 259 no. 21;"Deiatelnost tsentralnogo komiteta partii v dokumentakh," *Izvestiia TsK KPSS,* no. 6 (1990): 181: "Propose [*predlozhit*] to the 3-rd International not to accept the Borotbists into the International." Rakovskii and Zinoviev were present. Meijer, ed., *Trotsky Papers* I: 785. The Borotbist–CPU agreement was signed on 17 December. Bachynsky, ed., *Dokumenty*, 244.

94 Iefimenko, *Status USRR*, 108, 150–60.

95 The Russian CC had rejected the Borotbist application on 11 October, the same day they agreed to a military alliance with the UNR. They changed their minds between 8 and 11 November, when they also concluded the UNR alliance was unnecessary. Trotsky and Krestinskii agreed with Lenin and Stalin to give Zinoviev the decisive vote. The rejection of 29 November did not refer to the Ukrainian party as Communist, although the term was in its official name. G.M. Adibekov et al., *Politbiuro TsK RKP(b)-VKP(b) i komintern. 1919–1943. Dokumenty* (Moscow, 2004), 34. TsDAHO f. 57 op 2 sprava 376 no. 4; sprava 368 no. 182.

96 TsDAHO f. 57 op 2 sprava 367 nos. 235, 257, 289.

97 TsDAHO f. 57 op 2 sprava 367 nos. 301–2; (Kovaliv) nos. 309–10.

98 T. Rigby, *Communist Party Membership in the USSR, 1917–1967* (Princeton, 1968), 85–6.

99 TsDAHO f. 57 op 2 sprava 367 nos. 249–50, 269, 270, 274, 278, 281, 285.

100 TsDAHO f. 57 op 2 sprava 367 nos. 306–8, cited in Iefimenko, *Status USRR*, 105.

101 Iefimenko, *Status USRR*, 293–5.

102 TsDAHO f. 57 op 2 sprava 375 nos. 12–20.

103 TsDAHO f. 57 op 2 sprava 259 nos. 37, 39–41, 47, 57. Rakovskii's letter reproduced in Bachynsky, ed., *Dokumenty,* 258–9.

104 TsDAHO f. 57 op 2 sprava 259 nos. 57–8; op 2 sprava 375 no. 23. Critics wrote that the rejection stemmed from Russian domination of the CI. Bolshevism represented the centralist tendency in communism while the Borotbists, like the Italian and Swiss parties, represented the decentralized "federalist" tendency. This latter tendency would dominate, but the ascendancy of the former at the moment led to a decision injurious to communists' interests. *Borotbist,* 5 March 1920.

105 *Chernovyi prapor*, 8–10 August and 8 October 1924; TsDAHO f. 8 op 1 sprava 116. The Comintern secretary sent this application to Stalin with a note asking what to do. Stalin approved the rejection. Adibekov et al., *Politbiuro TsK RKP(b)-VKP(b)*, 293–4n.

106 Bachynsky, ed., *Dokumenty*, 553–5. Included was reference to a "blood tie" between the "Russian working class" and the "working class of Ukraine" – a wording that implied there was a Russian but no Ukrainian working class. (551).

Conclusion

1 Historians of Russian attitudes towards revolutionary France have not examined this issue. T. Kondratieva, *Bolcheviks et Jacobins* (Paris, 1989); E. Hobsbawm, *Echoes of the Marseillaise* (New Brunswick NJ, 1990); D. Shlapentokh, *The French Revolution and the Russian Anti-Democratic Tradition* (New Brunswick, 1997); idem, *The Counter-Revolution in Revolution* (New York, 1998). On republican justifications of imperial rule, see E.G. Andrew, *Imperial Republics: Revolution, War, and Territorial Expansion from the English Civil War to the French Revolution* (Toronto, 2011).

2 J.D. Young, "A Very English Socialism and the Celtic Fringe, 1880–1991," *History Workshop Journal* 35 (1993): 136–52; Stuart, *Marxism and National Identity*, 10–15; Adibekov et al., *VKP(b) Komitern i Iaponiia*, 285, 473, 509. S.D. Gupta, *Comintern and the Destiny of Communism in India, 1919–1943* (Calcutta, 2006), 154–8, 302–4.

3 Evicted by Ukrainians and the Whites in August 1919, Trotsky proposed sending CPU leaders to "conquer Siberia for the Soviet revolution." Meijer, ed., *The Trotsky Papers*, 625.

4 In his note, he implicitly associated Russian and not Esperanto with "the world language." Two years later, he gave a qualified apology. Iu. Mykytenko, "Slidamy odniiei zabutoi polemiky," *Slovo i chas* no. 6 (1991): 33–5. In 1923, in his afterward to the expurgated edition of Gusev-Orenburgskii's *Kniga o Evreiskikh pogromakh* (161), Gorky blamed the "Russian [*Russkoi*] nation" for the 1919 pogroms in Ukraine, seeing them as proof of "the inherent sadistic cruelty of the Russian [*russkomu*] nation." See also: Agurskii, ed., *Maksim Gorkii*, 279–80.

5 Stalin, *Works*, XIII: 25–6; V.A. Nevezhin, ed., *Zastolnye rechi Stalina* (Moscow, 2003), 44.

6 TsDAHO f. 57 op 6 sprava 12 no. 3; op 2 sprava 76 no. 179.

7 Potichnyi, ed., *On the Current Situation*, 176.

8 Khrystiuk, *Zamitky i materialy do istorii Ukrainskoi revoliutsii*, II: 59-62. Khrystiuk implies that the Bolsheviks feared that events in Kyiv would take the same course as in Petrograd but place Ukrainian left SDs and SRs in power instead of themselves. *Chervony prapor*, 14 February 1919.

9 Mazepa, *Bolshevizm i okupatsiia Ukrainy* , 83, 148, attributed Russian expansionism to the fact that Bolsheviks had come to power in a backward country that needed resources – which was doctrinally Leninist but not empirically true.

10 Lenin considered colonialist rule to be a bilateral phenomenon and overlooked the role of settler "creole" colonists as a third group within the relationship who could be either separatist or loyalist. He gave no analytical attention to settler imperial loyalism or "creole" settler-colonist-led independence movements that did not necessarily call for decolonization for native populations. Thus, Lenin supported the Boers – not the Bantus, whom British "imperialists" had recently freed from slavery.

11 L. Narangoa and R. Cribb, *Imperial Japan and National Identities in Asia, 1895–1945* (London, 2003).

12 V. Lypinsky, *Khliborobska Ukraina* (Vienna, 1920), I: 42.

13 Nahorny, *"Bilshovyzm ta Ukrainskyi national kommunizm,"* 128.

Index

CPSIA information can be obtained
at www.ICGtesting.com
Printed in the USA
BVHW042358070522
636315BV00001B/7